Access to Asylum

Is there still a right to seek asylum in a globalised world? Migration control has increasingly moved to the high seas or the territory of transit and origin countries, and is now commonly outsourced to private actors. Under threat of financial penalties airlines today reject any passenger not in possession of a valid visa, and private contractors are used to run detention centres and operate border crossings.

In this volume Thomas Gammeltoft-Hansen examines the impact of these new practices on refugees' access to asylum. A systematic analysis is provided of the reach and limits of international refugee law when migration control is carried out extraterritorially or by non-state actors. State practice from around the globe and case law from all the major human rights institutions are discussed. The arguments are further linked to wider debates in the fields of human rights, general international law and political science.

THOMAS GAMMELTOFT-HANSEN is Research Fellow at the Danish Institute for International Studies and External Lecturer at the University of Copenhagen, where he teaches international refugee law. He is also an associated legal expert to the European Council for Refugees and Exiles, a former policy analyst with the Danish Refugee Council and a regular consultant to a number of international organisations, governmental institutions and non-governmental organisations.

D1324804

CAMBRIDGE STUDIES IN INTERNATIONAL AND COMPARATIVE LAW

Established in 1946, this series produces high-quality scholarship in the fields of public and private international law and comparative law. Although these are distinct legal sub-disciplines, developments since 1946 confirm their interrelation.

Comparative law is increasingly used as a tool in the making of law at national, regional and international levels. Private international law is now often affected by international conventions, and the issues faced by classical conflicts rules are frequently dealt with by substantive harmonisation of law under international auspices. Mixed international arbitrations, especially those involving state economic activity, raise mixed questions of public and private international law, while in many fields (such as the protection of human rights and democratic standards, investment guarantees and international criminal law) international and national systems interact. National constitutional arrangements relating to 'foreign affairs', and to the implementation of international norms, are a focus of attention.

The Board welcomes works of a theoretical or interdisciplinary character, and those focusing on the new approaches to international or comparative law or conflicts of law. Studies of particular institutions or problems are equally welcome, as are translations of the best work published in other languages.

General Editors   James Crawford SC FBA
Whewell Professor of International Law, Faculty of Law, and Director, Lauterpacht Research Centre for International Law, University of Cambridge
John S. Bell FBA
Professor of Law, Faculty of Law, University of Cambridge

Editorial Board   Professor Hilary Charlesworth *Australian National University*
Professor Lori Damrosch *Columbia University Law School*
Professor John Dugard *Universiteit Leiden*
Professor Mary-Ann Glendon *Harvard Law School*
Professor Christopher Greenwood *London School of Economics*
Professor David Johnston *University of Edinburgh*
Professor Hein Kötz *Max-Planck-Institut, Hamburg*
Professor Donald McRae *University of Ottawa*
Professor Onuma Yasuaki *University of Tokyo*
Professor Reinhard Zimmermann *Universität Regensburg*

Advisory Committee Professor D. W. Bowett QC
Judge Rosalyn Higgins QC
Professor J. A. Jolowicz QC
Professor Sir Elihu Lauterpacht CBE QC
Judge Stephen Schwebel

A list of books in the series can be found at the end of this volume.

Access to Asylum
International Refugee Law and the Globalisation of Migration Control

Thomas Gammeltoft-Hansen

CAMBRIDGE
UNIVERSITY PRESS

CAMBRIDGE UNIVERSITY PRESS
Cambridge, New York, Melbourne, Madrid, Cape Town,
Singapore, São Paulo, Delhi, Mexico City

Cambridge University Press
The Edinburgh Building, Cambridge CB2 8RU, UK

Published in the United States of America by Cambridge University Press, New York

www.cambridge.org
Information on this title: www.cambridge.org/9781107621558

First published 2011
First paperback edition 2013

A catalogue record for this publication is available from the British Library

Library of Congress Cataloguing in Publication Data
Gammeltoft-Hansen, Thomas.
Access to asylum : international refugee law and the globalisation of migration control /
Thomas Gammeltoft-Hansen.
   p.   cm. – (Cambridge studies in international and comparative law)
Includes bibliographical references and index.
ISBN 978-1-107-00347-7 (hardback)
1. Asylum, Right of.   2. Political refugees – Legal status, laws, etc.   3. Law and
Globalization.   I. Title.   II. Series.
K3268.3.G36   2011
342.08′3 – dc22   2010052386

ISBN 978-1-107-62155-8 Paperback

Human laws cannot have the unerring quality of scientifically demonstrated conclusions. Not every rule need possess final infallibility and
certainty; as much as is possible in its class is enough.

St Thomas Aquinas (*Summa Theologica*, Ia–2ae, xci 3, ad 3)

Contents

Foreword

Most refugees today cannot travel to the developed world to seek recognition of their international legal right to protection. They instead face an ever-expanding array of mechanisms – carrier sanctions, border security systems, migration management regimes and the like – which seek to deflect them from wealthy states. This dilemma has been exacerbated in recent years by the rapid expansion of governmental efforts to contract out many migration management functions to transport companies, security firms and other non-state actors. Refugees may thus never be able to reach the territory of a country which has in principle agreed to receive them; they may never be in a position to state their claim to a person with the legal responsibility and authority to protect them; or both.

Distancing himself from those who proclaim a 'legal black hole' when refugees are encountered in extraterritorial settings, Thomas Gammeltoft-Hansen effectively shows that refugee law's core norm of *non-refoulement* is among a small number of vital rights that must be respected wherever a state exercises jurisdiction. And drawing on both principles of state responsibility and the duty of due diligence, he shows also that states cannot blithely invoke the traditional maxim that they bear no liability for private acts as a means of disavowing liability for deterrence effected by the non-state actors refugees are most likely to encounter.

But this book is no simplistic manifesto for refugee rights. To the contrary, Gammeltoft-Hansen forthrightly identifies and explores the critical areas of legal ambiguity – what is jurisdiction? when can private conduct truly be said to be authorised or controlled by a state? what level of diligence can reasonably be expected of a state in overseeing private actors? He rightly concedes that these areas of legal uncertainty afford states crucial 'wriggle room' within which to avoid their presumptive protection responsibilities, legally powerful though these may in theory be.

Most importantly, Gammeltoft-Hansen invites us to see the big picture of an asylum system in which powerful governments exploit legal ambiguity to distance themselves both horizontally and vertically from refugees. In his view, the power of extant international law is ironically a significant driver of the 'offshoring' and 'outsourcing' of protection. It is because international law has evolved to impose responsibility when refugees are subject to control in international spaces such as the high seas that effective avoidance now requires that some other sovereign receive the refugees. And it is because international law increasingly recognises liability for official acts even when committed abroad that wealthy states seeking some measure of control over the deflection process will seek to engage corporate or other non-state entities to exercise management functions for them.

The determination of powerful states to avoid legal strictures thus plays a critical role in generating an international and corporate market for migration control, including dealing with refugees. Because less developed countries with poor human rights records and rudimentary (if any) asylum systems are able to offer the most competitive deflection option, and because corporate or other non-state actors will be guided by concerns of efficiency and profit maximisation, the prospects for refugees are not good – in Gammeltoft-Hansen's words, likely amounting to no more than 'protection lite'. Equally disturbing, because scrutiny of protection in such circumstances is difficult if not impossible, even cases arguably governed by international law are less likely to be noticed.

This important book addresses what may well be the most pressing challenges in international refugee law today. It affirms the real power of refugee law even as it challenges us to concede the costs of refugee law's power. Most importantly, it makes a compelling case for creative engagement with the foundational principles of public international law that inform and constrain the ability of refugee law to mitigate sovereign authority in the interests of human rights protection.

James C. Hathaway
University of Michigan Law School
Ann Arbor
August 2010

Preface

This work reflects the law as it stood, to the best of the author's knowledge, on 20 June 2010. The topicality of the issues covered in this book means, however, that these areas of law are still very much developing. Readers are advised to pay attention to more recent case law. At the time of writing the following cases of particular interest were still pending before the European Court of Human Rights: *Hirsi and Others* v. *Italy*, European Court of Human Rights, Application No. 277765/09, lodged 26 May 2009 (concerning Italy's high-seas interception and pushback of migrants to Libya); *Al-Skeini and others* v. *the United Kingdom*, Application No. 55721/07, lodged 11 December 2007; and *Al-Jedda* v. *United Kingdom*, Application No. 27021/08, lodged 3 June 2008 (both concerning possible extraterritorial jurisdiction for actions of the United Kingdom in Iraq). All website addresses were accurate as at 20 June 2010.

Earlier versions of the author's arguments in the present work have been published elsewhere. Parts of the arguments in chapters 3 and 4 have appeared in 'Growing barriers: international refugee law', in M. Gibney and S. Skogly (eds.), *Universal Human Rights and Extraterritorial Obligations* (Philadelphia: University of Pennsylvania Press, 2010) and 'The refugee, the sovereign and the sea: EU interdiction policies in the Mediterranean', in R. Adler-Nissen and T. Gammeltoft-Hansen (eds.), *Sovereignty Games: Instrumentalizing Sovereignty in Europe and Beyond* (New York: Palgrave, 2008). An earlier version of section 2.3 has been published as part of 'The outsourcing of asylum in the EU and the advent of protection lite', in L. Bialasiewicz (ed.), *Europe in the World: EU Geopolitics and the Transformation of European Space* (Farnham: Ashgate, 2010).

Thomas Gammeltoft-Hansen
Christianshavn, 20 June 2010

Acknowledgements

No academic insight is ever achieved in isolation. Beyond the scholars cited in the following, a number of people and institutions have more directly contributed to the process through which this volume has materialised.

This book is an adaption of my doctoral dissertation, which was carried out in co-operation with Aarhus University, the Danish Institute for International Studies and the Danish Refugee Council. The single greatest debt of gratitude is owed to Jens Vedsted-Hansen, who has provided excellent guidance and constant encouragement. I am further indebted to Elspeth Guild, Mark Gibney and Jens Hartig Danielsen, who served as my dissertation committee members, for their critical insights and generous advice on how to improve the manuscript.

Throughout the last five years the Danish Institute for International Studies has provided me with the best possible research environment, professionally and personally. I should like to extend particularly warm thanks to all my colleagues at DIIS, in the migration unit and elsewhere, for providing support and encouragement of the kind that not only makes for great colleagues but also great friends. I am further grateful to colleagues and friends at the European University Institute, Aarhus University and Copenhagen University for providing inspiration and office space at various stages of this project.

For the duration of the present project I have simultaneously been employed by the Danish Refugee Council. I am very grateful to Anne la Cour, Thomas Thomsen and Andreas Kamm for providing me with the opportunity to undertake a Ph.D. with this unique set-up. It is also through the Danish Refugee Council that I have been given the opportunity to work with a number of European refugee-assisting organisations making up the European Council for Refugees and Exiles. The exchange of ideas with colleagues in both places has provided relief from, as well as stimulus to, the time otherwise spent in the ivory tower.

A number of other people have critically helped shape this book through their ideas and comments. For that I am particularly grateful to Tanja Aalberts, Rebecca Adler-Nissen, Rosemary Byrne, Morten Broberg, Guy Goodwin-Gill, Stefano Guzzini, Peter Vedel Kessing, Anja Klug, Nina Maria Lassen, Jesper Lindholm, Gregor Noll, Jorrit Rijpma, Simon Turner, Finn Stepputat and Ninna Nyberg Sørensen.

Nienke van Schaverbeke, Finola O'Sullivan, Daniel Dunlavey, Richard Woodham and others from Cambridge University Press have provided impeccable editorial support. I would like to thank the series editor, James Crawford, and the anonymous readers for their comments and suggestions. In addition, I would like to acknowledge Benedikte Granvig, Ida Marie Vammen and Ane Toubro for their great efforts in ensuring consistency and correctness in the references and citations. The responsibility for any omissions or errors remaining is mine alone.

Last, but not least, I am grateful to my family and many good friends for both their support and understanding in this endeavour. This book is dedicated to my parents, who in each their way continue to inspire me to work in this field.

Table of treaties and other international instruments

Table of cases

Permanent Court of International Justice

Island of Palmas, RIIA II, 4 April 1928
SS Lotus, PCIJ Ser. A, No. 10 (1927)
SS Wimbledon, PCIJ Ser. A, No. 1 (1923)

International Court of Justice

Application of the Convention on the Prevention and Punishment of the Crime of Genocide (Bosnia and Herzegovina v. Yugoslavia), Preliminary Objections, 11 July 1996
Application of the Convention on the Prevention and Punishment of the Crime of Genocide (Bosnia and Herzegovina v. Serbia and Montenegro), 26 February 2007
Armed Activities on the Territory of the Congo (Democratic Republic of the Congo v. Rwanda), 3 February 2006
Armed Activities on the Territory of the Congo (Democratic Republic of the Congo v. Uganda), 19 December 2005
Barcelona Traction, Light and Power Co. Case (Belgium v. Spain), Second Phase, 5 February 1970
Corfu Channel Case (United Kingdom v. Albania), 9 April 1949
Legal Consequences of the Construction of a Wall in the Occupied Palestinian Territory, Advisory Opinion, 9 July 2004
Legality of the Threat or Use of Nuclear Weapons, Advisory Opinion, 8 July 1996
Military and Paramilitary Activities in and against Nicaragua (Nicaragua v. United States of America), 27 June 1986
Namibia (South West Africa) Case, 26 January 1971

1   Introduction

1.1 The questions of extraterritoriality

1.1.1 Encountering the state

When does a refugee encounter the state? The straightforward answer to this question would be: when arriving at the border and surrendering him- or herself to the authorities, uttering the magic word, 'asylum'. Reality, however, seldom fits this picture. First of all, a substantial number of asylum-seekers only make their claim some time after actually entering the country of prospective asylum. Second, and more importantly, the last decades have seen a number of policy developments to extend migration control well beyond the borders of the state.

A person seeking asylum in, for example, Europe or the United States may thus encounter the authorities of these countries before even departing. It could be at the consulate when attempting to obtain a visa, at the airport of key departure or transit countries where immigration officers are deployed to advise airlines and foreign authorities on whom to allow onwards passage. It could be during an attempt to cross the Mediterranean or the Caribbean seas or any one of the many other places where ships, aircraft and radar systems operate to intercept even the smallest vessel before it can reach the territorial waters of the prospective destination state.

Alternatively, the refugee may not encounter the state *in persona*, but rather through delegation. Under bilateral and European Union (EU) agreements, Libya and Morocco, for example, are expected to carry out exit border control in co-operation with EU member states. Or the controlling authority may take the form of a private company. Most asylum countries today impose heavy fines on airline carriers for allowing passengers to board without proper documentation and visas, effectively making these companies responsible for carrying out rigorous migration control functions.

The above initiatives are the concrete expressions of the general trend in many states to extend the reach of migration control to destinations outside its territory and to employ agents other than the state's own authorities. Since the first comprehensive framework for a common European asylum and immigration policy was laid down at the EU summit in Tampere in 1999, co-operation with third countries in this area has been given top priority, and in 2005 a full strategy for the 'external dimension' of EU asylum and migration policy was presented.[1] Several scholars have observed how this 'external dimension' is increasingly 'colonising' the foreign policy agenda of many traditional asylum countries.[2] Similarly, the taking on of tasks in relation to asylum and immigration by private companies is becoming a fast-growing industry. Immigration detention centres are increasingly run by private companies; contracts have been awarded to, for example, Boeing to install surveillance systems along the United States–Mexican border; and private security companies are today operating several checkpoints along the border between Israel and the West Bank.

As political phenomena, the trend towards extraterritorialisation and the involvement of private actors may both be thought of as part of a globalisation process whereby migration control is simultaneously 'offshored' and 'outsourced'. These two processes constitute some of the most striking features in the development of migration policies of both developed and less developed countries. Migration control has traditionally focused strictly on the border as the natural sovereign delineation and on the official border guard as a natural expression of state authority. While private

---

[1] European Council, Presidency Conclusions of the Tampere European Council, SI (1999) 800, 16 October 1999; Council of the European Union, A Strategy for the External Dimension of JHA: Global Freedom, Security and Justice, 14366/1/05 JAI 417 RELEX 628, 24 November 2005.

[2] C. Rodier, 'Analysis of the external dimension of the EU's asylum and immigration policies', European Parliament, Directorate-General for External Policies of the Union Directorate B – Policy Department (2006); S. Lavenex, 'Shifting up and out: the foreign policy of European immigration control', (2006) 29 West European Politics 329–50; T. Gammeltoft-Hansen, 'Outsourcing migration management: EU, power, and the external dimension of asylum and immigration policy', DIIS Working Paper no. 2006/1, Danish Institute for International Studies (2006); C. Boswell, 'The "external dimension" of EU immigration and asylum policy', (2003) 79 International Affairs 619–38; V. Guiraudon, 'Before the EU border: remote control of the "huddled masses"', in K. Groenendijk, E. Guild and P. Minderhoud (eds.), In Search of Europe's Borders (The Hague: Kluwer Law International, 2002), pp. 191–214.

border guards and overseas immigration officers have far from replaced traditional border control, one thing seems safe to conclude: today, the classical dictum that a state's executive power is to be exercised by its own officials and confined within the scope of its territorial borders[3] can no longer be asserted with the same rigour.

1.1.2 The questions raised in this volume

For any refugee lawyer, the most pertinent question arising from the developments sketched above is the extent to which international refugee and human rights law gives rise to state responsibility when migration control is carried out extraterritorially and/or by private actors. The question is important for several reasons. Both scholars and refugee advocates have repeatedly argued that, for example, the interception of boat refugees or the rejection of asylum-seekers by airlines is fundamentally in violation of both the 1951 Convention Relating to the Status of Refugees (Refugee Convention) and general human rights law instruments. The concern is that privatisation and extraterritorialisation are used as a pretext for effectively circumventing basic human rights obligations, either because these are not applicable extraterritorially or when private actors carry out controls, or because these rights are simply not realised. Second, it has been argued that the 1951 Refugee Convention is inadequate in guaranteeing the rights of refugees beyond the territorial boundaries of states. The majority of rights are based on the premise that the refugee is present within the territory or at least at the border of the obliged state. The move towards privatisation and extraterritorial migration control may thus make redundant a number of treaty provisions, thereby undermining the ability of the present framework to guarantee refugee protection effectively.

From these considerations alone it becomes clear that any comprehensive answer to the above is premised on at least three different sub-questions. The first of these relates to the applicability *ratione loci* of international refugee law: to what extent does international refugee and human rights law apply to situations where states exercise migration control outside their territory? Several commentators have expressed concern that extraterritorial migration control appears to take place 'beyond

---

[3] *Case of the S.S. Lotus*, PCIJ, Ser. A, No. 10 (1927), 4, at 18. See also H. J. Morgenthau, 'The problem of sovereignty reconsidered', (1948) 48 *Columbia Law Review* 341–65, at 344.

the rule of law', in a 'rights vacuum' or 'legal black hole'.[4] A number of states seem to suggest that somehow international human rights and refugee law do not apply, or apply differently, when states act outside, as opposed to within, their territory. This is not peculiar to refugee law but finds parallels in a number of issues, ranging from offshore detention of prisoners to international tax havens.[5] As such, it begs both a specific examination of the geographical reach of core refugee obligations and a general analysis of the exact limits for state jurisdiction. In other words, is there such a thing as extraterritorial legal responsibility in cases of offshore migration control and, if so, how far does it extend?

The second question concerns the vertical application of international refugee law when states delegate authority to private actors: under what circumstances does migration control carried out by private actors give rise to state responsibility under refugee and human rights law? The outsourcing of control functions to airlines or other private actors has raised concerns that protection obligations are being undermined.[6] Carrier sanctions are generally operated regardless of protection concerns, and asylum-seekers are particularly likely to be rejected since they often lack proper documentation.[7] Concerns have further been raised that the use of private contractors to carry out border controls or operate immigration detention centres creates an accountability gap, where the 'corporate veil' blurs public oversight and states all too easily rid themselves of legal obligations otherwise owed.[8] Where privatised migration controls

---

[4] B. Vandvik, 'Extraterritorial border controls and responsibility: a view from ECRE', (2008) *Amsterdam Law Forum* 27–36, at 28; R. Wilde, 'Legal "black hole"? Extraterritorial state action and international treaty law on civil and political rights', (2005) 26 *Michigan Journal of International Law* 739–806.

[5] J. Steyn, 'Guantánamo Bay: the legal black hole', (2004) 53 *International and Comparative Law Quarterly* 1–15; R. Palan, *The Offshore World: Sovereign Markets, Virtual Places and Nomad Millionaires* (Ithaca: Cornell University Press, 2003).

[6] Amnesty International, 'No flights to safety: carrier sanctions: airline employees and the rights of refugees', ACT 34/21/97, November 1997; UNHCR, Position on Conventions Recently Concluded in Europe (Dublin and Schengen Conventions), Geneva, 16 August 1991; Council of Europe Parliamentary Assembly, Recommendation 1163 (1991) on the Arrival of Asylum-Seekers at European Airports.

[7] F. Nicholson, 'Implementation of the Immigration (Carriers' Liability) Act 1987: privatising immigration functions at the expense of international obligations', (1997) 46 *International and Comparative Law Quarterly* 586–634, at 598; E. Feller, 'Carrier sanctions and international law', (1989) 1 *International Journal of Refugee Law* 48–66.

[8] P. R. Verkuil, *Outsourcing Sovereignty: Why Privatization of Government Functions Threatens Democracy and What We Can Do About It* (Cambridge University Press, 2007); J. Vedsted-Hansen, 'Privatiseret Retshåndhævelse og Kontrol', in L. Adrian (ed.), *Ret og Privatisering* (Copenhagen: Gad Jura, 1995), pp. 159–79.

simultaneously operate extraterritorially these problems are only likely to be exacerbated. As is known from the parallel debate on the use of private military companies (PMCs), impunity of both private contractors and the outsourcing states is a recurrent problem.[9] The privatisation of migration control thus equally raises more general questions of international law: when and under what circumstances does private conduct give rise to state responsibility under international refugee and human rights law, and to what extent are these obligations affected by the *locus* of migration control and concomitant extraterritorialisation?

Last, but not least, it is crucial to look beyond the strictly legal analysis and ask how the actual realisation of rights under international refugee and human rights law is affected by the extraterritorialisation and privatisation of migration control. Access to legal aid, counselling and national complaint mechanisms may be severely impaired for a refugee who never sets foot on European soil. Several commentators have argued that moving migration control away from the territory or delegating it to private actors may entail an 'out of sight, out of mind' effect vis-à-vis constituencies and national monitoring mechanisms.[10] Many of the institutional mechanisms that normally ensure the realisation of human rights and the rule of law are essentially territorially limited. Similarly, the conceptual distinction between public and private that continues to permeate national and international law means that many of the ordinary accountability mechanisms do not operate effectively when otherwise governmental functions are delegated to private actors. Beyond questions of the extraterritorial applicability of refugee law and attribution of private conduct there is also, therefore, a concern that protection entitlements are simply not realised as the activities take place further away from the state and its territory, where little oversight is provided and access to the ordinary institutions guiding an asylum claim or human rights procedure is lacking.

---

[9] P. W. Singer, 'War, profits, and the vacuum of law: privatized military firms and international law', (2004) 42 *Columbia Journal of Transnational Law* 521–49.

[10] T. Gammeltoft-Hansen, 'The refugee, the sovereign and the sea: EU interdiction policies in the Mediterranean', in R. Adler-Nissen and T. Gammeltoft-Hansen (eds.), *Sovereignty Games: Instrumentalising Sovereignty in Europe and Beyond* (New York: Palgrave Macmillan, 2008) pp. 171–96; S. H. Legomsky, 'The USA and the Caribbean interdiction programme', (2006) 18 *International Journal of Refugee Law* 677–96, at 679; V. Guiraudon, 'Enlisting third parties in border control: a comparative study of its causes and consequences', paper presented at a workshop on 'Managing International and Inter-Agency Co-operation at the Border', Geneva Centre for the Democratic Control of Armed Forces, 13–15 March 2003.

1.1.3 Understanding the globalisation of migration control

Beyond the more legal questions set out above, the present volume also hopes to contribute indirectly to the more general understanding of the globalisation of migration control as a political phenomenon.

A growing number of scholars from a variety of disciplines are starting to engage with this question and, as one might expect, rather different frameworks have been presented to answer it. From an economic perspective, policies for offshore migration control and refugee protection have been argued to provide more cost-effective solutions. A number of scholars emphasise that the 'externalisation'[11] or 'externalities'[12] of asylum and immigration policy represent a natural response to more complex and diverse migration flows, a complexity which has made it important to extend control over the entire length of the journey[13] and to develop more preventive strategies focusing on the 'root causes' of migration.[14] Others argue that the 'colonisation' of the foreign policy agenda by hitherto domestic issues is a reflection of the growing politicisation of asylum and immigration issues. As domestic solutions are complicated by policy dilemmas and are difficult to realise, the venue for political action shifts outwards to avoid the constraints of domestic policy-making.[15] In particular, immigration is increasingly viewed as an 'internal security

[11]   Rodier, 'Analysis'; A. Betts, 'International co-operation between north and south to enhance refugee protection in regions of origin', RSC Working Paper No. 25, Refugee Studies Centre, Oxford, 2005; S. Sterkx, 'Curtailing the comprehensive approach: governance export in EU asylum and migration policy', paper presented at ECPR Joint Sessions of Workshops, Uppsala, 13–18 April 2004; I. Kruse, 'Creating Europe outside Europe: externalities of the EU migration regime', paper presented at ECPR conference, 'Theories of Europeanisation', Marburg, 18–21 September 2003.

[12]   S. Lavenex and E. M. Ucarer (eds.), *Migration and the Externalities of European Integration* (Lanham: Lexington Books, 2002).

[13]   S. Lavenex and E. M. Ucarer, 'The external dimension of Europeanization: the case of immigration policies', (2004) 39 *Cooperation and Conflict* 417–445; Boswell, '"External dimension"'; D. Bigo, 'When two become one: internal and external securitisations in Europe', in M. Kelstrup and M. C. Williams (eds.), *International Relations and the Politics of European Integration: Power, Security and Community* (London: Routledge, 2000), pp. 171–205.

[14]   S. Turner, J. Munive and N. N. Sørensen, 'European attitudes and policies towards the migration/development nexus', in N. N. Sørensen (ed.), *Mediterranean Transit Migration* (Copenhagen: Danish Institute for International Studies, 2006), pp. 67–100.

[15]   Lavenex and Ucarer, 'External dimension'; V. Guiraudon, 'The constitution of a European immigration policy domain: a political sociology approach', (2003) 10 *Journal of European Public Policy* 263–82; J. v. d. Klaauw, 'European asylum policy and the global protection regime: challenges for UNHCR', in Lavenex and Ucarer, *Migration and the Externalities of European Integration*, pp. 33–54; F. Pastore, 'Aeneas' route – Euro-Mediterranean relations and international migration', in ibid., pp. 105–123.

threat', albeit one that necessitates an international response in order to be effective.[16]

Equally, the involvement of private actors in migration control may be seen as part of a much larger trend to privatise tasks hitherto exclusively carried out by the state. Thus private migration control has been argued to be cost-saving through shifting the costs of control to, for example, carriers and creating competition among several bidding contractors.[17] Privately operated migration controls have also been seen as a response to the inability of national authorities to achieve effective control. By requiring airlines to carry out document checks an additional layer of control is installed at the crucial point of departure, when airlines have unique access to inbound passengers and their data.[18] Lastly, the privatisation of migration control has even been claimed to result in increased accountability as a competition parameter, and the use of privately contracted border guards to achieve a 'civilising' effect by presenting a more friendly face than that presented at borders operated by national border authorities or military personnel.[19]

The present volume, however, starts from the hypothesis that at least part of the explanation for the current drive towards offshore and privatised migration control should be found in the answers to the questions regarding the relationship between these policies and international legal structures. It is suggested that extraterritorial controls and the involvement of private actors are becoming increasingly fashionable largely because states believe that by delegating authority and moving beyond

[16] R. Furuseth, 'Creating security through immigration control: an analysis of European immigration discourse and the development towards a common EU asylum and immigration policy', NUPI Report 274, Norsk Utenrikspolitisk Institutt (2003); C. Rudolph, 'Globalization and security: migration and the evolving conceptions of security in statecraft and scholarship', (2003) 13 *Security Studies* 1–32; Guiraudon, 'Before the EU border'; D. Bigo, 'Security and immigration: towards a critique of the governmentality of unease', (2002) 27 *Alternatives* 63–92; Bigo, 'When two become one'; J. Huysmans, 'The European Union and the securitization of migration', (2000) 38 *Journal of Common Market Studies* 751–777.

[17] S. Scholten and P. Minderhoud, 'Regulating immigration control: carrier sanctions in the Netherlands', (2008) 10 *European Journal of Migration and Law* 123–147; Verkuil, *Outsourcing Sovereignty*.

[18] G. Noll, *Negotiating Asylum: The EU Acquis, Extraterritorial Protection and the Common Market of Deflection* (The Hague: Martinus Nijhoff, 2000), p. 108; Vedsted-Hansen, 'Privatiseret Retshåndhævelse', p. 160.

[19] L. Dickinson, 'Contract as a tool for regulating PMCs', in S. Chesterman and C. Lehnart (eds.), *From Mercenaries to Markets* (Oxford University Press, 2007), pp. 217–38, at p. 230; C. H. Logan, *Private Prisons: Cons and Pros* (Oxford University Press, 1990).

their territory they are able to release themselves – de facto or de jure – from some of the constraints otherwise imposed by international law.

In that context, the legal analysis set out above becomes a stepping stone to asking more critically to what extent offshoring and outsourcing policies enable states to realise migration control unconstrained by refugee and human rights law. As will be seen, this is not a question that may simply be answered by 'either–or', but rather one that requires nuanced answers and one in relation to which a certain amount of interpretative disagreement persists in some areas. Yet it is only through a more thorough understanding of the limits of legal responsibility and the areas where such responsibility may at least be contested that it is possible to understand how states enact and position offshore and outsourced migration control. Why is it that European states have been so keen to negotiate access in order to move migration control from the high seas and into the territorial waters of African states? And why is it that several states emphasise that immigration officers posted to foreign airports maintain only an advisory role with regard to the controls carried out by airline staff?

Lastly, it is hoped that the present analysis might contribute to a better understanding of how extraterritorialisation and privatisation practices fundamentally operate at the intersection between law and politics in today's world. The apparent difficulties in bringing refugee and human rights law fully to bear in all situations of extraterritorial and/or privatised migration control point to a deeper conflict between the universal purpose and idea behind human rights law, on the one hand, and the codification of human rights law as part of general international law building on principles of national sovereignty, on the other. It is in the context of this tension that extraterritorialisation and privatisation become attractive strategies, as they create a disjuncture between the increasingly global and market-oriented modes of governance pursued by states and an international legal framework still largely vested in a conceptualisation of the state building on territorial delineations and the distinction between public and private. The result is what may be termed the increasing commercialisation of sovereignty, in which sovereign prerogatives, territory and functions are strategically traded and commodified among states and between governments and private actors, a development that ultimately either threatens severely to undermine the effectiveness of human rights law or demands that some of the most fundamental principles of international law and our politico-legal conception of the state be readjusted.

1.2 Structure

The nexus between the globalisation of migration control and international refugee law raises three interrelated legal issues around which the following chapters are structured. The first concerns the geographical applicability of core norms under the Refugee Convention. Chapter 3 examines the extraterritorial application of the *non-refoulement* principle as set out in Article 33 of the Refugee Convention, which has been a hotly debated issue ever since its inception. The chapter summarises and seeks to structure the different arguments to be made from the language of the text, and the object and purpose of the article and the drafting documents. It then goes on to examine subsequent interpretation as set out in soft law, state practice and other formulations of *non-refoulement* principles in general human rights and customary law.

The second issue concerns the wider applicability of human rights law to situations of extraterritorial migration control. Chapter 4 analyses the basis for establishing extraterritorial jurisdiction, which is a threshold criterion for both Article 33 of the Refugee Convention and the majority of general human rights instruments. The chapter looks first at the meaning of jurisdiction in general international law and human rights law respectively. It then goes on to examine whether and under what circumstances jurisdiction may be brought about by migration control exercised in three different geographic spheres: areas where authority is withdrawn or territory legally excised, migration control carried out in international waters, and migration control carried out within the territorial jurisdiction of another state.

The third part of the legal analysis concerns the attribution of private conduct, and thus state responsibility, in cases where private actors exercise migration control or other forms of authority vis-à-vis asylum-seekers and refugees. Chapter 5 starts out by recalling different practices as regards private involvement for the purpose of migration control and the protection concerns voiced over the use of, for example, carrier sanctions and private contractors. It then goes on to examine when and under what circumstances migration control carried out by private actors may give rise to direct state responsibility. To this end the International Law Commission's Articles on State Responsibility (ILC Articles) are employed as a guiding framework. In addition, it is argued that states also retain certain due diligence obligations under refugee and human rights law in respect of private actors exercising migration control.

Ensuring access to asylum, however, does not stop here. While the legal analysis is a necessary and crucial first step, the refugee subjected to off-shore and outsourced migration control often finds him- or herself unable de facto to realise rights owed de jure. Chapter 6 thus sketches some of the more practical protection issues raised by extraterritorial and privatised migration control. As will be shown, offshoring and outsourcing tend to render the control practices themselves invisible and eclipse the ordinary human rights institutions and mechanisms aiding persons to launch an asylum claim and monitoring state behaviour.

Before all this, however, chapter 2 will attempt to establish a more general framework for understanding the relationship between inter-national refugee law and state policies to control migration flows in a globalised world. It first locates the refugee as a traditional marker of state sovereignty and traces the current drive towards extraterritorial and privatised migration control. It is then argued that the current devel-opments reflect a deeper tension between the universal claim of human rights and core norms pertaining to national sovereignty, linking human rights to the principle of territoriality and the public/private distinction. The result is the current bifurcation between the reach of refugee law and state practices to offshore and outsourced migration control.

Chapter 7 seeks to draw together the conclusions of the preceding analysis as well as to set out a few perspectives as regards the wider significance of these issues.

2 The refugee and the globalisation of migration control

> The refugee in international law occupies a legal space characterized, on the one hand, by the principle of State sovereignty and the related principles of territorial supremacy and self-preservation; and, on the other hand, by competing humanitarian principles deriving from general international law ... and from treaty.[1]

The refugee is both a product of, and remains closely embedded in, a complex interplay between state prerogatives and human rights, and politics and law. This chapter sets out to examine more generally this relationship in order to understand the drive towards extraterritorial and privatised migration control that we are currently witnessing.

As noted above, the nexus between the refugee and migration control has arguably always been a point of confrontation between sovereign rights and international law as exemplified by the 1951 Refugee Convention. Offshore and privatised migration control may in this sense be seen as political strategies by the state to bypass this confrontation and reclaim discretionary power. Yet in the process a new field of contestation opens up between universal and particularist claims to the applicability of international refugee and human rights law. It is argued that the difficulties in bringing international law to bear on offshore and privatisation policies reflect an underlying conflict between the universal purpose of human rights law on the one hand, and its formalisation as a matter of treaty law on the other.

This is particularly evident in the international refugee protection regime, which remains firmly vested in territorial principles for

---

[1] G. Goodwin-Gill and J. McAdam, *The Refugee in International Law*, 3rd edn (Oxford University Press, 2007), p. 1.

dividing and tailoring protection obligations. As a result, a growing market for migration control is emerging where sovereign territory and functions are commercialised, both between states and in the relation between governments and private actors. This commercialisation of sovereignty reflects and reinforces a disjuncture between the increasingly global and market-oriented forms of state governance and a legal framework still largely built on territorial and statist principles. It is in this tension that the legal debate surrounding extraterritorial human rights application and state responsibility for acts of private actors is waged, and the outcome of this debate is likely to have crucial implications not only in the field of refugee law but also for the future effectiveness of the human rights project at large.

2.1 The refugee as a marker of sovereignty

The refugee is an anomaly in a world where it is assumed that all individuals remain subjects of a territorial sovereign. Yet the refugee is also an integral part of the international system of states, a seemingly unavoidable side-effect of state sovereignty as we know it.[2]

In the first place, the refugee is a product of national sovereignty, the state's absolute and perpetual power within its commonwealth. The refugee emerges as a result of the state's unwillingness or failure to secure the ordinary protection offered to its citizens. From the expulsion of the French Huguenots as the first 'modern' refugees, the history of refugee flows reads not just as a history of political oppression, revolutions and violent conflict, but also as a history of state-building and of the Westphalian state system itself, where the exclusion of some has often been a deliberate strategy to reinforce the inclusion of others.[3]

As a legal figure, however, the refugee in the modern context is constructed in contrast to national sovereignty and as a marker of its limits. From the perspective of a potential asylum state, refugee law places a constraint on the otherwise well-established right of any state to decide who

---

[2] E. Haddad, 'The refugee: the individual between sovereigns', (2003) 17 *Global Society* 297–322, at 297.

[3] M. Weiner, 'Ethics, national sovereignty and the control of immigration', (1996) 30 *International Migration Review* 171–97, at 188; A. Zolberg, 'The formation of new states as a refugee-generating process', (1983) 467 *Annals of the American Academy of Political and Social Science* 24–38, at 36.

may enter and remain on its territory.[4] As an expression of international sovereignty and international law of co-operation, the refugee protection regime is an attempt, albeit imperfect, to resolve the problem of those occupying the undesirable and, in systemic terms, impossible position between mutually exclusive sovereign states.

It is this tension between human rights law and the exercise of sovereign powers that Goodwin-Gill points to in the quotation above. Both aspects refer back to the concept of sovereignty. The latter emanates from principles of *national* sovereignty that endow states with the freedom to act unconstrained and the right to exclude foreigners from their territory. The former is an expression of *international* sovereignty through which states have submitted themselves to binding treaties of international law, in this case human rights treaties that explicitly constrain this freedom to act and impose a corollary responsibility to respect the rights of individuals within their jurisdiction. The refugee is poised squarely between these two conceptions of sovereignty: sovereignty as freedom and sovereignty as responsibility.[5]

It is also this tension that comes to the fore in the initial encounter between the asylum-seeker and the border authorities of a potential asylum state. As is well known, international law stops short of granting an

---

[4] As Emmerich de Vattel notes in *The Law of Nations*, every sovereign nation retains the power, as inherent in sovereignty and essential to self-preservation, to forbid the entrance of foreigners within its dominions or to admit them only in such cases or on such conditions as it may see fit to prescribe. E. de Vattel, *The Law of Nations* (Philadelphia: T. & J.W. Johnson & Co., 1883), Book 2, paras. 94, 100.

[5] The dictum that sovereignty entails responsibility, even outside the realm of treaty law, was famously expressed by Judge Huber in the *Las Palmas* case:

> Territorial sovereignty... involves the exclusive right to display the activities of the State. This right has as a corollary a duty: the obligation to protect within the territory the rights of other States, in particular their right to integrity and their inviolability in peace and war, together with the rights which each State may claim for its nationals in foreign territory. Without manifesting its territorial sovereignty in a manner corresponding to the circumstances, the State cannot fulfil this duty. (*Case of the Island of Palmas*, PCIJ, Judgment of 4 April 1928, RIIA Vol. II)

On the conception of sovereignty as 'freedom' and sovereignty as 'responsibility' see further T. E. Aalberts and W. Werner, 'Sovereignty beyond borders: sovereignty, self-defense, and the disciplining of the state', in Adler-Nissen and Gammeltoft-Hansen, *Sovereignty Games*, pp. 129–50; W. Werner, 'State sovereignty and international legal discourse', in W. Werner and I. F. Dekker (eds.), *Governance and International Legal Theory* (Leiden: Brill Academic Publishers, 2004), pp. 125–58.

individual right of asylum.[6] Nonetheless, the key norm of refugee law, the principle of *non-refoulement*, bids states not to return any refugee to a country where they risk persecution. At the drafting committee of the 1951 Refugee Convention, the *non-refoulement* clause was thus described as 'an exceptional limitation of the sovereign right of states to turn back aliens to the frontiers of their country of origin'.[7] It is this 'trump card' that is available to the asylum-seeker and which in ordinary circumstances will require a state to suspend its rules of immigration control and undertake a refugee status determination procedure for all asylum-seekers arriving at its territory to determine if such a risk is present.[8]

The last twenty-five years, however, have seen an increased politicisation of asylum across both traditional and new asylum countries. Following the end of the Cold War, receiving refugees no longer entailed ideological points. From the 1970s, the welcoming labour immigration schemes of several European countries were abandoned. At the same time, globalisation has allowed new patterns of migration and refugee flight. For the 'jet-age asylum-seeker' knowledge of both destinations far away and transcontinental transportation is more readily available. And rather than conforming to the traditional image of the singular bona fide asylum-seeker, refugees are increasingly caught up in mixed flows of irregular migrants, often facilitated by human smugglers specialised in avoiding traditional forms of border control.[9]

---

[6] The right 'to seek and enjoy in other countries asylum from persecution', enshrined in Art. 14 of the Universal Declaration of Human Rights, has so far not been codified as a matter of universal treaty law. Further, the somewhat cryptic formulation has traditionally been interpreted as an extension of the much older humanitarian state prerogative to grant asylum and resist extradition; a right of the asylum state vis-à-vis the state of origin against the nationality jurisdiction of the latter. A. Grahl-Madsen, *Commentary on the Refugee Convention 1951, Articles 2–11, 13–37* (Geneva: Division of International Protection of the United High Commissioner for Refugees, 1963, repub. 1997), pp. 195–6. Whether this interpretation is entirely correct may, however, be disputed. Asylum as a right between states arguably has little to do with the notion of human rights. A closer reading of the drafting history further suggests that while the declaration falls short of an individual right to be *granted* asylum, a procedural right to *seek*, or in other words a right to an asylum process, was intended to remain. T. Gammeltoft-Hansen and H. Gammeltoft-Hansen, 'The right to seek revisited: on the UN Human Rights Declaration Article 14 and access to asylum procedures in the EU', (2008) 10 *European Journal of Migration and Law* 439–59.

[7] Remark made by the Israeli delegate, Nehemiah Robinson, Ad Hoc Committee on Statelessness and Related Problems, First Session, 20th meeting, E/AC.32/SR.20, para. 49.

[8] J. Hathaway (ed.), *Reconceiving International Refugee Law* (The Hague: Kluwer Law International, 1997), p. xix.

[9] M. J. Gibney and R. Hansen, 'Asylum policy in the West: past trends, future possibilities', WIDER Discussion Paper, UNU/WIDER, Helsinki, 2003; S. Castles and M. J. Miller, *The Age*

The response has been a general tightening of national asylum systems and border control. Recognition rates have gone down in a number of industrialised countries, and measures have been introduced to reduce the time of asylum processing and restrict the rights and benefits enjoyed during the stay. Second, legal mechanisms have been implemented to restrict arriving asylum-seekers' access to asylum procedures, introducing particularly expeditious examinations or *prima facie* rejecting asylum-seekers arriving from so-called 'safe countries of origin' or 'safe third countries'.[10]

Lastly, states have been keen to prevent asylum-seekers and irregular migrants from reaching their territories in the first place. The *non-refoulement* principle has been seen by some states as an open door or 'blank cheque' for any migrant claiming to be an asylum-seeker, leaving little control to states in determining how many must be admitted to its asylum procedures.[11] In practice, many states have further found it difficult to return failed asylum-seekers because of lack of nationality identification or a country willing to accept them. Intercepting asylum-seekers and irregular migrants before they reach their destination has thus become a particularly popular strategy for states looking both to reduce the numbers of asylum-seekers and to avoid the trouble and costs associated with returning those rejected.[12]

As a result, forms of extraterritorial or externalised migration control have been rapidly expanding across traditional asylum countries, in particular Australia, the United States and European countries. This involves, first, the *offshoring* of the state's own migration authorities. From the

of Migration: International Population Movements in the Modern World, 3rd edn (New York: Palgrave Macmillan, 2003); L. Barnett, 'Global governance and the evolution of the international refugee regime', New Issues in Refugee Research No. 54, UNHCR, Geneva (2002); A. Zolberg, 'Beyond the crisis', in P. M. Benda and A. Zolberg (eds.), *Global Migrants, Global Refugees* (New York: Berghahn Books, 2001), pp. 1–19.

[10] A. Hurwitz, *The Collective Responsibility of States to Protect Refugees* (Oxford University Press, 2009), pp. 45–66; E. Guild, 'The Europeanisation of Europe's asylum policy', (2006) 18 *International Journal of Refugee Law* 630–52; J. Vedsted-Hansen, 'Europe's response to the arrival of asylum seekers: refugee protection and immigration control', New Issues in Refugee Research No. 6, UNHCR, Geneva (1999), p. 17; Goodwin-Gill and McAdam, *Refugee in International Law*, p. 333.

[11] K. Bem, 'The coming of a "blank cheque" – Europe, the 1951 Convention and the 1967 Protocol', (2004) 16 *International Journal of Refugee Law* 609–27; Hathaway, *Reconceiving International Refugee Law*, p. xviii.

[12] Guild, 'Europeanisation'; S. Lavenex, 'Shifting up and out'; Guiraudon, 'Before the EU border'; Vedsted-Hansen, 'Europe's response'; J. Hathaway, 'The emerging politics of non-entrée', (1992) 91 *Refugees* 40–1.

enforcement of visa regulations at consulates to the sending of immigration liaison officers to key transit countries and the deployment of warships to intercept migrant boats on the high seas, migration control is no longer something that is being performed only at the perimeter of a state's sovereign territory, but rather is a set of progressive mechanisms to check travellers at every step of their prospective journey.[13]

Second, the externalisation of migration control has been carried out through delegation, as an *outsourcing* of control responsibilities and duties to third states and – the focus of the present volume – private parties. The international co-operation regarding migration management is illustrative of the fact that migration, and migration control in particular, has become a foreign policy issue in its own right, and transit and origin countries of migration are both directly and indirectly being wooed to carry out exit border control of national and transiting emigrants.[14] But authority and obligations are also shifted vertically, to private companies and corporations. Under threat of economic penalties, airlines and other carriers have long carried out elaborate document and visa checks at the point of departure.[15] In recent years, private security companies and other contractors have been increasingly employed by states to carry out migration control both at the borders and overseas.[16]

---

[13] S. Kneebone, 'The Pacific plan: the provision of "effective protection"?', (2006) 18 *International Journal of Refugee Law* 696–722; Legomsky, 'USA and the Caribbean interdiction programme'; T. Gammeltoft-Hansen, 'The risk of migration control: a reflexive analysis of the common EU asylum and immigration policy', master's thesis, University of Copenhagen, 2005.

[14] A. Geddes, 'Migration as foreign policy? The external dimension of EU action on migration and asylum', SIEPS Report 2009:2, Swedish Institute for European Policy Studies, Stockholm, 2009; M.-T. Gil-Bazo, 'The practice of Mediterranean states in the context of the European Union's Justice and Home Affairs External Dimension: the safe third country concept revisited', (2006) 18 *International Journal of Refugee Law* 571–600; Gammeltoft-Hansen, 'Outsourcing migration management'; Lavenex, 'Shifting up and out'; E. Guild, 'What is a neighbour? Examining the EU neighbourhood policy from the perspective of movement of persons', paper presented at Western NIS Forum for Refugee-Assisting NGOs, Yalta, 1–3 June 2005; V. Guiraudon and G. Lahav, 'The state sovereignty debate revisited: the case of migration control', (2000) 33 *Comparative Political Studies* 751–78.

[15] E. Guild, 'The borders of the European Union: visas and carrier sanctions', (2004) 7 *Tidsskriftet Politik* 34–43; Nicholson, 'Implementation'; Feller, 'Carrier sanctions'.

[16] Verkuil, *Outsourcing Sovereignty*; I. Gatev, 'Very remote control: policing the outer perimeter of the EU neighbourhood', paper presented at the European University Institute conference, 'The external dimension of European immigration policies', Florence, 23–24 November 2006.

Neither of these developments sits easily with the traditional picture of refugee law as a constraint on the prerogative of states to control entry into their territory. As part of extraterritorial controls, states have claimed that neither the *non-refoulement* principle nor other norms under international refugee law apply when refugees are intercepted outside the state's territory. Similarly, the argument that states incur any obligations under refugee law as a result of carrier controls has been rejected on the premise that these controls are a private matter, distinct from the state's own authorities and thus responsibility. As a consequence, few if any protection mechanisms are currently available to the refugee who encounters the immigration authorities or privately operated migration control extraterritorially. As a matter of political practice at least, the balance between national and international sovereignty, freedom and responsibility, established by modern refugee law, thus seems to tip and the refugee, now encountered extraterritorially, is once again submitted fully to the sovereign power and benevolence of the potential asylum state.

2.2 Between universal human rights and principles of national sovereignty

How may we conceptualise the developments sketched above? The case of refugees and migration control could be seen as signifying a more fundamental shift in the way states organise themselves and respond to global challenges. Just as migration control is being offshored, so are functions ranging from commercial business to the detention of terrorist suspects. Similarly, private involvement for the purpose of migration control is part of a much broader trend to privatise inherently sovereign functions, from the running of prisons to the use of private security companies for military operations at home and abroad. In each case the traditional assumption that states remain free to exercise sovereign powers within, and only within, their own territory is challenged, which in turn prompts questions on how to organise sovereign responsibilities relating to national and international human rights obligations.

These questions have occupied numerous political scientists and lawyers for well over the last decade. From very different viewpoints, scholars of both disciplines have heralded the developments above as evidence of the decline or even the 'end of sovereignty'.[17] First, those emphasising sovereignty as a de facto property of the state have argued that immigration is just one example of the fact that sovereignty, in the sense of the state's ability to control transborder flows and exercise power within its territory, is waning as a result of globalisation. Like migration, the global flow of capital and goods, the rise of transnational corporations, international crimes such as drug trafficking, and the effects of climate change all seem to undermine the state's ability to assert effective jurisdiction at its borders and within its territory.[18]

In this context, the extraterritorialisation and privatisation of migration control may be taken as evidence of the 'retreat of the state', and these policies thus ultimately take on a more symbolic function.[19] While control initiatives viewed in isolation can be said to be effective, the idea of controlling immigration perfectly – an impregnable 'Fortress Europe' – ultimately remains illusory.[20] First, aspiring to achieve complete control carries an inherent risk of establishing obstacles for the 'wanted' migrants. In the global economy, liberal states are deeply dependent on easy travel across borders, both for their own citizens and for business visitors, tourists and labour migrants. Second, when they nonetheless implement migration control, states are further caught in an impossible endeavour, where each expansion of control is likely to spawn an answering loss of control, as more migrants and asylum-seekers are driven to seek entry clandestinely, the profitability of human smuggling is driven up and new migratory routes open.[21]

Closely connected to the views above, others have argued that territorial and state-centric sovereignty principles as a normative framework for the organisation of state competences and rights in the international

[17] J. A. Camilleri and J. Falk, *The End of Sovereignty? The Politics of a Shrinking and Fragmenting World* (Aldershot: Edward Elgar, 1992).

[18] R. Falk, 'Human rights: a descending spiral', in R. A. Wilson (ed.), *War on Terror* (Cambridge University Press, 2005), pp. 225–41; S. D. Krasner, *Sovereignty – Organized Hypocrisy* (Princeton University Press, 1999); D. Held, A. McGrew, D. Goldblatt and J. Perraton, *Global Transformations: Politics, Economics, and Culture* (Stanford University Press, 1999); S. Sassen, *Losing Control? Sovereignty in an Age of Globalization* (New York: Columbia University Press, 1995).

[19] S. Strange, *The Retreat of the State* (Cambridge University Press, 1996).

[20] T. Gammeltoft-Hansen, 'EU's Umulige Grænsekontrol', (2006) 2 *Udenrigs* 69–79; S. Skogly and M. Gibney, 'Transnational human rights obligations', (2002) 24 *Human Rights Quarterly* 781–98, at 783, 787; Weiner, 'Ethics', 179–81.

[21] T. Gammeltoft-Hansen, 'Filtering out the risky migrant: migration control, risk theory and the EU', AMID Working Paper Series 52/2006, Academy for Migration Studies in Denmark, 2006.

system are at best superfluous and at worst directly misleading in today's world.[22] Globalisation provides not only challenges to traditional modes of governance, but also new possibilities. As a result, states themselves are becoming global actors, and the offshoring and outsourcing of government functions is a natural consequence in a world increasingly dominated by the international law of co-operation as opposed to coexistence.[23]

From a human rights perspective, these developments have been taken by some as support for a similar revision or more dynamic interpretation of human rights and other areas of international law, and of their ability to regulate the activities of states and non-state actors. If human rights are supposed to be universally applicable and remain effective, the emergence of policies to offshore and outsource otherwise governmental functions in themselves provides the strongest argument for similarly expanding the reach of these instruments and having international judiciaries respond more readily to human rights violations of signatory states wherever on the globe they may be occurring.[24] Similarly, it has been argued that the growing role of non-state actors on the international scene entails new responsibilities under international law for, to cite one example, transnational corporations.[25] Thus while offshore and privatised migration control may be accepted as a natural strategy to recoup efficiency in

---

[22] K. Nicolaidis and J. L. Tong, 'Diversity or cacophony? The continuing debate of new sources of international law', (2004) 25 *Michigan Journal of International Law* 1349–75, at 1354; L. Henkin, 'That "S" word: sovereignty, and globalization, and human rights, etc.', (1999) 68 *Fordham Law Review* 1–14; C. Clapham, 'Sovereignty and the Third World state', (1999) 47 *Political Studies* 522–37, at 522; P. Malanczuk, *Akehurst's Modern Introduction to International Law* (Oxford: Routledge, 1997); M. Koskenniemi, *From Apology to Utopia: The Structure of International Legal Argument* (Helsinki: Finnish Lawyers' Publishing Company, 1989), p. 198.

[23] S. Sakellaropoulos, 'Towards a declining state? The rise of the headquarters state', (2007) 71 *Science and Society* 7–34; Skogly and Gibney, 'Transnational human rights obligations', 784; J. A. C. Salcedo, 'Reflections on the existence of a hierarchy of norms in international law', (1997) 8 *European Journal of International Law* 583–95; W. Friedmann, *The Changing Structure of International Law* (London: Stevens & Sons, 1964); C. Leben, 'Symposium: the changing structure of international law revisited: by way of introduction', (1997) 8 *European Journal of International Law* 399–408.

[24] M. Gibney, *International Human Rights Law: Returning to Universal Principles* (Lanham, MD: Rowman & Littlefield, 2008); B. Vandvik, 'Extraterritorial border controls and responsibility: a view from ECRE', (2008) *Amsterdam Law Forum* 27–36; M. Scheinin, 'Extraterritorial effect of the International Covenant on Civil and Political Rights', in F. Coomans and M. T. Kamminga (eds.), *Extraterritorial Application of Human Rights Treaties* (Antwerp: Intersentia, 2004), pp. 73–82; T. Meron, 'Extraterritoriality of human rights treaties', (1995) 89 *American Journal of International Law* 78–82.

[25] A. Clapham, *Human Rights Obligations of Non-state Actors* (Oxford University Press, 2006).

response to global challenges, such activities cannot remain outside the scope of international refugee and human rights obligations.

In contrast to the different positions above, this volume does not identify a waning of state sovereignty, regardless of whether this elusive concept is defined as a set of material powers or as a normative framework. The idea of perfect border control may be illusory. Yet, like any other display of sovereign autonomy, full control over a state's external borders has probably always remained a somewhat unrealised ideal.[26] While states may be confronting new challenges in this regard, outsourcing and offshoring represent practices whereby exactly the same mechanisms of globalisation are employed to reassert regulatory capacity and control in areas where such capacity is otherwise restrained, either by the factual circumstances such as increased migratory pressures or by legal constraints such as national and international refugee and human rights obligations. Thus, paradoxically, shifting regulatory functions away from the territory and away from the state's own authorities seems to reinforce rather than diminish state power in this material sense.[27]

Furthermore, despite evocative references to a growing 'legal black hole', there is little to suggest that offshore and outsourced migration control takes place outside international and national law as such. First, arrangements to shift migration control to foreign territory or to delegate control functions to private entities tend to be facilitated precisely through international legal arrangements and national law. Second, as will be evidenced throughout the following chapters, both general principles of international law and a growing body of human rights case law affirm that human rights and refugee law obligations remain applicable even when states act extraterritorially or delegate authority to non-state actors.

Yet, contrary to the claims for a universal extension of state obligations, it is equally clear that the application of refugee and human rights instruments to situations of offshore or outsourced governmental activities is a far from straightforward matter. As will be seen, states are not bound in all situations, and the content and extent of obligations may change when migration control is shifted to foreign territories or private entities. In each case state responsibility is dependent on the establishment

---

[26] Krasner, *Sovereignty – Organized Hypocrisy*.

[27] Palan, *Offshore World*, p. 153; E. Guild, 'The border abroad – visas and border controls', in Groenendijk, Guild and Minderhoud, *In Search of Europe's Borders*, pp. 87–104, at p. 103; Guiraudon, 'Before the EU border'.

of extraterritorial jurisdiction over the human rights victim in question and, in cases of outsourcing, of control over the agent or actors perpetrating the human rights in question.[28] Consequently, while case law establishing state responsibility in these situations is growing, there has been some reluctance among both national and international judiciaries to extend unconditionally human rights obligations in cases of offshoring and outsourcing.

This reluctance reflects a potential clash with core norms of international law anchored in national sovereignty. The first of these is the principle of territoriality. Probably the most fundamental principle of international law is that each state's right to exercise power is limited to its sovereign territory. The territory is the state's primary physical manifestation vis-à-vis other states.[29] In a world composed of equal sovereign states, the claim legitimately to exercise power, or jurisdiction, is vested in the 'sovereign nation cage', horizontally encompassing the state's land territory and territorial sea, and vertically extending from the Kármán line – 100 km (approximately 62 miles) above sea level – down through the subsoil of the national territory and ending at the centre of the Earth.[30]

Territory thus serves in international law as the expression of national sovereignty, and as such has become instrumental in solving legal disputes. As was held by the Permanent Court of International Justice in the *Las Palmas* case,

Sovereignty in the relations between States signifies independence. Independence in regard to a portion of the globe is the right to exercise therein, to the exclusion of any other State, the functions of a State. The development of the national organisation of States during the last few centuries and, as a corollary, the development of international law, have established this principle of the exclusive competence of the State in regard to its own territory in such a way as to make it the point of departure in settling most questions that concern international relations.[31]

---

[28] Where migration control is both privatised and carried out extraterritorially, such as in the case of carrier sanctions, these requirements become cumulative. See further below, section 5.7.

[29] I. Brownlie, *Principles of Public International Law* (Oxford University Press, 1998), p. 105.

[30] O. Spiermann, *International Legal Argument in the Permanent Court of International Justice: The Rise of the International Judiciary* (Cambridge University Press, 2005), p. 83; Palan, *Offshore World*, p. 97; R. T. Ford, 'Law's territory (a history of jurisdiction)', (1999) 97 *Michigan Law Review* 843–930; J. G. Ruggie, 'Territoriality and beyond: problematizing modernity in international relations', (1993) 47 *International Organization* 139–74, at 151. See further below, section 4.2.1.

[31] *Case of the Island of Palmas*, p. 838.

In the human rights context, the territoriality principle has played an equally important role in setting boundaries for state responsibility.[32] Some instruments explicitly limit rights to beneficiaries present within the territory of the state in question. More generally, many human rights instruments are limited in their geographical application to the state's 'jurisdiction'. While the meaning of this term has been fiercely debated, it has been difficult to dissociate it from territory as the primary realm of state power. Thus in the *Banković* case the European Court of Human Rights held that 'jurisdiction', in the meaning of the Convention,

must be considered to reflect the ordinary and essentially territorial notion of jurisdiction, other bases of jurisdiction being exceptional and requiring special justification in the particular circumstances of each case.[33]

As will be discussed in chapter 4, jurisdiction and concomitant human rights responsibility may, in a range of situations, equally be established extraterritorially. Yet in the vast majority of cases jurisdiction is naturally understood in territorial terms and any extension beyond this requires the additional step of establishing the state's authority or control over the human rights victim or geographic area in question.

The second foundational norm is the distinction between public and private. The separation between public and private has been a constitutive element of both national and international law.[34] The state's monopoly of the legitimate exercise of power within its commonwealth necessitates that the state, and those acting as agents of the state, can be clearly defined in relation to those over whom power is to be exercised. Just as territoriality serves to delineate and define the state horizontally vis-à-vis other states, the public/private distinction thus serves to define the state vertically in relation to its subjects.[35]

---

[32] C. Tomuschat, *Human Rights: Between Idealism and Realism*, 2nd edn (Oxford University Press, 2008), p. 98.

[33] *Banković and Others v. Belgium, Czech Republic, Denmark, France, Germany, Greece, Hungary, Iceland, Italy, Luxembourg, Netherlands, Norway, Poland, Portugal, Spain, Turkey and the UK*, European Court of Human Rights, Application No. 52207/99, 12 December 2001, para. 61.

[34] P. Alston, 'The "not-a-cat" syndrome: can the international human rights regime accommodate non-state actors?', in P. Alston (ed.), *Non-state Actors and Human Rights* (Oxford University Press, 2005), pp. 3–36; C. Chinkin, 'A critique of the public/private dimension', (1999) 10 *European Journal of International Law* 387–95; R. Higgins, *Problems and Process: International Law and How We Use It* (Oxford: Clarendon Press, 1994), p. 153.

[35] The public/private distinction as a foundational norm of international law and the critique thereof is dealt with below, section 5.4.

A basic principle of international law has thus been that states cannot be held responsible for the conduct of private actors.[36] As noted by the International Court of Justice in the *Genocide* case,

the fundamental principle governing the law of international responsibility [is that] a State is responsible only for its own conduct, that is to say the conduct of persons acting, on whatever basis, on its behalf.[37]

Of course, real life seldom conforms to the neat separation between public authorities and private persons. Private involvement in the execution of otherwise governmental policies is no new phenomenon and a growing one, and a sharp distinction between public and private is consequently hard to uphold both de facto and de jure. Chapter 5 deals with situations where conduct of otherwise private actors may thus nonetheless be attributed to the state and thereby gives rise to human rights responsibility. But even so, the public/private distinction tends to remain the point of departure. An initial presumption against state responsibility for human rights violations seems to persist in most cases where governmental functions such as migration control are privatised, and this presumption must be rebutted in each specific case.

The result is a situation where the application of international refugee and human rights law to situations of offshore or outsourced migration control is increasingly contested. Interpretation of both specific refugee law provisions and general principles such as 'jurisdiction' and 'attribution' seems to oscillate between two opposing poles – on the one hand the universal claim underpinning both refugee and human rights law and, on the other, principles of national sovereignty anchoring responsibility to the state and its territory. In other words, each time human rights responsibility has to be established in situations of offshoring and outsourcing, the 'sovereignty threshold' has to be overcome.[38]

The difficulties in establishing human rights responsibility in cases of extraterritorial or privatised migration control thus inevitably point back to a deeper conflict within international refugee and human rights law itself. On the one hand human rights are declared to be universal; on

---

[36] R. P. J. Barnidge, *Non-state Actors and Terrorism: Applying the Law of State Responsibility and the Due Diligence Principle* (The Hague: Asser Press, 2008), p. 4; J. Crawford, *The International Law Commission's Articles on State Responsibility: Introduction, Text and Commentaries* (Cambridge University Press, 2002), p. 91; Higgins, *Problems and Process*, p. 153.

[37] *Application of the Convention on the Prevention and Punishment of the Crime of Genocide (Bosnia and Herzegovina v. Serbia and Montenegro)*, ICJ, 26 February 2007, para. 406.

[38] Skogly and Gibney, 'Transnational human rights obligations', 796.

the other hand human rights are part and parcel of the larger frame-work of international law and as such must pay homage to its underlying principles in order to remain law.[39] Borrowing a distinction from Kant, a difference thereby remains between the *sein* and the *sollen* of refugee and human rights law, between human rights codified as positive inter-national law and human rights as a universal normative ideal.[40] While the latter proceeds from the creed that wherever there is power there must be constraint of that power, the former fixes responsibility to a legal construction of the state built on the principles of territoriality and the public/private distinction.

2.3 The territoriality of the international refugee regime

The above is no less true of international refugee law. Despite its appear-ance and language of universality and the starting premise of escaping national sovereignty by ensuring refuge for subjects of other states, the international refugee protection regime is in the true sense of the word *inter*-national. Refugee protection is not guaranteed in a global homo-geneous juridical space, but materialises as a patchwork of commit-ments undertaken by individual states tied together by multilateral treaty agreements.[41] This becomes clear not only from looking at the global pro-vision of protection but also when examining the fundamental principles on which human rights and, in particular, refugee law are premised.

As noted above, to some extent territorial principles permeate human rights law in general. The subjects of human rights protection are nor-mally conceived to be either a state's own nationals or aliens within

---

[39] Neil MacCormick speaks of the 'positivisation' of human rights law that serves to institutionalise and make authoritative otherwise controversial and often inexact notions of rights. N. MacCormick, *Institutions of Law: An Essay in Legal Theory* (Oxford University Press, 2007), pp. 273–4.

[40] P.-M. Dupuy, 'International law: torn between coexistence, cooperation and globalization: general conclusions', (1998) 9 *European Journal of International Law* 278–86, at 285. Although partly related, the argument made above should not be confused with the dichotomy sometimes proposed by critical legal scholars between human rights as expressing human values and human rights as expressing state values: the utopia and the apology. See e.g. R. Burchill, 'International human rights law: struggling between apology and utopia', in A. Bullard (ed.), *Human Rights in Crisis* (Aldershot: Ashgate, 2008), pp. 49–68, and Koskenniemi, *From Apology to Utopia*. Whereas the view presented in this volume poses the conflict in terms of contrasting and competing interests in the service of human rights law, the tension identified above is structural and relates to a conflict between purpose and form.

[41] Palan, *Offshore World*, p. 87.

its territory. The major achievement of the human rights movement was exactly to introduce to international law a set of norms that did not simply concern the *horizontal* relationship between states, but a *vertical* obligation between each state and its subjects and others within its territory.[42] In codifying this vertical relationship as a matter of treaty law, the principle of territoriality is essentially reaffirmed once more. As Matthew Craven points out,

The general problem ... is that the international human rights project, far from being one that is essentially antithetical to the inter-state order, is one that relies upon a relatively sharp demarcation between respective realms of power and responsibility. Human rights obligations typically require not merely that states abstain from certain courses of action, but also act with 'due diligence' to protect individuals from others, and to progressively fulfil rights in certain circumstances. In order for these obligations to be in any way meaningful, some distinction has to be maintained between those contexts in which a state may reasonably be said to assume those responsibilities and those in which it does not.[43]

This is not to say that human rights obligations are under all circumstances limited to the territorial sphere. As will be evidenced throughout the following chapters and as is shown in a growing body of literature, human rights responsibility may involve an additional *diagonal* relationship between a state and individuals outside its territory,[44] but intra-state protection remains the starting point.

The international legal refugee protection regime is part and parcel of this development. Refugee law may be considered a branch of human rights law, and refugee protection has benefited substantially from the bolstering and patching of claims under specific refugee instruments with obligations derived from general human rights law.

That said, refugee law is distinctive in at least one respect. Whereas the thrust of the human rights movement is geared towards opening up the black box of the state hitherto so zealously guarded by principles of national sovereignty, refugee law is specific in dealing solely with the relationship between the state and the subjects of another

---

[42] H. Steiner, 'International protection of human rights', in M. D. Evans (ed.), *International Law*, 2nd edn (Oxford University Press, 2006), pp. 753–82, at p. 769; Skogly and Gibney, 'Transnational human rights obligations', 782.

[43] M. Craven, 'Human rights in the realm of order: sanctions and extraterritoriality', in Coomans and Kamminga, *Extraterritorial Application*, pp. 233–58, at p. 255.

[44] M. Gibney and S. Skogly (eds.), *Universal Human Rights Law and Extraterritorial Obligations* (Philadelphia: University of Pennsylvania Press, 2010); Coomans and Kamminga, *Extraterritorial Application*.

state. This relation may still be played out vertically within the host state, yet the fact that it is concerned solely with foreigners and not a state's own subjects means that the refugee regime, in certain ways, differs from the ordinary modus operandi of the broader human rights regime.

Much of the human rights movement has been geared towards pushing for increased state responsibility in ensuring rights owed to its citizens. The refugee regime, in contrast, takes as its starting point the fact that for some individuals the realisation of fundamental rights within their country of origin will never be possible. While both the human rights and the refugee regime share the same concern to avoid rights violations, the solution offered under the refugee regime is not state reform but protection in another state.[45] No onus is put on the obligations of countries of origin under international refugee law; rather, instruments have been explicit in stating that the granting of asylum is not to be considered as an 'unfriendly act' towards countries of origin.[46] Thus where the human rights regime in general is preventive and aimed at protection in the country of nationality, the refugee regime is by and large palliative and exilic.[47]

There have been several attempts to overcome this exilic bias. The movement by some scholars to 'reconceive refugee law as human rights' naturally involves an extension of protection obligations to states without a direct territorial affiliation to the refugee, to countries of origin for ending persecution and to more developed states for providing financial support to the countries of first asylum that continue to receive the majority of the world's refugees.[48] Similarly, current policy developments in a number of countries seem to emphasise 'protection in the region' or even

---

[45] J. Hathaway, 'Forced migration studies: could we agree just to "date"?', (2007) 20 *Journal of Refugee Studies* 349–69.

[46] See e.g. the Preamble of the UN Declaration on Territorial Asylum, UNGA Res. 2312 (XXII), 14 December 1967.

[47] J. Hathaway, 'New directions to avoid hard problems: the distortion of the palliative role of refugee protection', (1995) 8 *Journal of Refugee Studies* 288–94; Goodwin-Gill and McAdam, *Refugee in International Law*, pp. 2–5; B. S. Chimni, 'The geopolitics of refugee studies and the practice of international institutions: a view from the south', (1999) 11 *Journal of Refugee Studies* 350–74; G. Okoth-Obbo, 'Coping with a complex refugee crisis in Africa: issues, problems and constraints for refugee and international law', in V. Gowlland-Debbas (ed.), *The Problem of Refugees in the Light of Contemporary International Law: Papers Presented at the Colloquium Organized by the Graduate Institute of International Studies in Collaboration with the United Nations High Commissioner for Refugees, Geneva 26 and 27 May 1994* (Dordrecht: Martinus Nijhoff Publishers, 1996), pp. 7–17.

[48] Hathaway, *Reconceiving International Refugee Law*.

'in-country protection' as alternatives to asylum in, for example, Europe or the United States.[49]

In many respects these developments ought to be readily welcomed. For decades UNHCR has been trying to get the message across that 'refugees are human rights violations made visible'. A more equitable distribution of the global burden of refugee protection is no doubt needed if greater compliance with refugee protection standards is to be ensured. Yet, so far, financial commitment to these policies has remained limited. At the same time, efforts to ensure 'protection in the region' have in some instances been closely linked to offshore and outsourced migration control, pitching the former as a political compensation for the latter. The net result of such policies is thus not always increased burden sharing, but rather burden shifting.

The basic structure of international refugee law could be argued to provide a certain incentive for shifting protection obligations through offshore and privatised migration control. This concerns, first, the core principle that states may not send back, or *refouler*, a refugee to a place in which he or she risks persecution.[50] Normally, this prohibition is engaged as soon as a refugee or asylum-seeker arrives at the frontiers of a given state and in principle requires authorities to undertake a status determination procedure.[51] In this way, the division of refugee protection responsibilities generally follows territorial borders – whatever country refugees find themselves in, that state is responsible for not sending them back to persecution. The *non-refoulement* principle is reactive in the sense that it presupposes some kind of contact between the state and the asylum-seeker.

The importance of proximity and territorial delineations becomes even more evident when moving past this fundamental obligation and looking at the wider set of protections guaranteed by the international refugee

---

[49] S. Taylor, 'Protection elsewhere/nowhere', (2006) 181 *International Journal of Refugee Law* 283–312.

[50] In effect this also applies to asylum-seekers. Refugee status is declaratory, not constitutive, meaning that it is not dependent on formal recognition by a state, for example through a refugee status determination procedure. As a result, states are bound to respect the principle of *non-refoulement* presumptively until it has been proven that an asylum-seeker is not a refugee and therefore can be rejected or returned without a risk of harm.

[51] J. Fitzpatrick, 'Revitalizing the 1951 Refugee Convention', (1996) 9 *Harvard Human Rights Journal* 229–53; UNHCR, Advisory Opinion on the Extraterritorial Application of Non-refoulement Obligations under the 1951 Convention relating to the Status of Refugees and its 1967 Protocol, 26 January 2007.

protection regime. The rights stemming from the 1951 Refugee Convention are granted not *en bloc* but progressively, according to the 'level of attachment' a refugee obtains to a given country. Thus the more sophisticated rights, such as access to welfare, employment and legal aid, are only granted when the refugee is 'lawfully staying' or 'durably resident' in the territory of the host state. Conversely, refugees or asylum-seekers who are not present in a state's territory but are nonetheless under its jurisdiction, such as on the high seas or in the territory of a third state, are only entitled to a very basic set of rights centred on the *non-refoulement* obligation.[52]

This incremental approach reflects a seemingly sensible concern of the drafters not to extend the full scope of rights immediately in situations where refugees may arrive spontaneously in large numbers.[53] Yet, at a time when states are moving both migration control and the management of asylum outside their own territorial confines, this notion of progressiveness risks being cut short, as refugees and asylum-seekers may never reach the territory of the acting state.

Lastly, protection is not just protection. Despite the near-global applicability of instruments such as the 1951 Refugee Convention, the protection of refugees remains dependent on the individual sovereign states obliged to guarantee it. As such, the actual protection afforded to refugees has been seen to vary considerably, depending on the country bestowing it.

This variation can be seen to have at least three dimensions. First, one could ask whether it can be assumed that the rights owed to refugees under the Refugee Convention are actually afforded. This is most evident in the case of states that are not party to the Refugee Convention or other relevant human rights instruments and therefore under no obligation to guarantee the rights embedded in them.[54] Furthermore, as repeatedly pointed out by the agency responsible for supervising the application of the Refugee Convention, the degree of certainty with which it can be

---

[52] The most pertinent rights under the Refugee Convention that are specifically granted without reference to being present or staying at the territory include Art. 33 (*non-refoulement*), Art. 16 (access to courts) and Art. 3 (non-discrimination). Somewhat more specific and limited in their extraterritorial remit, Arts. 13 (property), 22 (education) and 20 (rationing) also apply extraterritorially. J. Hathaway, *The Rights of Refugees under International Law* (Cambridge University Press, 2005), pp. 160 ff.

[53] Hathaway, *Rights of Refugees*, p. 157.

[54] Except for obligations that may take the form of *jus cogens*, as some scholars argue is the case for the *non-refoulement* principle. See e.g. J. Allains, 'The *jus cogens* nature of *non-refoulement*', (2001) 13 *International Journal of Refugee Law* 533–58. See further below, section 3.6.9.

assumed that rights are realised and the obligations owed are adhered to should not be taken for granted, even for states that are a party to the Convention.[55] As the surge in restrictive asylum and immigration policies has taken hold among countries in the Global North, it becomes increasingly difficult to find 'model states'.

Second, even though adherence to the formal protection requirements is taken for granted, specific rights may not be implemented or may be implemented rather differently in different countries. Thus the scope of rights afforded can be said to vary. Of the thirty-three articles of the Refugee Convention specifying the rights of refugees (Arts. 2–34), only four (Arts. 3, 4, 16(1) and 33) are exempt from the possibility of reservations. In some cases, reservations have been employed to derogate from the way in which a specific right is granted. Denmark entered a reservation towards Article 17(1) (the right to paid employment), as it has been reluctant to extend to refugees access to the labour market similar to that enjoyed by 'most favoured nationals of a foreign country', which are those of the Nordic countries, with which Denmark has entered into special agreements.[56]

This leads to the third, and perhaps most important, aspect. A great number of rights pertaining to refugees are specifically granted at a level relative to how each country treats different categories of people. The freedom of religion guaranteed under Article 4 of the Refugee Convention is thus not absolute, but is only enjoyed in relation to the freedom of religion afforded to nationals of the country in question. This point is particularly pertinent to the social rights and services that can be claimed by refugees. The great differences between human rights and living standards in more and less developed countries are likely to make the refugee experience substantially different in, for example, Uganda as compared with the United Kingdom.

Together, these three dimensions can be termed the 'quality of protection', understood as the certainty, scope and level of rights afforded to refugees. They paint a rather chequered picture of the entitlements actually provided to refugees under the international refugee protection regime. Thus when states attempt to prevent the triggering of the

---

[55] UNHCR, *State of the World's Refugees: Human Displacement in the New Millennium* (Geneva: UNHCR, 2006).

[56] The wording of the reservation was changed to its current formulation on 25 March 1968. Denmark's reservation is still upheld, yet its practical significance is reduced if not entirely obviated by subsequent EU law granting similar rights to all EU nationals.

territorial mechanism that makes them responsible for granting certain rights to asylum-seekers (as in the case of interdiction schemes or carrier sanctions) or subsequently attempt to shift the burden of bestowing these rights onto third countries (as in the case of 'safe third country' rules or plans for 'protection in the region of origin'), it may be relevant to consider not only whether protection will be afforded elsewhere, but also the quality of this protection.

There has been a tendency to overlook or even deny this point when considering the transfer of responsibility for protection as, for example, under the 'safe third country' rule. As the UK House of Lords declared,

> the Convention is directed to a very important but very simple and very practical end, preventing the return of applicants to places where they will or may suffer persecution. Legal niceties and refinements should not be allowed to obstruct that purpose. It can never, save in extreme circumstances, be appropriate to compare an applicant's living conditions in different countries if, in each of them, he will be safe from persecution or the risk of it.[57]

Arguably, however, such an interpretation of the Refugee Convention fails to acknowledge the array of rights normally bestowed on any refugee having arrived in the territory, even if refugee status is not yet recognised.[58] But where the refugee is encountered extraterritorially, only a very limited set of rights under the 1951 Refugee Convention may potentially be claimed. In the processes of extraterritorialisation and privatisation, not only may the formal responsibility for *non-refoulement* shift, but the quality of protection owed is also likely to be substantially altered, depending on the territorial state in which migration control is carried out. To the extent that protection responsibility is deflected or transferred to less developed states, or to states with poor human rights records or undeveloped asylum systems – as has indeed been the case – this may effectively erode the quality of protection afforded under the present refugee regime.

The result is what could be termed 'protection lite', understood as the presence of formal protection, but with a lower degree of certainty about the scope and/or level of rights afforded. Like 'Coke Lite', it retains its brand name, but the content has substantially fewer calories. It is important to note that, within a strict or restrictive reading, this may well fall

---

[57] *R. v. Secretary of State for the Home Department, ex parte Yogathas,* UK House of Lords, [2002] UKHL 36, 17 October 2002, para. 9.

[58] Hathaway, *Rights of Refugees,* p. 332.

within the operational flexibility made possible by the international legal framework. Indeed, the territorial principle of dividing responsibility and bestowing rights relative to the practices and situation of each particular country enshrined in the 1951 Refugee Convention is the very premise for this development. Whether it is in the spirit of the present regime, however, is another question.

2.4 The commercialisation of sovereignty and the market for migration control

The difficulty in having international refugee law overcome the sovereignty threshold could be argued to stem from the fundamental change in the political logic around which migration control is organised. The territorial structures underpinning the international refugee protection regime not only provide an incentive to extraterritorialise migration control in order to reduce protection obligations owed; they also make it attractive to engage in co-operation with third states and private actors to shift migration control to the territory of states with perceived lower costs with regard to the quality of refugee protection. Designating migration control as 'extraterritorial' or 'private' in itself becomes an asset. Hence, from the perspective of the corporate actors taking on control responsibilities or the territorial state within whose jurisdiction migration control is enacted, these very traits become marketable.

As political practices, offshore and outsourced migration control could be seen as expressions of a growing 'commercialisation of sovereignty'. This term was originally coined by international political economists to explain the significance of tax havens and offshore economies. It describes how certain states have strategically deregulated areas of national legislation, often only for particular groups such as foreigners, for example for taxation purposes, or even for certain areas of their territory such as airport tax-free zones, tourist areas or the use of flags of convenience. It involves a bifurcation of the sovereign space into heavily and lightly regulated realms – all in order to attract international business and capital.[59] As a result, Liberia is, at least on paper, the largest shipping nation in

[59] R. Palan, 'Tax havens and the commercialization of state sovereignty', (2002) 56 *International Organization* 151–76; Palan, *Offshore World*.

the world, and the Cayman Islands is formally the world's fifth-largest economy.[60]

More generally, and in the wider sense in which this term is used in the present context, the commercialisation of sovereignty may be defined as the strategic disposition or commodification of state territory, rights, prerogatives and functions in the relation between states and between states and private actors. In the context of migration control, commercialisation of sovereignty is possible exactly because of the territorial principles underpinning refugee law in terms of the distribution of responsibility and the extent and quality of protection owed. In the patchwork of national refugee and human rights regimes, shifting the legal geography for migration control may simultaneously reduce the acting state's protection responsibilities and shift legal obligations to third states or private actors whose 'human rights obligations are either lower, less extensive or less precise than those of the destination State'.[61]

2.4.1 Jurisdiction shopping and the inter-state market for migration control

The result of the above is a growing international and corporate market for migration control. This market may be seen to have two dimensions. The first is horizontal and primarily related to extraterritorialisation. By moving control activities out of their national territory, states are engaging in 'jurisdiction shopping'.[62] Jurisdiction shopping may involve a unilateral decision to move control activities to the high seas, or *res communis*, and thereby bring about a reduction of rights owed under international refugee law compared with the territorial setting. Equally, some states have sought to excise parts of their territory, such as airports or exposed shorelines, to create consciously deregulated areas where ordinary procedures and law in regard to asylum-seekers and migrants does not apply. Most clearly, however, jurisdiction shopping may be observed when states shift migration control into the territory or territorial waters of another state willing to make available its sovereign jurisdiction for the specific purpose. In these instances, not only is the responsibility of the acting

[60] Palan, *Offshore World*, p. 3.
[61] G. Noll, 'The politics of saving lives: interception, search and rescue and the question of human rights at sea', paper presented at a workshop, The Future of Asylum Policy in the European Union, organised by the Finnish EU Presidency and the Odysseus Network, Turku, 10 October 2006, 1.
[62] Palan, 'Tax havens'.

state reduced, but a competing duty bearer is introduced into the equation that may be argued to have the primary responsibility for assessing the protection needs of any asylum claim made within its territory.

Examples where states have engaged in such bartering of sovereign authority for the purpose of migration management are several and growing. As part of the EU–co-ordinated HERA operations preventing irregular migration to the Canary Islands, Spain has thus signed agreements with Senegal and Mauritania to intercept and directly return irregular migrants within their territorial waters. Italy has signed a similar treaty with Libya that allows for joint patrolling in Libyan waters. Outside Europe, the United States has used the Guantánamo base leased from Cuba as a diversion point for asylum-seekers intercepted on the high seas and, in 2001, Australia negotiated an agreement with the island states of Nauru and Papua New Guinea to establish offshore processing centres for intercepted asylum-seekers.

The economic or other costs involved in these arrangements are often hard to gauge, as agreements may not be publicly available and arrangements for the purpose of migration control tied to other foreign policy areas such as trade or development aid.[63] In addition to costs associated with setting up a radar station in Tripoli and delivering six naval vessels, the joint patrol treaty between Italy and Libya was accompanied by an agreement that Italy would pay US$5 billion to Libya.[64] Whether such solutions are cost-effective in the strictly economic sense is, furthermore, uncertain. Non-governmental organisations (NGOs) estimate that, over a six-year period, ensuring third-state co-operation and relocating, housing and processing asylum-seekers at offshore locations have cost Australia close to A$1 billion, an amount much greater than that needed for processing the approximately 1,700 asylum-seekers concerned through ordinary territorial procedures.[65] Such calculations are, however, notoriously speculative and the calculations for other cases, especially where only access for control is negotiated, may, of course, look different. In any case,

---

[63] Geddes, 'Migration as Foreign Policy?', 33; Gammeltoft-Hansen, 'Outsourcing migration management'; Lavenex, 'Shifting up and out'; E. Guild, 'What is a neighbour'; J. Niessen and Y. Schibel, 'International migration and relations with third countries: European and US approaches', MPG Occasional Paper, Migration Policy Group, Berlin, May 2004.

[64] The funds were framed as a compensation and apology for the damages and misdeeds done during Italy's colonial rule of Libya. John Philips, 'Pact with Libya aims at curbing illegals', *Washington Times*, 31 August 2008.

[65] K. Bem et al., 'A price too high: the cost of Australia's approach to asylum-seekers', A Just Australia and Oxfam Australia (August 2007).

offshore migration control schemes appear to be driven just as much by political motivations and the estimated deterrent effect as for economic reasons alone.[66]

Closely related to the market for migration control, but somewhat beyond the scope of this volume, one may equally identify a growing 'market for refugee protection'.[67] The Australian case thus involves more than merely jurisdiction shopping for the purpose of migration control, but concerns an offshoring of the asylum procedure as a whole. Offshore asylum procedures, or at least screening, have equally been conducted by the United States in Cuba and, although never realised, were put forward as an EU-wide proposal by the United Kingdom in 2003.[68] Lastly, a number of states currently operate so-called 'protected entry procedures', which involve the possibility of submitting asylum applications at the embassies of third countries.[69]

While offshore asylum procedures have been shown to entail a number of problems relating both to costs and to the legal questions around the closed-camp type setting of most proposals,[70] policies that attempt to shift material protection obligations have generally fared better. In recent years policies to realise 'protection in the region' have thus been pursued by both the EU and a number of individual states.[71] The overall aim here is to improve the protection capacity of key transit or neighbouring countries and thus to prevent secondary movements and/or designate them as 'safe third countries'. The jurisdiction shopping and market-based logic of these schemes are equally clear: by shifting responsibility for refugees to less developed countries the territorial structure of the

---

[66] G. Noll, 'Visions of the exceptional: legal and theoretical issues raised by transit processing centres and protection zones', (2003) 5 *European Journal of Migration and Law* 303–41.

[67] T. Gammeltoft-Hansen, 'The extraterritorialisation of asylum and the advent of "protection lite"', Working Paper 2/2007, Danish Institute for International Studies, 2007.

[68] See further below, section 3.5.2.

[69] G. Noll, J. Fagerlund and F. Liebaut, 'Study on the feasibility of processing asylum claims outside the EU against the background of the common European asylum system and goal of a common asylum procedure', European Commission, 2003.

[70] Noll, 'Politics of saving lives'; Noll, 'Visions of the exceptional'.

[71] Gammeltoft-Hansen, 'Extraterritorialisation of asylum'; A. Betts, 'Towards a Mediterranean solution? Implications for the region of origin', (2006) 18 *International Journal of Refugee Law* 652–77; L. Peral, 'EU protection scheme for refugees in the region of origin: problems of conditionality and coherence', paper presented at ESIL Research Forum on International Law: Contemporary Issues, Geneva, 26–28 May 2005.

refugee regime is utilised to reduce the quality of protection owed and thereby get 'more protection for the Euro'.[72]

Interestingly, jurisdiction shopping for the purpose of migration control may be linked indirectly to the commercialisation of sovereignty for other purposes. Many of the vessels carrying irregular migrants setting off from Libya and the west African coast in the attempt to reach Europe are operated by former Ghanaian and Senegalese fishermen, prized by human smugglers for their navigational and seafaring skills.[73] Declining fish stocks have made it increasingly difficult for these people to maintain their traditional livelihood. According to critics, this depletion is itself caused by EU agreements with countries such as Senegal and Mauritania to buy access for European trawlers which increasingly operate within the territorial waters and exclusive economic zone of west African states.[74] Thus the EU and its member states first pay to ensure access for their trawlers and then again negotiate access to the same waters for the purpose of curbing irregular migration.

2.4.2 Privatisation and the corporate market for migration control

The second dynamic in the commercialisation of sovereignty relates to the increased marketisation of otherwise sovereign functions to non-state entities. In the same way that jurisdiction shopping creates a market for migration control between states, privatisation establishes a vertical market between a state and private contractors, companies and individuals. The trend towards privatisation of otherwise governmental functions is

---

[72] Noll et al., 'Processing asylum claims outside the EU', p. 5. The practice of designating 'safe third countries' may also in itself be conceptualised as part of an international market for refugee protection. While safe-third-country policies are unilateral instruments, the readmission agreements that permit actual return have been a key topic of foreign policy negotiations between traditional asylum countries and transit states, and have involved substantial financial compensation or other trade-offs. N. Coleman, *European Readmission Policy* (The Hague: Martinus Nijhoff Publishers, 2009); J.-P. Cassarino, 'Informalising readmission agreements in the EU neighbourhood', (2007) 42 *The International Spectator* 179–96; Gammeltoft-Hansen, 'Outsourcing migration management'; R. Byrne, G. Noll and J. Vedsted-Hansen, *New Asylum Countries? Migration Control and Refugee Protection in an Enlarged European Union* (The Hague: Kluwer Law International, 2002), IV, p. 19; S. Lavenex, *Safe Third Countries: Extending the EU Asylum and Immigration Policies to Central and Eastern Europe* (New York: Central European University Press, 1999), p. 189; K. Landgren, 'Deflecting international protection by treaty: bilateral and multilateral accords on extradition, readmission and the inadmissibility of asylum requests', New Issues in Refugee Research No. 10, UNHCR, Geneva (1999).

[73] H. Lucht, 'Ud af den globale verdens skygger', (2007) *Den Ny Verden* 73–82, at 74.

[74] Ibid.

closely linked to neo-liberalism and, more recently, the dominance of new public management theory.[75] It builds on the idea that 'the job of government is to steer, not row the boat'.[76] Steering is done through 'market-based governance', by designing and awarding contracts, and introducing economic incentives and sanctions.[77] As a result government control or influence is often less directly felt and observable.

In the privatisation of migration control one may observe several different modes of governance.[78] These include, first, the use of formal contractors supplementing national immigration authorities in carrying out a variety of tasks, from the designing and setting up of border control technology to acting as auxiliaries to, or completely replacing, national border guards. In the United States Boeing was thus awarded a US$2.5 billion contract to set up a high-tech surveillance system along the United States–Mexico border, and in Israel private security companies run several of the major checkpoints between Israel and the West Bank. In comparison, the co-optation of airlines and other carriers to perform document checks of their passengers is less contractually regulated. Instead, carrier sanctions and liability legislation rely on the negative economic logic that airlines will find it more cost-efficient to introduce the required control measures than incur financial penalties and the obligation to return any unauthorised passengers. Lastly, private actors may on their own initiative take on migration-control-related functions for ideological or economic purposes. This may be seen, for example, in the growing market for commercial visa processing companies or the rise of vigilante 'border guards' such as the self-proclaimed Minutemen patrolling the United States–Mexico border.

Beyond reasons of efficiency, the appeal of privatising migration control may equally lie in the distancing of the control functions from the state in order to avoid accountability. It creates the appearance that migration control is, precisely, private and thus external to the state itself. If the label 'private' is accepted, this may serve to remove certain legal obligations; as a matter of positive law only states are accountable under

---

[75] A. Leander, *Eroding State Authority? Private Military Companies and the Legitimate Use of Force* (Rome: Centro Militare di Studi Strategici, 2006), p. 43; P. J. Andrisani, S. Hakim and E. S. Savas, *The New Public Management: Lessons from Innovating Governors and Mayors* (Norwell, MA: Kluwer, 2002).

[76] E. S. Savas, quoted in D. Osbourne and T. Gaebler, *Reinventing Government* (New York: Addison-Wesley, 1992), p. 25.

[77] Verkuil, *Outsourcing Sovereignty*, pp. 168–71.

[78] All the following examples are dealt with more extensively below, in chapter 5.

international refugee law. The privatisation of migration control may further work to circumvent national or regional legislative constraints. In the European Union, concerns that the abolition of internal border checks would entail a loss of control were mitigated by legislation having carriers check passports or identity cards on all intra-EU routes.[79] Today, any passenger travelling through via an EU member state is thus likely to have his or her documents checked at least twice, once at check-in and once at the gate – in both instances by private transport officials.[80]

For both extraterritorialisation and privatisation, then, the market for migration control becomes a question of the choice of forum – between different national jurisdictions and between the public and the private. Commercialisation of sovereignty is in this sense facilitated by the international law of co-operation, contract law and market-driven governance techniques.[81] It is, for example, through bilateral agreements between Spain and Senegal that Spanish ships are allowed to carry out migration control inside Senegalese waters.[82] And it is within and through the framework laid down in the 1944 Chicago Convention and associated standards of the International Civil Aviation Organization (ICAO) that governments impose migration control obligations on airline companies.[83]

At the same time, however, these arrangements are premised on the existence of regulatory differences, either between states or in the distinction between public and private. In principle, only if there is a differential in terms of obligations and constraints incurred does it make sense to shift activities elsewhere. As such, the commercialisation of sovereignty may be viewed equally as a governmental technique of spatial and statist constraints that serves to reaffirm the importance of territorial boundaries and the public/private distinction.[84]

Both jurisdiction shopping and the privatisation of sovereign functions involve a disjuncture between actual practices of offshore and privatisation on the one hand, and international and national legal frameworks on the other. The commercialisation of sovereignty is made possible exactly because of the difficulty in capturing current political practices related

---

[79] G. Lahav, 'Migration and security: the role of non-state actors and civil liberties in liberal democracies', Second Coordination Meeting on International Migration, United Nations, Department of Economic and Social Affairs, Population Division (2003), p. 93.
[80] See further below, section 5.3.
[81] Palan, *Offshore World*, p. 86; Lahav, 'Migration and security', 92.
[82] See below, section 4.3.3.   [83] See below, section 5.3.   [84] Palan, *Offshore World*, p. 3.

to increased international co-operation and market-based governance within the legal norms of responsibility.[85] Paradoxically, it is the traditional norms of national sovereignty and the territorial structure of international refugee law that provide the preconditions for the proliferation of international co-operation and private contracts in the area of migration control.

The commercialisation of sovereignty is intimately dependent on this structural difference between law and politics. Thus the growth in offshore and privatisation practices has not, as one might have expected, been accompanied by a similar extension of legal frameworks to cover and regulate new forms of governance. Instead, offshore and privatisation policies rely on and reconstruct old norms of territoriality and the public/private distinction. As a result, the commercialisation of sovereignty, quite unlike Friedmann's original vision, describes a world in which the ever-growing international law of co-operation does not challenge but rather reaffirms principles of national sovereignty and the international law of coexistence.[86]

2.5 Conclusion and wider implications: offshore and privatisation as late-modern sovereignty games

This chapter has attempted to probe the deeper legal and political issues at stake in offshore and privatised migration control. Why is it so difficult to hold states accountable under international refugee and human rights law when migration control moves outside the territory or is delegated to private actors?

Arguably, the encounter between the refugee and the border authorities of a possible asylum state has always been a marker of sovereignty and as such a battleground between core sovereign prerogatives and international treaty obligations. While offshore and outsourcing may be perceived as strategies to circumvent the latter, they also open up a new field of contestation between universal and more particularist interpretations of international refugee and human rights law itself.

The difficulties in establishing state responsibility in cases of extraterritorial or privatised migration control inevitably point back to core norms

---

[85] R. Schwarz and O. Jütersonke, 'Divisible sovereignty and the reconstruction of Iraq', (2005) 26 *Third World Quarterly* 649–65, at 651; Palan, 'Tax Havens', 153.

[86] Friedmann, *Changing Structure of International Law*.

pertaining to national sovereignty, more specifically the principle of territoriality and the public/private distinction. A potential is hereby created for the commercialisation of sovereignty and a growing 'market for migration control', where states may trade access to sovereign territory or outsource sovereign functions in order to shift or deconstruct refugee and human rights obligations. As is particularly evident when examining the territorial structure of the Refugee Convention, international law itself plays a constitutive role in fostering these new practices by continuously emphasising territorial and public/private distinctions.

From the core of the commercialisation of sovereignty emerges a problem of matching political realities with legal norms. This is not a particularly new phenomenon. Writing more than six decades ago, Hans Morgenthau noted with regret a similar disjuncture:

> At the root of the perplexities which attend the problem of the loss of sovereignty there is the divorce, in contemporary legal and political theory, of the concept of sovereignty from the political reality to which the concept of sovereignty is supposed to give legal expression.[87]

More recently, scholars have pointed out that at the heart of this seeming paradox there is a 'descriptive fallacy'.[88] Those who argue that state sovereignty is being eroded as a consequence of immigration flows and difficulties in maintaining border control or other features of globalisation seem to assume that state sovereignty needs to correspond to something 'out there', a real state of world affairs. As Krasner points out, history is full of aberrations and few states have ever fully and simultaneously been able to claim the key features normally associated with sovereignty – internal authority, recognition by other states, autonomy in decision-making and control over transborder flows; indeed, striving for one of these may often fundamentally impair another.[89] Certain elements of state sovereignty seemingly go untouched despite fundamental changes at the level of political organisation. So far, no international institution has managed to escape the statist framework and legal basis conferred on it by independent states.[90] Similarly, despite the fashionable references to

---

[87] Morgenthau, 'Problem of Sovereignty Reconsidered', 348.

[88] N. Walker, 'Late sovereignty in the European Union', in N. Walker (ed.), *Sovereignty in Transition* (Oxford: Hart Publishing, 2003), pp. 3–32, at p. 7; W. Werner and J. De Wilde, 'The endurance of sovereignty', (2001) 7 *European Journal of International Relations* 283–313, at 285.

[89] Krasner, *Sovereignty – Organized Hypocrisy*, pp. 3, 220.

[90] S. Sur, 'The state between fragmentation and globalization', (1997) 8 *European Journal of International Law* 421–35, at 421; R. O. Keohane, 'Hobbes's dilemma and institutional

'failed states', it is surprising how resilient these entities remain in their ability to claim international legal sovereignty.[91]

Sovereignty should, perhaps, rather be understood as a *claim* to power circumscribed by law setting out the idea of the legitimate supreme power within a polity.[92] In this sense, sovereignty works as an 'institutional fact' – an organisational set of principles, the authenticity of which depends on the internalisation of the relevant norms by key actors.[93] Such a claim may become more complex to perform in an era of globalisation, yet it continues to be the only claim to exercise legitimate power and remains thereby the essential and existential reference point.

It would be wrong to assume, however, that no link exists between law and politics and that legal frameworks may thus remain completely unaffected by changing political practices. Rather, when political practices related to sovereignty such as offshore and outsourcing are dislocated from the traditional Bodinian and Vattelian picture of the state, a field of contestation opens where opposing claims to authority and responsibility may be made based on either de facto or de jure conceptualisations of sovereignty.

The current debate over state responsibility in cases of privatisation and the extraterritorial application of human rights is the strongest testimony to this fact. The majority of human rights lawyers start from practice when arguing, for example, that, in order to remain legitimate, the exercise of power by the United States at Guantánamo must be accompanied by a similar extension of national and international law to the individuals detained. Similarly, claims that states' own human rights obligations are strictly state-centric and territorially limited may appear somewhat fictitious if those same states are simultaneously engaged in widespread offshoring and outsourcing practices, thereby leaving an obvious human rights vacuum. Such a move may end up as 'sovereignty overstretching', where the gap between the normative construction of the state and concomitant boundaries for sovereign responsibility and political realities in the exercise of sovereign powers becomes too wide.[94]

---

change in world politics: sovereignty in international society', in H. H. Holm and G. Sørensen (eds.), *Whose World Order? Uneven Globalization and the End of the Cold War* (Boulder: Westview, 1995), pp. 63–87, at p. 72.

[91] G. Sørensen, 'Sovereignty: change and continuity in a fundamental institution', (1999) 47 *Political Studies* 590–604.

[92] Walker, 'Late sovereignty in the European Union', p. 6.

[93] MacCormick, *Institutions of Law*; Werner and De Wilde, 'The endurance of sovereignty'.

[94] Aalberts and Werner, 'Sovereignty beyond borders'.

This has not prevented states from doing exactly that, however. In particular, the long-standing debate as to the geographical application of the *non-refoulement* principle as enshrined in the 1951 Refugee Convention is illustrative of the fact that states continue to fall back on territorial principles in delimiting their own human rights obligations.[95] Beyond the blunt refusal of any and all extraterritorial obligations, however, the way in which claims for limited human rights responsibility are made is, interestingly, not simply by self-reference to the limited sphere of a state's own authority but rather, and more often, by reference to the responsibility of someone else.

This is a key feature of the commercialisation of sovereignty and what has elsewhere been described as 'late-modern sovereignty games'.[96] In the 'classical' sovereignty game, aspiring and established states are concerned with claims to their own legitimate authority as sovereigns, be this through territorial control, popular support or international recognition. The commercialisation of sovereignty, by contrast, essentially involves instrumentalising the authority of other polities and actors in order to limit the sovereignty, or at least sovereign responsibility, of the acting state. Put simply, as offshore and privatisation practices have moved to the fore, sovereignty games in this regard become a matter of *disclaiming* authority and sovereign responsibility over the polity or acts concerned.[97]

This is most evident in the case of jurisdiction shopping, where the sovereign territory of another state is instrumentalised in order to shift human rights obligations, exploitation rights or fiscal authority to another sovereign and thus duty bearer in the international system. It is only by subsuming offshore fishing to the sovereign exploitation rights and fishing quotas of Ghana that Spain and other European countries can maintain that their national fishing does not exceed internationally set quotas. Similarly, it is by reference to the territorial state as the guarantor of human rights obligations within its national borders that a presumption is created against similar obligations of states carrying out interception schemes in foreign territorial waters.[98]

A disclaiming of authority is equally at work in the context of privatisation. This is seen clearly where delegated tasks are simultaneously

---

[95] See below, chapter 3.

[96] T. Gammeltoft-Hansen and R. Adler-Nissen, 'An introduction to sovereignty games', in Adler-Nissen and Gammeltoft-Hansen, *Sovereignty Games*, pp. 1–17.

[97] Cf. Walker, 'Late sovereignty in the European Union', p. 5.

[98] See below, section 4.3.3.

carried out extraterritorially, such as in the case of imposing control responsibilities on private airline carriers. Here, privatisation not only works to distance the outsourcing state from the performance of control, but also the use of a private interlocutor in the exercise of authority avoids a possible sovereignty conflict with the territorial state and may thereby create an even stronger presumption for any refugee protection obligations to fall back on the territorial state. Disclaiming authority may, however, also work by reference to entities other than the state. While the public/private distinction has traditionally been used to limit the role of private actors as subjects of international law, more recent claims for direct responsibility of private actors under international law could be seen as an attempt to institutionalise alternative duty bearers that may indirectly distance states from similar responsibility.[99] In situations of both offshoring and outsourcing it thus becomes alluring to states to play the 'sovereignty card' – to emphasise national sovereignty norms and boundaries for responsibility not just on behalf of themselves but perhaps more so on behalf of others.

Consequently, the confrontation pertaining to this area is not merely one relating to differing interpretations of refugee and human rights law instruments, but equally a struggle over competing sovereignty claims of authority and responsibility. On the one side stand those stressing the actions of the offshoring and outsourcing states; on the other those pointing to the continued importance of national sovereignty in the determination of legal obligations. The first set of arguments moves from actual assertions of sovereign power to emphasising the correlated sovereign responsibility and the universal application of human rights. The second set of arguments starts from the legal construction of sovereign authority as circumscribed by territorial and statist norms and moves from there to simultaneously limiting sovereign responsibility for extraterritorial acts and non-state entities as well as emphasising the responsibility of the territorial states where control is performed.

In what follows a more traditional legal analysis is offered that attempts to trace the reach of international refugee law, human rights law and general international law in holding states accountable when offshoring and privatising migration control. Yet to understand the difficulties in

---

[99] Clapham, *Human Rights Obligations*; Alston, 'The "not-a-cat" syndrome'. See further below, section 5.4.

extending refugee and human rights obligations to all situations involving extraterritorial acts and situations of privatisation, it may be useful to keep in mind not just the inherent interpretative issues and complications brought about by the legal analysis, but also the deeper politico-legal framework in which legal interpretation is rooted.

3 Refugee protection and the reach of the *non-refoulement* principle

The *non-refoulement* principle is often referred to as the 'cornerstone' or 'centrepiece' of the international refugee protection regime. Short of a right to be granted asylum, the guarantee that no refugee will be sent back to a place where he or she will be persecuted constitutes the strongest commitment that the international community of states has been willing to make to those who are no longer able to avail themselves of the protection of their own government. At the same time the *non-refoulement* obligation serves as the entry point for all subsequent rights that may be claimed under the 1951 Refugee Convention. Without this, little else matters.

In the initial encounter between the refugee and the authorities of a potential asylum state, the protection against *refoulement* naturally becomes the first and most important consideration. This chapter examines the geographical reach of the *non-refoulement* principle as a first and crucial step in determining states' international obligations in cases of offshore migration control.

The *non-refoulement* principle as enshrined in Article 33 of the Refugee Convention reads as follows:

1) 'No Contracting State shall expel or return ('*refouler*') a refugee in any manner whatsoever to the frontiers of territories where his life or freedom would be threatened on account of his race, religion, nationality, membership of a particular social group or political opinion.
2) The benefit of the present provision may not, however, be claimed by a refugee whom there are reasonable grounds for regarding as a danger to the security of the country in which he is, or who, having been convicted by a final judgment of a particularly serious crime, constitutes a danger to the community of that country.'

Various interpreters have argued that the wording and meaning of this article are unambiguous.[1] Nonetheless, intense debate continues to rage over its exact application and scope. This is particularly true with regard to its geographical reach and the extent to which states are bound by this fundamental obligation with regard to refugees encountered extraterritorially. Most restrictively, the *non-refoulement* principle has been interpreted as applying solely within the territory of an acting state. While admitting that this is not a very satisfactory solution to the problem of asylum, Nehemiah Robinson concludes in his commentary that

Art. 33 concerns refugees who have gained entry into the territory of a Contracting State, legally or illegally, but not to [sic] refugees who ask entrance into this territory... In other words, if a refugee has succeeded in eluding the frontier guards, he is safe; if he has not, it is his hard luck.[2]

This interpretation has drawn support from other scholars, arguing that '[e]ven though "*refoulement*" may mean "non-admittance at the frontier", it is quite clear that the prohibition against "*refoulement*" in Article 33 of the 1951 Convention does not cover this aspect of the term "*refoulement*"'.[3] Several states have taken the same view when deciding to close their borders,[4] and the US Supreme Court took a similar position in a case involving US interdiction of Haitian boat refugees.[5]

A slightly more inclusive view would hold that the geographical scope must at least be extended to situations arising at the borders. The use of the phrase 'in any manner whatsoever' lends strong support to the interpretation that Article 33(1) also applies to situations involving non-admittance of refugees presenting themselves at the frontier of an asylum state.[6] Furthermore, both scholars and international bodies have argued that it would seem illogical that the refugee who succeeds in crossing the border illegally would enjoy greater protection than the

---

[1] See e.g. UNHCR, Advisory Opinion, para. 24, and the dissenting opinion by Justice Blackmun in *Sale, Acting Cmmr, Immigration and Naturalization Service v. Haitian Center Council*, US Supreme Court, 113 S.Ct. 2549, 509 US 155, 21 June 1993. See further *inter alia* G. Noll, 'Seeking asylum at embassies: a right to entry under international law?', (2005) 17 *International Journal of Refugee Law* 542–73, at 553.

[2] N. Robinson, *Convention Relating to the Status of Refugees: Its History, Contents and Interpretation – A Commentary* (New York: Institute for Jewish Affairs, 1953), p. 163.

[3] Grahl-Madsen, *Commentary on the Refugee Convention.*   [4] See further below, section 3.2.5.

[5] *Sale*. See also Goodwin-Gill and McAdam, *Refugee in International Law*, pp. 218 ff.

[6] P. Weis, *The Refugee Convention, 1951: The Travaux Préparatoires Analysed with a Commentary by the Late Dr Paul Weis* (Cambridge University Press, 1995), p. 341.

refugee who lawfully presents him- or herself to the authorities at the border.[7]

Others again have argued that with respect to the *refoulement* prohibition, states are responsible for conduct in relation to any refugee subject to or within their jurisdiction. While the notion of jurisdiction primarily refers to a state's territory, it does also cover situations in which states exercise effective control beyond their borders, such as on the high seas or within foreign territory. This position is supported by reference to the broader incorporation of the *non-refoulement* principle in universal and regional human rights instruments[8] that clearly oblige states even where jurisdiction is established extraterritorially.[9]

Lastly, it has been argued that the question of *from* where *refoulement* occurs is wholly immaterial. Article 33(1) is only concerned with *to* where a refugee might be returned. The principle of *non-refoulement* as enshrined in the Refugee Convention thus in principle enjoys universal application wherever a state may act.[10] Article 33(1) contains no explicit restrictions as to the lawful presence or residence of the refugee within the territory of the state in question, but explicitly prohibits *refoulement* in 'any manner

---

[7] See in particular Council of Europe Parliamentary Assembly, Report on the Granting of the Right of Asylum to European Refugees, Doc. 1986, 29 September 1965, p. 7. See also S. P. Sinha, *Asylum and International Law* (The Hague: Martinus Nijhoff, 1971), p. 111.

[8] See below, section 3.6.

[9] Hathaway, *Rights of Refugees*, pp. 160 ff.; R. Plender and N. Mole, 'Beyond the Geneva Convention: constructing a de facto right of asylum from international human rights instruments', in F. Nicholson and P. Twomey (eds.), *Refugee Rights and Realities* (Cambridge University Press, 1999), pp. 81–105, at 86.

[10] An obvious exception to this notion of universality, however, would seem to be the country of origin, as a persecuted person who has not yet left his or her country is not a refugee in the meaning of Art. 1 of the Refugee Convention. Goodwin-Gill and McAdam, *Refugee in International Law*, p. 244. This point has also been expressed in UNHCR, *Handbook on Procedures and Criteria for Determining Refugee Status*:

> It is a general requirement for refugee status that an applicant who has a nationality be outside the country of his nationality. There are no exceptions to this rule. International protection cannot come into play as long as a person is within the territorial jurisdiction of his home country. (UNHCR, *Handbook on Procedures and Criteria for Determining Refugee Status*, HCR/IP/4/Eng/Rev. 1st edn (Geneva: 1992 [1979]), para. 88)

Nonetheless, some scholars have suggested that as a general principle of international law, Art. 33 may also apply in circumstances in which the refugee or asylum seeker is within their country of origin yet under the protection of a third state. E. Lauterpacht and D. Bethlehem, 'The scope and content of the principle of *non-refoulement*: opinion', in E. Feller, V. Türk and F. Nicholson (eds.), *Refugee Protection in International Law: UNHCR's Global Consultations on International Protection* (Cambridge University Press, 2003), pp. 87–177, at p. 122. For a contrary view see Noll, 'Seeking asylum at embassies', 550 ff. See further below, section 3.6.8.

whatsoever'.[11] A similar argument has been made in an opinion prepared for UNHCR arguing that, as a wider principle of customary international law, the prohibition against *refoulement* binds all states and will engage their responsibility wherever conduct takes place.[12]

It should be clear just from this brief sketch that there is far from a consensus on the applicability *ratione loci* of Article 33 of the Refugee Convention. Through a more systematic interpretative approach this chapter seeks to dispel the present ambiguity. Yet, in reviewing the arguments made in favour of each of the different interpretative stances, the inherent potential of contesting the application of core norms when carrying out offshore migration control also comes to the fore.

3.1 The historical context of Article 33

Noting that the geographical scope of application attached to Article 33 of the Refugee Convention does at least appear ambiguous,[13] the following section will be dedicated to a brief analysis of its drafting history. This is not to give this source pre-eminence; as is quite evident from the 1969 Vienna Convention on the Law of Treaties, the *travaux préparatoires* are to be considered only a supplementary means of interpretation.[14] In this particular case, however, the discussions that took place during the drafting of the Refugee Convention serve as an important starting point for understanding the continued disagreement as to the exact applicability *ratione loci* of the *non-refoulement* principle and may thus provide a frame for the subsequent analysis.

3.1.1 The ad hoc committee

The Refugee Convention was first discussed by an ad hoc committee consisting of thirteen government representatives, which convened in two

---

[11] Goodwin-Gill and McAdam, *Refugee in International Law*, p. 246.

[12] Lauterpacht and Bethlehem, 'Scope and content', p. 149.

[13] Beyond the scholarly disagreements staked out above, this assessment also finds support in *R. (European Roma Rights Centre and Others) v. Immigration Officer at Prague Airport and Another*, UK House of Lords, [2004] UKHL 55, 9 December 2004, para. 17.

[14] Recollecting the rules of interpretation as set out in Art. 32 of the Vienna Convention on the Law of Treaties:

> Recourse may be had to supplementary means of interpretation, including the preparatory work of the treaty and the circumstances of its conclusion, in order to confirm the meaning resulting from the application of Article 31, or to determine the meaning when the interpretation according to Article 31:
>
> a. leaves the meaning ambiguous or obscure, or
> b. leads to a result which is manifestly absurd or unreasonable.

sessions in January and August 1950 to produce a draft text. The UN General Assembly decided not to deal with the substance of the draft but rather to convene a Conference of Plenipotentiaries in Geneva to ensure the widest possible debate, also including non-members of the UN.[15] The conference took place in July 1951; twenty-six states were represented and two were observing. On 25 July the final text was adopted by twenty-four votes to none.

From the outset there was a realisation that the *non-refoulement* principle was of key importance in ensuring a functional instrument and that it might place a considerable number of restrictions on state sovereignty. In both fora the provisions leading to Article 33 of the final text were thus discussed at length. In the first draft, prepared by the secretariat for the ad hoc committee, *non-refoulement* appeared in Article 24(3):

Each of the Contracting Parties undertakes in any case not to turn back refugees to the frontiers of their country or origin, or to territories where their life or freedom would be threatened on account of their race, religion, nationality or political opinions.

In addition, the draft Article 24(1) clearly referred both to 'expulsions' and to 'non-admittance at the frontier (*refoulement*)' as inspired by Article 3 of the 1933 Convention Relating to the International Status of Refugees.[16] The inclusion of non-admittance at the border was supported by the US representative, Louis Henkin, who argued that, even though an actual right to asylum had been deleted from the draft,

[it] did not, however, follow that the convention would not apply to persons fleeing from persecution who asked to enter the territory of the contracting parties. Whether it was a question of closing the frontier to a refugee who asked admittance, or of turning him back after he had crossed the frontier, or even of expelling him after he had been admitted to residence in the territory, the problem was more or less the same. Whatever the case might be, whether the refugee was in a regular position, he must not be turned back to a country where his life and freedom could be threatened.[17]

This interpretation received support from both the French and Israeli representatives.[18] The French representative emphasised the absolute nature of the *refoulement* prohibition, and argued that 'any possibility,

---

[15] Robinson, *Convention Relating to the Status of Refugees*, p. 5.

[16] Doc. E/AC.32/2. All references to drafting documents of the convention can be found in A. Takkenberg and C. Tahbaz, *The Collected Travaux Préparatoires of the 1951 Geneva Convention Relating to the Status of Refugees* (Amsterdam: Dutch Refugee Council, 1990).

[17] Doc. E/AC.32/SR.20, para. 54.   [18] Ibid., paras. 60, 63–64.

even in exceptional circumstances, of a genuine refugee being returned to his country of origin would not only be inhuman, but was contrary to the very purpose of the Convention'.[19] While the direct reference to non-admittance at the border was taken out in subsequent drafts,[20] it was emphasised that the French term 'refoulement' was thought to cover situations both of expulsion or of return from the territory and non-admittance at the frontier.[21]

Support for a wider geographical scope can also be found indirectly in the more general discussions of Article 33. A matter of considerable debate was the inclusion of exceptions in cases of national security or where refugees invited public disorder, when it was argued that an unrestrained *non-refoulement* obligation might require states to admit refugees whom they considered a threat.[22] Both the Belgian and the US representatives argued against such provisions, noting that even when a country was unwilling to admit a refugee on national security grounds, 'it would always be possible to direct him to territories where his life or his freedom would not be threatened'.[23]

This reasoning was further affirmed in the comments submitted in the report of the ad hoc committee after the first session, in which it was noted that '[t]his article does not imply that a refugee must in all cases be admitted to the country where he seeks entry'.[24] While not explicitly mentioned in the discussions, it is worth pointing out that if 'admitted' is to be understood as being physically allowed access to the territory, such a situation could only occur at or outside the territorial borders of the state in question. Logically Article 33(1) could thus not have been assumed to apply only to those who have already entered the territory.

Instrumental in the discussions of the ad hoc committee was establishing a broad principle prohibiting *refoulement* or return 'in any manner whatsoever' and to 'any territory where his life or freedom would thereby be endangered'.[25] To the extent that restrictions to the application *ratione loci* of this prohibition were proposed these were answered in the negative,

---

[19] Doc. E/AC.32/SR.40, para. 33.   [20] Doc. E/1850.

[21] Doc. E/AC.32/SR.21, paras. 13–26. Similarly, 'turn back' was replaced by 'return', yet this was seemingly intended only as a matter of style. Doc. E/AC.32/SR.22, para. 110.

[22] Robinson, *Convention Relating to the Status of Refugees*, pp. 164–5.

[23] Doc. E/AC.32/SR.20, para. 14.

[24] E/1618, Comments to Art. 28 [previously Art. 24] in the Report of the First Ad Hoc Committee on Statelessness and Related Problems, Takkenberg and Tahbaz, *Collected Travaux*, 421.

[25] Weis, *Refugee Convention*, p. 328.

supporting an interpretation that would at least embrace non-admission at the frontier and likely an even wider application.

3.1.2 The Conference of Plenipotentiaries

At the Conference of Plenipotentiaries in July the following year develop-ments, however, took a different turn. Several states represented at the conference were concerned that the ad hoc committee had set too abso-lute a standard in regard to the *non-refoulement* clause, and argued that the international situation had substantially changed since the initial work of the committee.[26]

During the first meeting at which the then Article 28 was discussed, Mr Zutter, the Swiss representative, questioned the exact meaning assigned to the operational words used in the draft text. In his opinion the word 'refoulement' in particular seemed to leave room for various interpreta-tions:

In the Swiss Government's view, the term 'expulsion' applied to a refugee who had already been admitted to the territory of a country. The term 'refoulement', on the other hand, had a vaguer meaning; it could not, however, be applied to a refugee who had not yet entered the territory of a country. The word 'return', used in the English text, gave that idea exactly.[27]

As reason for this interpretation the Swiss representative noted that states could not be compelled to allow large groups of persons claiming refugee status to cross its frontiers.[28] He further asked the conference that this point be made entirely clear and that Switzerland could only support the adoption of the text on the above interpretation.

The Swiss concern was recognised by a number of countries which all supported the Swiss interpretation.[29] At the final meeting the Dutch representative, Baron van Boetzelaer, recalled the Swiss remarks from the first reading, according to which 'Article 28 would not have involved any obligations in the possible case of mass migration across frontiers or of attempted mass migration' and stated that such an interpretation

---

[26] Hathaway, *Rights of Refugees*, p. 356; Robinson, *Convention Relating to the Status of Refugees*, p. 160. Notably, the article proposed by the ad hoc committee contained only the first paragraph cited above, what was to become Art. 33(1). It was the conference which, with reference to national security, inserted para. 33(2), limiting the *ratione personae* of the *non-refoulement* obligation for refugees considered a 'danger to the security of the country' and those having been convicted of a 'particularly serious crime'.

[27] Doc. A/CONF.2/SR.16, p. 6.   [28] Ibid.

[29] Notably France, Italy, Sweden, Netherlands and the Federal Republic of Germany. See Doc. A/CONF.2/SR.16, pp. 6 ff.

of the scope of the now Article 33 was of 'very great importance' to the Dutch government. In order to dispel any ambiguity he thus wished to have it officially noted that the conference was in agreement with such an interpretation. Since there were no objections, the president, Knud Larsen, ruled that this reading could be placed on the record.[30]

While this understanding was argued entirely on concerns regarding large-scale migration, the possibility of extraterritorial applicability was seemingly sacrificed solely for reasons of state fears of mass influx. At least, this is the interpretation of some of the early commentators. It is on the basis of the discussions at the conference that Robinson concludes that only the refugee who has succeeded in eluding the border guard is safe.[31] According to Grahl-Madsen this means that a contracting state that manages to fence off its entire territory 'may refuse admission to any corner of its territory without breaking its obligations under Article 33'.[32]

3.1.3 Between two readings

Two conflicting bases for establishing the applicability *ratione loci* of Article 33 of the Refugee Convention emerge when going through the drafting history. The ad hoc committee, placing its emphasis on *to* where, rather than *from* where, return is conducted, clearly supports a more universalist interpretation. Affirming the centrality of the *non-refoulement* provision, this argument could easily be extended to make Article 33 cover situations taking place beyond the borders of an acting state as well. On the other hand, the conference appears to have rejected unequivocally any extra- and ad-territorial application, and instead assumed a strictly territorial reading of obligations under this provision.

How this conflict should be resolved depends on the methodological approach pursued. Within the limited remit of the *travaux préparatoires*, resolving this conflict largely comes down to methodological preference. Proponents of a consensual approach are likely to lend authority to the territorialist interpretation. The question of geographical scope was raised repeatedly at the conference, and the rejection of extraterritorial and border applicability was fully argued and affirmed. The fact that the draft from the ad hoc committee was handed over to a Conference of Plenipotentiaries rather than dealt with during a UN General Assembly session could be taken to support the argument further that more substantial

---

[30] Doc. A/CONF.2/SR.35, p. 21.
[31] Robinson, *Convention Relating to the Status of Refugees*, p. 163.
[32] Grahl-Madsen, *Commentary on the Refugee Convention*.

revisions were envisioned for the initial draft, and thereby the argumentation provided by the ad hoc committee, to be superseded. On the other hand, the argumentation provided by the ad hoc committee clearly speaks to the purpose and object of Article 33, pointing out that its importance demands a broad scope. Further, while the restrictive interpretation proposed by the Swiss delegate was placed on the record with no objections, the actual existence of a consensus could be questioned, and no textual amendments were made to the draft text to cement this interpretation.[33] Lastly, the restrictive interpretation put forward by the Swiss and Dutch delegates concerned only a very specific set of circumstances, namely situations of mass influx. This need not, and may never have been intended to, entail a general restriction of the applicability *ratione loci* of Article 33.[34]

There has been a tendency among both scholars and practitioners to cite either the ad hoc committee or the Conference of Plenipotentiaries.[35] While this may serve to consolidate particular positions, needless to say it is not furthering genuine legal scholarship. The above has attempted to provide a balanced account, which is crucial if we want to understand how this duality between universal and territorial conceptualisations of sovereign human rights responsibilities continues to have a bearing on the interpretation of the geographical scope of the *non-refoulement* principle.

One should be careful not to assign too much importance to the drafting history in the interpretation of human rights treaties.[36] When the

---

[33] While the remarks were placed 'on the record', they were not 'agreed to' or 'adopted' as one could have expected of something which, given the broader interpretation suggested by the committee, would effectively constitute an amendment to the scope of the article. Dissenting opinion by Justice Blackmun in *Sale*. Whether the particular interpretation tabled at the conference did constitute an actual amendment is of course equally debatable.

[34] Indeed, the possibility of a more conditional or limited responsibility in cases of mass influx has been partly recognised in subsequent interpretation. See e.g. UNHCR Executive Committee Conclusion No. 100 (2004); and Conclusion No. 22 (XXXII) (1981); and UNHCR, Protection of Refugees in Mass Influx Situations: Overall Protection Framework, UN Doc. EC/GC/01/4, 19 February 2001. For an overview of the debate for and against a derogation or limits to the *non-refoulement* principle and other rights under the Refugee Convention in cases of mass influx see Goodwin-Gill and McAdam, *Refugee in International Law*, pp. 335–45; Hathaway, *Rights of Refugees*, pp. 355–63; F. Durieux and J. McAdam, '*Non-refoulement* through time: the case for a derogation clause to the Refugee Convention in mass influx emergencies', (2004) 16 *International Journal of Refugee Law* 4–24; M. Barutciski and A. Suhrke, 'Lessons from the Kosovo refugee crisis: innovations in protection and burden-sharing', (2001) 14 *Journal of Refugee Studies* 95–134.

[35] See e.g. UNHCR, Advisory Opinion; and *Sale*.

[36] The use and place of the preparatory works in the interpretation of international refugee law has been the subject of some debate. In his dissenting opinion to the *Sale*

historical remarks and interpretations nonetheless serve as an introduction to the present interpretative quest, it is because the drafting history clearly illustrates the competing understandings and interpretations of core refugee law principles. On the one hand, a universal interpretation was proposed that clearly builds on general human rights principles and the ideological promise that human rights may serve to constrain state power wherever it is exercised. On the other hand, a number of states at least seemed adamant about applying a territorial reading, referring back to principles of national sovereignty and strict Westphalian boundaries for state responsibility. It is in these discussions that the seeds of the legal disputes were planted that continue to occupy refugee lawyers more than half a century later.

Moving beyond the drafting history, we shall see how the above arguments feed into a more doctrinal legal inquiry into the scope of application *ratione loci* of the *non-refoulement* obligation. Notably, the discussions on application during the conference did not question the deliberations as to the object and purpose of the *non-refoulement* clause put forward by the ad hoc committee. Rather, the argument made by the Swiss delegate concerned the linguistic interpretation of the article, thus at the very outset sowing doubt as to what exactly is the ordinary meaning of the words 'return' and '*refoulement*'. Following the traditional order of treaty interpretation, the following section starts out by considering the language and meaning of the text. Second, arguments as to the object and purpose will be presented. Third, subsequent developments in both state practice and soft law will be considered and, lastly, the wider normative context of the *non-refoulement* principle in international law is discussed.

3.2 Language

3.2.1 'In any manner whatsoever'

What does the language of Article 33 tell us about the territorial scope of the *non-refoulement* principle? As noted above, on the more general level some scholars have argued that the particularly inclusive language of this article, prohibiting *non-refoulement* 'in any manner whatsoever', would suggest that it applies regardless of whether actions occur inside

case, Justice Blackmun argued that '[r]eliance on a treaty's negotiating history (travaux préparatoires) is a disfavoured alternative of last resort.' See also 'The Haitian Interdiction Case 1993 brief *amicus curiae*', (1994) 6 (1) *International Journal of Refugee Law* 85–102, at 99. On the other hand, James Hathaway had argued that the preparatory work is essential in determining the object and purpose of treaty text. Hathaway, *Rights of Refugees*, pp. 56 ff.

the territory of an acting state, at the border, or even beyond the national territory.[37]

This argument has a strong appeal on an immediate reading. Yet a closer analysis indicates that this is at least unlikely to have been the intended meaning. Going through the various drafts of the convention and surrounding discussion it becomes clear that the expression 'in any manner whatsoever' was not included out of any consideration as to geographical application. Rather, it was inserted to ensure that Article 33 covered any thinkable instance of *refoulement*, even when not submitted to a formal procedure. The use of 'in any manner whatsoever' thus prohibits all different acts and forms of return, expulsion or extradition, whether by judicial or administrative authorities.[38]

3.2.2 Level of attachment

Second, an argument has been made based on the negative inference that since nothing in the wording explicitly restricts the obligation to actions occurring within the territory or at the border, a broader scope of application *ratione loci* is called for. This reflects the overall structure of the treaty. The wording of the majority of provisions in the Refugee Convention specifically makes rights conditional on some kind of territorial affiliation (e.g. being physically present, lawfully present or lawfully staying). Article 33 is, however, one among a small number of rights to which no such conditions adhere and is thus applicable wherever a state exercises jurisdiction.[39]

This argument provides an important premise for claiming a wider scope for Article 33. Yet it remains questionable whether a wider application can be inferred from this alone. In other words, the fact that no territorial conditions are mentioned in Article 33(1) does not in itself call

---

[37] Goodwin-Gill and McAdam, *Refugee in International Law*, p. 246; Legomsky, 'USA and the Caribbean Interdiction Programme', 687; Hathaway, *Rights of Refugees*, p. 338; Weis, *Refugee Convention*, p. 341.

[38] Lauterpacht and Bethlehem, 'Scope and content', p. 122; Robinson, *Convention Relating to the Status of Refugees*, p. 162. Draft E/AC.32/L.25 introduced 'in any way' to refer to the 'various methods by which refugees could be expelled, refused admittance or removed'. While 'refused admittance' is mentioned, there is no reference to whether this includes border situations. See further Report of the First Ad Hoc Committee on Statelessness and Related Problems, Comments to Art. 28, Takkenberg and Tahbaz, *Collected Travaux*.

[39] 'Haitian Interdiction Case 1993', at 86. See also Hathaway, *Rights of Refugees*, pp. 160 ff.; Goodwin-Gill and McAdam, *Refugee in International Law*, p. 246. See further above, chapter 2.3.

for a wider geographical scope of application, but only defers argumentation to subsequent stages of interpretation.

3.2.3 Article 33(2)

Conversely, the US Supreme Court in the *Sale* case made an argument that the language of Article 33(2) does in fact imply that a physical presence in the territory is necessary to engage the *non-refoulement* provision.[40] Noting that this article exempts states from the *non-refoulement* obligation for refugees who constitute a 'danger to the security of a country in which he is', the court goes on to argue that since a refugee on the high seas is in no country at all, if the *non-refoulement* obligation was to apply there, it would create an anomaly where 'dangerous aliens on the high seas would be entitled to the benefits of 33(1) while those residing in the country that sought to expel them would not'.[41] Based on this reasoning the court finds it 'more reasonable to assume that the coverage of 33(2) was limited to those already in the country because it was understood that 33(1) obligated the signatory state only with respect to aliens within its own territory'.[42]

While Article 33(2) clearly represents a concession to national sovereignty by maintaining the right of states to expel refugees already on their territory who are causing security concerns,[43] the argument that this exception entails a territorial limitation of the *non-refoulement* obligation as such seems flawed in its underlying logic. Whereas Article 33(2) is clearly an exception to Article 33(1), referring to its scope *ratione loci, materiae* and *personae* and in itself setting out a subgroup of refugees for whom the protection against *refoulement* is waived, it does not follow that Article 33(1) is conversely limited by the scope of Article 33(2). Justice Blackmun succinctly pointed this out in his dissenting opinion:

One wonders what the majority would make of an exception that removed from the Article's protection all refugees who 'constitute a danger to their families'. By

---

[40] While the court held that the Refugee Convention and the 1967 Protocol was non-self-executing, thereby moving the main issue to the interpretation of the US implementing legislation, it did recognise that this statute was passed specifically to make US domestic legislation conform with the obligations spelled out in the convention and thus reserved some effort for deliberations over the interpretation of the scope *ratione loci* of Art. 33. See further Legomsky, 'USA and the Caribbean interdiction programme', 687 ff.

[41] *Sale*, p. 7.   [42] Ibid., p. 7.

[43] Legomsky, 'USA and the Caribbean Interdiction Programme', 689.

the majority's logic, the inclusion of such an exception presumably would render Art. 33(1) applicable only to refugees with families.[44]

Rather, one could argue that Article 33(2) may have been restricted to those present at the territory either because situations involving extraterritorial interception were not foreseen[45] and/or because it would be natural to assume that a refugee would only pose a real danger to the security of a country once he or she had entered its territory.[46]

3.2.4 'Refouler'

Next, it has been pointed out that the word '*refouler*', as known only in French and Belgian law, clearly also covers non-admission to the territory.[47] As both the French and the English texts are authoritative, the Council of Europe Parliamentary Assembly has thus noted that '*ne pas refouler*' without further ado can be interpreted as covering non-admission to the territory.[48] Further, it also appears from the drafting history that the style committee replaced the word 'turn back' with 'return' as the latter was considered the nearest equivalent to the French '*refouler*' around which the early discussions evolved.[49] To clear any doubts as to whether 'return' had a more restrictive meaning, the French term was even parenthetically included in the English text.[50]

Nonetheless, it has been argued that even though '*refouler*' may apply to non-admittance and the border in ordinary usage, '*refouler*' was given a special meaning by the parties to the Refugee Convention regardless of its ordinary usage consistent with Article 31(4) of the Vienna Convention.[51] As support for this argument, reference is made to the drafting history.

---

[44] Dissenting opinion by Justice Blackmun in *Sale*, p. 3.

[45] Legomsky, 'USA and the Caribbean Interdiction Programme', 689.

[46] Hathaway, *Rights of Refugees*, p. 336. As was also noted by Justice Blackmun in *Sale*, 'the tautological observation that only a refugee already in a country can pose a danger to the security of the country "in which he is" proves nothing' (p. 3). Further, even in the conceived instance where a refugee not in the country could pose a security threat, presumably the benefit of the exception, allowing *refoulement*, would make little difference.

[47] 'Haitian Interdiction Case 1993', 90; as noted above this was also recognised during the drafting discussions. See Doc. E/AC.32/SR.21, paras. 13–26; Hathaway, *Rights of Refugees*, pp. 336 ff.

[48] Council of Europe Parliamentary Assembly, Report on the Granting of the Right of Asylum to European Refugees, Doc. 1986, 29 September 1965, p. 6.

[49] Robinson, *Convention Relating to the Status of Refugees*, p. 162.   [50] Ibid.

[51] For the view that a special meaning was attached to the terms 'return' and '*refouler*', see *R. (European Roma Rights Centre and Others) v. Immigration Officer at Prague Airport*, House of Lords, para. 68.

If a genuine consensus was established based on the remarks of the Swiss and Dutch delegates regarding a special meaning of the term 'return', as suggested by commentators such as Robinson and Grahl-Madsen, no enquiry needs to be made into its usage elsewhere.

In her treatment of this question, however, Davy refuses to accept this suggestion on three grounds. First, deducing a 'special meaning' exclusively from the *travaux préparatoires* would effectively make these a primary source of interpretation, which would be inconsistent with the hierarchical structure of interpretation set out in the Vienna Convention, according to which the preparatory work is only to be relied on as a secondary, and clarifying, source. Second, it is not clear from the record and minutes that a decision was taken on a 'special meaning' during the conference. As discussed above, the remarks by the Swiss and Dutch delegates may have sowed doubt as to the meaning of these terms, yet it is a stretch from that to arguing that they constitute a new consensus on a special meaning. Lastly, in the light of the high number of states that have signed the convention, establishing a 'special meaning' would require more than remarks from a few states discussing the issue at the Conference of Plenipotentiaries.[52]

3.2.5 'To the frontiers of territories'

Lastly, there is the argument mentioned at the outset of this chapter that the question of *from* where a refugee is returned is irrelevant on a closer reading of the terms employed. Article 33 sets out two proscriptions, one regarding expulsion and one regarding return. As indicated by the use of 'or' between 'expel' and 'return' in the article, these two prohibitions should be read disjunctively. The first, expulsion, clearly refers solely to actions removing a refugee *from* a contracting state.[53] The second prohibition, however, bans actions returning refugees *to* the frontiers of any territories where their life or freedom would be threatened.[54] As noted by Justice Blackmun, a dictionary reading of 'return' would have it mean 'to bring, send or put (a person or thing) back to or in a former position'.[55]

---

[52] U. Davy, *Asyl und internationales Flüchtlingsrecht* (Vienna: Österreichische Staatsdruckerei, 1996), I: *Völkerrechtlicher Rahmen*, pp. 106–7.

[53] The prohibition against expulsion of refugees lawfully present is further set out in Art. 32 of the Convention.

[54] 'Haitian Interdiction Case 1993', at 87.

[55] Drawn from *Webster's Third New International Dictionary* (1986). Cited by Justice Blackmun in *Sale*, p. 2.

One could reasonably argue that any action undertaken by a state to intercept a refugee after commencing flight would be included in this reading if it were to result in a redirection of the refugee to a risk of persecution.[56]

3.2.6 Summary: arguments from the language of Article 33

These last two points are probably the strongest arguments drawn from the text itself in favour of a wider scope of Article 33. To the extent that these readings can be established as the ordinary meaning, one need not proceed further in the inquiry. Yet, on both accounts, this interpretation has been contested. Although scholars like Nehemiah Robinson and Atle Grahl-Madsen have acknowledged the reading of 'refouler' as including actions at the frontier, both still defer to the territorial interpretation based on the drafting history. From a methodological perspective the validity of relying so heavily on the subjective element of drafting intent is questionable. Under a strict application of the 1969 Vienna Convention, an objective interpretation of the wording will always take precedence.[57]

It may thus be concluded that 'the plain and ordinary meaning' of *refouler* supports an interpretation extending application of the *non-refoulement* requirement to situations occurring *at* the border. This, however, does not in itself aid in extending the scope *ratione loci* to include

---

[56] A variation of this argument was presented in the analysis of Art. 33 submitted to UNHCR's Global Consultations by Lauterpacht and Bethlehem:

> [I]t must be noted that the word used is 'territories' as opposed to 'countries' or 'States'. The implication of this is that the legal status of the place *to* which the individual may be sent is not material. The relevant issue will be whether it is a place where the person concerned will be at risk. This also has wider significance as it suggests that the principle of *non-refoulement* will apply also in circumstances in which the refugee or asylum seeker is within their country of origin but is nevertheless under the protection of another Contracting State. (Lauterpacht and Bethlehem, 'Scope and content', p. 122)

This argument faces at least one major difficulty, however, as it is hard to see how the conclusion can be reconciled with the requirement of Art. 1A(2) limiting the *ratione personae* of the convention to persons having fled their country of origin. Goodwin-Gill and McAdam, *Refugee in International Law*, pp. 250 ff. Beyond this, the argument would appear to fall back on the same intermediate premise as set out above, namely that it is not a question of *from* where, but *to* where a person is returned.

[57] U. Linderfalk, *Om tolkningen av traktater* (Lund: Lund University, 2001), pp. 261–64; Noll, *Negotiating Asylum*, p. 430; Davy, *Asyl und internationales Flüchtlingsrecht*, p. 105. Of course, neither Robinson nor Grahl-Madsen would have known of this instrument at the time of their writing, which may account for their stronger reliance on the preparatory works. On the other hand, the Vienna Convention is generally regarded as a codification of pre-existing customary international law.

situations where migration control is exercised extraterritorially. The majority ruling in the *Sale* case thus acknowledged the point that the inclusion of *'refouler'* in the English text would indicate that 'return' should be understood as a 'defensive act of resistance or exclusion at a border', yet proceeds from there to deny that the Convention applies to actions on the high seas.[58] While an examination of the language thus extends the scope *ratione loci* of Article 33 of the Refugee Convention to situations at the border, it does not bring clarity regarding any application beyond the physical frontiers.

3.3 Purpose and object

Beyond the strict interpretation of treaty language, any legal provision would have to be interpreted in the light of the purpose to which it is directed and the concerns it seeks to address. Looking for the *telos* of Article 33 of the Refugee Convention, several substantial arguments have emerged in favour of a wider geographical application of the article. Nonetheless, the rift between territorialist and universalist interpretations continues to be evident in the debate over the purpose and object of Article 33, not just in terms of the relative importance assigned to this aspect of interpretation, but also of the orientation chosen. The contours emerge of a conflict partly reflecting the disagreement evident during the drafting history but also pointing to a broader confrontation, between those emphasising general principles of human rights and universality and those who see human rights law as expressing a compromise between such aspirations and the realpolitik of what states eventually are willing to sign up to.

3.3.1 Towards a wider interpretation

For several scholars the natural starting point of searching for evidence of the essential object of Article 33 is again the drafting history of the

---

[58] *Sale*, pp. 7 ff. To the present author, however, the reasoning between these two statements does not appear entirely clear. The argument, best summarised, starts from the assertion that if *'refouler'* is limited to instances occurring behind or at the frontiers, its parenthetical insertion following 'return' would indicate a narrower meaning of this term as well. Second, based on previous litigation, border situations are interpreted as 'on the threshold of initial entry', which again is taken to refer to a refugee physically present, yet not resident. For a critique of this reasoning see 'Haitian Interdiction Case 1993', at 89 ff.

treaty.[59] In particular, the initial and substantial discussions of the ad hoc committee are often drawn on in favour of a wider interpretation. We may recall the remark by the US representative, Louis Henkin:

> Whether it was a question of closing the frontier to a refugee who asked admittance, or of turning him back after he had crossed the frontier, or even of expelling him after he had been admitted to residence in the territory, the problem was more or less the same. Whatever the case might be, whether the refugee was in a regular position, he must not be turned back to a country where his life and freedom could be threatened.[60]

This point essentially confirms the textual reading above, arguing that the purpose of Article 33 is to prevent a certain consequence, namely return *to* rather than *from* a specific territory. Consequently, limiting the geographical application to the territory would be 'inconsistent with the purpose, and is contrary to the spirit, of the UN Refugee Convention'.[61]

While Henkin's reasoning was addressed to border situations, it seems clear that a purposive interpretation could extend this reasoning to cover extraterritorial application as well. Henkin himself affirmed this in connection with the *Sale* case:

> It is incredible that states that had agreed not to force any human being back into the hands of his/her oppressors intended to leave themselves – and each other – free to reach out beyond the territory to seize a refugee and to return him/her to the country from which he sought to escape.[62]

Similarly, the purpose and object of Article 33 have been sought from the text itself. Replicating language arguments espoused above, it has thus been claimed that the 'essential purpose' of the *non-refoulement* principle is to prohibit 'return in *any manner whatsoever* of refugees to countries where they may face persecution'.[63]

Second, reference has been made to the context of the treaty. The preamble thus explicitly recognises 'the social and humanitarian character of

---

[59] Hathaway, *Rights of Refugees*, p. 56; H. Lauterpacht, 'Restrictive interpretation and the principle of effectiveness in the interpretation of treaties', (1949) 26 *British Yearbook of International Law* 48–85, at 83.

[60] Doc. E/AC.32/SR.20, para. 54.

[61] UNHCR, *The State of the World's Refugees: In Search of Solutions* (Oxford University Press, 1995), p. 204. See also G.-H. Gornig, *Das Refoulement-Verbot im Völkerrecht* (Vienna: Wilhelm Braumüller, 1987), XVIII, p. 21.

[62] L. Henkin, 'Notes from the president', *ASIL Newsletter*, September–October 1993, 1.

[63] Goodwin-Gill and McAdam, *Refugee in International Law*, p. 248 (emphasis added).

the problems of refugees'.[64] Further, noting the endeavour to 'assure refugees the widest possible exercise of these fundamental rights and freedoms' may be taken as support of a wide interpretation of both the material and geographical scope of the Convention.[65]

The historical context may further be invoked in support of a wider geographical application. As noted by Justice Blackmun in his dissent to the *Sale* verdict,

[T]he Convention... was enacted largely in response to the experience of Jewish refugees in Europe during the period of World War II. The tragic consequences of the world's indifference at that time are well known. The resulting ban on *refoulement*, as broad as the humanitarian purpose that inspired it, is easily applicable here... [66]

In this sense, the lack of any direct historical precedent for extraterritorial interception mechanisms may excuse Article 33 for not explicitly emphasising an extraterritorial scope.[67]

Following on from this it has been contended that a strictly territorial interpretation leads to a self-evidently arbitrary and unreasonable result. If a strictly territorial interpretation is applied, the most fundamental protection afforded by the Convention turns not on protection needs but on the ability of refugees to access clandestinely the country of asylum.[68] Recalling the regret of early commentators, it seems intuitively wrong to uphold an interpretation whereby the refugee who manages to elude the border guard and enter illegally will receive more protection than the refugee who honestly presents his or her asylum claim to the authorities at or before the border.[69]

---

[64] Lauterpacht and Bethlehem, 'Scope and content', pp. 106 ff.; E. Willheim, 'MV *Tampa*: the Australian response', (2003) 15 *International Journal of Refugee Law* 159–91, at 175.

[65] A. Fischer-Lescano and T. Löhr, *Border Control at Sea: Requirements under International Human Rights and Refugee Law* (Berlin: European Centre for Constitutional and Human Rights, 2007), p. 14.

[66] Justice Blackmun in *Sale*, p. 7.   [67] Hathaway, *Rights of Refugees*, p. 337.

[68] 'Haitian Interdiction Case 1993', at 92.

[69] Gornig, *Refoulement-Verbot*, p. 20; A. Grahl-Madsen, *Territorial Asylum* (Stockholm: Almqvist & Wiksell International, 1980), p. 85; Robinson, *Convention Relating to the Status of Refugees*, p. 163; Fischer-Lescano and Löhr, *Border Control at Sea*, p. 15. A similar point building on the wider norm context has been made with reference to Art. 31 of the Refugee Convention, exempting refugees from penalties related to illegal entry or presence. Noll asserts that if the convention prohibits states from penalising refugees from breaking national entry regulations, 'it must be concluded *a fortiori* that the Convention does not allow that the observance of the same regulations is enforced *ex ante* by the means of *refoulement*'. Noll, *Negotiating Asylum*, p. 430. See further Davy, *Asyl und internationales Flüchtlingsrecht*, p. 120.

3.3.2 *Against a wider interpretation*

In contrast to the above stand those who claim that the purpose of the Refugee Convention is essentially territorial in the commitments it asks states to undertake. The UK House of Lords has argued that the focus of the Convention is on the treatment of refugees within the receiving state. The Refugee Convention is explicitly an instrument relating to the *status* of refugees. Emphasis is thus on the rights owed to refugees that are assumed to be *within* the country of asylum.[70] Grahl-Madsen, while regretting the lack of applicability of Article 33 at the border, has argued that territorial affiliation may always be at the heart of states' willingness to take on human rights responsibilities:

> It must be remembered that the Refugee Convention to a certain extent is a result of the pressure by humanitarian interested persons on Governments, and that public opinion is apt to concern itself much more with the individual who has set foot on the nation's territory and thus is within the power of the national authorities, than with the people only seen as shadows or moving figures 'at the other side of the fence'. The latter have not materialized as human beings, and it is much easier to shed responsibility for a mass of unknown people than for the individual whose fate one has to decide.[71]

While Grahl-Madsen moves somewhat beyond the realm of strictly legal reasoning, he nonetheless points to the same underlying argument, that the Convention is essentially territorial in its inception and that states cannot reasonably be expected to oblige themselves on matters concerning refugees beyond this.

Yet the argumentation in both instances appears flawed. As discussed at the outset of this chapter, it is correct that the Refugee Convention operates on a principle of territorial approximation according to which different rights are accrued according to the level of attachment established between the refugee and the host state. Yet, exactly because of this complex structure *ratione loci*, it cannot simply be inferred that because most rights enshrined are triggered only after the refugee's presence within the territory that this is the geographical ambit of Article 33 as well. Indeed, it is clear from the drafting history that several rights under the Convention were intended to have an extraterritorial application. This is so for the right to property (Art. 13), where the drafters were keen to ensure refugees' ability to claim property in states where they are not

---

[70] Lord Bingham of Cornhill in R. *(European Roma Rights Centre and Others) v. Immigration Officer at Prague Airport and Another*, House of Lords, para. 16.

[71] Grahl-Madsen, *Commentary on the Refugee Convention*.

physically present.[72] Similar arguments were made for the right to tax equity (Art. 29) and, importantly, access to courts (Art. 16(1)). Common to these rights, like Article 33, is that no explicit reference is made to a certain level of attachment.

In respect of Grahl-Madsen's more general argument, one equally wonders if his premises apply in the globalised world of today. As argued above, the drafters of the Convention are unlikely to have foreseen that states would move their migration control to the high seas or foreign jurisdictions in order to prevent asylum-seekers from arriving at their borders. Although these practices may take place 'out of sight' of the controlling state's public oversight mechanisms,[73] there nevertheless is little doubt that offshore and outsourced migration control increasingly means that authorities decide the fate of refugees long before their arrival at their territory.

The second argument in favour of a more territorial interpretation builds on the consequentialist position that extraterritorial application of Article 33 would entail a de facto right of admission, which was explicitly excluded from the remit of the Convention. The underlying premise of this reasoning is that in practice adherence to the *non-refoulement* principle generally requires states to undertake a status determination procedure in order to ensure that a refugee is not returned to persecution. As such procedures cannot meaningfully be conducted on the high seas, for example, states would be required to admit any asylum-seeker for whom the *non-refoulement* principle is applicable to its territory for at least the duration of the asylum procedure.[74] Not only would this have immense implications for the legality of all types of offshore migration control mechanisms,[75] it would also seem to go against the intention of the drafters, who explicitly precluded a right of admission for those not already present.[76]

This view, however, may be refuted on several levels. First, it should be recognised that neither in theory nor in practice does the *non-refoulement* obligation amount to a right of admission in situations involving asylum-seekers at the border of a state or beyond. While, as Noll describes it, Article 33 may be said to entail a right of refugees to 'transgress an

---

[72] Hathaway, *Rights of Refugees*, p. 162.   [73] See below, chapter 6.

[74] R. Weinzierl, *Border Management and Human Rights: A Study of EU Law and the Law of the Sea* (Berlin: Deutches Institut für Menchenrechte, 2007), p. 19.

[75] Noll, 'Seeking asylum at embassies', 549.

[76] Doc. E/AC.32/SR.20, para. 54. Goodwin-Gill and McAdam, *Refugee in International Law*, p. 206.

administrative border', triggering the legal responsibility of a state, it does not entail a similar right to access physically the territory of the said state.[77] The fact that in practice states subsequently allow admission for asylum-seekers encountered at their frontiers or in international waters in order to instigate an asylum procedure does not amount to a right to admission.

Further, as discussed above, even the ad hoc committee made it quite clear that the *refoulement* prohibition does not entail that refugees must in all cases be admitted to the territory.[78] Rather, it was envisioned that a state which refused admission to its own territory might divert a refugee to a third country as long as no risk of persecution existed there.[79] Safe third-country policies and plans for extraterritorial processing of asylum-seekers are both examples of strategies that seek to carve out a space located exactly between the negative responsibility not to return a refugee to persecution and the positive obligation of allowing entry. Lastly, a reading of the drafting history suggests that while issues regarding admission and a right of asylum were omitted from the scope of the Convention, this reflected realpolitik and lack of consensus rather than an express intention or *telos* to deny admission in frontier situations.[80]

The last but most consistent set of arguments for a restrictive interpretation conceptualises the purpose of the Refugee Convention as being a compromise between competing interests: on the one hand the need to ensure protection for victims of persecution, on the other respect for the national sovereignty of both asylum and origin states.[81] From a pure protection perspective this has entailed a number of shortcomings. As dealt with above, no right to be granted asylum is guaranteed under the Refugee Convention, and states still maintain sovereign control over who gains access to their territory. Likewise, both the present refugee regime and that preceding it are fundamentally exilic or palliative in nature and no emphasis or obligations are placed on the countries of origin.[82]

---

[77] Noll, *Negotiating Asylum*, p. 387.

[78] E/1618, Report of the First Ad Hoc Committee on Statelessness and Related Problems, Comments to Art. 28.

[79] Doc. E/AC.32/SR.20, para. 14.   [80] Doc. E/AC.32/SR.19, p. 18; Doc. E/AC.32/SR.20, p. 7.

[81] Lord Bingham of Cornhill in *R. (European Roma Rights Centre and Others) v. Immigration Officer at Prague Airport and Another*, House of Lords, para. 16.

[82] Okoth-Obbo, 'Coping with a complex refugee crisis'; C. Tomuschat, 'State responsibility and the country of origin', in V. Gowlland-Debbas (ed.), *The Problem of Refugees in the Light of Contemporary International Law Issues* (The Hague: Kluwer, 1996), pp. 59–80; J. Hathaway, 'New directions to avoid hard problems: the distortion of the palliative role of refugee protection', (1995) 8 (3) *Journal of Refugee Studies* 288–94.

In the same way, a lack of extraterritorial scope of the *non-refoulement* prohibition may be viewed as a protection shortcoming that 'offends one's sense of fairness'.[83] Yet it does not follow that it was necessarily the purpose of the Convention to remedy these shortcomings. This argument was expressed clearly by the majority in the *Sale* case:

> The drafters... may not have contemplated that any nation would gather fleeing refugees [outside their national borders] and return them to the one country they had desperately sought to escape; such actions may even violate the spirit of Article 33; but a treaty cannot impose uncontemplated extraterritorial obligations on those who ratify it through no more than its general humanitarian intent. Because the text of Article 33 cannot reasonably be read to say anything at all about a nation's actions towards aliens outside its own territory, it does not prohibit such actions.[84]

3.3.3 General presumptions in the interpretation of telos

This brings us to a more fundamental discussion of what general presumptions underlie the arguments on each side and thus what actually counts as the object and purpose of a given legal instrument. Here the preliminary choices of interpretative position become decisive.[85] The restrictionist argumentation above expresses a strong preference in favour of voluntarist theory and related principles of national sovereignty.[86] According to this view, the scope of international law is determined entirely by the will of states at the moment of conception.[87] Lacking a clear interpretative basis for a wider scope within the text and drafting remarks, a residual principle of freedom or state sovereignty prescribes 'restrictive interpretation', choosing the permissible interpretation that involves the minimum of obligations for the state party, a maxim dubbed *in dubio mitius*.[88]

An interpretative position starting from international sovereignty and the state as an international law subject, however, would reject this view. Elihu Lauterpacht and Daniel Bethlehem have argued that the object and purpose of the Refugee Convention, like other treaties of a 'humanitarian

---

[83] Remark in relation to the *Sale* case by Simon Brown J in *R. (European Roma Rights Centre and Others) v. Immigration Officer at Prague Airport and Another*, UK Court of Appeal, [2004] QB 811, [2003] EWCA Civ 666, 20 May 2003.

[84] *Sale*, p. 8.   [85] Noll, *Negotiating Asylum*, p. 450.

[86] Indeed, the majority's decision in the *Sale* decision closely mimics that of the *Lotus* case:
> The rules of law binding upon States therefore emanate from their own free will as expressed in conventions... Restrictions upon the independence of States cannot therefore be assumed. (*Lotus*, p. 18)

[87] *Lotus* case, p. 18.   [88] *Case of the S.S. Wimbledon*, PCIJ Ser. A, No. 1 (1923), pp. 24 ff.

character', do not conform to this mode of reasoning, which represents, at best, a maxim relevant in regard to the international law of coexistence.[89] They cite an Advisory Opinion of the International Court of Justice on *Reservations to the Genocide Convention* in which it is contended that

In such a convention, the contracting States do not have any interests of their own; they merely have, one and all, a common interest, namely, the accomplishment of those higher purposes which are the *raison d'être* of the convention.[90]

More generally, we may ask whether taking the premise of national sovereignty and the presumptive freedom of action as a starting point for interpreting binding instruments aimed at constraining both is not somewhat self-defeating. In his famous article, 'Restrictive interpretation and the principle of effectiveness in the interpretation of treaties', Hersch Lauterpacht argued against restrictive interpretation:

The purpose of treaties – and of international law in general – is to limit the sovereignty of states in the particular sphere with which they are concerned. Their purposes are to lay down rules regulating conduct by restricting, in that particular sphere, the freedom of action of states. To a large extent treaties have no meaning except when conceived as fulfilling that function.[91]

The critique against *in dubio mitius* in treaty interpretation, and especially in regard to human rights instruments, has found support from a number of scholars.[92] What is essentially rejected here is an interpretative outlook in which national sovereignty is the sole starting point. Entering into binding international agreements is a function of the international sovereignty of states, and so it would be natural to base purposive interpretation on a conception of the state as an international law subject.

---

[89] Lauterpacht and Bethlehem, 'Scope and content', p. 104. In line with this view, Noll concludes that the *in dubio mitius* principle has been somewhat eclipsed by the proliferation of human rights:

> Where treaties aim at stipulating benefits for third parties not represented under treaty negotiations, the duty-minimising presumption of bilateral international law is no longer appropriate. (Noll, *Negotiating Asylum*, p. 409)

[90] *Reservations to the Convention on the Prevention of and Punishment of the Crime of Genocide, Advisory Opinion*, International Court of Justice, 28 May 1951, p. 23.

[91] H. Lauterpacht, 'Restrictive interpretation and the principle of effectiveness in the interpretation of treaties', (1949) 26 *British Yearbook of International Law* 48–85, at 60.

[92] See e.g. Hathaway, *Rights of Refugees*, p. 73; Noll, 'Politics of saving lives', 409; O. Spiermann, *Enten & Eller: Studier i suverænitetsbegreber* (Copenhagen: Jurist- og Økonomforbundets Forlag, 1995), p. 189. It should be noted that the principle is not mentioned in the Vienna Convention, nor is there evidence that it has ever found extensive application in the judgments of the International Court of Justice or its predecessor.

Variations on Hersch Lauterpacht's argument have been put forward by a broad array of refugee and human rights scholars. While the critique against restrictive interpretation as not taking account of the context of international sovereignty may be well placed, one should, however, be careful not simply to replace one bias with another. This concern is particularly relevant where human rights instruments are subjected to a particular interpretative methodology in which state interests may be disregarded in view of the higher, co-operative, purpose of the legal instrument.[93] The particular value or pitfalls of such a methodological distinction between human rights and general international law notwithstanding,[94] it is quite clear that the interpretative problem between the territorial and the universal positions is not solved as such, but only referred back to the underlying conflict, or preliminary choice, between national and international sovereignty.

3.4 Preliminary conclusions after the first stage of interpretation

The above has sought a solution to the scope of application *ratione loci* of Article 33 within the ordinary meaning of the text, the purpose and object of the article and, although formally categorised as 'supplementary', the drafting history. These categories represent the immutable basis of interpretation and thus the essential starting point of any positivist reading.

An examination of the language used does support extending the scope to include non-admission at the border but, as regards extraterritorial application, an inherent discordance seems to persist between restrictive and universal readings. This interpretative tension has been shown to exist in the very drafting process without explicitly having been resolved. Instead, a number of arguments around the language and the object and purpose of the article inevitably fall back on arguments already proposed during the drafting sessions, or different elements of the drafting history itself are enlisted in support of one position or the other.

[93] Lauterpacht and Bethlehem, 'Scope and content'. A similar view is taken by Hathaway, when noting that where treaties are designed to advance 'general goals for the international community as a whole...their very nature compels a more particularized approach to interpretation'. Hathaway, *Rights of Refugees*, p. 73.

[94] M. T. Kamminga and M. Scheinin, *The Impact of Human Rights Law on General International Law* (Oxford University Press, 2009); B. Simma, 'International human rights and general international law: a comparative analysis', in *Collected Courses of the Academy of European Law, Volume IV, Book 2* (The Hague: Kluwer Law International, 1995), pp. 153–236; A. Pellet, '"Human rightism" and international law', (2000) *Italian Yearbook of International Law* 3–16.

On balance, the arguments from the wording of the article and an analysis of the object and purpose provide relatively more support to a broader scope that includes at least border situations and possibly an even wider application. Yet nowhere does an interpretation present itself that convincingly narrows the field to yield a single authoritative result.

At the present stage one is thus tempted to concur with Gregor Noll's assessment that '[g]iven the richness of accumulated arguments, the battle over the proper interpretation of Article 33 GC can no longer be won on a substantial level. The decisive arguments are those relating to the interpretation of interpretative rules'.[95] This is clear not only in the debate over what sources to accord primacy, but equally in the underlying principles guiding interpretative choices.

Interpretation, however, does not stop here. Following the methodological approach outlined above, this is where informal sources and a wider contextual reading may aid legal interpretation. The following sections will seek to relate the primary interpretation arrived at above to sources that may exert an interstitial normative influence on the reading of Article 33. These fall into three main categories: first, non-binding resolutions, or soft law, as expressed by international or regional inter-state bodies; second, state practice as regards actual interpretation of the scope of Article 33 in situations involving migration control beyond the territory; and, lastly, expressions of the *non-refoulement* principle in other human rights instruments and general international law. While these sources do not possess an independent normative force, in the identification of the interpretative scope remaining after the interpretative application above, this secondary step in the legal analysis aims at narrowing, or conflating ambiguities in, the interpretation from the sources applied at the first stage.

3.5 Subsequent interpretation and state practice

3.5.1 Soft law

Looking to soft law, a substantial number of resolutions have appeared to deal with the interpretative problem of the geographical application of the *non-refoulement* obligation under Article 33. The majority of them have been directed to the issue of border applicability and largely

---

[95] Noll, *Negotiating Asylum*, p. 427.

replicate the various arguments for inclusive readings presented above. More recently, however, a similar consensus seems to have emerged in favour of extending the application of the *non-refoulement* principle to the entire jurisdiction of acting states.

3.5.1.1 At the frontiers

The UNHCR Executive Committee has passed numerous conclusions on the issue of *non-refoulement* and its interpretation under the Refugee Convention. An examination of this material makes it quite clear that the scope *ratione loci* of Article 33 was accepted early as encompassing situations at the border. A number of Conclusions have simply expressed concern over refugees being rejected at the frontier.[96] More directly, Conclusion No. 15 (XXX) 1979, paragraph (j), recommends that 'where an asylum-seeker addresses himself in the first instance to a frontier authority the latter should not reject his application without reference to a central authority'.[97] More strongly, 'the fundamental importance of the observance of the principle of *non-refoulement* – both at the border and within the territory of a State' was reaffirmed in Conclusion No. 6 (XXVIII) 1977, paragraph (c).[98]

Support may also be drawn from the 1967 UN Declaration on Territorial Asylum[99] and the 1977 Draft Convention on Territorial Asylum.[100] Article 3 of the Declaration and of the Convention cover *non-refoulement* and were explicitly intended to clarify the scope of Article 33 of the

---

[96] UNHCR Executive Committee, Conclusion No. 14 (XXX) (1979), para. (b), and Conclusion No. 21 (XXXII) (1981), para. (f).

[97] A similar recommendation that immigration officers act in respect of the principle of *non-refoulement* in border instances is expressed in UNHCR Executive Committee, Conclusion No. 8 (XXVIII) (1977), para. (e)(i).

[98] Since then, the view that observance of the *non-refoulement* principle simply entails non-rejection at the frontier has been set out in Conclusion No. 22 (XXXII) (1981), para. II(A)2; No. 81 (XLVIII) (1997), para. (h); No. 85 (XLIX) (1998), para. (q); and No. 99 (LV) (2004), para. l.

[99] United Nations General Assembly, Resolution 2312 (XXII) (14 December 1967). The Declaration found further support from the Committee of Ministers of the Council of Europe, Declaration on Territorial Asylum, 278th Meeting of the Ministers' Deputies, 18 November 1977.

[100] A number of different versions have been prepared for this Convention. For an overview see Grahl-Madsen, *Territorial Asylum*, pp. 174–211. All citations in the following relate to the draft presented at the UN Conference on Territorial Asylum, UN Doc. A/CONF.78/12, 4 February 1977. While in the end the conference could not agree to adopt the Convention, the provisions of the draft were discussed at length and seventy-six states expressed support for the Convention, and it may as such be considered a source of soft law. See Grahl-Madsen, *Territorial Asylum*, pp. 8 ff., 61–66.

Refugee Convention. Referring back to the original argument made by the Swiss and Dutch delegates in favour of a strictly territorial application, a clause was inserted in each instrument exempting the state in cases of mass influx. Yet, barring this situation, it is clear that the *non-refoulement* principle is otherwise to cover asylum-seekers 'at the frontier' and prohibit 'non-rejection at the frontier, return or expulsion, which would compel him to remain in or return to a territory with respect to which he has a well-founded fear of persecution'.[101]

The Council of Europe Parliamentary Assembly has taken a similar view. While acknowledging the strictly territorial interpretation possible on the basis of the *travaux préparatoires*, it is argued that not only can the concept '*ne pas refouler*' be interpreted to cover non-admission to the territory, it further 'seems illogical a priori that a person who has succeeded in crossing the frontier illegally should enjoy greater protection than someone who presents himself legally'.[102] Border applicability is further affirmed by a Council of Europe resolution urging member governments to ensure that 'no one shall be subjected to refusal at the frontier, rejection, expulsion, or any other measure which would have the result of compelling him to return to or remain in a territory where he would be in danger of persecution'.[103]

3.5.1.2 Within the jurisdiction

In more recent soft law instruments, support can equally be found for extending the geographical scope beyond the borders. While UNHCR itself has been quite explicit in expressing the view that the *non-refoulement* principle applies wherever a state acts,[104] evidence of a more expansive interpretation of the geographical scope is somewhat more subtle and nuanced in the Executive Committee conclusions. Particular attention

---

[101] UN Draft Convention on Territorial Asylum, UN Doc. A/CONF.78/12, 4 February 1977, Art. 3.

[102] Council of Europe Parliamentary Assembly, Report on the Granting of the Right of Asylum to European Refugees, Doc. 1986, 29 September 1965, pp. 6–7.

[103] Council of Europe, Resolution 14, Asylum to Persons in Danger of Persecution, 29 June 1967, para. 2.

[104] As argued,

> Since the purpose of the principle of *non-refoulement* is to ensure that refugees are protected against forcible return to situations of danger it applies both within a State's territory and to rejection at the borders. It also applies outside the territory of States. In essence, it is applicable wherever a State acts. (UNHCR, UNHCR Note on the Principle of Non-refoulement, EU seminar on the implementation of the 1995 EU Resolution on minimum guarantees for asylum procedures)

has been paid to interdiction and refugees rescued at sea. UNHCR's advisory opinion on extraterritorial application of the *non-refoulement* principle cites Conclusion No. 15 (XXX) 1979, paragraph (c), asserting that '[i]t is the humanitarian obligation of all coastal States to allow vessels in distress to seek haven in their waters and to grant asylum, or at least temporary refuge, to persons on board wishing to seek asylum.'[105] While this would seem to extend an obligation to vessels on the high seas or adjacent territorial seas, it is less clear that this obligation stems from the legal *non-refoulement* principle as enshrined in the Refugee Convention and not from a more general 'humanitarian obligation' and the law of the sea.[106]

The more recent Conclusion on Protection Safeguards in Interception Measures is clearer that the *non-refoulement* principle is intended to apply extraterritorially. Responding to new legal developments to allow migration control on the high seas or in foreign territorial waters, it is recommended that

Interception measures should not result in asylum-seekers and refugees being denied access to international protection, or result in those in need of international protection being returned, directly or indirectly, to the frontiers of territories where their life or freedom would be threatened on account of a Convention ground. (Conclusion No. 97 (LIV) 2003, para. (a)(iv)).

In the same conclusion, however, it is emphasised that 'The State within whose sovereign territory, or territorial waters, interception takes place has the primary responsibility for addressing any protection needs of intercepted persons' (para. a(i)). While it is a bit unclear how exactly 'primary responsibility' is to be understood, this limitation would seem to support an interpretation that states are obliged by the principle of *non-refoulement* wherever they exercise effective control. This is supported by Conclusion No. 74 (XLV) 1994, paragraph (g), calling on states 'to respect scrupulously the fundamental principle of *non-refoulement*, and to make every effort to ensure the safety and well-being of refugees within their jurisdiction'.

See further UNHCR, Advisory Opinion; Guy S. Goodwin-Gill, 'R. (ex parte European Roma Rights Centre et al) v. Immigration Officer at Prague Airport and another (UNHCR intervening)', (2005) 17 (2) *International Journal of Refugee Law* 426–53.

[105] UNHCR, Advisory Opinion, p. 15.

[106] See the 1982 United Nations Convention on the Law of the Sea, the 1974 International Convention for the Safety of Life at Sea (SOLAS), the 1979 International Convention on Maritime Search and Rescue (SAR) and the 1989 International Convention on Salvage.

Lastly, an interpretation extending the principle of *non-refoulement* to situations involving interdiction has been put forward by regional bodies. The Inter-American Commission on Human Rights issued a report following the Supreme Court ruling in the *Sale* case. The Commission specifically rejected the view taken by the Supreme Court, and gave support to the interpretation set out in UNHCR's *amicus curiae* brief that Article 33 does indeed apply to persons interdicted on the high seas as opposed to US territory.[107] Consequently, the United States was breaching the *non-refoulement* principle set out in the Refugee Convention.[108] Similarly, the Council of Europe has issued recommendations calling on member states to uphold their responsibilities under both the Refugee Convention and the European Convention on Human Rights when conducting immigration control at sea.[109]

3.5.2 State practice

While in discourse states thus appear to have affirmed a more expansive interpretation, actual practice may, however, tell a different story. It is in relation to concrete state actions that one is likely to find the most evident resistance to extraterritorial application of the *non-refoulement* principle.

3.5.2.1 State practice in the interpretation of human rights treaties

Following Article 31(3)(b) of the Vienna Convention, any subsequent practice in the application of the treaty may be taken into account if it establishes an agreement of the parties regarding its interpretation. Yet the value of state practice from an interpretative perspective continues to be a contested issue among refugee and human rights lawyers. On the one hand, legal realists have argued that human rights norms not backed up by consistent state practice are essentially meaningless, and observation of actual practice thus becomes the primary source if

---

[107] 'Haitian Interdiction Case 1993'.

[108] *Haitian Center for Human Rights v. United States ('US Interdiction of Haitians on the High Seas')*, Inter-American Commission on Human Rights, Case 10.675, Report No. 51/96, Doc. OEA/Ser. L/V/II.95 7, rev. 13 March 1997, paras. 156–8.

[109] Council of Europe Parliamentary Assembly, Access to Assistance and Protection for Asylum-Seekers at European Seaports and Coastal Areas, Recommendation 1645, 29 January 2004, para. (j). The preceding report further notes that 'these recommendations should apply as long as foreign nationals are under the jurisdiction of a member state'. Doc. 10011, 5 December 2003, para. 49.

one is to deduce valid norms.[110] Other scholars, conversely, have argued that it is only relevant to consider state practice insofar as it supports the purpose of the instrument in question.[111] According to this position, '[r]eports of non-compliance with the principle of *non-refoulement* on the high seas and occasionally expressed doubts of single EU states about the applicability of the principle of *non-refoulement* on the high seas are not relevant indications under international law for the interpretation of the Refugee Convention.'[112]

To the mind of the present author, neither of these positions is correct. While the relative value of state practice as a source of international law may be debated,[113] it is highly dubious to accord some practices normative importance while prima facie discarding others according to a preliminary determination of the purpose of the instrument.[114] On the other hand, ascribing normative influence to every breach of human rights norms as representative of a more restrictive interpretation amounts to little more than a refusal to recognise international human rights law as such.

Between these two extremes, a more correct starting point is to assess the influence of state practice on the interpretation of treaty law by using the same criteria as when looking for general custom. Thus state practice must be measured both on its consistency and on the extent to which it is borne by a conviction that such practice is permissible under the relevant legal rule (*opinio juris*). Positively identifying a state's conviction about its legal duty is often difficult, if not impossible, and this has lead to some methodological resistance to the importance of *opinio juris sive necessitatis* within customary international law.[115] Yet, in the present context, where the objective is to assess restrictive state practice and the concomitant absence of such convictions of legal obligations, it is conversely clear

---

[110] J. S. Watson, *Theory and Reality in the International Protection of Human Rights* (New York: Transnational Publishers Inc., 1999).

[111] Weinzierl, *Border Management and Human Rights*, p. 37.

[112] Weinzierl, *Border Management and Human Rights*, p. 37.

[113] Hathaway, *Rights of Refugees*, pp. 71 ff.; Watson, *Theory and Reality*, p. 34; U. Fastenrath, 'Relative normativity in international law', (1993) 4 *European Journal of International Law* 305–40, at 327.

[114] The problems of such an approach are further compounded in those instances where the determination of purpose is equally restricted by some preconceived assumption for or against national sovereignty and state interests. See above, section 3.3.3.

[115] O. Spiermann, *Moderne Folkeret*, 3rd edn (Copenhagen: Jurist- og Økonomforbundets Forlag, 2006), pp. 51 ff.; J. L. Goldsmith and E. A. Posner, *The Limits of International Law* (Oxford University Press, 2005), pp. 24 ff.

that where evidence of *opinio juris* is found to be incongruent with actual practice, such state practice may readily be discarded.[116]

3.5.2.2 General assessment

When looking for state practice in this area it is surprising how few examples one can find of states rejecting asylum-seekers at their borders or in international waters *and* simultaneously claiming that this is permissible under Article 33 of the Refugee Convention. Several of the states which opposed application at the frontier during the drafting sessions today apply the *non-refoulement* principle to border situations through their national legislation.[117] Notably, EU member states have established the *non-refoulement* obligation to apply in border situations.[118] While notorious examples of border closures clearly resulting in *refoulement* have been recorded, the majority of these instances have been followed by claims that those expelled were 'illegal immigrants' and not refugees, that the *non-refoulement* obligation could be derogated due to a situation of mass influx, or that local authorities were acting independently.[119] While such relabelling of refugees may pose a serious problem, and arguments that the *non-refoulement* principle does not apply in situations of mass influx are questionable, they do not, however, challenge the interpretation of the geographical scope of application of the *non-refoulement* obligation.

---

[116] This is consistent with the approach of the International Court of Justice in the *Nicaragua* case, pointing out that contrary practice does not undermine the formation of customary international law if the practice is condemned or the state in question does not claim to be acting as a matter of right. *Case Concerning Military and Paramilitary Activities in and against Nicaragua*, International Court of Justice, 27 June 1986.

[117] J. Rodger, 'Defining the parameters of the non-refoulement principle', LLM research paper, international law, Faculty of Law, Victoria University, Wellington, 2001, 15; S. Taylor, 'Australia's implementations of its non-refoulement obligations under the Convention against Torture and Other Cruel, Inhuman or Degrading Treatment or Punishment and the International Covenant on Civil and Political Rights', (1994) 17 *University of New South Wales Law Journal* 459; Gornig, 'Refoulement-Verbot, p. 23; K. Hailbronner, 'Asylrecht in Völkerrecht', in W. Beitz and M. Wollenschläger (eds.), *Handbuch des Asylrechts* (Baden-Baden: Nomos, 1980), p. 95.

[118] European Council, Establishing the Criteria and Mechanisms for Determining the Member State Responsible for Examining an Asylum Application Lodged in One of the Member States by a Third-Country National, Regulation 342/2003, 25 February 2003, Art. 3(1); and European Council, Minimum Standards on Procedures in Member States for Granting and Withdrawing Refugee Status, Directive 2005/85/EC, 1 December 2005, Arts. 3(1) and 35. Under Art. 35 of the directive member states are, however, allowed to apply national border procedures subject to fewer legal safeguards.

[119] Goodwin-Gill and McAdam, *Refugee in International Law*, p. 230.

Similarly, until the *Sale* case scholars have found it difficult to record a single historical precedent for similar extraterritorial deterrence mechanisms without some assumption of responsibility.[120] UNHCR equally noted that, to its knowledge, no other state has resorted to the implementation of a formal policy of intercepting refugees on the high seas and repatriating them against their will.[121] This has led Goodwin-Gill to conclude that while Article 33 may not have applied to situations beyond the border at the time of drafting, subsequent state practice has confirmed a wider scope *ratione loci*.[122]

Since *Sale*, however, one could point to some additional examples, most notably the Australian operation of the so-called 'Pacific Solution' and the British proposal for a 'new vision for refugees'. Before simply concluding that a general consensus of the parties has been established regarding the interpretation of the applicability *ratione loci* of Article 33, a critical look must therefore be taken at these cases and a few general caveats underlined.

First, it should be noted that only a limited number of states are likely ever to have confronted a situation where they have to take a deliberate stance for or against extraterritorial applicability of the *non-refoulement* principle. Naturally, this would be limited to coastal states or states applying extraterritorial migration control in the territory of third states, which so far has primarily been a feature of more developed countries.

Second, there is a time element to consider. As shown in the later chapters, extraterritorial migration control in its various forms has clearly become more popular in recent years, and the picture may thus be changing. Lastly, and this will be considered in more detail in the next chapter, it is necessary to nuance state interpretation of scope *ratione loci* rather more. While some states may accept liability in situations involving interdiction on the high seas, they may refuse to accept that the *non-refoulement* principle applies to actions undertaken on the sovereign territory of another state. That said, a closer look at the Australian, US and UK cases suggests that even practices in these countries do not uniformly support a strict territorial interpretation.

3.5.2.3 Australia

The Australian 'Pacific Solution' was developed following a stand-off concerning the Norwegian ship MV *Tampa*. In August 2001 the *Tampa*

---

[120] Hathaway, *Rights of Refugees*, p. 337.   [121] 'Haitian Interdiction Case 1993', at 92.
[122] Guy Goodwin-Gill, *The Refugee in International Law*, 2nd edn (Oxford University Press, 1996), pp. 121–124.

responded to a request by the Australian search and rescue authorities to investigate a distress call from an Indonesian vessel, which turned out to be carrying 433 mainly Afghan asylum-seekers. Australia refused to let the *Tampa* enter Australian waters. Health problems on board caused the *Tampa* to ignore this order, and the ship was subsequently boarded by Australian special forces. Following another week of negotiations, Australia struck deals with Papua New Guinea and Nauru that they would host the asylum-seekers while their claims were examined.[123]

The incident led the Australian government to pass three pieces of legislation.[124] First, the 2001 Border Protection Act established interdiction powers in the territorial sea, contiguous zone and international waters. Second, two amendments to the Migration Act were passed, one excising certain northern islands from its 'migration zone' and thus from that part of its territory from where an asylum claim can effectively be launched,[125] and one enabling Australian authorities to send interdicted asylum-seekers or persons having arrived at the excised territories to countries 'declared' to provide effective protection in accordance with relevant human rights standards.[126]

The Australian response attracted substantial criticism from the international community.[127] From a legal perspective, it is clear that Australia cannot simply define and delimit the territory on which international obligations are owed, as it is an established principle of international law that sovereign territory is defined not by individual announcement but by effective possession and exercise of power.[128] Second, the simple

---

[123] For more detailed analysis of the *Tampa* incident, see Kneebone, 'Pacific plan'; T. Magner, 'The less than "Pacific" solution for asylum seekers in Australia', (2004) 16 *International Journal of Refugee Law* 53–90; M. Pugh, 'Drowning not waving: boat people and humanitarianism at sea', (2004) 17 *Journal of Refugee Studies* 50–68; Willheim, 'MV *Tampa*'; C. M.-J. Bostock, 'The international legal obligations owed to the asylum seekers on the MV *Tampa*', (2002) 14 *International Journal of Refugee Law* 279–301; P. Mathew, 'Australian refugee protection in the wake of the *Tampa*', (2002) 96 *American Journal of International Law* 661–76.

[124] For a more detailed description, see Mathew, 'Australian refugee protection', 663 ff.

[125] Migration Amendment (Excision from Migration Zone) Act 2001. The migration zone delimits the territory from where application for a 'protection visa' can be launched, which in practice is how Australia accepts an application for asylum. Mathew, 'Australian refugee protection', 664.

[126] Migration Amendment (Consequential Provisions) Act 2001, Art. 198(A).

[127] Magner, 'Less than "Pacific" solution', 83; Willheim, 'MV *Tampa*', 191.

[128] Hathaway, *Rights of Refugees*, p. 321; Magner, 'Less than "Pacific" solution', 74 ff.; Goodwin-Gill, *Refugee in International Law*, p. 123; A. Ross, *Lærebog i Folkeret*, 4th edn (Copenhagen: Munksgaards Forlag, 1961), pp. 159 ff. Situations of excised territory and international zones are discussed in more detail below, section 4.3.1.

declaration of countries as providing effective protection creates a number of difficulties concerning transfer of protection responsibility, exacerbated by Australia's decision to sign an agreement with Nauru, which is not a signatory to the 1951 Refugee Convention.[129]

Yet, these issues notwithstanding, it is not clear that the Australian practice amounted to a rejection of the application of the *non-refoulement* principle to situations involving interdiction on the high seas. The asylum-seekers on board the *Tampa* and subsequently interdicted vessels were not returned to Afghanistan, Iran or Indonesia or other countries of origin. On the contrary, the Australian government made substantial efforts to negotiate agreements with third countries to ensure that asylum-seekers would receive some kind of protection and eventual asylum processing. Such a system may raise other issues under international refugee law, yet it is not, strictly speaking, inconsistent with Article 33 as long as no risk of *refoulement* exists in those third states.[130] Thus, while the 'Pacific Solution' was manifestly intended to avoid asylum procedures in Australia, the fact that another state was envisaged to provide at least temporary protection hardly constitutes state practice in support of a more restrictive interpretation of the *non-refoulement* principle.

3.5.2.4 United States

In contrast to Australia, the US government expressly held that Article 33 was not applicable to actions carried out by the US Coast Guard in international waters when arguing the *Sale* case. In 1989, the US delegate to the UNHCR Executive Committee had taken a similar position, arguing that there is a difference between a binding legal commitment and mere moral and political principles of refugee protection:

---

[129] Kneebone, 'Pacific plan'; S. H. Legomsky, 'Secondary refugee movements and the return of asylum seekers to third countries: the meaning of effective protection', (2003) 15 *International Journal of Refugee Law* 567–667. On the issue of transferring responsibility for status determination and refugee protection more generally, see N. Lassen, J. v. Selm and J. Doomernik, *The Transfer of Protection Status in the EU, against the Background of the Common European Asylum System and the Goal of a Uniform Status, Valid throughout the Union, for those Granted Asylum* (Brussels: European Commission, 2004).

[130] This has primarily been dealt with in the context of 'safe third country' policies. See e.g. Hurwitz, *Collective Responsibility*; Gil-Bazo, 'Practice of Mediterranean states'; J. v. Selm, *Access to Procedures, 'Safe Third Countries', 'Safe Countries of Origin' and 'Time Limits'*, Global Consultations on International Protection, Third Track, background paper (Geneva: UNHCR, 2001); N. Lassen and J. Hughes, *'Safe Third Countries': Policies in European Countries* (Copenhagen: Danish Refugee Council, 1997). See also Doc. E/AC.32/SR.20, para. 14.

As a matter of practice, the United States authorities did not return persons who were likely to be persecuted in their countries of origin . . . That was the practice, and . . . the policy of the United States, and not a principle of international law with which it conformed . . . It did not consider that the *non-refoulement* obligation under article 33 of the Convention included an obligation to admit an asylum-seeker. The obligation . . . pertained only to persons already in the country and not to those who arrived at the frontier or who were travelling with the intention of entering the country but had not yet arrived at their destination.[131]

More recently, the United States issued a set of observations in response to a 2007 advisory opinion by UNHCR on the extraterritorial application of the *non-refoulement* principle. In these observations, the United States underlines its 'long-standing interpretation' that 'Article 33 of the 1951 Refugee Convention applies only in respect of aliens within the territory of the Contracting State', and emphasises that any practice of the United States to respect the *non-refoulement* principle when carrying out interception on the high seas was a matter of national policy, not international legal obligation.[132]

While these statements are unambiguous, they have not drawn any support from other states. It is further noteworthy that the United States itself has hardly been consistent in applying this interpretation.[133] The Haitian interdiction programme was enacted following a 1981 agreement with the Haitian government authorising US officials to board Haitian vessels on the high seas and in US territorial waters.[134] Under this agreement, however, the United States promised not to return anyone found to be a refugee.[135] In section 3 of the concomitant Executive Order 12324, US authorities were further required to 'take whatever steps are necessary to ensure . . . the strict observance of our international obligations concerning those who genuinely flee persecution in their homeland'.[136]

---

[131] Remarks by Mr. Kelley, UN Doc. No. A/AC.96/SR.442, paras. 80–82. Cited in G. Goodwin-Gill, 'The Haitian refoulement case: a comment', (1994) 6 *International Journal of Refugee Law* 103–9, at 106.

[132] US Mission to the United Nations and other international organisations in Geneva, Observations of the United States on the Advisory Opinion of the UN High Commissioner for Refugees on the Extraterritorial Application of Non-refoulement Obligations under the 1951 Convention Relating to the Status of Refugees and its 1967 Protocol, 28 December 2007, p. 9.

[133] Goodwin-Gill and McAdam, *Refugee in International Law*, p. 224.

[134] Exchange of Diplomatic Letters between E. H. Preeg, US Ambassador to Haiti, and E. Francisque, Haiti's Secretary of State for Foreign Affairs, TIAS No. 10241, 23 September 1981.

[135] Legomsky, 'USA and the Caribbean interdiction programme', 679.

[136] United States, Executive Order 12324, 46 Federal Reg. 48109–10, 29 September 1981.

Thus, under coastguard guidelines, if interviews conducted on board suggested that persons had a legitimate claim to refugee status, passage to US territory for asylum processing would be arranged.[137] There is thus a strong argument that, until the Kennebunkport Order of 1992,[138] not only policy but also *opinio juris* existed in favour of an interpretation of the *non-refoulement* principle as applying on the high seas.

3.5.2.5 United Kingdom

In February 2003 a British proposal for a 'new vision' for refugee protection was leaked to the press. The proposal contained two main elements. The first was to improve regional protection and set up 'regional protection areas' as a means of reducing secondary movement and turning back failed asylum-seekers who for other reasons cannot be returned to their countries of origin.[139] It was the second half of the proposal, however, that sparked the most furious debate.[140] This part envisaged the establishment of 'transit processing centres' in third countries on the major transit routes to the EU. Asylum-seekers arriving spontaneously in the EU would thus as a rule be sent back for status determination to centres managed by the International Organization for Migration (IOM) and operating a screening procedure approved by UNHCR.[141]

In particular, the latter element of the proposal attracted substantial criticism for being inconsistent with international refugee law, and the whole scheme was eventually vetoed by Germany and Sweden. The adjoining analysis of the legal implications itself considered the need for possible revisions to the *non-refoulement* principle as enshrined in the Refugee Convention and the European Convention on Human Rights to avoid extraterritorial obligations, but ended up recommending a solution that, by establishing regional protection areas, would represent 'a new way

---

[137] H. H. Koh, 'The "Haiti paradigm" in United States human rights policy', (1994) 103 *Yale Law Journal* 2391–435, at 2393. As noted by Legomsky, however, the effectiveness of this procedure in avoiding *refoulement* was highly questionable. A total of 364 vessels were inspected from 1981 to 1990 and more than 21,000 Haitians returned, yet in the same period only six claims were found strong enough to warrant transfer to US territory. Legomsky, 'USA and the Caribbean Interdiction Programme', 679.

[138] United States, Executive Order 12807, 57 Federal Reg. 23133, 4 May 1992.

[139] UK Home Office, New Vision for Refugees, 7 March 2003, pp. 11 ff.

[140] The two parts were conflated in a later version presented to the EU Commission in March 2003 under the common heading of 'Regional protection areas', although subsequent discussion papers and a Danish Memorandum retained the distinction. For an overview of the different language and content of these documents, see Noll, 'Visions of the exceptional', 10 ff.

[141] UK Home Office, New Vision for Refugees, 7 March 2003, pp. 13 ff.

of providing protection with continued adherence to the *non-refoulement* principle'.[142] Thus not only was this plan never implemented in practice, but in similar fashion to Australia's 'Pacific Solution', extraterritorial application of the *non-refoulement* principle was not denied as such.

In other instances, however, the United Kingdom has been more direct in claiming a territorial interpretation. Following the positioning of British immigration officers at Prague Airport carrying out extraterritorial migration control, a case was submitted to the House of Lords by six rejected asylum-seekers of Roma origin.[143] Both the UK government and the House of Lords held that, as the Refugee Convention had been conceived, the scope of Article 33 is limited to those present in the territory (para. 17). The British government has taken a similar position in cases concerning the imposition of carrier sanctions and visa applications at British embassies.[144]

Nonetheless, on a closer reading of the reasoning in *Immigration Officer at Prague Airport*, the House of Lords asserts that, in view of the soft law developments cited above,

> there appears to be general acceptance of the principle that a person who leaves the state of his nationality and applies to the authorities of another state for asylum, whether at the frontier of the second state or from within it, should not be rejected or returned back to the first state without appropriate enquiry into the persecution of which he claims to have a well-founded fear.[145]

What distinguishes the operation of carrier sanctions and immigration officers in the above cases is not the geographical scope of Article 33 but the fact that the asylum-seekers had not left their country of origin and thus could not be considered refugees in the meaning of Article 1 of the Refugee Convention.

---

[142] Ibid., p. 10.

[143] *R. (European Roma Rights Centre and Others) v. Immigration Officer at Prague Airport and Another*, House of Lords.

[144] Nicholson, 'Immigration Act 1987', 614 ff. In *Sritharan*, the court similarly argued, 'Article 33 does not refer, and has never been understood to refer, to someone who has not yet arrived here ... even if the refusal to permit him to come here leads to his physical return by some other country to the country from which he is fleeing.' *Regina v. Secretary of State for the Home Department, ex parte Robert Denzil Sritharan and Benet Marianayagam*, UK High Court (England and Wales), [1993] Imm. A R 184, 24 February 1992.

[145] *R. (European Roma Rights Centre and Others) v. Immigration Officer at Prague Airport and Another*, House of Lords, para. 26. Elsewhere, however, the verdict specifically rejects extraterritorial application of the Refugee Convention in line with the *Sale* verdict (see para. 68, Lord Hope). See further discussion of this case in section 4.3.3.

3.5.3 Summary: soft law and state practice

Examples where states have sought either to circumvent the *non-refoulement* obligation or to deny outright its application outside the territory have become more prevalent. This is hardly surprising. At a time when concerns over asylum and immigration have led to more restrictive policies in the majority of developed countries, it becomes very tempting for states to reinvoke restrictive interpretations and principles of national sovereignty in cases where the exact scope of obligations is seen as unclear or unsettled.

What the above examples make clear, however, is that such restrictive interpretation is uniform in neither space nor time. What makes these cases stand out is the backdrop of both practice and discursive commitments confirming a more expansive reading of the *non-refoulement* principle enshrined in Article 33 of the Refugee Convention. This is richly confirmed in resolutions and recommendations. Early on border application was established, and more recently growing support has gathered in favour of a reading extending applicability *ratione loci* to the jurisdiction of the acting state.

As such, one should be careful in assigning too much importance to examples of restrictive state practice. While one cannot simply disregard these instances, from the standpoint of legal interpretation the prevalence, consistency and degree of legal conviction does not merit normative significance at present. That said, to the extent that these examples signify the start of a more general trend towards restrictive interpretation, this situation may of course change in the future.

3.6 The wider normative context of the *non-refoulement* principle

The *non-refoulement* principle finds expression in a number of other international instruments, both by name and by effect. At this stage looking to the wider normative context of Article 33 may legitimately aid the interpretation. Both national and international jurisprudence have emphasised the importance of interpreting the Refugee Convention as a 'living instrument' affected by subsequent legal developments.[146] As Hathaway further points out, since refugees are normally entitled to benefit from

---

[146] F. Nicholson and V. Türk, 'Refugee protection in international law: an overview', in Feller, Türk and Nicholson, *Refugee Protection*, pp. 3–42, at pp. 37–38.

general human rights protection and the content of the Refugee Convention and other human rights instruments overlaps on several issues, an interpretation should be sought that gives some coherence to cognate concepts under different treaties.[147]

3.6.1 Methodological appraisal of comparative interpretation

The question remains as to the weight to accord to coherence with other treaties when interpreting the geographical scope of the *non-refoulement* principle set out in the Refugee Convention. Arguments have been put forward that this may form part of the context by reference to Article 31(3)(c) of the Vienna Convention, stipulating that interpretation must take into account 'any relevant rules of international law applicable in the relations between the parties'.[148] For the most part, formulation of the *non-refoulement* principle in these instruments has been concluded or judicially developed after the drafting of the 1951 Refugee Convention. Interpreting treaties within their contemporary international legal context is, however, commonly accepted. Originally, draft Article 31(3)(c) of the Vienna Convention included a delimiting 'in force at the time of conclusion'. Yet this provision was intentionally dropped to allow for a more 'dynamic' or 'evolutionary' interpretation.[149]

More problematic, however, is the fact that rules must be 'applicable in the relations between the parties'. 'Parties' in this context is all signatory states.[150] Even though there is a broad coincidence of norms, the group of states bound by the Refugee Convention is not coextensive with the group of states bound by, for example, the European Convention on Human Rights or the International Covenant on Civil and Political Rights. For the present purpose, it is thus doubtful that these instruments can be considered a primary source under Article 31(3)(c) of the Vienna Convention.[151]

---

[147] Hathaway, *Rights of Refugees*, p. 64.

[148] M. Koskenniemi, 'Hierarchy in International Law: A Sketch', (1997) 8 *European Journal of International Law* 566–582.

[149] Spiermann, *Moderne Folkeret*, p. 130; L. Oppenheim, *Oppenheim's International Law*, Vol. 1: *Peace*, 9th edn, ed. R. Jennings and A. Watts (Harlow: Longman, 1992), p. 1282. As noted in connection with the *Namibia* case, 'interpretation cannot remain unaffected by subsequent development of law . . . an international instrument has to be interpreted and applied within the framework of the entire legal system prevailing at the time of the interpretation.' *Namibia (South West Africa) Case*, International Court of Justice, 26 January 1971, p. 31.

[150] Linderfalk, *Om tolkningen av traktater*, p. 203.

[151] Ibid., p. 292; Noll, 'Seeking asylum at embassies', 552.

Formulations of the *non-refoulement* principle in other binding international instruments, to the extent that they do concern themselves with norms whose content and form are in part similar to those of Article 33 of the Refugee Convention, may, however, be considered treaties *in pari materia*, and as such subsidiary sources of interpretation.[152] This approach has been generally confirmed by both the International Court of Justice and the European Court of Human Rights.[153] Comparative analysis may thus be used, albeit restrictively, to ensure a more systematic interpretation.

3.6.2 The 1933 Refugee Convention

The extended debate regarding the applicability of Article 33 of the 1951 Refugee Convention to non-admission at frontiers is somewhat surprising, considering that its predecessor, the 1933 Convention Relating to the International Status of Refugees explicitly included this obligation. The original formulation read, 'Elle s'engage, dans tous les cas, à ne pas refouler les réfugiés sur les frontières de leur pays d'origine.'[154] While some initial confusion during the drafting pertained as to the proper translation of the authoritative French text, the English text of Article 3 is unambiguous:

Each of the Contracting Parties undertakes not to remove or keep from its territory by application of police measures, such as expulsions or non-admittance at the frontier (*refoulement*), refugees who have been authorised to reside there regularly, unless the said measures are dictated by reasons of national security or public order. It undertakes in any case not to refuse entry to refugees at the frontier of their countries of origin.

The 1951 Refugee Convention specifically set out to revise the 1933 Convention. While a deliberately more restrictive approach in the successor instrument cannot be ruled out, the 1933 Convention must, however, be considered an important interpretative source in cases where the latter instrument lacks clarity regarding the same issue.[155] In terms of scope *ratione personae*, the protection offered by Article 3 of the 1933 Refugee Convention is, however, limited to 'refugees who have been authorised to reside there [the asylum country] regularly'. Thus protection against

---

[152] Ibid.   [153] Linderfalk, *Om tolkningen av traktater*, pp. 288–300.
[154] Cited in R. J. Beck, 'Britain and the 1933 Refugee Convention: national or state sovereignty?', (1999) 11 *International Journal of Refugee Law* 597–623, at 621.
[155] Hathaway, *Rights of Refugees*, p. 315; Noll, *Negotiating Asylum*, pp. 424–25; G. Fourlanos, *Sovereignty and the Ingress of Aliens* (Stockholm: Almquist and Wiksell International, 1986), p. 153; Robinson, *Convention Relating to the Status of Refugees*, p. 163.

non-admittance would only concern refugees who had already gained admission and residence previously.[156]

3.6.3 The International Covenant on Civil and Political Rights

The 1966 International Covenant on Civil and Political Rights contains no explicit references to *non-refoulement* or asylum. Yet in relation to Article 7 the Human Rights Committee has stressed that 'States parties must not expose individuals to the danger of torture or cruel, inhuman or degrading treatment or punishment upon return to another country by way of their extradition, expulsion or *refoulement*.'[157] Some disagreement exists as to the scope *ratione loci* of the covenant in general. Article 2(1) stipulates that states parties are to ensure the application of the rights of the covenants to all individuals 'within its territory and subject to its jurisdiction'. The wording of this article allows for both a cumulative reading, through which the Covenant would apply only within those parts of the territory where the state also has jurisdiction, and a disjunctive reading, setting territory as well as jurisdiction as the applicability *ratione loci* of the instrument.

Based on a cumulative reading, some scholars have rejected entirely extraterritorial application of the Covenant on Civil and Political Rights.[158] Similarly, not only has the United States argued that the disjunctive interpretation is unsustainable, but it also rejects the competence of the Human Rights Committee to issue authoritative interpretations of the text.[159]

Convincing arguments have, however, been advanced in favour of a disjunctive reading. A strictly territorial reading would lead to a manifestly absurd result such as, for example, the fact that the right to enter one's

---

[156] Robinson, *Convention Relating to the Status of Refugees*, p. 163.

[157] Human Rights Committee, General Comment to Art. 7 20/44, para. 9.

[158] Noll, 'Seeking asylum at embassies', 557–64; Noll, *Negotiating Asylum*, p. 440; C. F. Amerasinghe, *Local Remedies in International Law* (Cambridge University Press, 1990), pp. 147–9.

[159] United States Observations on General Comment 31, Human Rights Committee, Meeting of the 87th Session, United States of America (2nd and 3rd periodic report), Geneva (10–28 July 2006). See further United States Mission to the United Nations and other international organisations in Geneva, Observations of the United States on the Advisory Opinion of the UN High Commissioner for Refugees on the Extraterritorial Application of Non-refoulement Obligations under the 1951 Convention Relating to the Status of Refugees and its 1967 Protocol (28 December 2007), p. 8.

On the role of general comments by the Human Rights Committee in setting out interpretation, however, see T. Buergenthal, 'The UN Human Rights Committee', (2001) 5 *Max Planck Yearbook of United Nations Law* 341–98, at 386–90.

own country would be meaningless if individuals could not claim it from outside the territory of their country of origin.[160] A wider interpretation has further been applied by the Human Rights Committee, noting that 'a State Party must respect and ensure the rights laid down in the Covenant to anyone within the power or effective control of that State Party, even if not situated within the territory of the State Party'.[161] This reading has further been confirmed by the International Court of Justice.[162] If not the case at its inception, extraterritorial applicability of the International Covenant on Civil and Political Rights thus appears to have been established subsequently.

3.6.4 The Convention on the Rights of the Child

Article 2(1) of the 1989 Convention on the Rights of the Child obliges signatory states to 'respect and ensure the rights set forth in the present Convention to each child within their jurisdiction'. At the same time, Article 37 of the Convention indirectly prohibits *refoulement* of children to places where they would be at risk of being tortured.

In addition, other articles in the convention may attach and add to obligations owed under other instruments of national and international law. The 'best interest of the child' principle enshrined in Article 3 has thus been invoked in cases involving both admission and return of children and their families.[163] More specifically, Article 22(1) obliges states to 'take measures to ensure' that refugees or asylum-seekers falling under the personal scope of the convention 'receive appropriate protection and humanitarian assistance in the enjoyment of applicable rights set forth in the present Convention and in other international human rights or humanitarian instruments to which the said States are Parties'. As Noll shows, the latter may in some cases involve obligations in cases where asylum-seekers encounter authorities extraterritorially.[164]

---

[160] Hathaway, *Rights of Refugees*, p. 165; D. McGoldrick, 'Extraterritorial effect of the International Covenant on Civil and Political Rights', in Coomans and Kamminga, *Extraterritorial Application*, pp. 41–72, at p. 48; Meron, 'Extraterritoriality of human rights treaties', 80; M. Nowak, *UN Covenant on Civil and Political Rights: CCPR Commentary* (Kehl am Rhein: Engel, 1993), p. 41.

[161] Human Rights Committee, General Comment No. 31, UN Doc. HRI/GEN/1/Rev. 7, 12 May 2004, p. 192.

[162] *Legal Consequences of the Construction of a Wall in the Occupied Palestinian Territory*, International Court of Justice, 9 July 2004, para. 109.

[163] J. McAdam, 'Seeking asylum under the Convention on the Rights of the Child: a case for complementary protection', (2006) 14 *International Journal of Children's Rights* 251–74.

[164] Noll, 'Seeking asylum at embassies', 570–72.

3.6.5 *The Convention against Torture*

The 1984 Convention against Torture and Other Cruel, Inhuman and Degrading Treatment or Punishment resembles the Refugee Convention in the sense that applicability *ratione loci* is not set out in a single article, but differing scopes pertain to each of the obligations placed upon signatory states. A number of articles specify 'any territory under its jurisdiction', which would allow for extraterritorial application in at least the instances where a state exercises effective control over a geographical area beyond its national territory.[165] Other articles, however, contain no explicit geographical limitations. Among these are Article 3, which prohibits parties from returning, extraditing or *refouling* any person to a state 'where there are substantial grounds for believing that he would be in danger of being subjected to torture'. The Committee against Torture has reaffirmed a wider, protection-based application of this article to asylum-seekers fearing *refoulement* on numerous occasions.[166] The lack of a specific geographical limitation has led some commentators to suggest that the *non-refoulement* principle flowing from Article 3 of the Convention against Torture regulates state action 'wherever it takes place'.[167] Even under a more restrictive interpretation, the Committee against Torture has affirmed that applicability *ratione loci* of Article 3 is not limited to the territory, but must be extended to all situations in which a state exercises effective control, whether over territory or individuals.[168]

3.6.6 *The OAU Convention on Refugees*

At the regional level, the 1969 OAU Convention Governing Specific Aspects of Refugee Problems in Africa contains a broad *non-refoulement* clause that clearly embraces border applicability. Article II(3) reads,

---

[165] Arts. 2, 5, 7, 11, 12, 13, and 16.

[166] B. Gorlick, 'The Convention and the Committee against Torture: a complementary protection regime for refugees', (1999) 11 *International Journal of Refugee Law* 479–95, at 486–8.

[167] Goodwin-Gill and McAdam, *Refugee in International Law*, p. 248.

[168] UN Committee against Torture, Conclusions and Recommendations of the Committee against Torture, UN Doc. CAT/C/USA/CO/2, 25 July 2006, para. 14. The United States and the United Kingdom have rejected this view on various grounds. For a refutation of their argumentation, see P. V. Kessing, 'Terrorbekæmpelse og menneskeret', Ph.D. dissertation, Faculty of Law, Copenhagen University, 2008, pp. 234–7. See also UNHCR, Advisory Opinion, p. 17.

No person shall be subjected...to measures such as rejection at the frontier, return or expulsion, which would compel him to return to or remain in a territory where his life, physical integrity or liberty would be threatened.

3.6.7 The American Convention on Human Rights

Article 22(8) of the 1989 American Convention on Human Rights reads,

In no case may an alien be deported or returned to a country, regardless of whether or not it is his country of origin, if in that country his right to life or personal freedom is in danger of being violated because of his race, nationality, religion, social status, or political opinions.

Article 1(1) of the convention contains much the same jurisdiction formulation as used in the Convention on the Rights of the Child, 'to ensure to all persons subject to their jurisdiction the free and full exercise of those rights and freedoms', with no territorial reference as in the Covenant on Civil and Political Rights.

3.6.8 The European Convention on Human Rights

Lastly, Article 1 of the 1950 European Convention on Human Rights states, 'The High Contracting parties shall secure to everyone within their jurisdiction the rights and freedoms defined in Section I of this Convention.' While the convention does not include an explicit *non-refoulement* clause, Article 3 has consistently been interpreted to include the prohibition of *refoulement* to places where individuals may fear torture, inhuman or degrading treatment or punishment.[169] The jurisprudence of the European Court of Human Rights has repeatedly affirmed that the term 'jurisdiction' may in some circumstances extend beyond the territory – the decisive criterion being whether or not a state exercises 'effective control'.[170]

---

[169] Noll, *Negotiating Asylum*, pp. 441–6; Nicholson, 'Immigration Act 1987', 627. The application of Art. 3 to instances of *non-refoulement* was first affirmed by the Court in *Soering v. United Kingdom*, European Court of Human Rights, Application No. 14038/88, 7 July 1989. Subsequently the court has held that it is 'well-established in case law that the fundamentally important prohibition against torture and inhuman and degrading treatment under Article 3, read in conjunction with Article 1 of the Convention to "secure to everyone within their jurisdiction the rights and freedoms defined in the Convention", imposes an obligation on Contracting States not to expel a person to a country where substantial grounds have been shown for believing that he would face a real risk of being subjected to treatment contrary to Article 3.' *T.I. v. United Kingdom*, European Court of Human Rights, Application No. 43844/98, 7 March 2000 (Admissibility), para. 228.

[170] UNHCR, Advisory Opinion, paras. 39–40. The meaning of 'jurisdiction' and 'effective control' is discussed more extensively in chapter 4.

3.6.9 Non-refoulement as part of customary international law

The widespread adherence to the *non-refoulement* principle as enshrined in different international instruments has lead some to suggest that *non-refoulement* is part of customary international law and as such may have a wider scope of application *ratione loci*.[171] As part of UNHCR's Agenda for Protection, all parties to the Refugee Convention formally acknowledged 'the principle of *non-refoulement*, whose applicability is imbedded in customary international law'.[172] Similarly, in their analysis of the *non-refoulement* principle, Elihu Lauterpacht and Daniel Bethlehem draw support for customary status both from the parallel formulations of the principle in other instruments of international law and the fact that around 90 per cent of all UN states are party to one or more conventions that include a direct or indirect *non-refoulement* obligation.[173] According to Lauterpacht and Bethlehem, establishing *non-refoulement* as part of customary international law dictates 'that the responsibility of a State will be engaged in circumstances in which acts or omissions are attributable to that State wherever these may occur'.[174]

Two issues are at stake here. The first concerns whether or not the *non-refoulement* principle can be considered part of customary international law. While UNHCR and a number of refugee lawyers argue that this is so, there is still some disagreement on this issue. More critical scholars maintain that while adherence to some principle of *non-refoulement* is widespread, the standard of customary law simply has not yet been met.[175]

The second issue concerns the geographic scope of such a custom. Even if the argument about customary status is accepted, the argument that

---

[171] G. Goodwin-Gill, '*Non-refoulement* and the new asylum seekers', in D. Martin (ed.), *The New Asylum Seekers: Refugee Law in the 1980s* (Dordrecht: Martinus Nijhoff Publishers, 1986), p. 103. See further Goodwin-Gill, '*R. v. Immigration Officer at Prague Airport*', at 436–40; and 'Haitian Interdiction Case 1993', at 94. Some scholars have even argued that *non-refoulement* may be considered *jus cogens*: J. Allains, 'The *jus cogens* nature of *non-refoulement*', (2001) 13 *International Journal of Refugee Law* 533–58.

[172] UNHCR, Declaration of States Parties to the 1951 Convention and/or Its 1967 Protocol relating to the Status of Refugees, UN Doc. HCR/MMSP/2001/09, 16 January 2002, para. 4. See also Hathaway, *Rights of Refugees*, p. 364.

[173] Lauterpacht and Bethlehem, 'Scope and content', p. 147.   [174] Ibid., p. 160.

[175] J. Hathaway, 'Leveraging asylum', (2010) 45 (3) *Texas International Law Journal* 503–36; K. Hailbronner, 'Non-refoulement and "humanitarian" refugees: customary international law or wishful legal thinking?', in D. Martin (ed.), *The New Asylum Seekers: Refugee Law in the 1980s* (Dordrecht: Martinus Nijhoff Publishers, 1988), pp. 128–36. For an overview of earlier positions taken as regards this issue, see Noll, *Negotiating Asylum*, p. 363, n. 1059.

this entails universal application *ratione loci* easily becomes circuitous. The debate surrounding customary status has mainly evolved around whether or not the *non-refoulement* principle can be extended to protect a wider set of beneficiaries than those mentioned in Article 1 of the Refugee Convention and whether the *non-refoulement* principle is binding for all states. To wit, the question of whether states not signatory to the Refugee Convention or other instruments are bound by the *non-refoulement* principle remains different from that concerning the scope *ratione loci* of this obligation in triggering the individual responsibility of each state when encountering the refugee. In other words, it would require further evidence to presume that the geographical scope of a customary principle of international law is broader than the explicit formulations of this principle in treaty law on which its claim as customary international law is in this case partly founded. Any claim for a wider scope *ratione loci* for a customary principle of *non-refoulement* will thus have to be independently underpinned by systematic analysis of state practice and *opinio juris*.

3.6.10 Jurisdiction as a standard scope of application ratione loci in human rights law

Another argument proposed on the basis of a comparative analysis is that, as a general proposition, states are responsible under international human rights law in relation to any person subject to or within their jurisdiction.[176] The argument appears to build on the assumption that in the absence of explicit specification to the contrary, jurisdiction is the 'standard' scope of application *ratione loci* for a state's obligations under public international law.[177] As noted by Theodor Meron, 'Narrow territorial interpretation of human rights treaties is anathema to the basic idea of human rights, which is to ensure that a state should respect human rights of persons over whom it exercises jurisdiction.'[178]

Unlike the argument for customary status of the *non-refoulement* principle specifically, this line of reasoning does not depend on the existence or inference of *non-refoulement* principles in other human rights treaties.

---

[176] UNHCR, Advisory Opinion, p. 16. See also Goodwin-Gill and McAdam, *Refugee in International Law*, pp. 244–5; Lauterpacht and Bethlehem, 'Scope and content', pp. 110–12; Plender and Mole, 'Beyond the Geneva Convention', p. 86.
[177] Hathaway, *Rights of Refugees*, p. 161.
[178] Meron, 'Extraterritoriality of human rights treaties', 82.

In support of this position, one may thus look to human rights treaties in general, international humanitarian law and general principles of public international law in order to bolster the claim that states are, as a general rule, responsible under international human rights law for anyone within or subject to their jurisdiction.

On closer scrutiny, however, the argument seems to falter. First of all, a significant number of international human rights treaties actually have a wider geographical scope than jurisdiction in their geographical application. Notably, the Genocide Convention contains no geographic restrictions whatsoever,[179] and the 1949 Geneva Convention obliges states parties 'in all circumstances' (Art. 1). The 1965 Convention on the Elimination of All Forms of Racial Discrimination does include a jurisdiction clause in Article 3 in setting the positive obligations of states parties, but is otherwise silent on the matter.[180] Second, a number of instruments have a more complex structure, prescribing different scopes *ratione loci* for different articles, which speaks against such a general assumption. This goes for the Refugee Convention and the Convention against Torture mentioned above. As an additional example, the 1966 International Convention on Economic, Social and Cultural Rights obliges states to 'take steps individually and through international assistance and co-operation' in order to achieve the realisation of the rights enshrined in the covenant. Yet the possible extraterritorial dimension remains debatable in relation to the precise nature and content of each article.[181]

A general principle that states are responsible for anyone within their jurisdiction cannot therefore be deduced from a comparative analysis. The introduction of a 'standard scope of application *ratione loci*' seems most of all a preliminary choice that defies ordinary interpretative methodology.[182] To appreciate this, one needs only to draw a parallel to the *Sale* case, in which a similar standard applicability *ratione loci* amounting to state territory was relied upon as an important premise of the court's verdict.[183] The flaws of this reasoning were pointed out both by the dissenting Justice Blackmun and by subsequent commentators, and

---

[179] *Application of the Convention on the Prevention and Punishment of the Crime of Genocide (Bosnia and Herzegovina v. Yugoslavia)*, Preliminary Objections, International Court of Justice, 11 July 1996, para. 31.

[180] See also the 1979 Convention on the Elimination of Discrimination Against Women.

[181] Coomans and Kamminga, *Extraterritorial Application*, p. 2.

[182] Noll, 'Seeking asylum at embassies', 552.   [183] *Sale*.

the US Supreme Court soon afterwards overturned it in its litigation involving competition law.[184]

3.6.11 Conclusions: the wider normative context of the non-refoulement principle

A comparative analysis of explicit and implicit *non-refoulement* obligations set out in binding human rights instruments other than the Refugee Convention shows that states parties to one or more of these instruments are bound by some variation of the *non-refoulement* principle, even beyond their territory. The 1933 predecessor of the 1951 Refugee Convention explicitly obliged signatories to respect the *refoulement* prohibition in instances occurring at the frontiers. A norm of *non-refoulement* extending to state jurisdiction can further be deduced from both the Covenant on Civil and Political Rights and the European Convention on Human Rights. Both the Human Rights Committee and the European Court of Human Rights have established that such jurisdiction is not limited to state territory but can extend both to actions undertaken on the high seas and to actions undertaken in the territory of a foreign sovereign. A similar *non-refoulement* obligation is further contained in Article 3 of the Convention against Torture. While this instrument does not explicitly delimit the applicability *ratione loci* of this article, even a more restrictive interpretation would have it apply extraterritorially to the extent that signatory states exercise effective control.

The impact of these observations, however, should not be unduly extrapolated. The view that *non-refoulement* today forms part of customary international law and therefore applies to state action wherever it occurs must be rejected, if not on its premise then on the missing justification why the conclusion follows from this premise. Similarly, the argument that, in the absence of explicit specification to the contrary, jurisdiction may be assumed to be the 'standard' scope of application *ratione loci* of all human rights treaties sits uneasy with a critical analysis of human rights treaties which shows a considerable variation in the designation of geographical application between and within instruments.

On the other hand, it is clear that in the interpretation of Article 33 of the Refugee Convention the instruments examined above may be considered treaties *in pari materia* and that formulations and development of

---

[184] Hathaway, *Rights of Refugees*, p. 339; Koh, "'Haiti Paradigm'", 2428.

non-refoulement obligations in this wider normative context may be considered a subsidiary source of interpretation. From a systematic viewpoint it is thus noteworthy that an interpretation of Article 33 of the Refugee Convention as applying wherever a state exercises jurisdiction is consonant with the parallel obligations stemming from the International Covenant on Civil and Political Rights, the Convention on the Rights of the Child and the European Convention on Human Rights. For the Convention against Torture, a more universalist interpretation may extend the application of Article 3 even further, but as a minimum the *non-refoulement* obligation established from this provision must be understood as extending to everyone within a state's jurisdiction.

General human rights law has always been relied on as providing important additional avenues to ensure protection for many refugees.[185] From a pragmatic perspective, this creates a basic presumption for any state party to one or more of the above instruments to respect the *non-refoulement* principle in any situation where jurisdiction can be established. The *non-refoulement* principles set out in instruments other than the Refugee Convention further expand both *ratione personae* and *ratione materiae* in comparison with Article 33. Thus the *refoulement* prohibitions stemming from, for example, the Convention against Torture or the European Convention on Human Rights do not allow for derogations for reasons of national security as set out in Article 33(2), nor are they limited to persons fearing persecution for reasons connected to race, religion, political opinion or affiliation to a certain social group as set out by Article 1 of the Refugee Convention.[186] In addition, while Article 1 of the Refugee Convention arguably excludes application in cases where potential asylum-seekers have not yet left their country of origin,[187] neither the OAU Convention nor any of the general human rights instruments carry this limitation.

The latter points should not be taken to imply that Article 33 of the Refugee Convention may also be interpreted as applying inside the country of origin or encompassing a wider group of beneficiaries. This would fly in the face of the language employed in Article 1 of the Refugee Convention, and no subsidiary source of interpretation can change that. What it does mean, however, is that to the extent that the interpretation of

---

[185] Plender and Mole, 'Beyond the Geneva Convention', p. 86.

[186] This does not preclude, however, the possibility of Art. 33 of the Refugee Convention being in some instances applicable in cases that do not amount to torture, inhuman or degrading treatment or punishment.

[187] *R. (European Roma Rights Centre and Others) v. Immigration Officer at Prague Airport and Another*, House of Lords, paras. 15, 26.

Article 33 in the Refugee Convention is still contested, the above provisions give additional support to an interpretation extending the applicability *ratione loci* to state jurisdiction for Article 33 as well.

3.7 A note on delimitations *ratione loci*

The above analysis has been operationalised around four concentric conceptions of applicability *ratione loci* of the *non-refoulement* principle enshrined in Article 33 of the Refugee Convention – 'within the territory', 'at the frontier', 'within a state's jurisdiction' and 'wherever a state acts'. These delimitations were chosen because they reflect the main positions in the existing debate to determine the geographical scope of the *non-refoulement* principle. In order justifiably to portray the existing views in their original context it has thus been necessary to replicate these categorisations even though they are not entirely unproblematic. A number of gradations or further differentiations are possible. One such important case is application inside the country of origin of an asylum-seeker. Whereas most scholarly work, including the present analysis, would insist that this is excluded under an immediate reading of Article 1 of the Refugee Convention, some scholars have claimed, as seen above, that this is conceivable in certain situations where a refugee is within their country of origin, but nonetheless subject to the jurisdiction of another state.[188] Moreover, while the notions of 'in the territory' or 'anywhere a state acts' are reasonably self-explanatory, 'at the frontier' and 'within the jurisdiction' are not. The concept of 'jurisdiction' will be the subject of the following chapter, but the question of singling out 'at the frontiers' as an intermediate category between inside and outside a state's territory may warrant a small digression here.

Exactly where is a refugee when at the border of a potential host state? Among social scientists it has become increasingly popular to speak of 'virtual' or 'blurry' borders in order to describe how migration control is increasingly carried out on each side of the geographic boundary.[189] Similarly, under current EU law member states may apply less favourable standards to asylum-seekers in designated border zones.[190] Yet, as a legal concept signifying a separate geographical sphere, 'at the border' makes

---

[188] Lauterpacht and Bethlehem, 'Scope and content', p. 122.
[189] Gammeltoft-Hansen, 'Filtering out the risky migrant', p. 31.
[190] See e.g. European Council, Minimum Standards on Procedures in Member States for Granting and Withdrawing Refugee Status, Directive 2005/85/EC, 1 December 2005, Art. 35.

little sense and it finds little support elsewhere in international law.[191] By common definition, the border is where one state's territory meets the territory of another state or international waters.[192] In a world occupied by mutually sovereign territories, it is difficult to see how, logically, 'at the frontier' can be maintained as anything more than a fixture without any independent extension. In other words, the refugee is either in the territory or outside – there is no dancing on the line.

Such considerations are not new. Goodwin-Gill has bluntly asserted that '[a]s a matter of fact, anyone presenting themselves at the frontier post, port or airport will already be within state territory and jurisdiction.'[193] As the actual border checkpoint is presumably located inside the territory of the host state this is consequently where the asylum-seeker meets the state.[194] This interpretation of course dissolves the dispute between territorial and border application by simply subsuming the latter delimitation within the former.

However, the argument could just as well be made the other way round. If border instances of *refoulement* are accepted as taking place before the refugee has entered the territory, the wide support for border applicability may, *mutatis mutandis*, be taken to support an interpretation of extraterritorial applicability. Put differently, if situations 'at the frontier' are not coextensive with 'in the territory', the former logically occur either in international waters or within the sovereign territory of a third state.

3.8 Conclusion

This chapter has sought to probe the protective reach of the 1951 Refugee Convention. In this enquiry the *non-refoulement* principle enshrined in Article 33(1) of this instrument acts as a threshold. For the refugee first encountering a state's migration control, the protection against *refoulement* is the right on which access to virtually all other rights depends.

Great controversy has persisted as to the geographical application of this principle, in the first instance whether it applies to rejection at the

---

[191] Few examples of distinct bilateral legal regimes in relation to the borders or frontiers are known, e.g. the notion of *voisinage* or the few instances of internationally controlled border zones, but they generally contain few hard rules beyond co-operation among the parties. V. Lowe, *International Law* (Oxford University Press, 2007), pp. 150 ff.

[192] Ibid., p. 151.

[193] Goodwin-Gill, *Refugee in International Law*, 2nd edn, p. 75; see also Hathaway, 'New directions to avoid hard problems', 6.

[194] Noll, 'Seeking asylum at embassies', 552.

border, and in the second instance whether it extends to state actions undertaken extraterritorially. A host of arguments in favour of different interpretations have been put forward throughout the last almost six decades, yet no clear and convincing answer to the resolution of this question has emerged.

A doctrinal analysis of the language alone does clearly extend geographical application of the *non-refoulement* principle to situations involving non-admittance at the frontier, something reaffirmed by the ad hoc committee during the drafting and by subsequent soft law and state practice. As to the possibility of extraterritorial application, however, no conclusive answer appears from an analysis of the wording, purpose and object of Article 33. Nor can the issue be resolved by looking to the *travaux préparatoires*. As Goodwin-Gill has noted, '[p]robably the most accurate assessment of States' view in 1951 is that there was no unanimity, perhaps deliberately so.'[195]

A broader contextual interpretation taking account of subsequent developments, however, somehow changes this picture. Support for an interpretation of the *non-refoulement* principle as extending to state jurisdiction has been expressed by both the Inter-American Commission on Human Rights and the UNHCR Executive Committee in relation to interdiction schemes undertaken on the high seas. An analysis comparing Article 33 with *non-refoulement* principles set out in other human rights treaties may further bolster this view. In particular, the International Covenant on Civil and Political Rights, the Convention against Torture and the European Convention on Human Rights all entail *non-refoulement* obligations that apply *ratione loci* everywhere a state can be shown to exercise jurisdiction.

As regards state practice, the recent surge in extraterritorial migration control schemes does not support a more expansive scope of Article 33. Yet a critical analysis of states operating extraterritorial migration control and/or asylum processing shows that actual practice and *opinio juris* are seldom unequivocal in rejecting extraterritorial application of the *non-refoulement* principle. Either such schemes incorporate some sort of mechanism, however incomplete, to avoid direct *refoulement*, or extraterritorial rejection is carried out while simultaneously paying lip service to the *refoulement* obligation at the rhetorical level.

In the opinion of the present author, it must thus be concluded that there has been a dynamic development in the application of the *non-refoulement* principle as enshrined in Article 33(1) of the Refugee

---

[195] G. Goodwin-Gill, *The Refugee in International Law* (Oxford: Clarendon Press, 1983), p. 74.

Convention. Although the issue may have been left unclear at the time of drafting and more than one interpretation is thus possible based on the wording of Article 33, this interpretative space has been substantially narrowed as subsequent developments in soft law and other human rights instruments point consistently towards a wider interpretation.

As state practices have developed, so has the normative reach of the Refugee Convention. From early on the *non-refoulement* principle has been challenged by states rejecting refugees at the borders, and as a reply a wide number of resolutions and other soft law instruments have certified and affirmed the application of Article 33 to these instances. In more recent years, states acting extraterritorially have prompted a similar response, not just with regard to the Refugee Convention, but more generally in international courts and supervisory bodies affirming the extraterritorial application of major human rights instruments to all instances where a state exercises jurisdiction.

The *non-refoulement* obligation set out in the Refugee Convention must be understood within this context. In the interplay between new state practices to extend control beyond the borders and normative developments to affirm extraterritorial human rights obligations, Article 33(1) cannot be left unaffected. The question remains, however, how far one may reasonably stretch application. While the humanitarian *telos* of the Convention in principle speaks for universal application, the national lawyer may conversely be concerned that unrealistic obligations are not placed on states parties.

3.8.1 A compromise: non-refoulement as effectiveness

In trying to resolve this issue, recourse may finally be had to the doctrine of effectiveness developed by Hersch Lauterpacht.[196] Much in line with the above, Lauterpacht argues that interpretation of the intention of the parties must not be used in isolation when discerning the purpose of a treaty. Rather the original *raison d'être* must be combined with a sense of

---

[196] H. Lauterpacht, *The Development of International Law by the Permanent Court of Justice* (New York: Longman, Green & Co., 1934), pp. 69 ff., and Lauterpacht, *The Development of International Law by the Permanent Court of International Justice*, 2nd edn (London: Stevens & Sons, 1958), pp. 225 ff. On Lauterpacht's use of this principle see I. Scobbie, 'The theorist as a judge: Hersch Lauterpacht's concept of the international judicial function', (1997) 8 *European Journal of International Law* 264–98. Lauterpacht's doctrine of effectiveness should not be confused with the so-called 'principle of effectiveness' in international law, stating that a state's jurisdiction is defined by the territory or individuals over which it exerts effective control. See further section 4.2.1.

its current usage and implementation in order to ensure that the treaty remains effective rather than becomes ineffective. In his own words, 'the maximum of effectiveness should be given to [an instrument] consistent with the intention – the common intention – of the parties'.[197] Thus an interpretation loyal to the wording and intention of the drafters at the time of conceptualisation may still be void if it fails to consider the applicability of this interpretation to the current context and practices. A similar argument has been made by reference to the obligation enshrined in Article 26 of the Vienna Convention that interpretation must be carried out in 'good faith' in order to ensure the performance of the treaty.[198]

One should be wary, however, of attempts to extend the notion of 'good faith' or 'effectiveness' as an independent legal basis for furthering expansive interpretations. The principle of good faith only operates to suggest giving preference to the interpretation that ensures the most effectiveness or actual performance of the treaty within the scope of possible interpretations set out by the text itself, its wording and the intentions of the drafters.[199] As noted by Hersch Lauterpacht,

This means that on occasions, if such was the intention of the parties, good faith may require that the effectiveness of the instrument should fall short of its apparent and desirable scope. The principle of effectiveness cannot transform a mere declaration of lofty purposes – such as the Universal Declaration of Human Rights – into a source of legal rights and obligations.[200]

Still, the Refugee Convention is a binding legal instrument and, as evidenced above, an interpretative scope does exist in the determination of the scope *ratione loci* of Article 33. How, then, would the introduction of a principle of effectiveness affect interpretation? On the one hand, if the purpose of Article 33 is to prevent a certain consequence, namely the return of refugees to persecution, there is no *a priori* reason to limit this obligation to a state's territory.[201] The fact that extraterritorial interception practices were not contemplated at the time of drafting cannot be taken as a valid argument for restrictive interpretation. Rather, in order to remain effective, the *non-refoulement* principle must be interpreted in

---

[197] Lauterpacht, *Development of International Law* (1958), p. 229.

[198] Hathaway, *Rights of Refugees*, p. 62. See further references therein.

[199] This view has been seconded by both refugee scholars and national judiciaries. See Hathaway, *Rights of Refugees*, p. 62, and *R. (European Roma Rights Centre and Others) v. Immigration Officer at Prague Airport and Another*, House of Lords, paras. 229, 249.

[200] Lauterpacht, *Development of International Law* (1958), p. 292.

[201] Meron, 'Extraterritoriality of human rights treaties', 80.

a way that, while consistent with the text and overall intention of the drafters, does not make it redundant in the light of evolving state practice to establish migration control beyond state territory. Consequently, a basis of both border and extraterritorial applicability could arguably be said to have been established much more firmly today much more than in 1951.[202]

On the other hand, a national sovereign perspective may equally rely on the principle of effectiveness as at least tempering somewhat what would otherwise be a claim for universal application. Acting or appearing extraterritorially, states may face a number of practical concerns and particular circumstances complicating their fulfilment of human rights obligations. An interpretation that binds state officials by a *non-refoulement* obligation in each and every situation in which a refugee is encountered may thus be practically impossible and thus ultimately ineffective. In view of this, the scope of Article 33 may conversely be limited to situations in which states can be said to exercise a sufficient degree of power over either the refugee encountered or the geographic area in which control takes place.[203]

This would extend application of Article 33 of the Refugee Convention to anywhere a state exercises jurisdiction. As will be discussed in the subsequent chapter, this is by no means as straightforward a matter as some refugee scholars would like it to be. Nor is it an interpretation that necessarily favours an expansive *ratione loci*. As in the discussions over Article 33, legal considerations to the concept of jurisdiction are equally wrought by competing claims between territorial and universalist positions.

Having considered the language and object of the *non-refoulement* obligation under the Refugee Convention, as well as the context, drafting history and subsequent developments in soft law, state practice and other instruments of human rights law, the uncertainty regarding the scope *ratione loci* of this provision can thus be resolved. A systematic analysis, consideration of subsequent development and the introduction of a principle

---

[202] To this end Hathaway even speaks of an 'evolutionary principle'. Hathaway, *Rights of Refugees*, p. 67.

[203] A similar view has been expressed by Hathaway and Dent, noting that

> Article 33 was not intended to compel States to take on protection responsibilities in the world at large, but it was clearly intended to constrain treatment of refugees within the scope of each State's authority. (J. Hathaway and J. A. Dent, *Refugee Rights: Report on a Comparative Survey*, Toronto: York Lanes Press, 1995, p. 9)

of effectiveness yield a clear result that extends application *ratione loci* to the jurisdiction of the acting state.

Nonetheless, this has not prevented a number of states from still maintaining that Article 33 of the Refugee Convention applies only within the territory or at most at the borders of the state in question. The United States thus continues to uphold the position that Article 33 does not apply extraterritorially.[204] Similarly, a former German minister of the interior, Otto Schily, declared in 2005 that the *non-refoulement* principle 'has no application on the high seas'.[205] While these views must be considered incorrect, their persistence may perhaps equally be understood in the light of the above analysis. The difficulty in reaching a clear interpretative result and the plethora of arguments in favour of different positions accumulated over the past six decades inevitably provide scope for contestation, where governments may seek to pick and choose among arguments to bolster whatever reading is found to be most desirable.

[204] US Mission, Observations on the Advisory Opinion.
[205] M. Garlick, 'The EU discussions on extraterritorial processing', (2006) 18 *International Journal of Refugee Law* 601–30, at 620.

4 Offshore migration control and the concept of extraterritorial jurisdiction

It was submitted in the previous chapter that the core protection offered by the 1951 Refugee Convention – the *non-refoulement* obligation – may be claimed by refugees as soon as they find themselves within a state's jurisdiction. As also has been shown, such an interpretation essentially brings the applicability *ratione loci* of Article 33 into line with the scope of a number of other human rights instruments. The question is, however, how much is gained by this. While refugee scholars have debated intensely the geographical reach of the *non-refoulement* principle, few of those arguing in favour of jurisdiction have actually undertaken a systematic analysis of what this concept entails.

A number of refugee scholars seem to assume that any exercise of migration control, whether inside, at or beyond the border, necessarily entails an exercise of jurisdiction.[1] This view, however, finds little support under general international law and current human rights jurisprudence. For the purpose of engaging human rights responsibilities the concept of jurisdiction is generally bound by a premise of effective control over either territory or individuals. Within the territory, this control is assumed to flow from the formal entitlement to exercise sovereign authority. Beyond the territory, however, the test for establishing such control is substantially more demanding. Not all actions undertaken by a state outside its territory appear to bring about jurisdiction. Yet the establishment of jurisdiction is, conversely, the premise for subjecting such states to relevant obligations under international refugee and human rights law.

The fundamental question addressed in this chapter may thus be phrased as follows: when, if ever, is extraterritorial migration control

---

[1] Lauterpacht and Bethlehem, 'Scope and content', p. 111; Willheim, 'MV *Tampa*', 175.

equivalent to effective control and, as a corollary, may offshore migration control under any other circumstances bring about jurisdiction?

In trying to answer this question, the chapter will first proceed by examining the notion of extraterritorial jurisdiction as employed in general international law and human rights law respectively. Second, the chapter moves on to analyse the most important international human rights litigation in respect of this issue and its application to different practices of extraterritorial migration control. The chapter seeks to elucidate how the existing human rights jurisprudence seems to be split between two fundamentally different interpretative starting points. The first extends from national sovereignty and the territoriality principle and emphasises the absolute and exclusive nature of jurisdiction even when established extraterritorially. The second starts from the basic tenet that 'power entails responsibility' and thus stresses the functional or causal relationship between the individual and the state in regard to a specific action or omission. Both perspectives may be evident in individual cases, but which remains dominant appears to depend on legal geography. When looking to establish jurisdiction in cases of extraterritorial migration control, one may thus usefully distinguish between three spheres: first, the excision of territory or denial of territorial jurisdiction, second, situations occurring in *terrae nullius* or on the high seas, and, lastly, cases where migration control is enacted within the territory or territorial waters of another state.

4.1 Rights owed to refugees within a state's jurisdiction

Before going into the more conceptual analysis of the meaning of jurisdiction, it may be useful to review briefly the legal protection available to the refugee who is presumed to be within a state's jurisdiction, yet still outside its territory. Moving beyond the *non-refoulement* obligation, what other rights are then applicable under international refugee law?

Looking to the Refugee Convention itself, the immediate answer would have to be 'relatively few'. As has been described in chapter 2, the Convention follows an incremental structure in which more and more rights are granted according to the level of attachment established between the refugee and the host state. By far the majority of entitlements are thus reserved for refugees who are already physically present within the territory or have some higher attachment to the host state. Where refugees have not yet reached the territory a state's obligations are immediately reduced to a few core rights under the Convention for which no particular level of attachment is specified. In addition to the *non-refoulement* principle, these include access to courts (Art. 16) and non-discrimination (Art. 3), as well as the somewhat more specific issues concerning property (Art. 13), education (Art. 22) and rationing (Art. 20). If the analysis of the geographical scope of Article 33 set out in the previous chapter is to be trusted we may assume, *mutatis mutandis*, that these obligations are similarly owed anywhere a state is held to exercise jurisdiction.[2]

Additional protection may, of course, still be derived from general human rights law. As set out in the previous chapter, a number of key human rights instruments all extend the scope of application *ratione loci* to state jurisdiction, including the Covenant on Civil and Political Rights, the Convention on the Rights of the Child, the Convention against Torture (in regard to some articles), the American Convention on Human Rights and the European Convention on Human Rights. As shown by several scholars, a broad set of protections for refugees may be developed from these general human rights instruments; in some respects these are more encompassing than the protection offered by the *lex specialis* of the Refugee Convention.[3] On the other hand, while these instruments may all in principle be invoked wherever a state exercises jurisdiction, important differences may pertain between and within instruments in triggering protection obligations in the context of migration control.[4]

The additional protection provided by general human rights instruments may be particularly important in scenarios where extraterritorial migration control is coupled to schemes for extraterritorial asylum procedures in offshore or third-country locations and the ordinary progression of rights under the Refugee Convention that flow from gaining access to the territory is thus cut short. Similarly, policies summarily to deflect asylum-seekers to designated 'safe third countries' may raise additional concerns when coupled with extraterritorial migration control. The present author concurs with the view that while 'safe third country' rules are not explicitly prohibited under international refugee law,

---

[2] Hathaway, *Rights of Refugees*, pp. 160 ff.

[3] J. McAdam, *Complementary Protection in International Refugee Law* (Oxford University Press, 2007); R. Mandal, 'Protection mechanisms outside of [*sic*] the 1951 Convention ("complementary protection")', Legal and Protection Policy Research Series, UNHCR, Geneva, 2005; D. E. Anker, 'Refugee law, gender and the human rights paradigm', (2002) 15 *Harvard Human Rights Journal* 133–54; Plender and Mole, 'Beyond the Geneva Convention'; Gorlick, 'Convention and the Committee against Torture'.

[4] Noll, 'Seeking asylum at embassies'.

such transfers of protection from one state to another do, as a minimum, require that the second state respects the full catalogue of rights already obtained by the refugee in the first state.[5] This means that a refugee arriving at the territory of a more developed country would be entitled to any right owed by that country according to the level of attachment of the refugee as 'physically present' even when deflected to a third state with more derogations to the Refugee Convention or a different interpretation of its obligations. Any shortcomings in this regard may entail the liability of the sending state.[6] Yet for the refugee who never sets foot on the soil of the controlling state before being deflected *en route* to a third country, the acting state will be bound only to guarantee that the limited number of rights pertaining to refugees 'within the jurisdiction' is guaranteed in the third country.

In addition, a particular concern may arise where migration control is carried out by a third state from within the country of origin. This can be the case where naval interception is granted permission to patrol the territorial waters of foreign states, where immigration liaison officers operate control in foreign airports, or by the simple denial of visas at consulates thereby impairing the possibility of exiting the country of persecution.[7] In such cases all rights under the Refugee Convention are lost, since refugee status is premised on having left the country of origin (Art. 1). By moving control so far forward that it even precedes flight the very label 'refugee' is deconstructed. Here again, the protection offered by general human rights law becomes particularly important, and it should be noted that the *non-refoulement* principles flowing from general human rights law instruments do not have the 'outside his country of origin' requirement.[8] In addition, exercising migration control with the effect that individuals are prevented from leaving their country of origin may, depending on the circumstances, amount to a violation of the right to

---

[5] Hathaway, *Rights of Refugees*, p. 333; Legomsky, 'Secondary refugee movements', 612 ff.

[6] *T.I. v. United Kingdom.*   [7] Byrne et al., *New Asylum Countries?*, pp. 10 ff.

[8] See further above, section 3.6. This point appears to have been gravely overlooked in *R. (European Roma Rights Centre and Others) v. Immigration Officer at Prague Airport and Another*, House of Lords. It should also be remembered that a difference may still remain as to the amount of actual control a state exercises and the de facto possibilities for it to extend protection benefits between a situation where a state encounters a protection-seeker in the territory of a third state and the situation in which the protection-seeker is still within his or her country of origin. In particular, situations are conceivable in which the country of origin resists or prevents the granting of protection benefits by the extraterritorial state and even onward passage out of the country by reference to its territorial sovereignty.

leave as established in, for example, Article 12 of the Covenant on Civil and Political Rights.[9]

Beyond these scenarios, it is nonetheless fair to assume that respect for these core protection obligations, owed wherever a state exercises jurisdiction, in practice will entail the transfer of asylum-seekers to the territory of the state for the purpose of engaging in an asylum procedure. From there on the rest of the rights catalogue guaranteed by the Refugee Convention will eventually unfold itself. This is in line with the analysis in the previous chapter and flows from the fact that meeting the requirements of the *refoulement* prohibition ordinarily involves a refugee status determination process which again, in the majority of situations, entails access to the territory. Following on from the previous chapters, an essential question from a refugee protection perspective is thus establishing the meaning of jurisdiction for human rights purposes.

4.2 The general basis for conceiving of extraterritorial jurisdiction

4.2.1 Jurisdiction as a matter of public international law

A state's jurisdiction normally describes the limits of its legal competence or regulatory authority.[10] As a concept concerned with boundaries, jurisdiction is thus best understood as one state's claim to exercise power vis-à-vis other states.[11] Within the Westphalian state system this claim is positively based on a state's own claim to territorial sovereignty and

---

[9] C. Harvey and R. P. J. Barnidge, 'Human rights, free movement, and the right to leave in international law', (2007) 19 *International Journal of Refugee Law* 1–21; Weinzierl, *Border Management and Human Rights*, p. 49; G. Goodwin-Gill, 'The right to leave, return and remain', in V. Gowlland-Debbas (ed.), *The Problem of Refugees in the Light of Contemporary International Law Issues* (The Hague: Martinus Nijhoff Publishers, 1996), pp. 93–108, at p. 95. However, and as pointed out by several scholars, the right to leave is by no means an absolute right, but is subject to certain permissible restrictions, national security, public order, public health. From the perspective of the state to which entry is sought, passport control and visa requirements, for example, are in themselves unlikely to constitute a breach of Art. 12 of the Covenant. Goodwin-Gill, 'Right to leave, return and remain', p. 96; K. Hailbronner, 'Comments on the right to leave, return and remain', in Gowlland-Debbas, *Problem of Refugees*, pp. 109–18, at p. 111. First and foremost, the right to leave may thus be claimed vis-à-vis the home state if arbitrary exit control is imposed. Hathaway, *Rights of Refugees*, pp. 308–9, 897–902. See also Human Rights Committee, General Comment No. 27: Freedom of Movement (Art. 12), UN Doc. CCPR/C/21/Rev.1/Add.9, 2 November 1999, para. 10.

[10] V. Lowe, 'Jurisdiction', in Evans, *International Law*, pp. 335–60, at p. 335; Oppenheim, *Oppenheim's International Law*, p. 456.

[11] F. Berman, 'Jurisdiction: the state', in P. Capps, M. D. Evans and S. Konstadinidis (eds.), *Asserting Jurisdiction* (Portland: Hart Publishing, 2003), pp. 2–15, at p. 4.

is negatively limited by competing claims to authority by other states similarly claiming exclusive authority within their territory.

Doctrinal analysis of extraterritorial jurisdiction normally distinguishes between a state's prescriptive jurisdiction and its enforcement jurisdiction.[12] As regards prescriptive jurisdiction, states are generally assumed to have a wider margin for extraterritorial application of laws and national courts. This was perhaps expressed most clearly in the 1927 *Lotus* case, in which the Permanent Court of International Justice held that

> Far from laying down a general prohibition to the effect that States may not extend the application of their laws and the jurisdiction of their courts to person, property and acts outside their territory, [international law] leaves them in this respect a wide measure of discretion which is only limited in certain cases by prohibitive rules.[13]

While this general presumption in favour of extraterritoriality has since been somewhat moderated in the light of egregious claims for extraterritorial jurisdiction, extraterritorial prescriptive jurisdiction is still accepted as long as the acting state can show some meaningful link with those over whom jurisdiction is asserted. Firmly established bases for doing this include territory and nationality: allowing states to assert legislative and judicial jurisdiction in extraterritorial incidents with a clear intraterritorial effect, or over nationals even though they are not present within the territory.[14] Claims for extraterritorial prescriptive jurisdiction have expanded in recent years, especially in the fields of security and international crime. This includes the proliferation of treaty-based agreements to allow extraditions, claims to extraterritorial jurisdiction based on the protection of a state's vital interests (the protective principle), and claims for universal jurisdiction in relation to certain international crimes, for example piracy and genocide.[15]

---

[12] R. Higgins, 'The legal bases of jurisdiction', in C. J. Olmstead (ed.), *Extra-territorial Application of Laws and Responses Thereto* (Oxford: International Law Association/ESC Publishing Lim., 1984), pp. 3–14; P. Weil, 'Towards relative normativity in international law?', (1983) 77 *American Journal of International Law* 413–42. Some authors further single out a third category of 'judicial jurisdiction'. To the present author this is a source of confusion, as judicial activity in the wider sense is arguably a composite of legislative and enforcement activities. In the present chapter, judicial decisions in themselves are considered as pertaining to prescriptive jurisdiction, whereas the enforcement of judicial decisions remains a feature of enforcement jurisdiction.

[13] *Lotus* case, p. 19.   [14] Lowe, *International Law*, pp. 340–56.

[15] L. Reydams, *Universal Jurisdiction: International and Municipal Legal Perspectives* (Oxford University Press, 2003); Capps et al., *Asserting Jurisdiction*; A. Cassese, *Terrorism, Politics and the Law* (Cambridge: Polity Press, 1989).

With regard to enforcement jurisdiction, the traditional presumption has been prohibitive rather than permissive. As was equally established in the *Lotus* case,

Now the first and foremost restriction imposed by international law upon a State is that – failing the existence of a permissive rule to the contrary – it may not exercise its power in any form in the territory of another State.[16]

As such, enforcement jurisdiction is in principle limited to the territory of the state and, with some limitations, the *res communis* such as the high seas.[17] Nonetheless, although this is the starting point and may cover the vast majority of a state's dealings, it is equally clear that jurisdiction cannot be entirely limited to the territory. As noted by the International Law Commission as early as 1975, 'international life provides abundant examples of activities carried on in the territory of a state by agents of another state acting on the latter's behalf'.[18] Common examples of extraterritorial enforcement jurisdiction within a foreign territorial jurisdiction include consular activities and deployment of military personnel abroad. In addition, a treaty basis for extraterritorial enforcement jurisdiction is likewise developing; examples include the 'hot pursuit' rules under the Schengen framework allowing cross-border access for EU member state law enforcement agencies, and the 'shiprider' agreements allowing US vessels access to the territorial waters and to board flag vessels of a number of Caribbean states to intercept drug smugglers. The latter in particular is conceptually very similar to the agreements such as that signed between Spain and Senegal to carry out migration control in Senegalese territorial waters. Lastly, under the law of the sea, states hold jurisdiction on board any vessel flying its flag (flag sovereignty), and states are permitted to extend enforcement jurisdiction, for customs and immigration purposes, for example to parts of the high seas, namely the twelve-mile contiguous zone extending from territorial waters, and for exploration purposes to the exclusive economic zone extending up to 200 miles.[19]

In sum, while jurisdiction as a concept of general and public international law does set out from territorial principles, the legal bases for extraterritorial jurisdiction are well developed regarding prescriptive

---

[16] *Lotus* case, p. 14.   [17] Lowe, 'Jurisdiction', p. 374.
[18] International Law Commission, *Yearbook of the ILC* (1975), II, p. 83.
[19] 1958 Convention on the Territorial Sea and Contiguous Zone, Art. 33. M. Gavouneli, *Functional Jurisdiction in the Law of the Sea* (The Hague: Martinus Nijhoff Publishers, 2007).

jurisdiction and situations of extraterritorial enforcement jurisdiction are hardly exceptional. As has been noted by one scholar, the entire law of jurisdiction essentially concerns exceptions to the principle of territoriality.[20] It is true, however, that issues of extraterritorial jurisdiction have always drawn contestation, both as a matter of state practice and within the legal field. Despite a surge in academic interest, jurisdiction is hardly an established field of legal enquiry and a variety of approaches is employed in different fields of international law.[21] As shall be seen, this is no less true for the issue of extraterritorial jurisdiction as applied in the human rights context.

4.2.2 Extraterritorial jurisdiction in the human rights context

The notion and function of jurisdiction in human rights law fundamentally differ in at least one respect from the notion of jurisdiction as employed in public international law. In the human rights context, the question of jurisdiction is not about whether a state's claim to exercise authority or some legal competence is lawful, but, rather, whether in a specific instance a particular state is bound to respect relevant human rights obligations.[22] What matters here is not simply legal entitlement to exercise authority, but, more often, the de facto power or control exercised by the state in relation to a specific territory or individual.[23] Establishing de jure jurisdiction for the purpose of exercising certain powers abroad may be a premise for evaluating the actual power, yet it is not a necessary one. While different from the scenario above, this is still in line with general public international law. As was held by the International Court of Justice in *Namibia*, 'Physical control of a territory, and not sovereignty or legitimacy of title, is the basis for state liability for acts affecting other states.'[24]

Keeping this distinction in mind, the notion of jurisdiction developed in human rights case law nonetheless still draws on the public international law doctrine of jurisdiction in important respects. Most crucially, human

[20] M. Milanovic, 'From compromise to principle: clarifying the concept of state jurisdiction in human rights treaties', (2008) 8 *Human Rights Law Review* 411–48, at 421.

[21] Capps et al., *Asserting Jurisdiction*, p. xvii.

[22] E. Roxstrom, M. Gibney and T. Einarsen, 'The NATO bombing case (*Banković et al. v. Belgium et al.*) and the limits of Western human rights protection', (2005) 23 *Boston University International Law Journal* 56–136, at 112.

[23] M. Milanovic, 'From compromise to principle', at 423; R. Lawson, 'Life after *Banković*: on the extraterritorial application of the European Convention on Human Rights', in Coomans and Kamminga, *Extraterritorial Application*, pp. 83–123, at p. 87.

[24] *Namibia (South West Africa) Case*, para. 53.

rights litigation has taken 'jurisdiction' to be understood in primarily territorial terms. In the *Banković* case, involving the NATO bombing of a Serbian radio station which killed sixteen employees, the Grand Chamber of the European Court of Human Rights had the opportunity to discuss the notion of jurisdiction at length, and concluded that

Article 1 of the Convention must be considered to reflect the ordinary and essentially territorial notion of jurisdiction, other bases of jurisdiction being exceptional and requiring special justification in the particular circumstances of each case.[25]

Consequently, the Court unanimously declared the *Banković* case inadmissible as the deceased were not deemed to be within the jurisdiction of the NATO states during the attack. Notwithstanding the criticism that this case and its conclusion have attracted, the premise set out here – that a territorial limitation is ordinarily assumed in the exercise of state jurisdiction – is both in line with public international law and generally supported in the international human rights jurisprudence.[26] The quotation, however, also concedes that jurisdiction does in some instances extend extraterritorially. When reviewing existing case law at least four distinctive bases for establishing extraterritorial jurisdiction for human

---

[25] *Banković*, para. 61.

[26] See e.g. Milanovic, 'From compromise to principle'; L. G. Loucaides, 'Determining the extra-territorial effect of the European Convention: facts, jurisprudence and the *Banković* case', (2006) 4 *European Human Rights Law Review* 391–407; V. Mantouvalou, 'Extending judicial control in international law: human rights treaties and extraterritoriality', (2005) 9 *International Journal of Human Rights* 147–63, at 157; Roxstrom et al., 'NATO bombing case', Lawson, 'Life after *Banković*'. *Banković* has further been read by some as setting out a geographical restriction to extraterritorial application, namely that the Convention is essentially regional and situations of extraterritoriality thus are only applicable within the legal space or '*espace juridique*' of the convention, i.e. only in the territory of another contracting state (para. 80). Such an interpretation, however, is both out of line with previous and subsequent case law of the Court. See e.g. *X and Y v. Switzerland*, European Commission of Human Rights, Application No. 7289/75 and 7349/76, 14 July 1977 (Liechtenstein was not at the time a party to the Convention), and *Issa and Others v. Turkey*, European Court of Human Rights, Application No. 31821/96, 16 November 2004. For a rebuttal of the restrictive *espace juridique* interpretation see e.g. J. Cerone, 'Out of bounds? Considering the reach of international human rights law', Working Paper No. 5, Center for Human Rights and Global Justice, New York, 2006, pp. 19–20; M. Gondek, 'Extraterritorial application of the European Convention on Human Rights: territorial focus in the age of globalization', (2005) *Netherlands International Law Review* 348–87, at 375–7; Lawson, 'Life after *Banković*', pp. 111–15; and R. Wilde, 'Opinion: The "legal space" or "*espace juridique*" of the European Convention on Human Rights: is it relevant to extraterritorial state action?', (2005) 2 *European Human Rights Law Review* 115–24.

rights purposes can be identified, some of which clearly derive from similar, or at least parallel, bases of extraterritorial jurisdiction as applied in other spheres of international law.

The first of these concerns treaty-based assertions of administrative, legislative or judiciary jurisdiction within another state.[27] Thus in *X and Y v. Switzerland* an immigrant prohibited entry into Liechtenstein was held to be subject to Swiss jurisdiction, as Switzerland legislated on immigration matters for both territories.[28] From this it follows that where extraterritorial migration control would amount to a direct exercise of judiciary or legislative powers abroad, there is a strong presumption that such exercise of authority will amount to extraterritorial jurisdiction in respect of individuals being subjected to that authority. While such arrangements are likely to be highly extraordinary, this line of cases may be relevant to some instances of offshore asylum processing.

Second, especially in regard to extradition and *refoulement* situations, an extraterritorial effects principle has developed. In *Soering v. United Kingdom*, the European Commission of Human Rights held that the extradition of a German national facing capital murder charges in the United States engaged the jurisdiction of the United Kingdom, from where he had been extradited, as the act of extradition itself contained a foreseeable risk of leading to a violation of Article 3.[29] While the judgment has been important in cementing the reach of the *non-refoulement* principle, this line of cases is not directly relevant to the present enquiry, as it concerns individuals already present in the territory of the state in question.

The last two bases for establishing extraterritorial jurisdiction for the purpose of human rights responsibility are more directly related to the factual qualification of the authority exerted as opposed to formal principles under international law or any international agreement between the parties. In these cases, jurisdiction is dependent on establishing that the state exercises effective control or authority – either over a defined *territory* or over an *individual*.

Extraterritorial jurisdiction over territory could be argued to follow from the general principle of effective sovereignty, extending

---

[27] *Drozd and Janousek v. France and Spain*, European Court of Human Rights, Application No. 12747/87, 26 June 1992; *Gentilhomme and Others v. France*, European Court of Human Rights, Application Nos. 48205/99, 48207/99 and 48209/99, 14 May 2002.

[28] *X and Y v. Switzerland*.

[29] *Soering*. The extraterritorial effects notion has since been confirmed in e.g. *Chahal v. the UK*, European Court of Human Rights, Application No. 22414/93, 15 November 1996; a similar approach has been taken by the Human Rights Committee in *Ng v. Canada*, UN Doc. A/49/40, 5 November 1993; and *Kindler v. Canada*, UN Doc. A/46/50, 30 July 1993.

jurisdiction to all geographical areas where a state exercises de facto control.[30] In *Banković*, the European Court established that extraterritorial jurisdiction may come about where a state 'through the effective control of the relevant territory and its inhabitants abroad as a consequence of military occupation or through the consent, invitation or acquiescence of the Government of that territory, exercises all or some of the public powers normally to be exercised by that Government'.[31] As was shown in *Cyprus v. Turkey*, responsibility in such situations pertains not only to acts of government agents but to any act or omission leading to human rights violations conducted in the area where effective control is upheld.[32]

Extraterritorial jurisdiction conceived as effective control over an individual flows from the reasoning that 'a State may also be held accountable for violation of . . . rights and freedoms of persons who are in the territory of another State but who are found to be under the former State's authority and control through its agents operating – whether lawfully or unlawfully – in the latter State'.[33] This category was also acknowledged in *Banković*, although referring more specifically to 'the activities of diplomatic and consular agents acting abroad and on board craft and vessels registered in, or flying the flag of, that State'.[34] Again, this category may to some extent reflect similar bases of extraterritorial jurisdiction for consular activities or flag-state jurisdiction established under general international law.[35]

The cases falling under this category involve, first, actions undertaken by consular authorities at or in conjunction with embassies or consulates. Some of these are specifically connected to actions in regard to nationals

---

[30] *Namibia (South West Africa) Case*, para. 53.
[31] *Banković*, para. 71. See further *Loizidou v. Turkey*, European Court of Human Rights, Application No. 15318/89, 18 December 1996; *Coard et al. v. United States*, Inter-American Commission on Human Rights, Case 10.951, 29 September 1999; *Salas and Others v. the United States ('US military intervention in Panama')*, Inter-American Commission for Human Rights, Case No. 10.573, Report No. 31/93, Annual Report IACHR 1993, 312, 14 October 1993. See also *Legal Consequences of the Construction of a Wall in the Occupied Palestinian Territory*, paras. 102–114.
[32] *Cyprus v. Turkey*, European Court of Human Rights, Application No. 25781/94, 10 May 2001, para. 77.
[33] *Issa and Others v. Turkey*, ECtHR, para. 71.
[34] *Banković*, para. 73. See also *Medvedyev and Others v. France*, European Court of Human Rights, Application No. 3394/03, 10 July 2008.
[35] See e.g. *Lotus* case; L. Oppenheim, *International Law: A Treatise*, 7th edn, ed. H. Lauterpacht (London: Longman, 1948), I, p. 548.

and are thus not directly relevant to the present enquiry.[36] Yet extraterritorial jurisdiction over foreigners in regard to consular activities has similarly been established.[37] Second, this notion of extraterritorial jurisdiction has been applied in a number of cases involving kidnapping or arrest of individuals on foreign territory and subsequent extradition to the territory of the acting state.[38] Although one could emphasise the inter-temporal aspect of subsequently bringing individuals to the territory, case law in these cases has generally emphasised that jurisdiction was established 'directly after' the arrest or handover to the authorities in question.[39] The correctness of this interpretation is supported by a number of cases where extraterritorial jurisdiction over individuals has been established in cases with no subsequent extradition, but where individuals have been physically detained or imprisoned abroad.[40]

Both for cases concerning effective control over territory and for those concerning authority over individuals, a tension is often evident between the universalist claim of human rights on one side and, on the other, the seeming primacy and exclusivity of the territorial jurisdiction. Positively establishing extraterritorial jurisdiction has thus been motivated by a desire to avoid double standards or 'a gap or vacuum in human

---

[36] See e.g. *X. v. Federal Republic of Germany*, European Commission on Human Rights, Application No. 1611/62, 25 September 1965; *X v. United Kingdom*, European Commission of Human Rights, Application No. 7547/76, 15 December 1977.

[37] *W.M. v. Denmark*, European Commission of Human Rights, Application No. 17393/90, 14 October 1992; *W. v. Ireland*, European Court of Human Rights, Application No. 9360/81, 28 February 1983.

[38] See e.g. *López Burgos v. Uruguay*, Human Rights Committee, UN Doc. A/36/40, 6 June 1979; *Lilian Celiberti de Casariego v. Uruguay*, Human Rights Committee, UN Doc. CCPR/C/OP/1, 29 July 1981; *Freda v. Italy*, European Commission on Human Rights, 8916/80, 7 October 1980; *Reinette v. France*, European Court of Human Rights, Application No. 14009/88, 2 October 1989; *Stocke v. Germany*, European Court of Human Rights, Series A, No. 199, 19 March 1991; *Ramirez Sánchez v. France*, European Commission of Human Rights, Application No. 28780/95, 24 June 1996; *Öcalan v. Turkey*, European Court of Human Rights, Application No. 46221/99, 12 March 2003.

[39] Gondek, 'Extraterritorial application', 374. See e.g. *Öcalan*, para. 91.

[40] See e.g. *Ilse Hess v. United Kingdom*, European Commission of Human Rights, Application No. 6231/73, 28 May 1975. Although the case was rejected due to the alleged impossibility of attributing the violation to any one of the four occupying powers holding Rudolf Hess, the Commission noted that 'there is, in principle, from a legal point of view, no reason why acts of the British authorities in Berlin should not entail the liability of the United Kingdom under the Convention' (para. 72). As a national example, see e.g. *Al-Skeini and others v. Secretary of State for Defence*, UK House of Lords, [2007] UKHL 26, 13 June 2006. In this case, involving detention and mistreatment resulting in the death of an Iraqi national, the basis for jurisdiction was established by, among other things, drawing a parallel to the embassy cases; see e.g. para. 132.

rights protection',[41] as it would be 'unconscionable...to permit a State party to perpetrate violations of the Covenant in the territory of another State, which violations it could not perpetrate within its own territory'.[42] Yet, and especially regarding situations involving potential clashes with foreign territorial jurisdictions, this consideration is tempered by the primacy of the territorial state's jurisdiction. As a result, the test for extraterritorial jurisdiction in these cases becomes more demanding and in practice needs de facto to exclude the competing authority of the territorial state. In cases involving control over a geographical area, establishment of extraterritorial jurisdiction has thus so far demanded a high degree of structural control over a well-defined area. For extraterritorial jurisdiction over individuals within a foreign jurisdiction, affirmative case law has similarly primarily involved instances involving physical custody or detention.

4.2.3 A methodological note

At this stage a few remarks about the methodological approach pursued may be in order. As may already be clear from the exposition above, the following analysis makes two assumptions of parsimony for the sake of clarity in the interpretation. The first is that an analysis of extraterritorial jurisdiction in human rights law cannot be divorced from considerations of how the concept of jurisdiction is employed in public international law. Reflecting a more 'fragmentary' approach, some scholars have argued that human rights law has developed a relatively autonomous status, in which questions of extraterritorial applicability cannot be limited by considerations such as that of how extraterritorial jurisdiction is understood within the more contractual framework of public international law.[43] The difference, as described above, between usage of jurisdiction to signify legal entitlement under public international law and jurisdiction as a premise of human rights responsibility should no doubt be borne in mind, and the warning that the two may easily be confused is thus

---

[41] *Cyprus v. Turkey*, para. 78.

[42] *López Burgos v. Uruguay*, para. 12(3); *Issa and Others v. Turkey*, para. 71.

[43] Milanovic, 'From compromise to principle', 447; Scheinin, 'Extraterritorial effect', pp. 78–9. See more generally Pellet, '"Human rightism" and international law', (2000) *Italian Yearbook of International Law* 3–16; Simma, 'International human rights'. Martin Scheinin has since lent support to a more 'reconciliatory' approach; see M. T. Kamminga and M. Scheinin (eds.), *The Impact of Human Rights Law on General International Law* (Oxford University Press, 2009).

apt. Yet, while distinct, the interpretation of extraterritorial jurisdiction in the human rights context cannot be completely dissociated from the jurisdictional framework in public international law.[44] This is especially evident when looking at the human rights case law on this issue as it is often explicitly informed by and reasoned from jurisdictional principles and typologies derived from general international law – correct or not.[45] Moreover, there is no need to think that such a starting point necessarily yields a more restrictive interpretation of extraterritorial jurisdiction. First, human rights case law may equally inform general international law.[46] Second, as will be demonstrated, an 'integrationist' approach that draws in perspectives from other areas of general international law may support just as well a more expansive interpretation of extraterritorial jurisdiction.[47]

The second assumption concerns the case law from which interpretation is drawn. Some scholars argue that there are substantial differences among the human rights instruments and, more importantly, between different geographic human rights bodies and institutions in how extraterritorial jurisdiction is conceived and established.[48] While this is almost inevitably true to some extent, the jurisprudence does not, to the mind of the present author, seem, as presented by other authors, to vary systematically on this particular issue. On the contrary, it is noteworthy that the different human rights institutions on several occasions cite and refer to each other on issues involving extraterritorial jurisdiction.[49] Furthermore, it may be hard to draw convincing conclusions as to systematic differences from the relatively limited amount of case law under some institutions.[50] In the following analysis an interpretation is thus presented in which legal geography or the extraterritorial venue of the

---

[44] McGoldrick, 'Extraterritorial effect', p. 42.

[45] Milanovic, 'From compromise to principle', 419. See e.g. *Issa and Others v. Turkey*, para. 71; *Gentilhomme and Others v. France*, para. 20, and *Banković*, paras. 59–61.

[46] Kamminga and Scheinin, *Impact of Human Rights Law*.

[47] S. Skogly, *Beyond National Borders: States' Human Rights Obligations in International Cooperation* (Antwerp: Intersentia, 2006).

[48] Gondek, 'Extraterritorial application'; Coomans and Kamminga, *Extraterritorial Application*, p. 4; Scheinin, 'Extraterritorial effect'.

[49] Hathaway, *Rights of Refugees*, p. 165; C. M. Cerna, 'Extraterritorial application of the human rights instruments of the inter-American system', in Coomans and Kamminga, *Extraterritorial Application*, pp. 141–74, at p. 145; McGoldrick, 'Extraterritorial effect', p. 68.

[50] Cerna, 'Extraterritorial application'; McGoldrick, 'Extraterritorial effect'.

act concerned, as opposed to institutional geography, is the organising principle.[51]

Lastly, the present chapter will draw its analysis primarily from international case law and general comments. As such, the chapter will not go into a doctrinal analysis of the meaning of 'jurisdiction' as set out in each of the relevant human rights instruments.[52] Rather, it is the current usage and different interpretations being proposed in the predominantly recent and still growing case law that is of particular interest to the present enquiry. It could, however, be objected that existing case law as regards extraterritorial jurisdiction is scarce, and may still be too limited too constitute a solid foundation for a more systematic interpretation. As Richard O'Boyle notes, 'the law on jurisdiction is still in its infancy'.[53]

4.3 Extraterritorial jurisdiction and migration control

In the following, establishing extraterritorial jurisdiction in cases of offshore migration control shall be considered with regard to three distinct spheres. The first sets out by examining not where extraterritorial obligations end, but, rather, where they start. State practices to excise parts

---

[51] A similar analytical framework has been adopted by two other studies, though both these focus more specifically on border controls at sea; see Fischer-Lescano and Löhr, *Border Control at Sea*, and Weinzierl, *Border Management and Human Rights*. As will be shown below, distinguishing between extraterritorial acts occurring on the high seas or in international airspace and acts occurring within a foreign territorial jurisdiction may account, for example, for the different approach taken by the European Court of Human Rights and the Inter-American Commission as pointed out by e.g. Coomans and Kamminga, *Extraterritorial Application*, p. 4.

[52] Some aspects of this issue have already been touched on in the previous chapter; see above, section 3.6. For a list of jurisdiction clauses in human rights treaties see Coomans and Kamminga, *Extraterritorial Application*, pp. 271–4. For an analysis of the origins of jurisdiction clauses in human rights treaties, see Milanovic, 'From compromise to principle', 429–34. For examples of a doctrinal analysis of the jurisdiction clause as set out in the European Convention on Human Rights, see M. P. Pedersen, 'Territorial jurisdiction in Article 1 of the European Convention on Human Rights', (2004) 73 *Nordic Journal of International Law* 279–305; A. Orakhelashvili, 'Restrictive interpretation of human rights treaties in the recent jurisprudence of the European Court of Human Rights', (2003) 14 *European Journal of International Law* 529–68. Lastly, a more comprehensive analysis of extraterritorial human rights obligations across different treaties has been undertaken by Michal Gondek, *The Reach of Human Rights in a Globalising World: Extraterritorial Application of Human Rights Treaties* (Antwerp: Intersentia, 2009); and in regard to international co-operation by Sigrun Skogly, *Beyond National Borders*.

[53] R. O'Boyle, 'The European Convention on Human Rights and Extraterritorial Jurisdiction: A Comment on Life after *Banković*', in Coomans and Kamminga, *Extraterritorial Application*, p. 139.

of their territory or designate 'international zones' have become increasingly popular, but do they qualify as extraterritorial? Second, the 'basic' or 'pure' situations of extraterritorial obligations are analysed, such as when migration control is moved to the high seas or *terrae nullius*. And, third, the more 'complex' question of establishing extraterritorial jurisdiction where extraterritorial migration control is carried out within the territory or territorial waters of another state is taken on. Finally, the impact of other legal frameworks, such as the law of the sea and bilateral treaties, is considered.

4.3.1 Withdrawal of authority and excision of territory

There has been a growing trend of withdrawing authority from parts of a state's territory for the purpose of migration control, either by simple declaration or by excising certain geographic areas through national legislation. This may be argued by some to fall outside a discussion of extraterritoriality. Yet it is a logical corollary to applying the jurisdiction approach in order to delimit the scope of application *ratione loci* of state responsibilities towards refugees. If it is submitted that jurisdiction is primarily territorial and flows from a state's effective control over a given geographical area, does state jurisdiction collapse when this control ceases, either because another polity takes it over or because a state self-imposes restrictions on its territorial sway? The latter situation is particularly interesting, as an affirmative answer would suggest that extraterritoriality can be constructed at will when states declare that part of or all their authority is henceforth withdrawn from a given area.

A number of states seem to think that this is the case and have adopted national legislation and policies that either de jure denies the applicability of international obligations or de facto limits access to asylum in parts of their territory. In addition to its interdiction policies on the high seas, the United States has maintained a 'wet-foot, dry-foot' policy with regard to Cuban asylum-seekers that effectively exempts US territorial waters for asylum purposes. Under the 1995 Cuban Migration Agreement all Cubans intercepted, whether on the high seas or in territorial waters ('wet-foots'), have thereby been returned directly to Cuba; whereas those who manage to reach the shores of the United States ('dry-foots') have been allowed to stay. The radical distinction reached absurd dimensions when, on 5 January 2006, fifteen Cubans clinging to a bridge in the Florida Keys were repatriated by the coastguard with the argument that the decommissioned bridge had been physically cut off from the beach and thus did not constitute US soil.[54]

The US policy did, however, contain a screening procedure for those interdicted at sea who expressed a fear of persecution if returned to Cuba. Until 2003, 170 persons were found to have a legitimate claim and have thus been resettled in third countries. Further, the agreement with Cuba includes a concomitant obligation for Cuba not to subject those returned to reprisals. Yet the US State Department itself has acknowledged that its ability to monitor the subsequent fate of those returned is limited.[55]

From 2001 onwards Australia has passed legislation to 'excise' more than 3,000 islands, certain coastal ports and northern coastal stretches as well as its territorial waters from its 'migration zone'.[56] Asylum-seekers who arrive in the excised territories, dubbed 'offshore entry persons', may apply for asylum with the UNHCR, but Australia has no obligation to grant them a visa or entry to mainland territory. Asylum-seekers encountered within the 'excised' areas have instead been transferred to Nauru or Papua New Guinea, or, since 2007, to the excised territory of Christmas Island, for offshore asylum processing.[57]

Lastly, a number of states have claimed that 'international zones' or 'transit areas' in ports and airports do not legally form part of their national territory. Under the Immigration Act 1987 an asylum-seeker arriving in the United Kingdom by ship or aircraft has legally not entered the United Kingdom if not disembarked or still within designated arrival areas.[58] In a case before the European Court of Human Rights, France similarly held that the international zone at Paris-Orly airport was different from French territory.[59] Within the zone no interpreters, legal

---

[54] R. E. Wasem, 'Cuban migration policy and issues', CRS Report for Congress RS20468, Congressional Research Service, Washington, 2007.

[55] M. C. Werlau, 'International law and other considerations on the repatriation of the Cuban balseros by the United States', (2004) 14 *Cuba in Transition* 202–12, at 211.

[56] Migration Amendment (Excision from Migration Zone) Act 2001; Kneebone, 'Pacific plan', 697. The degree to which the legislation represents an actual retraction of Australian sovereignty as a matter of international law is questionable. The amendments has no effect on Australia's sovereign claims in other respects. Australia has continued to exercise jurisdiction within the excised areas for all other purposes, and the excision explicitly does not affect the rights of Australian citizens or permanent residents.

[57] Goodwin-Gill and McAdam, *Refugee in International Law*, p. 256.

[58] Immigration Act 1987, Part I, s. 11(1); Nicholson, 'Immigration Act 1987', 617.

[59] *Amuur* v. *France*, European Court of Human Rights, Application No. 19776/92, 25 June 1996.

assistance or private assistance was allowed to asylum-seekers, and the French Office for the Protection of Refugees denied the applicants access to the asylum procedure on the grounds that it lacked jurisdiction.[60] With the increased delegation of migration control to private carriers and security companies,[61] refugees may find themselves unable to access such authorities post-arrival and instead be confined to these international zones effectively under private authority. Thus the transit zone at Moscow airport has been known to hold refugees denied onward flight to western Europe with no access to Russian immigration authorities and thus nowhere to direct asylum claims.[62]

From the standpoint of international law, however, such arrangements for withdrawing specific exercises of executive power from geographical areas otherwise regarded as a state's sovereign territory have little merit. Under international maritime law the territorial waters of coastal states, no more than and generally equal to twelve nautical miles, all form part of that state's sovereign geographical sphere and thus do not differ from the ordinary land territory for purposes of establishing state jurisdiction.[63]

The question of international airport zones was specifically dealt with by the European Court of Human Rights in *Amuur* v. *France*,[64] concerning the detention and subsequent removal of four Somali asylum-seekers from the international zone of Paris-Orly airport. Contrary to the French view that the international zone did not form part of French territory, the Court assertively concluded that '[d]espite its name, the international zone does not have extraterritorial status', and that regardless of national legislation to the opposite, holding the applicants in this zone made them subject to French law (para. 52). In its judgment the Court placed emphasis on the fact that, for all other purposes, France exercised sovereign authority in this zone and thus that the protections afforded under both

---

[60] J. H. Bello and J. Kokott, '*Amuur* v. *France*', (1997) 91 *American Journal of International Law* 147–52, at 148.

[61] Guiraudon, 'Before the EU border'.

[62] J. Hughes and F. Liebaut (eds.), *Detention of Asylum-Seekers in Europe: Analysis and Perspectives* (The Hague: Martinus Nijhoff, 1998), pp. 71–2; Nicholson, 'Immigration Act 1987', 598 ff.

[63] 1982 UN Convention on the Law of the Sea, Art 2(1). As other scholars have pointed out, the twelve-mile delimitation in practice reflects customary international law. Fischer-Lescano and Löhr, *Border Control at Sea*, p. 17. The territorial sea should in this sense be distinguished from the contiguous zone (extending up to 24 miles) and the exclusive economic zone (EEZ). In both of these areas, states may claim certain sovereign rights, yet these zones do not amount to sovereign sea territory.

[64] *Amuur* v. *France*.

the Refugee Convention and the European Convention on Human Rights had to be afforded (para. 43).

Even in cases where such authority and control can be questioned, case law seems to support the rule that jurisdiction extends to the entirety of a state's formally recognised territory. In *Ilaşcu and Others* v. *Moldova and Russia*,[65] concerning acts committed by the authorities of the Moldavian Republic of Transnistria (a self-proclaimed independent polity not internationally recognised), the Grand Chamber of the European Court of Human Rights held that both Russia and Moldova had jurisdiction: Russia by the fact that it asserted decisive influence over the regional regime and thus exercised effective control, Moldova by the fact that it held de jure sovereignty over the area. Notably, it was held that even though Moldova was 'prevented from exercising its authority over the whole of its territory . . . it does not thereby cease to have jurisdiction within the meaning of Article 1 of the Convention over that part of its territory' (para. 333). The Court, however, did emphasise that 'such a factual situation reduces the scope of that jurisdiction in that the undertaking given by the state under Article 1 must be considered by the Court only in the light of the Contracting State's positive obligations towards persons within its territory' (para. 334), meaning that Moldova had an obligation to use all available legal, political and diplomatic means to ensure that the rights of the Convention were respected, even if unable to ensure these rights directly. The establishment of Moldavian responsibility has been substantially criticised as leapfrogging the necessary link between human rights obligations and the actual ability of states to ensure them,[66] yet the ruling does underline the primacy of formal territorial readings in ascribing human rights responsibility.

From the perspective of refugee rights, these rulings are important in cementing the conclusion that jurisdiction cannot be retracted at will, and thus that, as a matter of international law, situations of extraterritoriality do not arise despite the legal fictions attempted through national policies or legislation. This position finds ample support in the case law of other international human rights institutions. The principle that a state must be assumed to exercise jurisdiction within its entire territory, unless this assumption can specifically be rebutted, was thus affirmed by the International Court of Justice in its opinion on the *Construction of*

---

[65] *Ilaşcu and Others v. Moldova and Russia*, European Court of Human Rights, Application No. 48787/99, 8 July 2004.

[66] Skogly, *Beyond National Borders*, p. 182; Roxstrom et al., 'NATO bombing case', 127.

a Wall in the Occupied Palestinian Territories,[67] and again by the European Court of Human Rights in *Assanidze* v. *Georgia*.[68]

The general principles set out in these cases may inform the ensuing quest to determine extraterritorial obligations vis-à-vis refugees on the high seas and in foreign territorial jurisdictions. The principal lesson from *Amuur* is that states cannot assume sovereign powers for one purpose while excluding them regarding others – authority in regard to migration control entails concomitant responsibilities in respect of asylum-seekers and refugees. From *Ilaşcu* it appears that even an actual withdrawal of authority over parts of the territory does not relieve states of all their obligations under international human rights and refugee law to asylum-seekers who might arrive there. A state is presumed to exercise jurisdiction throughout its entire territory, and this presumption can only be rebutted in exceptional circumstances.[69] Even in the case of foreign occupation or where effective control over parts of the territory is taken by a separatist movement supported by a foreign state, certain positive obligations to ensure human rights may still remain with the territorial state.

Yet, even if there is no question that a state's jurisdiction extends to its entire territory, differentiating regulation for such 'international zones' or 'border areas' may still be a legal-political strategy from a national perspective.

The applicability of international refugee law does not preclude states from installing special border procedures under national law as long as they are consistent with international obligations. Notably, Australia's 'Pacific Solution' never challenged the existence of international obligations in case of asylum-seekers arriving in the 'excised' areas, but maintained either offshore asylum procedures or special procedures in the excised areas.[70] Similarly, a number of countries maintain particular expedient asylum procedures for those arriving at international airports or who are intercepted within territorial waters, and the EU Asylum

---

[67] *Legal Consequences of the Construction of a Wall in the Occupied Palestinian Territory*, paras. 109–110.

[68] *Assanidze* v. *Georgia*, European Court of Human Rights, Application No. 71503/01, 8 April 2004, paras. 137–43.

[69] K. M. Larsen, 'Territorial non-application of the European Convention on Human Rights', (2009) 78 *Nordic Journal of International Law* 73–93, at 93.

[70] Fischer-Lescano and Löhr, *Border Control at Sea*, p. 17; Kneebone, 'Pacific plan'. Whether the asylum procedures there are in conformity with international law, however, may well be questioned.

Procedures Directive permits special and accelerated procedures for applications made at the borders, including airports.[71]

These policies may be seen as national strategies of jurisdiction shopping or, perhaps more correctly, jurisdiction bifurcation, through which states with more developed asylum systems that normally ensure a wide and comprehensive rights catalogue to asylum-seekers remain free to withdraw the application of any or all of these rights for certain parts of their territories as long as the resulting treatment does not fall short of international obligations. Yet, needless to say, the risk of falling below this threshold increases the more closely a state seeks to approximate its policy thereto. This causes a particular concern for spontaneously arriving asylum-seekers who, if they even make it that far, often encounter the state within these marginal zones.

4.3.2 Interception on the high seas

Moving beyond the claims to extraterritoriality within a state's formal territory, the first real situation of extraterritoriality appears when states act in geographical areas not pertaining to the territorial jurisdiction of any sovereign, such as international waters or *terrae nullius*. Such considerations may in practice be limited to the high seas, but could also become relevant in cases where refugees find themselves in territories with no effective sovereign, such as in the case of buffer zones under international administration or so-called 'failed' states.

Shifting migration control to international waters is not a new phenomenon. With the rise of boat refugees in the 1970s and 1980s, high-seas interception practices quickly became a favoured response of coastal states concerned with situations of mass influx.

The US interception programme regarding Haitian boat refugees has already been mentioned. Similarly, the Australian 'Pacific Solution' also included interception of unauthorised migrant vessels in international waters.[72] In southern Europe, migration control on the high seas has been carried out by Italy in the Adriatic Sea, by Italy, France and Greece in the Mediterranean, and by Spain both in the Mediterranean and in the Atlantic Ocean around the Canary Islands.[73] Following the implementation of Italian–Libyan co-operation on interceptions in May 2009, Italian

---

[71] Council Directive 2005/85/EC, 13 December 2005, Art. 35.

[72] Kneebone, 'Pacific plan'; Magner, 'Less than "Pacific" solution'.

[73] D. Lutterbeck, 'Policing migration in the Mediterranean', (2006) 11 *Mediterranean Politics* 59–82.

authorities thus intercepted and directly returned 850 persons in 2009. Despite the identification of asylum-seekers and *bona fide* refugees among those returned by UNHCR, no screening procedures or opportunity to apply for asylum was provided by Italy.[74]

In the European context, maritime interception policies have expanded in recent years, operational activities being co-ordinated by the EU's border agency, Frontex.[75] Several of these involve interdiction outside EU territorial waters. One is 'Operation Nautilus', which started in October 2006 and involves patrols in the international waters of the Mediterranean to prevent migration from Libya reaching Malta, Sicily or Lampedusa.[76] During the first years of the operation few migrants were diverted back due to a lack of co-operation with Libya and disagreement between Italy and Malta surrounding the disembarkation of persons rescued at sea. However, following the bilateral agreement signed between Italy and Libya, Frontex vessels have been reported as assisting in intercepting and diverting persons back to Libya.[77] Similarly, 'Operation Hera' was initiated in August 2006 to curb the migration flow towards the Canary Islands. Its operational zones cover both international waters and also, through bilateral agreements signed by Spain, the territorial waters of Senegal, Mauritania and Cape Verde. In 2008, 5,969 persons were reported to have been diverted back, although no specification was made as to whether these persons had been intercepted on the high seas or inside foreign territorial waters.[78]

To what extent are states undertaking such interdiction operations on the high seas bound by international law not to return those intercepted claiming asylum or fearing torture? So far, national courts and governments have varied somewhat in their interpretation of the

---

[74] 'Immigrati/Maroni: in un anno rimandati in Libia 850 "clandestini"', *l'Unita*, 10 May 2010, available at www.unita.it; UNHCR, 'UNHCR interviews asylum seekers pushed back to Libya', Briefing Note, 14 July 2009, available at www.unhcr.org.

[75] In 2010 Frontex-co-ordinated sea operations included 'Chronos' (previously 'Nautilus'), 'Hera', 'Hermes', 'Indalo', 'Minerva' and 'Poseidon', stretching across the Mediterranean Sea and the Atlantic Ocean off Senegal, Mauritania and Morocco.

[76] In April 2010 'Operation Nautilus' was renamed 'Operation Chronos'.

[77] On 18 June 2009, a German Puma helicopter operating as part of Operation Nautilus IV co-ordinated Italian coastguard interception of a boat carrying about seventy-five migrants 29 miles south of Lampedusa. The Italian coastguard reportedly handed the migrants over to a Libyan patrol boat. Human Rights Watch, 'Pushed back, pushed around: Italy's forced return of boat migrants and asylum seekers, Libya's mistreatment of migrants and asylum seekers', September 2009, p. 37.

[78] Frontex, 'Hera 2008 and Nautilus 2008 Statistics', news releases, 17 February 2009, available at http://frontex.europa.eu.

jurisdictional implications. The Haitian interdiction scheme operated by the United States was based on an exclusively territorial conception of the international *non-refoulement* obligation. This understanding was upheld by the US Supreme Court in *Sale*, which not only proposed a strictly territorial reading of the Refugee Convention, but also denied that the United States had jurisdiction when operating coastguard vessels in international waters with reference to a general presumption against extraterritoriality emanating from principles of national sovereignty.[79]

Both the reasoning and the conclusions of the *Sale* verdict have, however, been widely criticised.[80] Clearly there are exceptions to such a presumption against extraterritorial jurisdiction, and the US Supreme Court has since somewhat abandoned it.[81] The UK Court of Appeal bluntly concluded that *Sale* was 'wrongly decided; it certainly offends one's sense of fairness'.[82] *Sale* in this sense provides an excellent example of why national court decisions, even from the highest instance, should not be regarded as final settlements. As Harold Koh has pointed out, even though such cases are considered waypoints in the 'complex enforcement' of the otherwise self-executing Refugee Convention, in Europe such decisions are today regularly overturned by the European Court of Human Rights.[83]

Looking instead to the jurisprudence of international human rights institutions, the Inter-American Commission specifically rejected the Supreme Court's ruling in *Sale* and positively affirmed the applicability of Article 33 of the Refugee Convention in situations involving migration control on the high seas.[84] This decision is fully in line with previous case law of the Inter-American Commission extending the notion of effective control over individuals in cases concerning international areas. In *Brothers to the Rescue*,[85] Cuba was never held to control any specific geographical area of the high seas or international air space when it shot down two aircraft outside Cuba's twelve miles of territorial waters. Yet the Commission

---

[79] *Sale*.
[80] Hathaway, *Rights of Refugees*, p. 339; G. Goodwin-Gill, 'The Haitian Refoulement Case: A Comment', (1994) 6 *International Journal of Refugee Law* 103–109.
[81] Koh, '"Haiti Paradigm"', 2418.
[82] *R. (European Roma Rights Centre and Others) v. Immigration Officer at Prague Airport and Another*, Court of Appeal, para. 34.
[83] Koh, '"Haiti Paradigm"', 2406.
[84] *Haitian Center for Human Rights v. United States*, Inter-American Commission on Human Rights, Case 10.675, 13 March 1997, paras. 156–157.
[85] *Armando Alejandre Jr. and Others v. Cuba ('Brothers to the Rescue')*, Inter-American Commission on Human Rights, Case 11.589, 29 September 1999.

argued that a state's jurisdiction encompasses 'all the persons under their actual authority and responsibility' (para. 24) and that since an analysis of the facts found that 'the victims died as consequence of direct actions of agents of the Cuban State', this was 'sufficient evidence to show that the agents of the Cuban State, despite being outside its territory, subjected to their authority the civil pilots' (para. 25).

A similar line of reasoning is proposed by the European Court of Human Rights in *Isaak*.[86] The applicant crossed into the UN buffer zone in Cyprus and was beaten to death by Turkish-controlled TRNC authorities and Turkish-Cypriot protesters. Despite Turkish arguments that it exercised no jurisdiction within the buffer zone, the Court held that

even if the acts complained of took place in the neutral UN buffer zone, the Court considers that the deceased was under the authority and/or effective control of the respondent State through its agents.[87]

It concludes, accordingly, that the matters complained of in the present application fall within the 'jurisdiction' of Turkey within the meaning of Article 1 of the Convention and therefore entail the respondent state's responsibility under the Convention.

A precedent for establishing jurisdiction in situations involving migration control in international waters can further be found in the jurisprudence of the European Court of Human Rights. In *Xhavara*,[88] an Italian navy vessel seeking to stop and inspect suspected irregular migrants on board the Albanian vessel *Kater I Rades* ended up colliding with and sinking the ship. The incident became known as the 'Otranto tragedy' and eighty-three people are assumed to have died as a result of the collision, although not all the bodies could be recovered. Italy operated under a bilateral agreement with Albania allowing them to board Albanian vessels wherever encountered, but the collision occurred in international waters, 35 miles off the Italian coast in the strait of Otranto. While the case was declared inadmissible *ratione temporae*, the Court did consider Italy to have exercised jurisdiction and in principle held Italy responsible for instigating a full and independent investigation into the deaths under Article 2 – a requirement that Italy was considered to have already

---

[86] *Isaak and Others* v. *Turkey*, European Court of Human Rights, Application No. 44587/98, 28 September 2006 (admissibility).

[87] Ibid., p. 16.

[88] *Xhavara and others* v. *Italy and Albania*, European Court of Human Rights, Application No. 39473/98, 11 January 2001 (admissibility).

fulfilled by having initiated proceedings against the master of the Italian vessel.[89]

In sum, the presumption that states do incur obligations under international refugee and human rights law when exercising migration control on the high seas is strong. Looking beyond rare examples of strictly territorial interpretations by national courts, international human rights jurisprudence uniformly supports an interpretation that jurisdiction is established when state agents undertake sovereign functions or otherwise assert authority in international airspace or on the high seas. In doing so, both the Inter-American Commission and the European Court of Human Rights seemingly accept a lower threshold for establishing extraterritorial jurisdiction over individuals. While there is little doubt that bringing intercepted asylum-seekers on board vessels of the intercepting states would reach the threshold of effective control over an individual set by cases such as *Öcalan* or *López Burgos*, the victims of *Xhavara* or *Brothers to the Rescue* were not physically apprehended or detained by the acting state. From a doctrinal perspective, one might equally emphasise flag-state jurisdiction, or that jurisdiction was established by prior treaty in some of these cases, yet neither of these avenues appear to have been decisive or especially relied on in the reasoning provided.[90]

Rather, the argumentation in these cases appears to follow what could be termed a *functional* approach to jurisdiction. What matters is not a generalised test of personal or geographical control, but rather the specific power or authority assumed by the state acting extraterritorially in a given capacity. The concept of 'functional jurisdiction' is well known in international maritime law, where on the high seas extraterritorial jurisdictional interplays between flag states, coastal states and port states are the norm rather than the exception, and 'sovereign rights' short of full jurisdiction may be claimed in relation to specific interests, for example for exploitation or protective purposes.[91]

---

[89] At the time of writing a further case has been submitted to the European Court of Human Rights by twenty-three Eritreans and Somalis who as part of a larger group of 231 migrants were intercepted in the Strait of Sicily, 35 miles south of Lampedusa on 6 May 2009. The migrants were taken aboard Italian vessels and subsequently handed over to the Libyan authorities in Tripoli under the Italian–Libyan agreement. *Hirsi and Others* v. *Italy*, European Court of Human Rights, Application No. 277765/09. Undecided, complaint submitted 26 May 2009.

[90] In *Banković*, however, the European Court of Human Rights did emphasise that in *Xhavara* jurisdiction 'was shared by written agreement between the respondent States'. *Banković*, para. 37.

[91] Gavouneli, *Functional Jurisdiction*; B. D. Smith, *State Responsibility and the Marine Environment: The Rules of Decision* (Oxford: Clarendon Press, 1988).

In the human rights context, jurisdiction in this sense flows from the de facto relationship established between the individual and the state through the very act itself, or the potential of acting. As is also evident from *Brothers to the Rescue*, rather than having a general test as a distinct issue of admissibility, the issue of jurisdiction hereby becomes integrated in the analysis of the facts and the liability of the state in question. This approach stands in some contrast to the examples of formal territorialism that may be relied on in situations of excision and that have been expressed in cases such as *Ilaşcu*, where the lack of such a relationship was overlooked in favour of official sovereign entitlements. Under a functional conception of extraterritorial jurisdiction, the test becomes entirely case-specific. Certain situations involving interception at sea may continue to fall below the threshold for establishing jurisdiction. Yet a case that on its merits would hold a state responsible under the *non-refoulement* prohibition for actions occurring within the territory could be argued by this fact alone to engage the jurisdiction of states in similar instances occurring on the high seas.

Little thus changes in the jurisdictional analysis by moving migration control to the high seas. A strong presumption prevails that any interdiction measure, even if not amounting to effective control over individuals or a geographical area, through the act itself would entail jurisdiction and thus an obligation on behalf of the acting state to respect basic rights under international refugee and human rights law. This has not prevented some countries from arguing otherwise, however. Denying extraterritorial jurisdiction or the extraterritorial applicability of relevant human rights provisions still occasionally appears in the reasoning of governments and national courts. Furthermore, just as in the case of international zones, from the perspective of national law shifting the venue of regulation to the high seas may provide a context for denying certain protections under domestic legislation. Beyond the questioning of the extraterritorial applicability of international *non-refoulement* obligations, the US Supreme Court in *Sale* equally held that national asylum legislation, specifically §243(h)(1) of the 1952 Immigration and Nationality Act, did not protect aliens in international waters against *refoulement*.[92]

4.3.3 Migration control within a foreign territorial jurisdiction

Compared with the practices of excision or interception in international waters, migration control within a third state's territorial jurisdiction

---

[92] *Sale*, pp. 15–21.

encompasses a much wider range of policies. From the control performed at visa consulates, over the deployment of immigration officers at foreign airports, to interception within foreign territorial waters, policies to bring the different layers of migration control closer and closer to the sites of departure have expanded substantially over the last years.

The role and degree of control exercised by states engaging in these activities varies. The EU network of immigration liaison officers posted to airports, border crossings and national immigration authorities of key transit and origin countries emphasise that such officers 'do not carry out any tasks relating to the sovereignty of States',[93] yet in practice they 'advise' and 'support' national border guards and airline officials, and in some situations have extended access to foreign police and border records.[94] In other instances authority is asserted more directly. Under the juxtaposed control scheme the United Kingdom thus carries out migration control within demarcated zones at the ports of Calais, Dunkirk and Boulogne. Pursuant to agreements with France, within these zones British migration law is enforced directly by the UK Border Agency. Under more recent amendments the actual control may even be partly outsourced to private contractors.[95]

Similarly, in extension of the Frontex interception mission outside the Canary Islands, Spain has signed bilateral agreements to allow interception not just on the high seas but also within the territorial seas, contiguous zones and airspace of Cape Verde, Senegal and Mauritania. Any vessel intercepted within the territorial waters of the co-operating states is turned back to either its port of departure or a port in the territorial waters where the interception occurred. In 2006, according to Frontex statistics, 3,665 persons were intercepted in these zones and directly returned. No possibility of initiating asylum claims with European authorities was provided.[96]

Does the jurisdictional assessment change when migration control is moved onwards from the high seas to the territory or territorial waters

[93] Council of the European Union, Proposal for a Comprehensive Plan to Combat Illegal Immigration and Trafficking of Human Beings in the European Union, 6621/1/02, 27 February 2002, para. 67.

[94] Gatev, 'Very Remote Control', p. 10. On the 'advisory' role of immigration liaison officers in regard to private airlines, see further below, chapter 5.

[95] Immigration, Asylum and Nationality Act 2006, ss. 40 and 41. See further below, section 5.1.

[96] Frontex, 'Longest Frontex-coordinated operation – HERA, the Canary Islands', news release, 19 December 2006, available at http://frontex.europa.eu.

of another state? In cases where migration control is carried out as part of a state's control over a geographic area the presumption of jurisdiction would be strong, even for acts not directly associated with or carried out by the agents of the controlling state.[97] When, if ever, could such a situation apply to the issue of migration control? In the majority of the existing cases the establishment of jurisdiction over a geographic area has depended on the military occupation of larger territories and a certain duration of such presence, making its application to situations of extraterritorial migration control highly extraordinary. Yet in *Issa*, somewhat nuancing its previous practice in the *Cyprus* line of cases, the European Court specifically rejected both these requirements and held that in principle Turkey could have exercised 'effective overall control', even though it had established its military presence only temporarily and only over smaller areas in northern Iraq.[98]

This opens up the possibility of a more inclusive approach, where any exercise of overall control even over smaller parts of territory would suffice for the purpose of establishing jurisdiction.[99] This could be argued to be the case in instances such as the UK juxtaposed control scheme operating at the French ports of Dunkirk, Boulogne and Calais. At each port a defined zone is appropriated within which the UK Border Agency has exclusive control over enforcing its domestic immigration laws, carrying out controls and retaining records, including fingerprints.[100]

Alternatively, jurisdiction in cases of extraterritorial migration control may be established where states can be said to exercise sufficient authority over the individual asylum-seeker or migrant. The general recognition that extraterritorial jurisdiction may flow from 'the activities of diplomatic and consular agents acting abroad and on board craft and vessels registered in, or flying the flag of, that State'[101] could at face value

---

[97] *Cyprus v. Turkey.*

[98] *Issa and Others v. Turkey*, para. 74. See also *Banković*, para. 80. The reasoning in the *Issa* judgment has, however, been criticised for somewhat mixing arguments concerning effective control over an area or territory and effective control over an individual. Gondek, 'Extraterritorial application', 374–5.

[99] N. Mole, 'Case analysis: *Issa* v. *Turkey*: delineating the extra-territorial effect of the European Convention on Human Rights', (2005) *European Human Rights Law Review* 86–91, at 90.

[100] At the international level, the juxtaposed control scheme is provided for by the Touquet treaty, which was signed on 4 February 2003, and given domestic effect by the Nationality, Immigration and Asylum Act 2002 (Juxtaposed Controls). Similar control arrangements have been made to give access to UK immigration officers to perform migration control at Eurostar railway stations in France and Belgium.

[101] *Banković*, para. 73.

encompass most types of migration control enacted by states themselves in the territory of another state.

Yet, case law has so far set a high threshold for personal control, demanding that individuals are either in the physical custody of the extraterritorially acting state, or are on board vessels or in premises over which the extraterritorial state exerts some recognised form of extraterritorial jurisdiction. What was rejected in *Banković* was exactly the cause-and-effect notion of jurisdiction, as the court did not find that the killing of relatives of the applicants by NATO smart bombs was enough to establish personal authority over the individuals in question. More recently, the boundaries of effective control in the personal sense was examined by the House of Lords in *Al-Skeini*, with an extensive analysis of relevant international case law.[102] The case concerned the deaths of six Iraqi civilians. Five of them had been shot by armed forces of the United Kingdom or caught in crossfire during British patrols. The last claimant, Mr Mousa, had been detained at a British military base in Basra, when he was severely beaten and subsequently died from his wounds. Yet according to the House of Lords only this last case fell within the jurisdiction of the United Kingdom.

As regards actions taking place in the territory of a foreign state it thus appears that a distinction is made between cases where states exercise complete and physical control over an individual, such as in the case of arrest or custody, and situations that result only in violations of human rights on foreign soil or territorial waters, even when these instances are so important that they infringe the right to life. Failing this test, jurisdiction conflicts are resolved by returning to the basic territorial principles for dividing responsibilities. Under such a reading it becomes substantially harder to establish refugee and human rights responsibility when a state operates migration control within the territorial jurisdiction of a foreign state. Does rejection of onward passage by an immigration officer entail effective control in the personal sense? Does turning back a ship in foreign territorial waters?

Situations where migration control is followed by, or includes, transfer of asylum-seekers to defined camps or enclosures located outside the territory are likely to fulfil the criteria for establishing jurisdiction.[103] As part

---

[102] *Al-Skeini v. Secretary of State for Defence.* This case has been submitted to the European Court of Human Rights and referred to the Grand Chamber for a ruling, but is of yet undecided. *Al-Skeini and others v. the United Kingdom*, Application No. 55721/07.

[103] See e.g. *Ilse Hess v. United Kingdom* and *Al-Skeini and others v. Secretary of State for Defence.*

of the US interception of Haitian boat refugees, upwards of 4,000 Haitians were at one stage directed to the US naval base in Guantánamo where they were promised 'safe haven'. When they were subsequently forced back to Haiti, several refugee organisations considered this to constitute *refoulement*.[104] In 2003 the United Kingdom proposed a similar model, whereby all asylum-seekers intercepted in the Mediterranean or at the borders of an EU country would be sent back to 'transit processing centres' in countries such as Morocco.[105] Even though the plan was never realised, the exercise of such authority within a confined place would in all likelihood entail obligations under the European Convention on Human Rights.[106]

In the *Marine I* case the Committee against Torture explicitly affirmed that extraterritorial detention of migrants amounts to jurisdiction.[107] On 31 January 2007, the cargo vessel, *Marine I*, carrying 369 migrants of Asian and African origin, had capsized in international waters off the west African coast. Following eight days of diplomatic negotiations between Mauritania, Senegal and Spain, the Spanish Civil Guard boarded the vessel to provide immediate health care, but then proceeded to tow the *Marine I* to the Mauritanian port of Nouadhibou. Under an agreement with Mauritania, the migrants were disembarked and placed at a former fishing plant under Spanish authority. In the following days the majority of the migrants were repatriated to Guinea, India and Pakistan. Twenty-three people, however, resisted repatriation and remained at the fishing plant, guarded by Spanish security forces for five months. Ten of the twenty-three were eventually granted access to Spain and Portugal on humanitarian grounds and the final thirteen returned to Pakistan. In terms of the jurisdictional assessment, the Committee against Torture concluded that

jurisdiction must also include situations where a State party exercises, directly or indirectly, de facto or de jure control over persons in detention... In the present case, the Committee observes that the State party maintained control over all persons on board the *Marine I* from the time the vessel was rescued and throughout the identification and repatriation process that took place at Nouadhibou. In particular, the State party exercised, by virtue of a diplomatic agreement concluded with Mauritania, constant de facto control over the alleged victims during their detention in Nouadhibou. Consequently, the Committee considers that the

---

[104] Legomsky, 'USA and the Caribbean interdiction programme'.
[105] UK Home Office, New Vision for Refugees.
[106] For a discussion of the human rights implications of the UK proposal see Noll, 'Visions of the exceptional'.
[107] *J.H.A v. Spain*, Committee against Torture, CAT/C/41/D/323/2007, 21 November 2007.

alleged victims are subject to Spanish jurisdiction insofar as the complaint that forms the subject of the present communication is concerned.[108]

That Spain was held to exercise jurisdiction from the time of boarding the *Marine I* is in line with general international law and other case law. A ship exercising government functions is normally recognised as holding jurisdictional entitlements under international maritime law. Where ships operating interdiction schemes in foreign territorial waters physically board migrant vessels or bring on board individuals, a strong parallel would further be established to, for example, *Öcalan* and *López Burgos*. In *Medvedyev* the European Court of Human Rights thus held France to have exercised jurisdiction following the boarding and towing of a vessel flying the Cambodian flag suspected of drug smuggling. The vessel was intercepted in international waters off Cape Verde and subsequently brought to the French port of Brest. It may be assumed that such a scenario would similarly suffice to establish jurisdiction over the individuals detained on board a vessel even if intercepted within foreign territorial waters.[109] Whether this jurisdictional basis extends to activities not actually aboard intercepting vessels is more questionable. Taking into account the reasoning in *Banković* and *Al-Skeini*, merely denying onward passage or escorting vessels back may thus be insufficient to establish extraterritorial jurisdiction over the individuals concerned.[110]

Another issue to consider is whether the activities of immigration officers posted at airports or at border crossings of third states, for example, may entail the jurisdiction of the posting state. As noted above, the use of such officers has become increasingly popular. As an example, more than twenty-two European and North American countries have deployed immigration liaison officers to the vulnerable and hard-to-patrol borderlands between Russia and Ukraine.[111] In the United Kingdom, the network of UK airline liaison officers (ALOs) alone spans thirty-two countries, mainly in Africa, Asia and Europe. While the Border Agency notes that 'ALOs have no legal powers in foreign jurisdiction . . . the decision to carry a passenger or to deny boarding is always made by the airline',[112] the Home Office

---

[108] Para. 8(2). The case was however declared inadmissible as the complainant was not expressly authorised to act on behalf of the victims.

[109] *Medvedyev and Others v. France.* France appealed to the Grand Chamber, which upheld the jurisdictional ruling (paras. 63–66) in its ruling of 29 March 2010.

[110] But see section 4.5.

[111] Gatev, 'Very remote control', p. 10.

[112] UK Border Agency, Entry Clearance Guidelines, 2008, available at www.ukvisas.gov.uk, ch. 1, Annex 7.

nonetheless claims to have 'assisted in preventing nearly 180,000 inadequately documented passengers from boarding planes' in the period 2003–7.[113] Similarly, following the transfer of migration control to the Department of Homeland Security, the United States has expanded its network of Customs and Border Protection Officers at strategic airports. These officers carry out individual checks and interviews but officially do not have legal authority to prevent individuals from boarding. As emphasised by the head of Customs and Border Protection, however, economic penalties for bringing in unauthorised migrants make it 'very likely' that airlines would follow any recommendations by immigration officers.[114] While such situations are unlikely to amount to direct assertions of jurisdiction in the light of the existing case law, they may well, of course, give rise to indirect responsibility as a matter of outsourcing.[115]

In other cases, however, immigration officers exercise authority more directly, and may thus be argued to establish extraterritorial jurisdiction in the personal sense as government agents or consular officers acting abroad. Following a rise in Roma asylum-seekers arriving from the Czech Republic, the United Kingdom in February 2001 negotiated an agreement to install pre-clearance checks at Prague airport, giving posted British immigration officers powers to conduct interviews and grant or deny onward access to the United Kingdom. The scheme gave rise to complaints not only that refusing entry for asylum-seekers was likely to result in *refoulement*, but also that the operation was highly discriminatory in its targeting of Romas.

The case reached the House of Lords. Guy Goodwin-Gill, intervening on behalf of UNHCR, argued that having 'effectively extended its frontiers into the Czech Republic', the United Kingdom exercised jurisdiction and thus had to respect international human rights obligations, including the *non-refoulement* obligation.[116] The House of Lords appears to have been somewhat divided on the jurisdiction issue. The duty to respect the *non-refoulement* obligation was rejected. First, the applicants were not outside their country of origin and thus did not fall within the scope of the Refugee Convention.[117] More generally, Lord Bingham,

---

[113] *Hansard*, HL, vol. 693, col. WA104, 25 June 2007.

[114] Commissioner Robert C. Bonner, 'Remarks on the immigration and security initiative', paper read at Transnational Threats Audit Conference, Washington, DC, 11 February 2004.

[115] See below, chapter 5.

[116] Goodwin-Gill, '*R. v. Immigration Officer at Prague Airport*', paras. 103–6.

[117] *R. (European Roma Rights Centre and Others)* v. *Immigration Officer at Prague Airport and Another*, House of Lords, para. 18. While this argument is valid when considering only

citing *Banković*, expressed 'the very greatest doubt whether the functions performed by the immigration officers at Prague, even though they were formally treated as consular officials, could possibly be said to be an exercise of jurisdiction in any relevant sense over non-UK nationals such as the appellants'.[118]

The appeal was allowed, however, on grounds of racial discrimination. The House of Lords relied mainly on national legislation in this regard, and held that the specific targeting of travellers of Roma origin was contrary to section 1(1)a of the Race Relations Act 1976 (para. 104). Yet consideration was equally given to international human rights treaties, and in particular whether the pre-clearance operation was contrary to Article 26 of the International Covenant on Civil and Political Rights. Lord Steyn specifically held that

> The United Kingdom purported to exercise governmental authority at Prague Airport. The operation carried out at Prague placed the United Kingdom in breach of the International Covenant.[119]

While the concept of jurisdiction is not explicitly discussed, it is clear that the operations were thought to constitute an extraterritorial exercise of 'governmental authority' by the United Kingdom. For the responsibility of the Covenant to be engaged, the applicants would further have to be within the jurisdiction of the United Kingdom as specifically required by Article 2(1).[120]

It is equally hard to reach a conclusive answer from the precedent set by existing international human rights case law. The threshold for establishing extraterritorial jurisdiction over an individual has so far only been met in cases involving full physical control. While there is therefore little doubt that extraterritorial jurisdiction will be established in situations where offshore migration controls entail the detention or otherwise apprehension or confinement of those intercepted, it remains

---

the 1951 Refugee Convention, the House did not consider similar *non-refoulement* obligations arising from other instruments of human rights law, or whether the scheme could be considered a violation of the right to leave under Art. 12 of the International Covenant on Civil and Political Rights. See above, section 4.1, and Hathaway, *Rights of Refugees*, pp. 308–9.

[118] R. *(European Roma Rights Centre and Others) v. Immigration Officer at Prague Airport and Another*, House of Lords, para. 21. Lord Bingham's analysis of the asylum issue was in general agreed to by Baroness Hale (para. 72) and Lord Carswell (para. 108).

[119] Para. 45. Baroness Hale further specifically held the Prague Airport scheme to be in violation of the Covenant on Civil and Political Rights (paras. 98–99).

[120] See above, section 3.6.3.

questionable whether merely carrying out immigration interviews and rejecting onward passage, as was the situation in the *Prague Airport* case, will meet the test set by, for example, *López Burgos*, *Öcalan* and, as a national example, *Al-Skeini*.

Lastly, a particularly vexing question remains as to whether the enforcement of visa requirements is sufficient to bring applicants within the jurisdiction of the imposing state and whether a denial of such visas may consequently amount to a violation of the *non-refoulement* principle and other relevant norms of human rights law. Visas constitute one of the oldest and most widespread tools of extraterritorial migration control.[121] While visa requirements are often justified by reference to general immigration purposes, it is clear that asylum-seekers and refugees are likely to be particularly affected. The EU has introduced common rules requiring visas for nationals of 128 countries, covering most of Africa, Asia and large parts of Central America.[122] A special airport transit visa, limiting the otherwise established principle of free airport transit, is further required for nationals of those countries with particularly high asylum rates.[123] The obstacles presented to asylum-seekers through the visa regime are equally evident in the criteria set out for granting or refusing visas. The Common Consular Instructions direct consular officers to be 'particularly vigilant when dealing with . . . unemployed persons or those with irregular income' and to require supporting documentation in such 'high risk' cases. It should be clear that asylum-seekers are likely to fall into this category and are often unable to produce such documentation.[124]

---

[121] E. Guild, 'Jurisprudence of the ECHR: lessons for the EU asylum policy', in M. C. D. U. de Sousa and P. de Bruycker (eds.), *The Emergence of a European Asylum Policy* (Brussels: Bruylant, 2004), pp. 329–342; Guild, 'The border abroad'; Guiraudon, 'Before the EU border'; Goodwin-Gill, *Refugee in International Law*, 2nd edn, pp. 139–93. Visas were first introduced by the United States in 1924, effectively moving migration control abroad as consular offices became responsible for pre-screening passengers. A. Zolberg, 'Matters of state', in C. Hirschman, P. Kasinitz and J. DeWind (eds.), *The Handbook on International Immigration* (New York: Russell Sage Foundation, 1999), pp. 71–93, at p. 75.

[122] Guild, 'Jurisprudence of the ECHR'. European Council, Regulation (EC) No. 539/2001, 15 March 2001. The list is set out in the Common Consular Instructions on Visas for the Diplomatic Missions and Consular Posts, 2005/C 326/01, 22 December 2005, Annex 1, as amended.

[123] Common Consular Instructions on Visas, Annex 3, as amended. At the time of writing these include Afghanistan, Bangladesh, Democratic Republic of the Congo, Eritrea, Ethiopia, Ghana, Iran, Iraq, Nigeria, Pakistan, Somalia and Sri Lanka. Each member state may require similar visas for nationals of additional countries.

[124] Ibid., Section V. In addition, the cost of the visa itself works to reinforce this point. Whereas an early directive (68/360) relating to the issuing of visas for third-country nationals who are members of the family of Community nationals working in another

There is some support for the notion that visa applicants may under certain circumstances come under the jurisdiction of the granting or denying state. In *W.M. v. Denmark*,[125] seventeen citizens of the then German Democratic Republic (DDR) entered the Danish embassy for the purpose of seeking help to reach the Federal Republic of Germany. After having stayed on the embassy premises for one night, they were handed back to the DDR police and detained. On this basis, the Commission held that the applicants did come within Danish jurisdiction. International law regarding consulates and embassies further provides the sending state with a recognised jurisdictional basis and certain immunities from the jurisdictional competence of the territorial state.[126] From this it could be argued that any asylum-seeker or refugee actually on the premises of an embassy or consulate may come under the jurisdiction of the sending state. As Noll concludes, the denial of a visa may thus in exceptional conditions trigger responsibility under the European Convention on Human Rights, including respect of the *non-refoulement* requirement that flows from Article 3.[127]

In general, however, granting or denying a visa, even if conducted directly by consular or embassy agents, has seldom been considered sufficient to constitute *refoulement*.[128] Merely refusing a visa does not necessarily provide a sufficient causal link to any future violation of the *non-refoulement* principle,[129] and visa controls in general thus seem to have been accepted as legitimate measures even by UNHCR.[130] The enforcement of visa requirements may on the other hand lead to *refoulement*. Yet

---

Community country specifically required that such visas be issued free of charge, the price of a Schengen visa is currently €60.00. Guild, 'The border abroad', p. 89.

[125] *W.M. v. Denmark.*

[126] Noll, 'Seeking asylum at embassies', 567.

[127] In his analysis, however, Noll considers that responsibility only emerges as far as a positive duty to protect can be deduced in regard to the specific right violated. Ibid., 567, 569–70. See also section 4.5.

[128] Hathaway, *Rights of Refugees*, p. 310; Goodwin-Gill, *Refugee in International Law*, 2nd edn, p. 252.

[129] Even though jurisdiction was established in *W.M. v. Denmark*, the European Commission of Human Rights did not consequently find that the handing over of the applicant to DDR police and subsequent detention amounted to any violation of Convention rights attributable to Denmark, and the case was thus declared inadmissible *ratione materiae*.

[130] UNHCR, Interception of Asylum-Seekers and Refugees: The International Framework and Recommendations for a Comprehensive Approach, UN Doc. EC/50/SC/CRP.17, 9 June 2000, para. 17. See further discussion in Hathaway, *Rights of Refugees*, p. 311. Noll, however, maintains that in the instances where such a causal link between the rejection of a visa and a high risk of subjecting such applicants to a situation of persecution, torture or other ill-treatment is evident, an obligation under, e.g., Art. 3 of

the denial of onward travel to an asylum-seeker because of lack of a visa will in most cases either take place when the asylum-seeker arrives at the border of the destination state or will be enforced by migration authorities of the territorial state and private carrier companies which, for fear of being fined, take on control functions pre-departure.[131]

Further, the claim for extraterritorial jurisdiction is likely to diminish where visa processing is conducted outside embassies and consulates.[132] A number of states today require visa applicants to go and submit applications at visa application centres operated by private contractors, thus simultaneously moving visa processing away from member state embassies and outsourcing it in part to non-state agents.[133] The EU has further tabled plans for common visa application centres, including the possibility of private companies obtaining and forwarding visa applications.[134] Visa controls may, lastly, operate entirely passively, with no need for the state to establish its presence extraterritorially. In these cases visa applications may be handled, for example, by the consulates of a third state or be submitted online.

In sum, moving migration control on to the territory or into territorial waters of another state complicates the jurisdictional assessment. The existing case law appears to balance opposing concerns, between universal responsibility for extraterritorially acting states and a continued emphasis on principles of national sovereignty and primacy of the territorial jurisdiction. The result is an increasing difficulty in attaining legal clarity in terms of the exact reach of international refugee and human rights law, as quickly becomes apparent when considering different scenarios for extraterritorial migration control. A further complicating factor arises as control practices within foreign territorial jurisdictions show a growing overlap between situations where states act extraterritorially

the European Convention on Human Rights may arise. Noll, 'Seeking asylum at embassies', 564–70.

[131] The question of attributed state responsibility in regard to migration control carried out by carriers is discussed in chapter 5.

[132] Noll, 'Seeking asylum at embassies', 568.

[133] Guild, 'Jurisprudence of the ECHR', p. 39. Australia, the United States, the United Kingdom and several other EU member states thus require visa applicants in a range of countries to go through visa application centres operated by commercial partners such as VFS Global. At the time of writing, VFS Global facilitated visa applications for thirty-one countries and operated visa application centres in forty-six countries. See www.vfsglobal.com.

[134] European Commission, Draft Proposal for a Regulation of the European Parliament and of the Council Establishing a Community Code on Visas, COM(2006) 403, 19 July 2006, Arts. 37 and 38.

in their own capacity, and varying degrees of delegation or outsourcing to private actors or the authorities of the territorial state in question.

4.3.4 Jurisdiction and human smuggling

In addition to the geographical dimension, the jurisdictional assessment has been argued to change as interception activities relate to other areas of international law. This concerns, first, the still growing legal framework concerning human smuggling and trafficking.[135] Under the Protocol against Human Smuggling on Land, Sea and Air, states may intercept vessels on the high seas following consultation with the flag state if there is reason to suspect that the vessel is engaged in the smuggling of migrants, thereby superseding the otherwise established norm prohibiting states from boarding or obstructing passage for vessels flying the flag, and thus subject to the jurisdiction, of another state.[136]

These instruments have been referred to as legal basis by several countries engaged in extraterritorial migration control. Italy has thus argued that the return of migrants to Libya and Algeria was in conformity with the UN Convention against Transnational Organized Crime and the Protocol against the Smuggling of Migrants.[137]

While the Protocol may indeed provide a legal basis for intercepting and boarding, it does not, however, relieve states of their *non-refoulement* obligations under international human rights and refugee law. On the contrary, Article 19(1) of the Protocol explicitly states that

Nothing in this Protocol shall affect the other rights, obligations and responsibilities of States and individuals under international law, including international humanitarian law and, in particular, where applicable, the 1951 Convention and the 1967 Protocol relating to the Status of Refugees and the principle of *non-refoulement* as contained therein.

4.3.5 Extraterritorial jurisdiction and bilateral agreements

A second issue to consider is whether the assessment of extraterritorial jurisdiction changes where bilateral treaties or other agreements establish that one or the other state holds jurisdiction. Compared with interdiction on the high seas, the majority of migration control carried out within

---

[135] See in particular the 2000 UN Convention against Transnational Organized Crime and the associated Protocol against Human Smuggling on Land, Sea and Air and Protocol to Suppress and Punish Trafficking in Persons, Especially Women and Children.

[136] Smuggling Protocol, Art. 19, and similarly Trafficking Protocol, Art. 14. See further the 1958 Geneva Convention on the Territorial Sea and the Contiguous Zone, Art. 19.

[137] UNHCR, Submission by the Office of the United Nations High Commissioner for Refugees in the Case of *Hirsi and Others* v. *Italy*, March 2010, para. 2(1)(1).

foreign territory or territorial waters is specifically governed by political, administrative or treaty-based arrangements setting out the powers and competences of the extraterritorially acting state. As part of the HERA Frontex operation, Spain has thus signed memoranda of understanding with Senegal and Mauritania to bring on board Senegalese and Mauritanian immigration officers for interceptions carried out in their respective territorial waters.[138]

This sort of arrangement, commonly referred to as a 'shiprider' agreement, is well known in the field of maritime policing for combating drug smuggling, but also finds several precedents in regard to illegal migration. In 1997 Italy and Albania signed a protocol to interdict migrants in international waters and Albanian waters, and to bring Albanian officials on board two Italian naval vessels.[139] Similarly, under the 2003 interdiction agreement between the United States and the Dominican Republic, each country brought officials on board the other's vessels carrying out patrols in their respective territorial waters.[140]

How do such agreements affect the establishment of extraterritorial jurisdiction? Drawing a reference to the notion of extraterritorial jurisdiction in general public international law, one could on the one hand argue that extraterritorial jurisdiction for the purpose of human rights responsibility in some instances would flow from these arrangements themselves. In *Banković*, the European Court of Human Rights did emphasise that in cases such as *Xhavara*, 'common jurisdiction was established by written agreement'.[141] It is less evident, however, looking at the case itself, that this was the deciding factor. Since little comparable case law is available, it may be safer to argue that pre-established agreements between the territorial and the acting states may constitute part of the assessment when positively establishing extraterritorial jurisdictional claims and, more importantly, indirect responsibility in cases of outsourcing. It

---

[138] J. Rijpma, 'Building borders: the regulatory framework for the management of the external border of the European Union', doctoral dissertation, European University Institute, Florence, 2009, pp. 341–2.

[139] Protocol Between Italy and Albania to Prevent Certain Illegal Acts and Render Humanitarian Assistance to Those Leaving Albania, 2 April, *Gazzetta Ufficiale della Repubblica Italiana*, No. 163, 15 July 1997. See further D. Guilfoyle, *Shipping Interdiction and the Law of the Sea* (Cambridge University Press, 2009), p. 210.

[140] Agreement between the Government of the United States of America and the Government of the Dominican Republic Concerning Cooperation in Maritime Migration Law Enforcement 2003, KAV 6187. Guilfoyle, *Shipping Interdiction*, p. 196.

[141] *Banković*, para. 37.

should be remembered, however, that in most cases concerning migration control, such agreements are not readily available or are conducted more informally, perhaps exactly to avoid public scrutiny. Furthermore, if the very purpose of carrying out controls in foreign territory or territorial waters is to shift jurisdictional responsibility, such agreements are unlikely to contain clauses or provisions explicitly acknowledging jurisdiction of the extraterritorially acting state.[142]

In the above examples, bilateral agreements even seem intended to distance responsibility further from the interdicting state. Shiprider agreements may in this sense be used to argue not only that migration control takes place in foreign territorial waters, but also that the authority to deny onward passage is legally placed with the authorities of the territorial state. Under the United States–Dominican Republic Migrant Agreement any boarding, search and seizure may thus only be performed by officials in whose territorial waters interdiction takes place.

Whether shiprider agreements may be used as a pretext to shift obligations as a matter of refugee and human rights law is more questionable. As long as the intercepting vessel sails under, for example, Spanish flag and command, Spain arguably retains effective control on board. Bilateral agreements or shipriders do not appear to change much in this regard. In *Xhavara*, the European Court of Human Rights held that since the Albanian ship sank as a direct consequence of the collision with the Italian warship, Italy held sole jurisdiction: the Italian–Albanian Agreement 'cannot, by itself, engage the responsibility of the State under the Convention for any action taken by Italian authorities in the implementation of this agreement'.[143] The European Court of Human Rights further considered the impact of bilateral agreements when establishing extraterritorial jurisdiction in *Al-Saadoon and Mufdhi*.[144] The applicants were both detained by UK forces in Iraq, and complained that their transfer to the Iraqi authorities would constitute *refoulement* in relation to Article 2, as there was a serious risk that they would be subjected to the death penalty. The United Kingdom for its part argued that it had a legal obligation to transfer them to the Iraqi authorities, since UK forces were operating in

---

[142] So far, Frontex has thus denied access to the co-operation agreements signed between e.g. Spain, on the one hand, and Senegal and Mauritania, on the other, that were the legal basis for the Frontex HERA operations to prevent migrants from reaching the Canary Islands. See further Rijpma, 'Building borders', pp. 341–2.

[143] *Xhavara and Others v. Italy and Albania*, p. 4 (author's translation of the French text).

[144] *Al-Saadoon and Mufdhi v. United Kingdom*, European Court of Human Rights, Application No. 61498/08, 2 March 2010.

Iraq subject to a memorandum of understanding also establishing Iraqi overall jurisdiction.

The Court on the one hand recalled its previous jurisprudence that 'the Convention should be interpreted as far as possible in harmony with other principles of international law . . . [and] . . . recognises the importance of international cooperation'.[145] Yet immediately afterwards it goes on to emphasise the 'special character of the Convention as a treaty for the collective enforcement of human rights and fundamental freedoms' in guiding interpretation (para. 127), and then concludes that

> a Contracting Party is responsible under Article 1 of the Convention for all acts and omissions of its organs regardless of whether the act or omission in question was a consequence of domestic law or of the necessity to comply with international legal obligations. Article 1 makes no distinction as to the type of rule or measure concerned and does not exclude any part of the Contracting Party's 'jurisdiction' from scrutiny under the Convention. (para. 128)

In other words, the fact that a subsequent treaty or other agreement has been signed shifting jurisdiction or requiring that intercepted persons are handed over to the territorial state does not affect Convention liability. This conclusion further seems to follow naturally from the criteria on which extraterritorial jurisdiction is established. As noted above, for the purpose of human rights responsibility, extraterritorial jurisdiction does not rely on legal entitlements or competence but on factual control and exercise of authority.[146] While shiprider or other bilateral agreements may be taken into account in the assessment of the degree of control exercised by the extraterritorially acting state, they cannot serve to trade away human rights obligations at will.

Where the relationship of authority between territorial and extraterritorially acting states is turned around, however, the jurisdictional assessment may potentially differ. The operation of joint interception patrols by Libya and Italy has thus seen Italy supplying interception vessels to Libya, operating under the Libyan flag but with a shiprider agreement allowing Italian officials on board.[147] While it is somewhat unclear exactly what kind of authority the Italian authorities exercise on board, the case

---

[145] Para. 126. See further *Al-Adsani v. United Kingdom*, European Court of Human Rights, Application No. 35763/97, 21 November 2001, para. 55; *Banković*, para. 55; *Bosphorus Airways v. Ireland*, European Court of Human Rights, Application No. 45036/98, 30 June 2005, para. 150.

[146] Milanovic, 'From compromise to principle', pp. 422–26.

[147] 'Italy, Libya sign deal for joint patrol of Libyan coasts against illegal immigration', *International Herald Tribune*, 29 December 2007, available at www.iht.com. On the

for establishing direct Italian jurisdiction is likely to be somewhat more difficult.

The above example may be part of a more general trend where practices to shift migration control to third-country territories may perhaps equally be characterised as processes of outsourcing or delegation rather than merely offshore or extraterritorialisation. For the purpose of determining extraterritorial legal obligations, this raises a number of additional challenges. Establishing the international responsibility of states aiding and abetting other states or directing or instructing a private party in committing acts violating international refugee law introduces a question of attribution in addition to that of jurisdiction. Moreover, when the actual practices are examined, clearly characterising a particular situation as the one or the other easily becomes difficult, and creative labelling itself in some instances seems to be a strategy for avoiding correlated human rights obligations.

While the involvement or complete outsourcing of migration control to the authorities or another state may weaken claims for extraterritorial jurisdiction, it does not mean, however, that responsibility is simply shifted. In such cases, recourse may be had to, for example, the International Law Commission's Articles on State Responsibility.[148] As a general principle of international law a state may thus be held internationally responsible for the act of another state if it 'aids or assists' these acts,[149] 'directs and controls' them,[150] or 'coerces' the state into committing them.[151]

4.3.6 Jurisdiction and rescue at sea

Lastly, the shift towards carrying out interception in international waters may complicate the jurisdictional assessment as interdiction activities are increasingly intermingled with situations of distress at sea, thereby

---

history of Italian–Libyan co-operation in this area see further Lutterbeck, 'Policing migration in the Mediterranean'; Lavenex, 'Shifting up and out'.

[148] A full analysis of state responsibility in cases where migration control is outsourced to third states is outside the scope of the present work. However, the next chapter investigates situations where migration control is wholly or partly outsourced to non-state actors; for a discussion of the general relevance of the ILC Articles in human rights cases see section 5.5. See also Crawford, *International Law Commission's Articles*, pp. 58–60.

[149] Art. 16.   [150] Art. 17.

[151] Art. 18. In all instances it is, however, a requirement that the first state has knowledge of the act in question and that the act is equally considered an international wrong by that state.

triggering the legal framework of search and rescue (SAR) under the law of the sea. In practice, interception operations may quickly change to a situation of search and rescue. The condition of many vessels setting off to Lampedusa, the Florida Keys or Ashmore Islands is often deplorable, and over the last decades more than 10,000 refugees and migrants have died trying to cross the Mediterranean.[152] In addition, the actual encounter between intercepting and migrant vessels may provoke capsizing, either deliberately as migrants seek to provoke a rescue operation, or involuntarily if the weight of those on board the often overcrowded ships shifts too much to one side.[153]

The international search and rescue regime itself represents a notable exception to the territoriality principle in imposing duties on all coastal and seafaring states, not only within their territorial waters but also on the high seas and in foreign territorial waters. Under the UN Convention on the Law of Sea, every state must require the master of a vessel flying its flag to 'render assistance to any person found at sea in danger of being lost' and 'to proceed with all possible speed to the rescue of persons in distress, if informed of their need of assistance'.[154] Beyond imposing an obligation on both official and private vessels to rescue anyone encountered in distress, coastal states further have a positive duty to maintain 'an adequate and effective search and rescue service' and to ensure co-ordination of search and rescue operations.[155]

---

[152] The number is based on press reviews and as such is somewhat uncertain. 'Immigrants dead at the frontiers of Europe', Fortress Europe, L'Osservatorio sulle Vittime Del'Immigratizione, 14 January 2010, available at http://fortresseurope.blogspot.com. A somewhat lower number of 6,404 drowning deaths for the period 1993–2007 is reported by UNITED, 'The deadly consequences of "Fortress Europe"', Information Leaflet No. 24, May 2009. It should be noted that reinforcement of controls and expansion of interception may in themselves bear part of the blame for such loss of life. As the risk of getting caught on the shorter or easier crossings increases, many find themselves forced to take longer and more dangerous routes. Legomsky, 'USA and the Caribbean interdiction programme'; Lutterbeck, 'Policing migration in the Mediterranean'; Pugh, 'Drowning not waving'.

[153] Interview with Spanish naval captain, Las Palmas, 23 April 2007.

[154] United Nations Convention on the Law of the Sea (UNCLOS), Art. 98(1), and 1974 International Convention on the Safety of Life at Sea (SOLAS), Chapter V, Regulations 10(a) and 33. This entails a positive duty on flag states to adopt domestic legislation that imposes penalties on shipmasters who ignore or fail to provide assistance. In practice, however, many states have failed to do so and enforcement is difficult. Pugh, 'Drowning not waving'; S. Cacciaguidi-Fahy, 'The Law of the Sea and Human Rights', (2007) 19 *Sri Lanka Journal of International Law* 85–107.

[155] UNCLOS, Art. 98(2).

In order to ensure co-ordination, the Maritime Safety Committee has divided the world's oceans into thirteen search and rescue areas. In each region, the states affected are responsible for negotiating individual search and rescue areas, effectively partitioning responsibility for the high seas along geographic lines, within which each coastal state is responsible for co-ordinating search and rescue operations.[156]

While few states have challenged the existence of the basic duty to render assistance to persons in distress at sea, other issues as to the division of responsibilities remain contested. In particular, the search and rescue regime has been marred by the lack of clear rules for deciding where rescued persons should be put ashore and of an explicit obligation for states to allow disembarkation. This became a particularly problematic issue following the rise of 'boat people' in the 1970s, which made states concerned that asylum processing and protection responsibilities would follow from the hitherto relatively straightforward issue of the disembarkation and subsequent return to their country of origin of sailors rescued at sea. This has led to a number of stand-offs in which coastal states, flag states of the rescuing vessel and states of next port of call have all argued against taking responsibility themselves.[157]

In 2004, amendments were made to the 1979 Convention on Maritime Search and Rescue and the 1974 International Convention for the Safety

---

[156] The considerable requirements imposed on coastal states to set up installations and take on SAR obligations has, however, meant that development of regional SAR plans has been slow and still lacking in several regions.

[157] Kneebone, 'Pacific plan'; R. Barnes, 'Refugee law at sea', (2004) 53 *International and Comparative Law Quarterly* 47–77; Pugh, 'Drowning not waving'.

   An example of such a stand-off is the '*Budafel*' incident. In May 2007, the Maltese tugboat *Budafel* discovered twenty-seven migrants clinging to a floating tuna pen some 60 miles off the coast of Libya. The migrants, all men, had set off from the Libyan port of Al Zwarah nine days earlier and came from various countries including Ghana, Ivory Coast, Niger, Nigeria, Senegal and Sudan. On their sixth day at sea they had come across the tuna pen and managed to leave their waterlogged boat and hold on to a 50 cm-wide walkway and some buoys holding up the net. When the master of the *Budafel* found them twenty-four hours later he alerted the Maltese maritime authorities; from here on a diplomatic stand-off ensued. The Maltese authorities refused to let the *Budafel* tow the migrants to Malta since they had been encountered in international waters, 23 nautical miles outside Malta's search and rescue (SAR) area. Instead they alerted the Libyan authorities, asking them to respond to the incident, arguing that the migrants had been found within the Libyan SAR area. Libya for its part did not see fit to launch a rescue operation intercepting the tuna pen, and has long contested the SAR area divisions and embarkation obligations. An Italian naval vessel rescued the twenty-seven migrants only after three days of clinging to the tuna pen, and brought them to the Italian immigration centre on Lampedusa. Consiglio Italiano per i Rifugiati, Report Regarding Recent Search and Rescue Operations in the Mediterranean, 1 June 2007.

of Life at Sea (SOLAS), attempting to clarify, among other things, disembarkation responsibilities.[158] The amended annex to the SAR Convention reads,

The Party responsible for the search and rescue region in which such assistance is rendered shall exercise primary responsibility for ensuring that such co-ordination and co-operation occurs, so that survivors assisted are disembarked from the assisting ship and delivered to a place of safety, taking into account the particular circumstances of the case and guidelines developed by the [International Maritime] Organization.[159]

This formulation arguably falls short of explicitly setting out and imposing on each coastal state an ultimate responsibility to receive rescued persons. While there has been some disagreement as to the exact meaning of 'primary responsibility' in this context, the dominant view among states seems to be that disembarkation responsibilities thereby follow the geographic SAR area divisions, if no other state offers itself.[160]

While these amendments have broadly been celebrated as closing a vital gap in the search and rescue regime, they may at the same time be seen to provide a legal pretext for shifting asylum and refugee protection obligations. As interdiction schemes are increasingly moved into foreign search and rescue areas, the argument has been put forward that any persons rescued should be disembarked there and any concomitant protection issues similarly addressed by the state in whose SAR area rescue took place.[161] The potential for jurisdiction shopping in such instances is

---

[158] The amendments to both conventions were adopted by the International Maritime Organization in 2004 and entered into force on 1 July 2006. See Maritime Safety Committee, 78/26/Add. 1, Annex 3 and 5 respectively.

[159] Para. 3(1)(9). Similar wording occurs in para. 1(1) of the SOLAS Convention. See further Maritime Safety Committee, Guidelines on the Treatment of Persons Rescued at Sea, IMO Resolution MSC.167(78), 20 May 2004, para. 2(5).

[160] As emphasised by the IMO Facilitation Committee,

If disembarkation from the rescuing ship cannot be arranged swiftly elsewhere, the Government responsible for the SAR area should accept the disembarkation of the persons rescued in accordance with immigration laws and regulations of each Member State into a place of safety under its control in which the persons can have timely access to post rescue support. (International Maritime Organization, Principles Relating to Administrative Procedures for Disembarking Persons Rescued at Sea, FAL.3/Circ. 194, 22 January 2009, para. 2(3))

[161] The *Budafel* incident mentioned above is a case in point. EU guidelines on the matter even emphasise that for persons rescued on the high seas 'priority should be given to disembarkation in the third country from where the persons departed or through the territorial waters or search and rescue region of [sic] which the persons transited'.

exacerbated by the fact that none of the maritime conventions provide a solid definition of what constitutes 'distress'.[162] Instead, the master of the intercepting vessel has authority to evaluate whether a vessel is in need of rescue or is merely unseaworthy by modern standards.[163]

Yet, from a refugee and human rights perspective, it is unclear that the existence of a search and rescue situation ought substantially to affect the jurisdictional assessment in the case of asylum-seekers. Defining a situation as a rescue operation does not legally supersede any direct responsibilities vis-à-vis asylum-seekers on behalf of the acting state. The conventions in question do not deal specifically with asylum or protection issues. As such, there is no reason to think that states are relieved of protection obligations or referred to *lex specialis* in this regard when carrying out rescue operations. Given the above case law, and especially when taking rescued persons on board government vessels, there is a strong presumption that any such rescue operation would engage the jurisdiction of the acting state. Even if responsibility is thus subsequently transferred to the state in whose search and rescue area asylum-seekers have been picked up, an indirect responsibility thus remains to avoid chain-*refoulement*.[164] The guidelines adopted by the Maritime Safety Committee of the International Maritime Organization similarly emphasise that consideration should be given to avoid 'disembarkation in territories where the lives and freedoms of those alleging a well-founded fear of

---

Council of the European Union, Council Decision Supplementing the Schengen Borders Code as Regards the Surveillance of the Sea External Borders in the Context of Operational Co-operation Co-ordinated by Frontex, 2010/252/EU, 26 April 2010, Part II, 2(1).

[162] Pugh, 'Drowning not waving', 58.

[163] This has led some countries to apply a narrower definition of what constitutes distress in order to avoid taking on rescue operations or to shift the responsibility to neighbouring states. Malta, which has a particularly large SAR area covering 250,000 sq km, has thus been reported as encouraging migrant vessels to carry on towards Italy and supplying them with water and gas. According to a senior officer of the Armed Forces of Malta, 'distress' is defined as 'the imminent danger of loss of lives, so if they are sinking it is distress. If they are not sinking it is not distress.' S. Klepp, 'A double bind: Malta and rescue of unwanted migrants at sea', paper presented at Exploratory Workshop: The Human Costs of Border Control in the Context of EU Maritime Migration Systems, Vreije University, Amsterdam, 25–27 October 2009, p. 7; T. Gammeltoft-Hansen and T. Aalberts, 'Sovereignty at sea: the law and politics of saving lives in the *Mare Liberum*', DIIS Working Paper 2010/18, Danish Institute for International Studies, 2010.

[164] Fischer-Lescano and Löhr, *Border Control at Sea*, p. 40; Weinzierl, *Border Management and Human Rights*, p. 6; *Soering*.

persecution would be threatened'.[165] Lastly, UNHCR's Executive Committee has reaffirmed the continued applicability of protection norms, including both *non-refoulement* and non-penalisation, when states act under search and rescue rules or to combat human smuggling.[166]

In practice, however, it seems that the amalgamation of interception and search and rescue activities easily makes questions regarding refugee protection a secondary consideration. By referring solely to the legal regime surrounding search and rescue, any protection burden may be shifted away from the acting state and responsibilities assigned according to territorial or zone divisions as agreed among the states in the region.[167] Despite the fact that Libya is not a signatory to the 1951 Refugee Convention, both Malta and Italy have in several cases claimed that responsibility for disembarking persons rescued within the Libyan SAR area rested solely with Libya, and no considerations were seemingly made as to any protection issues.

While emphasising the disembarkation responsibilities of the state in whose search and rescue area measures take place is likely to be the most practical solution to the long-standing issue of disembarkation, it may, however, also serve as a pretext for burden shifting, and in some cases it carries a high likelihood of *refoulement*.

4.4 Double standards and jurisdiction shopping in the area of migration control

The above analysis set out to examine how the concept of 'jurisdiction' is applied in three distinct spheres. For situations involving excision of territory and claims of non-responsibility in 'international zones' the case law is so far unequivocal. States are not free to withdraw jurisdiction from certain parts of their territory and, even in cases where effective control is doubtful, the presumption of jurisdiction may remain based on de jure sovereignty. In the second sphere – state actions undertaken on the high seas or in *terrae nullius* – the approach to jurisdiction has been quite different. The emphasis has not been on testing effective control *strictu sensu*, but on establishing a meaningful jurisdictional link based on the actual relation between the state and the individual in the specific situation and

---

[165] Maritime Safety Committee, Guidelines, para. 6(17).
[166] UNHCR Executive Committee, Protection Safeguards in Interception Measures, Conclusion No. 97 (LIV) (2003). See also Conclusions No. 23 (XXXII) and No. 20 (XXXI).
[167] Noll, 'Politics of saving lives', p. 5.

in regard to the rights violation in question. The interpretation in these cases seems to apply a somewhat broader, functional concept of extraterritorial jurisdiction in which the guiding principle is a concern to avoid 'double standards'.

For cases where extraterritorial actions occur within the realm of another territorial sovereign, yet another approach is taken. In this sphere the two lenses applied above are seemingly combined. The aim of avoiding a 'gap or vacuum in human rights protection'[168] in such situations remains, yet it is tempered by the conflicting concern that stresses territoriality as the primary basis for establishing jurisdiction. The result is the exceedingly abstract 'effective control' test employed in cases such as *Banković*. In this line of reasoning, jurisdiction is neither taken as a given nor necessarily linked to the question of state responsibility. Instead, it becomes a separate test in which the conflicting basis for territorial jurisdiction has to be overcome in order for the 'exceptional' situation of extraterritorial jurisdiction to materialise.[169]

Just as in the doctrinal approach to enforcement jurisdiction under public international law, the human rights case law as regards extraterritorial jurisdiction is driven by a strong desire to avoid overlapping or competing claims to jurisdiction by several states. For situations involving extraterritorial control over a geographical area, this conflict is easier to resolve, as a sufficient degree of structural and/or military authority would normally exclude the possibility of similar control being exercised by the territorial state within that area. In cases involving control or power exercised over an individual, the test becomes more difficult. The personal notion of jurisdiction does not exclude the presence of a territorial state holding simultaneous jurisdiction. Yet, from the existing case law, the result seems to be a retreat to a micro-variation of the territorial interpretation. Extraterritorial jurisdiction in these cases has so far only been established when the individual is under the exclusive and full physical control of the extraterritorially acting state, which in practice is likely to nullify any competing authority in regard to human rights violations occurring. Anything short of this threshold by default falls within the jurisdiction of the territorial state.

From the perspective of the refugee and other human rights victims, the regrettable thing about this jurisprudence is that it effectively ends up doing exactly what it set out to avoid. A double standard is clearly created, whereby states apparently remain free to engage in human rights

---

[168] *Cyprus v. Turkey*, para. 78.   [169] *Banković*, paras. 59–61.

violations on foreign soil that would in principle entail responsibility if similar conduct occurred at home and probably also if carried out on the high seas. In so doing, the jurisprudence on extraterritorial jurisdiction retains a structural incentive for states to engage in offshore migration control.

By shifting control to the territory or territorial waters of third states a space is carved out where the sovereign prerogative to control entry into its territory may be asserted without the constraints ordinarily posed by refugee and human rights law. In the process, correlated protection obligations otherwise owed are either deconstructed or at best shifted to third states. Contrary to classical assumptions, the regulatory capacity and power to enforce migration control seem to expand the further these acts are removed from the territory, as the link between the de facto exercise of sovereign powers and the de jure responsibilities assumed to flow from these is strategically breached.

Notably, this move is premised on exactly the same principles that cement a state's protection obligations within its own territory. As migration control is extraterritorialised, the sovereignty and territorial jurisdiction of another state is invoked, which in turn creates an initial presumption against jurisdiction of the acting state. This is the core dynamic behind what may be characterised as a growing trend towards 'jurisdiction shopping' in the field of migration control. The more resourceful and traditional asylum countries increasingly negotiate access to carry out control within the territory of foreign states who, in turn, commercialise their sovereignty either for threats of sanctions or positive concessions – most often a combination of both.[170]

The analysis above identifies several other dynamics which achieve the same or a similar effect. Common to these moves is that, by shifting migration control further from state territory both geographically and conceptually, control may be asserted more unconstrainedly, de jure or de facto.

The first of these concerns strategies to nationally deregulate parts of the sovereign territory, typically border zones, offshore locations or

---

[170] F. Pastore, 'Aeneas' Route – Euro-Mediterranean relations and international migration', in S. Lavenex and E. M. Ucarer (eds.), *Migration and the Externalities of European Integration* (Lanham: Lexington Books, 2002), pp. 105–123; Lutterbeck, 'Policing migration in the Mediterranean'; Gammeltoft-Hansen, 'Outsourcing migration management'; Lavenex, 'Shifting up and out'; J. Niessen and Y. Schibel, 'International migration and relations with third countries: European and US approaches', MPG Occasional Paper, Migration Policy Group, Berlin, May 2004.

airports. What is created here is in effect a separate regulatory jurisdiction as a matter of domestic law, in which procedural and/or substantive protection guarantees are deliberately reduced compared with those applicable to asylum-seekers who manage to launch their claim from within the 'territory proper' of the state in question. Just as the tax-free zones of most international airports are meant to attract international currency, special migration zones operating in the same physical space are intended as a disincentive to asylum claims and a lowering of the cost associated with processing them through the application of, for example, 'manifestly unfounded' procedures. While such arrangements remain a legal fiction from the perspective of international law, the differentiation of national legislation may serve to approximate treatment to the very minimum of obligations owed under international refugee and human rights law and reduce the legal safeguards and procedural rights that in practice ensure their fulfilment.

The same logic applies to situations where migration control is moved to the high seas. While this jurisdictional move is unlikely to relieve states of jurisdictional obligations under international law, it may equally reduce obligations under domestic law and further open up a strategy for shifting protection obligations by shifting legal regimes. The definition of search and rescue zones represents in effect a remapping of the *res communis* for the purpose of dividing disembarkation responsibilities along geographical boundaries. Even though the implications of the recent amendments to the SAR and SOLAS Conventions as regards disembarkation remain disputed and some states continue to challenge SAR area divisions, they still serve as a basis for intercepting states to argue that persons 'rescued' in foreign search and rescue zones do not have a protection claim in regard to the acting state. In cases where the state in whose search and rescue area operations take place accepts this argument, this can be seen as an expansion of the notion of jurisdiction shopping, as protection obligations are in practice shifted – despite the conclusion above that rescuing states retain jurisdictional human rights obligations when operating on the high seas. In cases where the SAR state in question does not accept this argument, the result is likely to be an impasse which operates to the detriment of the wellbeing and safety of migrants and asylum-seekers.

The practices described in this chapter have been characterised by some commentators as being 'outside the law' or creating a 'legal vacuum'. While evocative, these descriptions are strictly speaking incorrect. What this analysis has attempted to elucidate is that it is exactly through law that extraterritorial migration control becomes a feasible and attractive strategy for states keen to avoid protection responsibilities. It is the invocation of principles of national sovereignty and the primacy of territorial jurisdiction that establish the presumption against extraterritorial obligations in cases where migration control is carried out within foreign jurisdictions. Similarly, it is by reference to the Law of the Sea and related rules on search and rescue that intercepting states argue for shifting disembarkation and protection responsibilities to the state in whose search and rescue zone operations take place. Practices of extraterritorial migration control in this sense are not about moving outside the law, neither are they a question of non-compliance but, on the contrary, they demonstrate the employment of creative strategies to shift refugee and human rights responsibilities within the structures afforded by international law.

Furthermore, it must be remembered that since jurisdiction shopping is realised precisely by reference to the jurisdiction and obligations of another state, the result is not necessarily a protection vacuum. Rather, human rights and protection responsibilities in principle remain with the territorial state. In practice, however, this shifting of protection obligations raises a number of additional questions and concerns. Not only may certain rights not be realised in this transfer; as discussed in chapter 2 the content and extent of these obligations may substantially change as well.

4.5 Towards a functional reading of extraterritorial jurisdiction?

The above has attempted to present an analysis based on a doctrinal approach and an interpretation of the international human rights jurisprudence as it stands at present. Nonetheless, as is also evident above, somewhat different readings continue to be put forward, and state practices denying extraterritorial jurisdiction both on the high seas and especially within third territory or territorial waters are still common. On a more general level, the debate regarding when states exercise extraterritorial jurisdiction is ongoing and has implications far beyond the issue of offshore migration control. Court cases to do with human rights responsibility during military missions abroad or responsibility when detaining suspected terrorists at Guantánamo or at secret detention facilities in third countries are likely to mark the resolution of this trench warfare, where opposing arguments grounded in universalism and territorialism continue to provide ample cannon fodder.

As such, the dominant reading may well change and develop. Not only has the *Banković* ruling been severely criticised, some scholars argue that we may already be seeing the contours of a jurisprudence deviating from the strict 'effective controls' test.[171] At least in a few cases, the European Court of Human Rights does seem to have applied what might be identified as a more functional test, even in cases concerning extraterritorial jurisdiction within the territory of another state. In *Issa*, the Court argued that the question of jurisdiction was too closely linked to the facts of the case and thus reserved it for the merits stage.[172] More expressly, *Andreou* seems to accept the cause and effect approach to jurisdiction explicitly denied in *Banković*. The case concerned Turkish authorities positioned behind the border but shooting down a demonstrator inside the UN-controlled demilitarised zone. In this case the European Court of Human Rights held that 'even though the applicant sustained her injuries in territory over which Turkey exercised no control, the opening of fire on the crowd from close range, which was the direct and immediate cause of those injuries, was such that the applicant must be regarded as within the jurisdiction of Turkey'.[173]

Furthermore, some scholars have suggested that offshore migration control, as an extension of essentially territorial, or *ad*-territorial, activities, lends itself particularly well to a jurisdictional approach based on functionalist criteria:

Border control measures, wherever they are carried out, have a functional territorial reference point since they are linked to the enforcement of state jurisdiction. This factually substantiated territorial reference significantly relativises extraterritoriality and means that sovereign measures linked to border control activities fall within the ECHR's scope.[174]

---

[171] Cerone, 'Out of bounds?', pp. 14–19; R. Lawson, 'Moving beyond *Banković*: the gradually expanding reach of the European Convention on Human Rights', paper presented at International Society for Military Law and the Law of War XVIIth Congress, Scheveningen, 16–21 May, 2006; Loucaides, 'Determining the extra-territorial effect'; Mantouvalou, 'Extending judicial control', 159.

[172] *Issa and Others v. Turkey*, para. 74.

[173] *Georgia Andreou v. Turkey*, European Court of Human Rights, Application No. 45653/99, 3 June 2008 (Admissibility), p. 11. It could, of course, be contended that this case should be considered an example of 'extraterritorial-effect jurisdiction', as the soldier firing was within Turkish jurisdiction. Yet, unlike in *Soering*, the applicant and human rights victim was not within Turkish jurisdiction. Importantly, the reasoning of the Court did not emphasise the act of shooting or the Turkish soldier as the jurisdictional base, but instead declared that by its actions, Turkey had brought the applicant within its jurisdiction.

[174] Fischer-Lescano and Löhr, *Border Control at Sea*, p. 29.

However, when a functional approach to extraterritorial jurisdiction has yet to gain a secure foothold, it may point back to a more fundamental inability of legal interpretation in this field to escape principles of national sovereignty. For the purpose of jurisdiction this seems to entail at least two dogmas. First, jurisdiction is conceived to be *exclusive*. This can be derived from the *Lotus* quotation, above, establishing the principle *par in parem non habet imperium* – a state has no authority within another state. Regardless of the fact that in most situations of extraterritorial migration control permission is granted by the territorial state, the jurisdiction case law seems adamant about avoiding conflicting claims. As a result, the test of effective control becomes a question of either–or, with any doubt resolved in favour of the territorial state. The second dogma is that jurisdiction is conceived to be all-inclusive or *total*. As professed in *Banković*, 'Article 1 does not provide any support that...jurisdiction can be divided and tailored in accordance with the particular circumstances of the extra-territorial act in question'.[175] This view is equally derived from a territorial conceptualisation of jurisdiction, and has been readily transferred to cases involving spatial extraterritorial control.[176]

However, the question is whether these two creeds can continue to be upheld in an increasingly globalised world. Both broader examples and specific case law seem to open up alternative interpretations. As for exclusivity, the proliferation of auxiliary legal bases for jurisdiction makes coexisting and competing jurisdictional claims unavoidable. This is most evident under the law of the sea, where the potential for concurrent jurisdictions is obvious, and where co-operative arrangements for dividing or sharing liability are far from uncommon.[177] But even for jurisdictional conflicts within the territorial jurisdiction of one state, deferral to territorial primacy may not always be the preferred solution.[178] The EU could be described as an example of a functionally limited polity essentially operating within the same geographical area as its sovereign member states that demands that we conceive of autonomy without territorial exclusivity.[179] Finally, while one may disagree with the premise for asserting Moldavian jurisdiction in *Ilaşcu*, it does set an important precedent for establishing double jurisdiction.

---

[175] *Banković*, para. 75.
[176] Roxstrom et al., 'NATO bombing case', 84. See e.g. *Cyprus v. Turkey*, and *Loizidou v. Turkey*.
[177] Gavouneli, 'Functional jurisdiction', pp. 49, 53.   [178] Lowe, *International Law*, p. 181.
[179] Walker, 'Late sovereignty in the European Union', p. 23.

With regard to the question of *totality*, the conclusion that extraterritorial jurisdiction must necessarily entail 'all or nothing' in terms of guaranteeing the entire rights catalogue seems equally flawed. Again, both the law of the sea and the EU spring to mind. The notion of the exclusive economic zone allows states a certain flexibility in terms of substantive contents, which allows the coastal state essentially to pick and choose the specific functions it wishes to exercise in the marine area it decides to designate as such.[180] Similarly, the EU and its member states constitute an example where authority is clearly divided and tailored according to different competences and subject matters. Lastly, while rare, historical examples of legal arrangements of shared or mixed jurisdiction over the same territory do exist.[181]

In contrast to the conception of jurisdiction flowing from national sovereignty, the case law concerning state actions in international airspace, waters and *terrae nullius* is illuminating and provides another pathway into the problem of extraterritorial jurisdiction. Within a functional conception of extraterritorial jurisdiction, the deciding factor is not 'the place where the violation occurred, but rather the relationship between the individual and the State in relation to a violation of any of the rights set forth in the Covenant, wherever they occurred'.[182] This approach applies the basic principle of human rights law that power entails obligations.[183] In the words of Cassel, summarising the jurisprudence of the Inter-American Commission, 'Where a State can kill a person outside its territory, it exercises sufficient control over that person to be held accountable for violating his right to life.'[184]

In accepting a functional approach to jurisdiction for human rights purposes, two issues arise that need to be resolved. The first concerns limiting the range and extent of state obligations to what is realistic and practicable. Under the 1951 Refugee Convention itself this is less of an issue, as the rights are specifically afforded incrementally, taking heed of state concerns that not all obligations may be realisable as soon as state

---

[180] Gavouneli, 'Functional jurisdiction', pp. 94–6.

[181] One such being the Anglo-French condominium over the New Hebrides. J. Turpin, 'The jurisdictional art of separation: the role of jurisdiction in the management of territorial and self-determination disputes – mixed jurisdiction in the Anglo-French condominium of the New Hebrides 1906-1980', doctoral dissertation, European University Institute, Florence, 2002.

[182] *López Burgos v. Uruguay*, para. 12(2).   [183] Lawson, 'Life after *Banković*', p. 86.

[184] D. Cassel, 'Extraterritorial application of inter-American human rights instruments', in Coomans and Kamminga, *Extraterritorial Application*, pp. 175–82, at p. 177.

responsibility is triggered. A state establishing jurisdiction by virtue of exercising offshore migration control would thus only be responsible for ensuring a limited number of rights, centred on the *non-refoulement* obligation. Under instruments like the European Convention on Human Rights or the Covenant on Civil and Political Rights, however, no similarly differentiated structure exists. It is clear that accepting a functional approach to jurisdiction would place an enormous burden on states if they were to guarantee the entire nexus of rights owed under, for example, the European Convention on Human Rights merely by denying onward access to an individual encountered on the high seas or in the territory of another state.[185]

Yet there is no logical reason to assume that the extent of obligations cannot change and be adapted to the particular circumstances as a state moves outside its territory. Several avenues could be envisioned for so doing. First, one might seek to distinguish between positive and negative obligations. While a state would be under the obligation to abstain from any direct action that would result in rights violations, such as the rejection of an individual or their return to persecution or torture, the scope of positive duties to secure human rights would be more narrowly circumscribed by the practical possibilities of ensuring such rights. This is already acknowledged in cases such as *Loizidou* and *Cyprus* v. *Turkey*, where positive extraterritorial obligations are imposed only to the extent that continued control over a geographical area and the presence of more permanent military and administrative structures merit it.[186]

---

[185] This point is similarly made by Craven:

> The general problem . . . is that the international human rights project, far from being one that is essentially antithetical to the inter-state order, is one that relies upon a relatively sharp demarcation between respective realms of power and responsibility. Human rights obligations typically require not merely that states abstain from certain courses of action, but also act with 'due diligence' to protect individuals from others, and to progressively fulfil rights in certain circumstances. In order for these obligations to be in any way meaningful, some distinction has to be maintained between those contexts in which a state may reasonably be said to assume those responsibilities and those in which it does not. The test of 'effective control' seems to provide an initial basis for doing so. (Craven, 'Human rights in the realm of order', p. 255)

Craven nonetheless acknowledges that there is no logical reason why states may not be held responsible for specific conduct or actions that undermine the enjoyment of rights in other parts of the globe, even beyond the realm of their effective control. Ibid., p. 255.

[186] *Loizidou* v. *Turkey* and *Cyprus* v. *Turkey*. Conversely, in *Ilaşcu* Moldova was held to have jurisdiction and retain a positive obligation to take diplomatic or other measures within its power, even though it did not have effective control over the area in

Given the principal difficulties in properly distinguishing between negative and positive human rights obligations, one could, however, also imagine an approach where the scope and application of rights is more broadly assessed in relation to the degree of control and authority exercised in the specific situation. This was essentially the approach taken by the US Supreme Court in *Boumediene*.[187] The case concerned the constitutional right to habeas corpus for detainees at Guantánamo, who have explicitly been barred from ordinary judicial review under the Detainee Treatment Act 2005. In its judgment the Court first rejected the 'formalistic, sovereignty-based test' put forward by the government[188] and denied that arrangements to commercialise sovereignty mean that states can disclaim constitutional obligations:

the Government's view is that the Constitution had no effect there, at least as to noncitizens, because the United States disclaimed sovereignty in the formal sense of the term. The necessary implication of the argument is that by surrendering formal sovereignty over any unincorporated territory to a third party, while at the same time entering into a lease that grants total control over the territory back to the United States, it would be possible for political branches to govern without legal constraint.

Our basic charter cannot be contracted away like this.[189]

But, even more interestingly, the Court further advanced what they termed a 'functional approach' in establishing both where constitutional rights apply and how they may be interpreted. While the majority considered it to be clear that fundamental constitutional rights cannot be denied, given the degree of actual control by the United States over detainees at Guantánamo, the 'inherent practical difficulties of ensuring all constitutional provisions always and anywhere' nonetheless had to be acknowledged.[190] Rather than restricting the extraterritorial application of the Constitution per se, however, the solution adopted in *Boumediene* was to draw on the common law tradition and accept that habeas corpus has always been considered 'an adaptable remedy. Its precise application and scope changed depending upon the circumstances.'[191]

In developing a functional approach to extraterritorial jurisdiction under international refugee and human rights law, at least two sets of practical difficulties may similarly serve to limit the application and scope

---

question. For a discussion of 'positive' or 'due diligence' obligations, see further below, section 5.8.

[187] *Boumediene et al. v. Bush*, 553 US 723 (2008), 12 June 2008.

[188] Ibid., p. 33.   [189] Ibid., p. 35.   [190] Ibid., p. 29.   [191] Ibid., p. 50.

of rights owed. First, one should take heed of the fact that certain rights presuppose a specific institutional context that may be realisable in the territorial context, but not, or only to a more limited extent, extraterritorially. While states may be expected to respect the *non-refoulement* obligation anywhere they exercise offshore migration control, ensuring certain procedural and material rights may only be practicable where extraterritorial jurisdiction has a more permanent character and/or involves effective control over local administrative structures.[192] This is most evident in cases concerning interception at sea. In *Medvedyev*, concerning the boarding of a ship flying the Cambodian flag suspected of drug smuggling in international waters, the European Court of Human Rights thus held that while France was exercising jurisdiction on board, it could not be held responsible for not immediately bringing the crew deprived of their liberty before a judge in accordance with Article 5(3) of the Convention during the thirteen days it took before the ship arrived at the French port of Brest.[193] Second, the scope of a state's obligations must be assessed in the light of the possibility of its enforcing such rights vis-à-vis any territorial sovereign. Again, where a state holds exclusive sway over an offshore geographical area this may be less of a problem, but where jurisdiction is merely exercised for the purpose of something such as migration control, the extraterritorially acting state is unlikely to be able proactively to intervene in regard to wider human rights issues without triggering a sovereignty conflict with the territorial state.

The second issue arising if one adopts a functional jurisdiction test is of a more practical character. While the effective control test, as argued above, essentially serves to exclude any competing jurisdictional claims over the territory or individual concerned, a functional approach to jurisdiction would entail a plethora of situations where more than one state might exercise jurisdiction in a given situation or over an individual.

If it is accepted that jurisdiction is non-exclusive, the need arises to determine which among several competing states would take on and fulfil actual obligations. In the refugee context both the territorial state and the state exercising offshore migration control may be expected to

---

[192] *Loizidou v. Turkey.* In *Boumediene* emphasis was similarly put on the long-standing and exclusive control over Guantánamo exercised by the United States, and that in this light the Detainee Treatment Act was not an adequate substitute for habeas corpus (p. 67). For a similar analysis see Tomuschat, *Human Rights*, p. 131.

[193] France was, however, held to be in violation of Art. 5(1), since a proper legal base for depriving the applicants of their liberty was not established. *Medvedyev and Others v. France.*

respect the *non-refoulement* obligation, yet only one state will presumably be able to undertake a refugee status determination process and take on any subsequent protection responsibilities.

Today, the division of protection responsibilities among several states is often carried out by means of mutual agreements, yet international law contains few clues as to how to resolve any conflicts in this regard. A natural recourse may of course be to emphasise the primacy of the territorial jurisdiction. This finds support from UNHCR's Executive Committee:

[t]he State within whose sovereign territory, or territorial waters, interception takes place has the primary responsibility for addressing any protection needs of intercepted persons.[194]

This principle would seem to suggest that to the extent that full and effective protection can be guaranteed by the territorial state, this would be the preferred party to take on protection obligations. However, crucial in this interpretation is the establishment that where this is not the case an underlying responsibility is borne by the state exercising extraterritorial jurisdiction for ensuring that protection obligations are met, and this may involve initiating asylum procedures and relocation to the territory of the acting state where refugee rights cannot be guaranteed by the territorial state.[195]

Realising this underlying, or subsidiary, human rights responsibility will be particularly important in cases where offshore migration is carried out within the territory of a state evidently lacking refugee protection and human rights standards. It is in this sense highly questionable whether current efforts by Italy to carry out migration control within Libyan territorial waters would in any way relieve the extraterritorially acting state of legal obligations in regard to asylum-seekers, given that

---

[194] UNHCR Executive Committee, Conclusion No. 97 (LIV) (2003).

[195] A similar principle of concomitant responsibility has arguably already been established by the European Court of Human Rights. In regard to the European Dublin Convention, the Court in *T.I. v. United Kingdom* held that the indirect removal of an asylum-seeker from the United Kingdom to an intermediary country, even if under a mutual agreement that this country would carry out a status determination procedure, did not absolve the United Kingdom from its obligations under Art. 3 in case that country (in this case Germany) did not fulfil its commitments.

This principle is easily transferred to cases where interception involves co-operative arrangements and the establishment of more than one state's jurisdiction. While a state carrying out offshore migration control may under agreement transfer any asylum-seekers to the authorities of the territorial state, this does not relieve the offshoring state of its international obligations under refugee and human rights law where the territorial state does not ensure refugee protection.

Libya is not a signatory to the 1951 Refugee Convention and has a track record of summarily expelling both migrants and refugees.

What has been suggested above is that a functional approach to extraterritorial jurisdiction not only is desirable from a human rights perspective, but is also an entirely possible reading as the concept of jurisdiction has developed in both general international law and human rights law specifically. Nonetheless, it is clear that what is suggested above would go squarely against the reasoning put forward in *Banković*, for example, which explicitly held that the rights under the convention cannot be 'divided and tailored' to a given situation.[196] I, for one, find this to be an unduly conservative and frankly incorrect assumption. As indicated above, the notion of functionally divided competencies and rights is firmly entrenched in several other areas of international law. Moreover, a number of both national and international cases have already established that account needs to be taken of the context in which states operate and the scope and application of rights tailored accordingly, especially when states exercise extraterritorial jurisdiction.

It remains to be seen whether national and international judiciaries will continue to cling to notions of national sovereignty or whether a functional conception more in line with progressions in other areas of international law will eventually find its way even in cases involving extraterritorial acts committed on a foreign state's territory. So far, it is as if there is a fundamental barrier that is hard to move past, a conceptual history that makes it cognitively difficult to conceive of jurisdiction not tied to territorial claims.

---

[196] *Banković*, para. 75.

5 The privatisation of migration control and state responsibility

The 'externalisation' of migration control is not limited to states' own actions on the high seas or in foreign territory. In tandem with the horizontal shift in locations for migration control, a shift may also be traced in terms of the actors engaged. This includes, first, the increasing inter-state co-operation touched on in the previous chapter that has elevated migration management into a prominent foreign policy issue for the EU and many traditional asylum countries.[1] Equally, however, migration and border control seem to have expanded vertically, enlisting private actors to perform crucial functions in regard to immigration control.

This chapter starts out by tracing the developments in private involvement for the purpose of migration control. As will be seen, private actors today occupy an increasing and varied role in migration management systems, and the effect of private migration control is increasingly felt by asylum-seekers and refugees.

Second, the chapter tries to elucidate when and under what circumstances states may be held responsible under international refugee and human rights law when migration control is delegated to private actors, such as airlines, border contractors or private security companies. Attempts to this end have so far been marred by difficulties in matching the traditional dictum that states are not responsible for the conduct of private actors with the current political reality and increased privatisation. International refugee law itself does not foresee that refugees are met by any other than a state's own officials. Nonetheless, the general principles of international law, such as the Articles on State Responsibility and the notion of due diligence, both provide avenues for establishing

---

[1] Gammeltoft-Hansen, 'Outsourcing migration management'; Lavenex, 'Shifting up and out'; Niessen and Schibel, 'International migration'.

state accountability: in the first case when a state actively engages private parties and their actions thus become directly attributable to the state, and in the second instance when states fail to take appropriate action to prevent non-state actors violating refugee rights and thus become indirectly responsible for any subsequent human rights violations.

In each case, however, the requirements for establishing state responsibility and obligations remain high, and ensuring accountability for privately operated migration control may thus be difficult both de jure and de facto. Despite the popularity of privatisation as a form of governance in an ever increasing number of fields, state responsibility for human rights violations in such cases relies on general principles of attribution and indirect responsibility, the application of which remains complex. Limited case law further exists to help draw clearer thresholds for when states incur responsibility and what level of obligations may be expected. Lastly, as in the case of extraterritorialisation, determining legal responsibility depends closely on establishing the factual relationship between a state, private actors and the human rights violation in question. Privatisation seldom lends itself to extensive public oversight, and scrutiny and determining the reach of international refugee law may therefore be particularly complicated when private migration control is carried out extraterritorially.

The following uses the term 'privatisation' loosely, as a shorthand for a wide set of circumstances in which private actors carry out otherwise governmental functions, and contains no implication as to whether these activities are in fact an act of state or not. The investigative purpose on the one hand necessitates that an initial assumption of separateness between private actors and state authorities is maintained, since the purpose of the analysis is precisely to show when private conduct may nonetheless be attributed to the state. Privatisation for the present purposes thus includes instances where it is evidently hard to separate private contractors or seconded staff from ordinary authorities. Conversely, the analysis also includes situations where there is hardly any formal link between states and private actors and where the state cannot be said to have actively instigated or even endorsed privately conducted migration control. As will be shown, however, states may nonetheless retain indirect obligations where it is likely and foreseeable that the acts of such actors will lead to refugee and human rights violations. In the following, the 'privatisation of migration control' thus embraces all forms of involvement by non-state actors in the design, setting up and enforcement of migration controls.

5.1 The rise of the private border guard

Before embarking on the legal analysis, it may first be useful to trace the developments in private involvement for the purpose of migration control. While the co-optation or incorporation of private actors for the purpose of migration control is as such not a recent phenomenon, the last decades have seen a substantial expansion of privatisation, and non-state actors today appear in a multitude of different settings connected to border control and migration management.

In the context of migration control, the oldest and most widespread example of privatisation is the imposition of carrier sanctions on private airlines and other international transportation companies. Transporters bringing in passengers without the required documents or visas are fined and made responsible for taking back and/or detaining passengers rejected by the immigration authorities. The threat of such fines has made private airline companies take on a number of control functions related to document checks, and lacking a visa or suspicions of document forgery are likely to lead to carriers rejecting a passenger at the point of departure. While the concept of carrier sanctions originally dates back to the early twentieth century,[2] legislation penalising and placing migration control obligations on carriers became popular and more developed from the second half of the 1980s, largely as a response to increasing number of 'jet age' asylum-seekers.[3] Today, carrier sanctions thus constitute a primary tool for ensuring pre-arrival migration control and a major obstacle for many refugees in reaching the territory of their prospective destination state and applying for asylum.

---

[2] Scholten and Minderhoud, 'Regulating immigration control', 123; Lahav, 'Migration and security', 92; Zolberg, 'Matters of state', 75. As early as 1902, the US Passenger Act demanded that shipmasters sign an affidavit to verify that all passengers were in good physical and mental health. Yet, unlike the modern variants, the original legislation did not invoke penal law but merely a civil law responsibility to take back those found inadmissible by US immigration officers.

[3] In the United States, in addition to the 1902 Passenger Act, carrier liability for bringing in aliens without valid passports and visas has been part of the Immigration and Nationality Act since 1952 (the MacCarran-Walter Act, Section 273). In Canada, similarly, rules were introduced as part of the 1976 Immigration Act. In the European context, legislation to impose obligations and concurrent fines on carriers was implemented by Belgium, Germany and the United Kingdom in 1987. A. Cruz, *Shifting Responsibility: Carriers' Liability in the Member States of the European Union and North America* (Stoke-on-Trent: Trentham Books, 1995), p. 5. In Denmark legislation was passed in 1986, but it only came into force in 1989. Article 26 of the 1990 Schengen Convention further imposes an obligation on signatory states to impose sanctions on all carriers who transport aliens without the necessary travel documents.

Yet the involvement of private actors for the purpose of migration control is far from limited to the case of carrier liability. At the physical border a number of states today make use of private contractors to assist national border authorities in performing immigration and security checks. Under the Immigration Asylum and Nationality Act 2006, the power to search vehicles, vessels and trains in the United Kingdom may be transferred to private contractors certified by the Secretary of State.[4] As part of the Secure Borders Initiative a number of private security and defence companies have been contracted by the United States to assist national border control. Recently, Boeing won the bid for setting up SBInet: a US$2.5 billion high-tech border surveillance system along the United States–Mexico border including sensor towers, radar scanners and possibly aerial surveillance drones. The contract involves Boeing designing and setting up the system as well as Boeing operators directing US border guards to intercept irregular border crossers.[5]

In other instances border security is being completely outsourced to private contractors. As part of the general privatisation trend entire ports and airports in both Europe and North America are now run and owned by private companies.[6] Since 2005 Israel has privatised border control at the major crossing points between Israel and the West Bank. In several places Israeli officials have been withdrawn from the border check areas, and inspections are handled solely by private contractors such as the private military company Modiin Ezrahi. The ministries of Defence and Public Security have justified privatisation on grounds related to efficiency and better service, yet several complaints have been filed by border crossers regarding harsh treatment, and voices have been raised that privatisation is first and foremost a way for the Israeli authorities to absolve themselves of legal responsibility.[7]

Moreover, a number of countries have contracted private companies to operate immigration detention facilities as well as to organise and carry out deportations. In the United Kingdom and Australia immigration detention, along with a number of prisons, is run by Group 4

---

[4] Ss. 40 and 41.
[5] J. Richey, 'Fencing the Border: Boeing's high-tech plan falters', *Corpwatch*, 9 July 2007, available at www.warprofiteers.com.
[6] M. B. Salter, 'Governmentalities of an airport: heterotopia and confession', (2007) 1 *International Political Sociology* 49–66, at 50.
[7] M. Rapoport, 'Outsourcing the checkpoints', *Hareetz*, 2 October 2007; G. Auda, 'Checkpoints go private', *France 24*, 17 March 2008; T. Buch, 'Israeli shift to private security draws fire', *Financial Times*, 3 June 2008.

Securicor.[8] In the United States, Haliburton was awarded a $410.2 million contract to expand detention and removal facilities, and companies such as Corrections Corporation of America already run a number of immigration detention facilities.[9] Similarly, in 2006 Geo Group was given a $250 million contract to provide buses and armed security for deportations from the United States.[10] The same year, the United Kingdom paid £12,391,175 to escort companies carrying out enforced removals.[11]

Finally, private involvement in migration control is not necessarily initiated or even endorsed by the respective states or governments. In the United States both private associations and individuals have taken up border control functions on their own initiative. The self-proclaimed 'Minutemen' carry out armed patrols on the United States–Mexico border, claiming to provide 'extra eyes and ears for national border security'.[12] Their relationship to official US Border Patrols is unclear. While the Department of Homeland Security has described the Minutemen as 'vigilantes' and asked them to step down activities, local border patrol authorities have in some instances endorsed them as providing support and a positive supplement to official controls.[13] The actual activities and effects of these groups are difficult to gauge, although NGOs have reported a number of incidents in which both border-crossers and irregularly staying migrants have been subjected to violence and physical restraint.[14]

---

[8] In 2004 Group 4 sold off part of their UK detention activities under the name 'Global Solutions Limited'. Other private immigration detention actors in the United Kingdom include Premier Detention Services and United Kingdom Detention Services. C. Bacon, 'The evolution of immigration detention in the UK: the involvement of private prison companies', RSC Working Paper No. 27, Refugee Studies Centre, Oxford (2005).

[9] J. Richey, 'Border for sale: privatizing immigration control', *Corpwatch*, 5 July 2006, available at www.corpwatch.org.

[10] Ibid.

[11] The main contractor for this purpose is Group 4 Securicor, but a number of other private security firms are approved and are used on a case-by-case basis. F. Arnold, E. Ginn and H. Wistrich, 'Outsourcing abuse: the use and misuse of state-sanctioned force during the detention and removal of asylum-seekers', joint report by Birnberg Peirce and Partners, Medical Justice and National Coalition of Anti-Deportation Campaigns, July 2008.

[12] 'Armed Americans patrol B.C.–Washington border', CTV Global Media, 2 October 2005, available at www.ctv.ca.

[13] Ibid.

[14] 'Unlawful imprisonment of immigrant by Minuteman volunteer', American Civil Liberties Union, 7 April 2005, available at www.aclu.org.

As in the case of carrier sanctions, several elements of this privatisation have a concurrent extraterritorial dimension by simultaneously shifting control away from the physical border. Amendments to the United Kingdom's juxtaposed control scheme operated at French ports has extended the role of private contractors in carrying out border controls at overseas control zones.[15] Under the amended legislation, private search officers are able to act independently of government immigration officers to search vehicles and detain and escort to the nearest immigration detention facility any persons found.[16]

Another example concerns the enlisting of private visa application agents, who collect, organise and present visa applications to the embassies or immigration authorities of the respective states. This practice is in some instances closely connected to or carried out by carriers themselves, as due to the sanctions system transportation companies have a vested interest in ensuring that travellers will be accepted by the destination state.[17] Yet the use of visa handling agents also seems to be a growing business outside the carrier framework. From the perspective of the state, the use of a trusted intermediary to vouch for visa applicants may reduce the examination carried out by consular visa officers and, from the perspective of the applicant, visa agents may of course increase the chances of a successful application.[18]

Under EU law the use of commercial intermediaries in visa applications is open to each member state, and the Common Consular Instructions provide for private agents performing tasks ranging from the basic supply of identity and other supporting documents to tour organisers taking care of travel documents, insurance and internal transfers.[19] Private companies engaged in this field seem to operate in a grey zone between independent commercial interests and government structures. On the one hand, visa facilitation seems to be a budding and lucrative market and, on the other, such agents are often closely connected to airlines eager to avoid refused passengers or carrier fines. In some countries embassies refuse to process visa applications unless applicants go through a pre-approved handling

---

[15] See above, section 4.3.3.

[16] Nationality, Immigration and Asylum Act 2002 (Juxtaposed Controls).

[17] E. Guild, 'Moving the borders of Europe', inaugural professorial lecture delivered at CPO Wisselleerstoel at the University of Nijmegen, 30 May 2001, p. 49.

[18] Ibid., p. 50.

[19] Common Consular Instructions on Visas for the Diplomatic Missions and Consular Posts, 2005/C 326/01, 22 December 2005, Section VIII(5).

agent. Moreover, policy proposals for common EU visa application centres foresee the possibility of outsourcing obtaining visa applications entirely to private contractors.[20]

Finally, the delegation of migration control to private carriers in some instances entails the responsibility of carriers for taking custody of rejected passengers in transit or at the point of destination until they can be returned. Consequently, carriers effectively become responsible for detaining migrants and asylum-seekers. A number of cases have thus emerged where passengers have been held either at hotels under guard by private security companies, or in privately managed detention zones at the airport.[21] A notorious example is the transit zone at the 'Sheremetyevo 2' airport in Moscow, which, according to Nicholson, 'has held up to 20 passengers at any one time, including refugees who have been denied flights to Western European States'.[22] While agreements or contracts with the host state have in some instances been formalised for the purpose of carrying out these tasks, detention zones are generally operated by airline companies with de facto no possibility of launching asylum claims.[23]

Parallel to the expansion of the forms of private involvement in migration control, one might also point to a number of qualitative changes and developments in the way in which private controls are enacted. The first of these is closely connected to the increased security concerns in regard to migration and border control. The requirements placed on carriers to perform security checks, scanning and verifying documents and submitting data to national authorities, have increased substantially since the attacks on the United States of 11 September 2001.[24] Both the United States and the European Union now operate schemes requiring carriers to deliver to the authorities of the destination state advance passenger

---

[20] European Commission, Proposal for a Regulation of the European Parliament and of the Council Amending the Common Consular Instructions on Visas for Diplomatic Missions and Consular Posts in relation to the Introduction of Biometrics Including Provisions on the Organisation of the Reception and Processing of Visa Applications, COM(2006) 269, 31 May 2006.

[21] R. I. R. Abeyratne, 'Air carrier liability and state responsibility for the carriage of inadmissible persons and refugees', (1998) 10 *International Journal of Refugee Law* 675–87, at 681; Hughes and Liebaut, *Detention of Asylum-Seekers in Europe*, pp. 108–9.

[22] Nicholson, 'Immigration Act 1987', 598 ff.

[23] Guild, 'Borders of the European Union'; Guiraudon, 'Before the EU border', p. 203; Nicholson, 'Immigration Act 1987', 598.

[24] Salter, 'Governmentalities of an airport', 54; Guiraudon, 'Enlisting third parties', pp. 11–12.

information (API) data on all passengers before landing.[25] At the same time, profiling and behavioural techniques aimed at identifying potential security threats may inadvertently target asylum-seekers; the fear and desperation leading to flight are easily mistaken by security officers for risk factors leading to a denial of boarding.[26] Lastly, given the nature of the attacks, airlines themselves are becoming increasingly concerned about security risks and thus occasionally of their own accord implement additional passenger screening and security procedures.

In some respects, the heightened security concerns could be argued to work against the privatisation of migration control. Before the 2001 attacks, airport security in the United States, including passenger screening, was largely assigned to airlines and private airport companies under the oversight of the Federal Aviation Administration (FAA).[27] Yet in November 2001 legislation was passed to renationalise airport security under the newly established Transport Security Administration, leading to the creation of more than 60,000 new federal employee posts.[28] Similarly, the bid by Dubai Ports World, a government-owned company of the United Arab Emirates, to purchase six already privately owned ports in the United States started a national debate about the security impact of completely privatised port facilities.[29] No policy changes resulted from this debate, however, and despite the introduction of federal immigration officers, the use of and obligations placed on private agents for the purpose of migration control have continued to grow in other areas.

Second, the privatisation of migration control is becoming increasingly multi-layered. The imposition of control obligations on carriers has resulted not only in carriers hiring and training their own security and inspection staff but also in a growing use of sub-contractors and thus

---

[25] European Council, On the Obligation of Carriers to Communicate Passenger Data, Directive 2004/82/EC, 29 April 2004. A number of carriers have complained that the categories of data required are too broad and put excessive demands on the airline companies. Furthermore, exchange of passenger name record (PNR) data between the United States and the EU has caused some concern with respect to data protection. See Agreement between the European Union and the United States of America on the processing and transfer of Passenger Name Record (PNR) data by air carriers to the US Department of Homeland Security (2007 PNR Agreement), 4 August 2007.

[26] Refugee Council, 'Remote controls: how UK border controls are endangering the lives of refugees', December 2008, p. 46.

[27] Verkuil, *Outsourcing Sovereignty*, p. 58.

[28] The Aviation and Transportation Security Act 2001, 115 Stat. 597, 19 November 2001. Verkuil, *Outsourcing Sovereignty*, p. 59.

[29] Ibid., p. 69.

further outsourcing. As the demands and standards required of airlines, sea transporters and port companies by destination states keep developing, hiring specialised security agents to carry out these functions is becoming more attractive and, to some companies, often the only viable option.[30] More than a hundred private sub-contractors have thus been engaged by Boeing under the SBInet programme. Information about which companies have been subcontracted and what tasks they are performing has not been made publicly available.[31]

Similarly, private contractors are increasingly acting as intermediaries in the implementation of interstate co-operation in regard to migration management. In the border region between Ukraine and Russia, a number of private or quasi-public companies funded by the EU and individual member states have thus provided technical material for border control, including document scanners, communications equipment and aircraft, as well as training Ukrainian border authorities in profiling techniques, deployment and organisational set-up.[32] This equally complicates the question of legal responsibility. While migration control is not carried out directly by these companies, they arguably aid the Ukrainian authorities in establishing controls in a country with a known record for refusing asylum-seekers and refugees at the border.[33]

Third, and finally, private involvement in migration control is being embedded in more complex arrangements between the relevant actors. While the imposition of, for example, carrier sanctions in principle leave the organisation and modes of control up to the airlines and transportation companies, in practice states exercise a great deal of influence over the control functions carried out, and more intimate relationships are thus developing between national immigration officers and airline employees.[34] The United Kingdom has thus offered to waive fines if airlines agree to comply with its 'approved gate-check' regulations. This involves British immigration officers training airline staff in

---

[30] Ibid., p. 68; Kruse, 'Creating Europe outside Europe', p. 15; Guiraudon, 'Constitution of a European immigration policy domain', 9; Cruz, *Shifting Responsibility*.

[31] Richey, 'Fencing the border'.

[32] I. Gatev, 'Border security in the eastern neighbourhood: where biopolitics and geopolitics meet', (2008) 13 *European Affairs Review* 97–116, at 110–11.

[33] See e.g. Human Rights Watch, 'Ukraine: on the margins – Rights violations against migrants and asylum seekers at the new Eastern border of the European Union', New York, 29 November 2005; UNHCR, 'UN condemns refoulement of Sri Lankan asylum seekers from Ukraine', press release, 10 March 2008, available at www.unhcr.org.ua.

[34] Scholten and Minderhoud, 'Regulating immigration control', 136; Vedsted-Hansen, 'Privatiseret Retshåndhævelse', pp. 173–5.

profiling techniques and detecting forged documents, the institution of an additional control procedure immediately prior to boarding and regular audits of airline performance by government officials.[35]

In a number of countries such training and monitoring is today carried out through the secondment of immigration liaison officers working with airlines at points of departure and transit.[36] While such officers seldom have the authority to carry out migration control directly, they often advise carriers whether to take on board or deny individual passengers. In addition countries such as the United Kingdom and the United States have introduced procedures requiring carriers to forward passenger bio-data to the destination country at check-in, thereby allowing national immigration authorities time to check relevant databases and on that basis notify carriers as to whether to board passengers.[37] In sum, more hybrid public/private partnerships appear to be developing as part of the privatisation of migration control. As the intersections between public and private are becoming increasingly blurred and hard to disentangle, determining where private involvement begins and public authority ends likewise becomes difficult.

5.2 The logic and consequences of privatising migration control

From the perspective of the outsourcing state, the appeal of privatising migration control may be found on several levels. To some extent, private involvement for the purpose of migration control may be seen as part of a much broader trend. The last decades have seen a rapid expansion in the privatisation and outsourcing of activities hitherto carried out exclusively by the state, from health services and prisons to international security and peacekeeping.[38]

The motivation for privatisation is often argued in cost-efficiency terms – states will outsource certain tasks either if it is cheaper to do

---

[35] Nicholson, 'Immigration Act 1987', 592–3.

[36] Scholten and Minderhoud, 'Regulating immigration control', 137; Goodwin-Gill and McAdam, *Refugee in International Law*, p. 379; Guild, 'Jurisprudence of the ECHR', p. 41. On the role of immigration liaison officers see above, section 4.3.3.

[37] In the United Kingdom this is known as the e-Borders programme and is provided for by the 2006 Immigration, Asylum and Nationality Act. Developing the technology and setting up the programme has similarly been outsourced, and a £650 million contract has thus been given to the US defence supply company Raytheon.

[38] P. Alston, 'The myopia of handmaidens: international lawyers and globalization', (1997) 8 *European Journal of International Law* 435–48, at 442.

so or if it leads to a more efficient accomplishment of the task in hand.[39] In the case of migration control both these may apply, or at least be perceived to apply. Several authors have explained private involvement as a reaction to the alleged failure of traditional and state-led means of border control.[40] By delegating control to, for example, airlines, states introduce a new layer of migration control that may effectively enforce visa requirements and reject undocumented travellers before they reach the physical border.[41] At the same time, control is carried out by actors with a unique access to inbound immigrants and their data, and at locations, such as foreign airports, that may otherwise be inaccessible to national immigration authorities.[42] Similarly, it has been argued that carrier sanctions are perceived to be cost-saving by largely shifting costs for training and maintaining control personnel to transport companies, as well as allowing control to take place before the border, thus saving costs connected to asylum processing, accommodation and, potentially, expulsion and return.[43]

In the particular context of migration control, however, the regulatory rationale of enlisting private actors may be seen to serve at least two additional purposes – avoiding legal obligations vis-à-vis protection seekers and avoiding sovereignty conflicts when installing extraterritorial migration control. As regards the first of these, privatisation of migration control replaces the encounter between an asylum-seeker and the state, typically represented by national immigration or border authorities, with an encounter between two private parties, neither of which can be made directly responsible under international refugee and human rights law. The privatisation of migration control has thus been described as a strategy to circumvent legal constraints that states otherwise face when carrying out border control.[44]

---

[39] Scholten and Minderhoud, 'Regulating immigration control', 129; Lahav, 'Migration and security', p. 91; Vedsted-Hansen, 'Privatiseret Retshåndhævelse', pp. 160–1.

[40] J. Ayling and P. Grabosky, 'Policing by command: enhancing law enforcement capacity through coercion', (2006) 28 *Law and Policy* 420–43; V. Guiraudon and G. Lahav, 'State sovereignty debate revisited', 164.

[41] Noll, *Negotiating Asylum*, pp. 108–9.

[42] Vedsted-Hansen, 'Privatiseret Retshåndhævelse', pp. 160–1.

[43] Scholten and Minderhoud, 'Regulating immigration control', 129. Other costs may nonetheless be associated with the delegation itself and ensuring its effective implementation. Save for the examples of carrier sanctions, visa agents and vigilante border guards such as the Minutemen, states bear the cost of contractors. Further, as noted above, in many instances training of carrier personnel is still carried out by state officials and the enforcement of control monitored by deployed immigration liaison officers.

[44] Lahav, 'Migration and security', pp. 89, 98; Guiraudon, 'Before the EU border', p. 195; Vedsted-Hansen, 'Europe's response', p. 20.

Second, to the extent that migration control is carried out extraterritori-ally, privatisation could be argued to avoid a potential sovereignty conflict with the territorial state. The posting of immigration officers exercising direct authority in foreign territory has so far been limited, and requires detailed legal agreements between the sending and hosting state. As was evidenced in the previous chapter, many states emphasise that immigra-tion liaison officers do not hold any direct authority and as such do not interfere with the sovereign competence of the host state.[45] By having a private entity enforcing actual controls and rejections, the complicated and traditionally undesirable situation of overlapping enforcement juris-dictions is seemingly avoided.

On both accounts, however, the logic may at least be questioned. As will be shown in the following, as a matter of international law both car-rier sanctions and other forms of privatised migration control do, under certain circumstances, incur state responsibility for violations of interna-tional refugee and human rights law. In particular, to the extent that a sufficient link between the state and the private actor can be established, the conduct of private agents is essentially identified with the outsourcing state for the purpose of any violation of international norms. Nonethe-less, establishment of state responsibility with regard to private migration control is no straightforward matter and establishing the required link to hold states accountable may not always be possible.

5.3 Private migration control and international refugee law

The adverse effects of carrier sanctions and other forms of privatised migration control on those seeking protection have been pointed out repeatedly.[46] Carrier sanctions are generally operated regardless of

---

[45] Council of the European Union, Proposal for a Comprehensive Plan to Combat Illegal Immigration and Trafficking of Human Beings in the European Union, 6621/1/02, 27 February 2002, para. 67.

[46] Abeyratne, 'Air carrier liability'; Nicholson, 'Immigration Act 1987'; S. Collinson, 'Visa requirements, carrier sanctions, "safe third countries" and "readmission": the development of an asylum "buffer zone" in Europe', (1996) 21 *Transactions* 76–90; Cruz, *Shifting Responsibility*; Vedsted-Hansen, 'Privatiseret Retshåndhævelse'; Feller, 'Carrier sanctions'; A. Ruff, 'The Immigration (Carriers' Liability) Act 1987: its implications for refugees and airlines', (1989) 1 *International Journal of Refugee Law* 481–500; H. Meijers, 'Possibilities for guaranteeing transport to refugees', in M. Kjærum (ed.), *The Role of Airline Companies in the Asylum Procedure* (Copenhagen: Danish Refugee Council, 1988), pp. 16–23.
     For refugee and human rights organisations see in particular Refugee Council, 'Remote controls', pp. 44–51; European Council for Refugees and Exiles, 'Defending refugees' access to protection in Europe', December 2007, pp. 29–31; and Amnesty

protection concerns and asylum-seekers are particularly likely to be rejected, as they naturally tend to lack full documentation and are unlikely to have been granted a visa.[47] As pointed out by UNHCR,

> Forcing carriers to verify visas and other travel documentation helps to shift the burden of determining the need for protection to those whose motivation is to avoid monetary penalties to their corporate employer, rather than to provide protection to individuals. In so doing, it contributes to placing this very important responsibility in the hands of those (a) unauthorized to make asylum determinations on behalf of States, (b) thoroughly untrained in the nuances and procedures of refugee and asylum principles, and (c) motivated by economic rather than humanitarian considerations.[48]

Placing obligations on private actors such as carriers thus not only shifts responsibility for migration control but in effect and to the same extent responsibility for identifying asylum-seekers and refugees. Not only are private actors likely to lack the competence to take on such a task, but the outsourcing structure, in this case employing economic sanctions, is likely to work against private actors taking any risks in admitting asylum-seekers without the required documentation. Lastly, very little is known about the actual operation of private actors. Supervision and reporting are often lacking as control is shifted to private agents and, to the extent that

International, 'No flights to safety: airline employees and the rights of refugees', ACT 34/21/97, November 1997; Group of Experts under the European Consultation on Refugee and Exiles, 'The effects of carrier sanctions on the asylum system', Danish Refugee Council/Danish Center of Human Rights, October 1991; Group of Experts under the European Consultation on Refugee and Exiles, 'The role of airline companies in the asylum procedure', Danish Refugee Council, July 1988.

[47] Goodwin-Gill and McAdam, *Refugee in International Law*, p. 377; Nicholson, 'Immigration Act 1987', 598; D. Matas, 'Carrier sanctions: alternatives or amendments to existing legislation', in M. Kjærum (ed.), *The Effects of Carrier Sanctions on the Asylum System* (Copenhagen: Danish Refugee Council and the Danish Center of Human Rights, 1991), pp. 27–34, at p. 27. See further above, section 4.3.3.

[48] UNHCR, Position on Conventions Recently Concluded in Europe (Dublin and Schengen Conventions), 16 August 1991. See further UNHCR, Position on Visa Requirements and Carrier Sanctions, Geneva, September 1995. A similar position has been taken by the Parliamentary Assembly of the Council of Europe:

> Airline sanctions ... undermine the basic principles of refugee protection and the right of refugees to claim asylum, while placing a considerable legal, administrative and financial burden upon carriers and moving the responsibility away from immigration officers. (Council of Europe Parliamentary Assembly, Recommendation 1163 on the arrival of asylum-seekers at European Airports, 23 September 1991, para. 10)

they are implemented extraterritorially, access to those rejected becomes inherently difficult.[49]

In the light of these concerns, it becomes natural to question the extent to which carrier sanctions or other instances of privatised migration control conflict with obligations under international refugee and human rights law. While these questions have been flagged by refugee lawyers for more than two decades,[50] it arguably still remains a somewhat underdeveloped area, and few attempts have been made towards a more systematic analysis of when states incur obligations under international refugee law as a result of the actions of private actors. The reasons for this may be several. The cases that have been brought before national courts mostly concern either the legality of upholding sanctions on carriers for persons already arrived or, occasionally, private suits brought against the airlines for refusal to permit boarding.[51] Second, lack of access to and monitoring of asylum-seekers denied embarkation or actively turned back by private actors has left both NGOs and lawyers with rather few case studies.[52]

The potential conflict between the control practices of carriers and international refugee law has indirectly been acknowledged as part of carrier legislation itself. Article 26(2) of the Schengen Convention thus reads,

The Contracting Parties undertake, subject to the obligations arising out of their accession to the Geneva Convention of 28 July 1951 relating to the Status of Refugees, as amended by the New York Protocol of 31 January 1967, and in accordance with their constitutional law, to impose penalties on carriers who transport aliens who do not possess the necessary travel documents by air or sea from Third States to their territories.[53]

---

[49] Nicholson, 'Immigration Act 1987', 598; Verkuil, *Outsourcing Sovereignty*, p. 71; and Vedsted-Hansen, 'Privatiseret Retshåndhævelse', p. 176. Nicholson goes on to note that even when airlines are asked to provide 'denied boarding' figures, they do not always do so, and that the UK Immigration Service has been reluctant to make data publicly available.

[50] E. Feller, 'Transport carriers and refugee protection', in Kjærum, *Role of Airline Companies*, pp. 6–13; Meijers, 'Possibilities for guaranteeing transport to refugees'; J. Vedsted-Hansen, 'Transporters' responsibilities under the Chicago Convention on International Civil Aviation', in Kjærum, *Role of Airline Companies*, pp. 14–16.

[51] See e.g. *Case Regarding Carrier Responsibilities*, Austrian Federal Constitutional Court (Verfassungsgerichtshof), G224/01, 1 October 2001; and *Scandinavian Airlines Flight SK 911 in Fine Proceedings*, Board of Immigration Appeals, NYC 10/52.6793, Interim Decision 3149, 26 February 1991. For further examples see Cruz, *Shifting Responsibility*.

[52] Nicholson, 'Immigration Act 1987', 598.

[53] A similar formulation was introduced in 1990 under the ninth edition of the ICAO standards under the 1944 Chicago Convention as an interpretative note to Standard

Very different interpretations have been applied by the various Schengen states and little effect has in practice been given to this clause.[54] In an attempt to remedy this, Article 4(2) of the 2001 European Council Carrier Liability Directive introduced a slightly different formulation:

Article 4(1) is without prejudice to Member States' obligations in cases where a third country national seeks international protection.[55]

While this formulation is wider in referring not only to obligations arising out of the 1951 Refugee Convention, it does, however, continue to spawn disagreement over interpretation. First, in referring to Article 4(1) setting out the obligation to pay fines, it is not clear whether other obligations, for example to return inadmissible passengers, are similarly waived in the case of protection seekers whose case is declared manifestly unfounded or eventually rejected. Second, national implementation seems to differ between member states as to whether fines are waived or reimbursed only when asylum or subsidiary protection is granted, or whether fines are waived for all passengers requesting asylum.[56]

A number of scholars have in addition argued that the imposition of carrier fines is inconsistent with Article 31 of the Refugee Convention.[57]

3(36)1, stating that 'nothing in this provision or in Note 1 is be constructed so as to allow the return of a person seeking asylum in the territory of a Contracting State, to a country where his life or freedom would be threatened on account of his race, religion, nationality, membership of a particular social group or political opinion'. Cruz, *Shifting Responsibility*, p. 70. The note does not, however, appear to have been carried over in later editions. Furthermore, no standard or recommendation is contained regarding non-penalisation for protection seekers or refugees, nor reference ever made to obligations in general human rights instruments.

54 Some countries, such as France, Italy and the Netherlands, have waived or reimbursed fines in those cases where the person in question is subsequently admitted to the asylum system, as long as the case is not considered 'manifestly unfounded'. Other countries, such as Germany and the United Kingdom, have argued that there is no connection between the transporting of a passenger without valid papers and the fact that they are asylum-seekers, fining carriers regardless of protection concerns. The latter argument seems somewhat inconsistent with the actual implementation. Consequently, the United Kingdom has been seen to reimburse fines levied for those who eventually receive refugee status (although not subsidiary forms of protection) and Denmark conversely in periods only fined insufficiently documented asylum-seekers, but not bona fide tourists. Cruz, *Shifting Responsibility*, pp. 41, 50.

55 Council Directive 2001/51/EC, 28 June 2001.

56 In 2003 UNHCR thus approached the Irish authorities for exemption from fines in cases involving persons seeking refugee protection. The Irish Minister of Justice refused to do this on the grounds that such a policy would make controls unworkable and further encourage false asylum claims. Hathaway, *Rights of Refugees*, p. 385.

57 Hathaway, *Rights of Refugees*, p. 386; Cruz, *Shifting Responsibility*, p. 74; J. Vedsted-Hansen, 'Sanktioner mod transportselskaber med "inadmissible passengers"', (1989) 71 *Juristen*

Article 31 obliges states not to penalise refugees for irregular access to their territory, and was specifically inserted as recognition that refugees may occasionally have an overriding need to seek entry, even if under false pretences or not in possession of proper documentation.[58] It should be remembered, however, that Article 31 is not an absolute prohibition, and according to Article 31(2) states may still uphold 'necessary' restrictions on the movement of refugees and other immigrants.[59] While it may be applicable in some instances, it is thus uncertain whether it prohibits measures such as carrier sanctions more generally. Where countries explicitly waive fines in cases where inadmissible passengers subsequently seek asylum, this would seem at least to partly pre-empt the argument. Furthermore, to the present author it remains questionable whether carrier liability legislation may meaningfully be described as a penalisation of refugees as long as the carrier, and not the refugee, is fined. Nonetheless, some carriers have been seen to introduce clauses into their general conditions of carriage that make passengers liable for any fines or other expenditure incurred as a result of improper documentation.[60] In such cases it is arguable that carrier legislation indirectly leads to a penalisation of asylum-seekers in potential violation of Article 31.

Even if these concerns are acknowledged and addressed by implementing states, however, neither is in practice likely to prove an effective guarantee for those in need of protection. Article 31 only applies to refugees who have already entered the territory of the host state. As long as airline companies are faced with a prospect of substantial economic penalisation for erroneous decisions regarding undocumented asylum-seekers,

---

219–33; Feller, 'Carrier sanctions', 58. In addition, Cruz argues that the effect of carrier sanctions in preventing refugees from boarding aircraft in order to seek asylum may amount to a violation of Art. 31(2) prohibiting restrictions to the movement of refugees other than those necessary. Cruz, *Shifting Responsibility*, p. 75. The argument, however, seems to overlook the territorial structure of the Refugee Convention. The application of this article is limited to refugees already 'in the country of refuge' and thus cannot apply to pre-departure rejection by carriers.

[58] Goodwin-Gill and McAdam, *Refugee in International Law*, p. 384; Vedsted-Hansen, 'Sanktioner mod transportselskaber', 130.

[59] G. Goodwin-Gill, 'Article 31 of the 1951 Convention Relating to the Status of Refugees: non-penalisation, detention, and protection', in Feller, Türk and Nicholson, *Refugee Protection*, pp. 185–252, at p. 185.

[60] A. la Cour Bødtcher and J. Hughes, 'The effects of legislation imposing fines on airlines for transporting undocumented passengers', in Kjærum, *Effects of Carrier Sanctions*, pp. 6–13, at p. 10. Further, the ICAO Standards under the 1944 Chicago Convention provide that airlines may attempt to recover costs related to removal and return flights from inadmissible passengers. Annex 9, Standard 5(10).

they are likely to adopt a preventive logic of 'if in doubt, leave them out'.[61] Second, even in cases where governments have made exceptional arrangements to ensure that asylum-seekers may board without visas, a number of cases have been documented in which airlines have opted to reject passengers regardless.[62] While the above considerations may thus bolster the position of asylum-seekers who have already arrived, they bring little consolation to those turned away by private agents at the border or point of departure.[63]

This leads us to the more fundamental question, namely whether rejection by airlines or other private enforcers of migration control may raise state responsibility in regard to core refugee obligations, in particular the principle of *non-refoulement*. It has been argued that carrier sanctions and similar use of private agents undermines the effectiveness of the *non-refoulement* principle and other core refugee protection obligations, and that as such these practices are therefore incompatible with an interpretation and implementation of Article 33 of the Refugee Convention and similar requirements in 'good faith'.[64] Similarly, general concern over the effect of carrier sanctions has been expressed by the Human Rights Committee with regard to the right to leave any country expressed in Article 12(2) of the International Covenant on Civil and Political Rights.[65]

Nonetheless, states have insisted on their right to impose carrier sanctions and have generally rejected the notion that such measures entail any human rights responsibility on behalf of the state implementing carrier legislation.[66] Equally, in the *Prague Airport* case, the UK House of Lords argued that the long-standing and widespread state practice regarding visa regimes and carrier sanctions could not be interpreted as being contrary to international law.[67] Rather than relate to arguments concerning the effectiveness or good faith interpretation of refugee and human rights

---

[61] Hathaway, *Rights of Refugees*, p. 384; Noll, *Negotiating Asylum*, p. 177.

[62] La Cour Bødtcher and Hughes, 'Effects of legislation', pp. 6–7.

[63] Nicholson, 'Immigration Act 1987', 617.

[64] Goodwin-Gill and McAdam, *Refugee in International Law*, pp. 377–80, 387–90; Nicholson, 'Immigration Act 1987', 618; Feller, 'Carrier sanctions', 59.

[65] Human Rights Committee, Concluding Observations of the Human Rights Committee: Austria, UN Doc. CCPR/C/79/Add.103, 19 November 1998, para. 11.

[66] Goodwin-Gill, *Refugee in International Law*, 2nd edn, p. 252.

[67] *R. (European Roma Rights Centre and Others) v. Immigration Officer at Prague Airport and Another*, House of Lords, para. 28. See further Goodwin-Gill and McAdam, *Refugee in International Law*, p. 371. The principal matter of the case, however, did not concern the use of carrier sanctions, but rather the responsibility of the United Kingdom's own authorities under the 1951 Refugee Convention and other human rights instruments when acting abroad. See discussions above in sections 3.5.2.5 and 4.3.3.

obligations, the main arguments for rejecting state responsibility under international refugee law seem to rely on the two premises that these measures are implemented by private actors and not states, and often extraterritorially, beyond the sanctioning state's effective control.

The expansion of private involvement in migration control in recent years thus raises two questions. The first concerns when, if ever, the actions of private entities may give rise to state responsibility under refugee and human rights law. The second question is whether the geographical venue of such privatised migration controls matters in the assessment of possible state responsibility. As will be seen, although the fundamental distinction between public and private affects state responsibility in this field, principled exceptions nonetheless exist to hold states accountable for human rights violations carried out by non-state entities under international law.

5.4 The public/private distinction

In both national and international law the dualism between public and private creates an initial presumption against engaging the responsibility of a state for actions not carried out by agents of the state.[68] As noted by the International Court of Justice in the *Genocide* case,

the fundamental principle governing the law of international responsibility [is that] a State is responsible only for its own conduct, that is to say the conduct of persons acting, on whatever basis, on its behalf.[69]

Put plainly, private conduct is not in principle attributable to the state.[70] The separation between the public and private spheres has been a constitutive element of liberal societies and remains a key norm of both domestic and international law.[71] In the modern vision of the nation state, regulatory functions and the exercise of power came to be centralised and monopolised by the state. Outside this, the market and private relations are both considered to be apolitical and thus subject to regulation under

---

[68] O. D. Schutter, 'Extraterritorial jurisdiction as a tool for improving the human rights accountability of transnational corporations', background paper to the SRSG on human rights and transnational corporations, UN High Commissioner for Human Rights, 2006, p. 18.

[69] *Bosnia and Herzegovina v. Serbia and Montenegro*, para. 406.

[70] Higgins, *Problems and Process*, p. 153.

[71] Chinkin, 'Critique of the public/private dimension', 389.

distinct legal regimes both at the national and the international levels.[72] Just as principles of national sovereignty and territory serve to delineate the state horizontally, the public/private distinction could thus be argued to delineate the state vertically, towards its subjects.

Arguably, the strict public/private dichotomy is a somewhat artificial legal construction. Neither historically, nor today, may clear and objective lines be drawn between the entities labelled 'private' and 'public'.[73] This concerns, first, the extent to which private actors, such as transnational companies and international commercial institutions, independently exercise authority that may sometimes parallel or even challenge that of the state.[74] Second, and more directly related to the present enquiry, private parties have always played a role in carrying out delegated government functions or assisting states in implementing governmental policies.[75] As was noted above, the last decades have seen a rapid expansion in the privatisation and outsourcing of activities hitherto carried out exclusively by the state. In these processes, it not only becomes more difficult to draw a firm line between public and private entities, the very notion of governmental activity and functions becomes equally blurred.[76]

From the perspective of accountability under international law, privatisation prompts two questions. The first concerns the extent to which non-state actors themselves may be considered subjects of international law. Strong arguments have been put forward in favour of the view that non-state actors, such as transnational corporations or international organisations, do, in principle, have certain human rights obligations, both when

---

[72] S. Sassen, *Territory, Authority, Rights: From Medieval to Global Assemblages* (Princeton University Press, 2006), pp. 187 ff.; Guild, 'Moving the borders of Europe', p. 45.

[73] Sassen, *Territory, Authority, Rights*, p. 188; M. Flinders, 'The politics of public–private partnerships', (2006) 7 *British Journal of Politics and International Relations* 215–39; Chinkin, 'Critique of the public/private dimension', 389; A. Clapham, *Human Rights in the Private Sphere* (Oxford: Clarendon Press, 1993), p. 188.

[74] Sassen to this extent talks about the rise of 'a new institutional zone of privatized agents' comprising different entities such as international arbitration systems, debt security and bond-rating agencies and international professional associations that all act to shift governance of the global economy from the public to the private sphere'. Sassen, *Territory, Authority, Rights*, p. 246. Another example includes the rise of private urban governance through home-owner and condominium associations – what McKenzie describes as 'privatopia'. E. McKenzie, *Privatopia* (New Haven: Yale University Press, 1994).

[75] Flinders, 'Politics of public-private partnerships', 224.

[76] Clapham, *Human Rights Obligations*, p. 11; Chinkin, 'Critique of the public-private dimension', 390.

acting independently and as a matter of complicity when acting in collaboration with other states.[77] From a practical perspective, however, this position meets a number of challenges. As expressed in treaty law, human rights are arguably designed to limit the exercise of *state* power and as such impose obligations only on states.[78] Under none of the regional human rights courts nor UN human rights complaint mechanisms may a claim be lodged against an individual or a private actor. As a matter of positive law, the effectiveness of international human rights law as it stands at present is thus dependent either on directly attributing violations to a state party or on establishing an indirect obligation of the state in regard to the violation in question.[79]

This leads us to the second question and the focus of the present chapter, namely the extent to which the state may nonetheless be held accountable for violations of human rights by private actors. This can occur in two instances. The first concerns situations where violations of human rights are directly attributable to a state, despite the fact that the violation itself was caused by a private actor. To this end, a useful starting point is provided by the Articles on the Responsibility of States for Internationally Wrongful Acts. As shall be seen, the privatisation of migration control may entail state responsibility in several situations, although the threshold for attribution remains high. A state's human rights obligations may, however, also be engaged even in situations where the conduct of private

---

[77] See in particular Clapham, *Human Rights Obligations* and further references at p. 58.

[78] R. Lawson, 'Out of control – state responsibility and human rights: will the ILC's definition of the "act of state" meet the challenges of the nation state in the 21st century?', in M. C. Castermans-Holleman, G. Hoof and J. Smith (eds.), *The Role of the Nation State in the 21st Century – Essays in Honour of Peter Baehr* (The Hague: Martinus Nijhoff, 1998), pp. 91–116, at p. 92.

[79] See for example Art. 34 of the European Convention on Human Rights, Art. 44 of the American Convention on Human Rights, Art. 1 of the Optional Protocol to the International Covenant on Civil and Political Rights, and Art. 22 of the UN Convention against Torture. Lawson, 'Out of control', p. 92. The question further remains as to how the establishment of human rights obligations of non-state actors would relate to obligations of states in respect of the same actions. Even though the two perspectives are often conceived of as being complementary (Clapham, *Human Rights Obligations*, p. 23), the present author is inclined to take the view that in practice the assignment of obligations with non-state actors themselves easily becomes a pretext for simultaneously disavowing responsibility of the outsourcing state and legitimising the competence of non-state actors to carry out functions such as migration control. For a contrary view and discussion of this objection, see the contributions in G. Teubner (ed.), *Global Law without a State* (Aldershot: Dartmouth, 1997). For a general overview of the debate and arguments for and against human rights responsibility of non-state actors, see Clapham, *Human Rights Obligations*, pp. 25–58.

actors is not, under the above framework, directly attributable to the state. This stems from the fact that human rights law places certain obligations on states to take measures to prevent, regulate or prosecute actions by private actors that violate human rights. In particular, all states have an obligation to exercise due diligence in regard to the conduct of private actors.

In both instances, however, the public/private distinction remains significant. While principles of international and human rights law do foresee a number of situations where states are responsible for wrongful acts of non-state actors, a presumption against this situation remains the starting point, and only on fulfilling certain tests may this presumption be successfully rebutted. And although the world is rife with examples of privatisation and concurrent state responsibility, as a matter of legal analysis the attribution of private conduct to the state in this sense remains an exception to the primary rule.[80]

In the case of direct attribution, overcoming the public/private dichotomy is, furthermore, only the first step in establishing human rights responsibility. Any human rights claim will also depend on the ability to establish the jurisdiction of the state in question and thus refers analysis back to the different jurisdictional tests set out in the previous chapter. Establishing human rights obligation of states outsourcing migration control to private agents acting abroad thus becomes doubly exceptional. In the case of due diligence obligations, however, the situation is potentially different. As will be discussed, here it is not the location of private actors or human rights violations that matters, but the acts or omissions by the state in encouraging or not acting to prevent such violations. That said, whether or not a state is exercising de jure jurisdiction and the extent of actual control over the private actor are, however, still likely to impact on the extent and degree of a state's due diligence obligations.

The legal difficulties in ensuring state responsibility for private conduct may appear somewhat paradoxical in the light of the fact that privatisation today constitutes a systemic feature of modern governance. Most

---

[80] The ILC Articles on State Responsibility have equally been criticised as reproducing an overly rigid public/private distinction. Chinkin thus argues that the Articles on State Responsibility fail to reflect the penetration of the private sphere indicated by state practice and growing jurisprudence and that if a state claims jurisdiction over the totality of functions under its territorial control, it might then be appropriate to assert its responsibility for all wrongful acts emanating from it, or from nationals subject to its jurisdiction. Chinkin, 'Critique of the public-private dimension', 389.

legal responses have been characterised by ad hoc solutions with little co-ordination and a sometimes circular logic.[81] The very definition of the private sphere is based on its consisting of *non*-state actors, *inter alia* autonomous and independent of government funding, control, authority or direction. By defining private actors simply by what they are not, it first of all becomes difficult to distinguish between the very different actors in this field and their rather different relationships to the state, from bands of private vigilantes to international security or military contractors. Second, and more fundamentally, this dichotomous definition serves to reinforce the notion that private actors are prima facie removed from the sphere of public international law.[82] It is in this sense that establishing state responsibility in cases of privatisation becomes problematic, as it sets out by assuming a distinction that may simply not be there in the first place.

5.5 Private actors exercising governmental authority

The previous chapters have dealt primarily with the level and extent of obligations for extraterritorial acts, yet the key question in regard to private involvement in migration control is whether conduct by private actors can even be attributed to the state. In such an enquiry recourse may be had to the International Law Commission's Articles on State Responsibility, which set out a number of general secondary norms regarding attribution and consequences of internationally wrongful acts. While not binding as a matter of treaty law, the principles may be considered customary international law.[83] That these principles are further applicable to human rights and refugee law has been affirmed both in the commentary to the Articles and through the reflection on and application of the principles contained by the human rights treaty bodies.[84]

---

[81] Flinders, 'Politics of public-private partnerships', 299.

[82] Alston, 'The "not-a-cat" syndrome', p. 3.

[83] R. McCorquodale and P. Simons, 'Responsibility beyond borders', (2007) 70 *Modern Law Review* 598–625, at 601; Lauterpacht and Bethlehem, 'Scope and content', p. 108. For an overview of the debate on codifying the Articles as a UN Convention, see J. Crawford and S. Olleson, 'The continuing debate on a UN convention on state responsibility', (2005) 54 *International and Comparative Law Quarterly* 959–68.

[84] McCorquodale and Simons, 'Responsibility beyond borders', 602; McGoldrick, 'Extraterritorial effect'; Crawford, *Articles on State Responsibility*, p. 25; Lawson, 'Out of control', p. 115. As noted in, for example, *Banković*, 'the Court recalls that the principles underlying the Convention cannot be interpreted and applied in a vacuum. The Court must also take into account any relevant rules of international law when examining

Under the ILC Articles, state responsibility may arise in two types of instances when functions are delegated to private actors: where such actors are empowered to exercise governmental authority, and where states authorise, direct or control otherwise private conduct. The first of these is set out in Article 5:

The conduct of a person or entity which is not an organ of the State under article 4 but which is empowered by law of that State to exercise elements of the governmental authority shall be considered an act of the State under international law, provided the person or entity is acting in that capacity in the particular instance.

This article was specifically included to take account of the growing number of situations in which governmental functions are outsourced or privatised to corporations, semi-public entities or public agencies. In such instances, otherwise private actors may be considered 'para-statal entities' to the extent that they are empowered to exercise specified elements of governmental authority.[85]

Importantly, the justification for attributing conduct of such entities to a state does not depend on the state exercising specific control in regard to the conduct, but rather on the conferral of authority through domestic law. The extent to which states carry out direct supervision and monitoring is thus not important. Neither is it decisive whether the conduct of private companies or other entities is carried out within or outside the territory; the link between the state and the entity is national law.[86]

questions concerning its jurisdiction and, consequently, determine State responsibility in conformity with the governing principles of international law.' *Banković*, para. 57.

Contrary to this, some scholars have argued that human rights constitute *lex specialis* or a legal regime *sui generis* and as such are specifically exempted from the scope of the ILC Articles under Art. 55. According to Evans and Clapham, the Articles on State Responsibility are best seen as 'operating in an altogether different realm' from human rights and as such should not be considered appropriate in the interpretation of human rights instruments, which do not operate as inter-state treaties. M. D. Evans, 'State responsibility and the European Convention on Human Rights: role and realm', in M. Fitzmaurice and D. Sarooshi (eds.), *Issues of State Responsibility before International Judicial Institutions* (Oxford: Hart Publishing, 2004), pp. 139–60, at p. 160; Clapham, *Human Rights in the Private Sphere*, p. 188.

To the present author, however, it does not appear from refugee and human rights instruments that they constitute *lex specialis* or a legal regime *sui generis* in this regard. For an overview of this discussion and a critique of Clapham's and Evans' position see Lawson, 'Out of control' and the references therein.

[85] Crawford, *Articles on State Responsibility*, p. 100.   [86] Ibid., p. 101.

Yet it is equally underscored that attribution of conduct under Article 5 should be understood as a 'narrow category' and that its application is limited in several respects.[87] First, the law in question must specifically authorise the conduct as involving the exercise of public authority. Second, the conduct leading to a breach of an international obligation must be related to the exercise of this public authority or governmental activity and not other actions, private or commercial, by the actor in question.

Consequently, the scope of attribution clearly depends on how 'government authority' is conceived. The article itself is silent on this issue, nor does the commentary attempt any actual definition. The emphasis in the commentary that the actors in question are considered 'para-statal' entities could be read in at least two ways. In the first instance, attribution will depend on the authority exercised by non-state agents to *substitute* or replace regulation that would otherwise be carried out by the state itself. As an example of this, Crawford mentions the contracting of private prison guards to exercise public powers of detention pursuant to judicial sentencing or prison regulations.[88] The test of attribution is in this case rigorous and dependent on the authority exercised being a *necessary* governmental function.

A more contextual reading could, however, also be established. In this instance, attribution will depend on the extent to which authority is conferred on private actors to carry out regulatory functions in extension of and *parallel* to similar functions and powers exercised by the state. The nuances between these two tests may be subtle, yet they are likely to carry particular importance in regard to the present enquiry. Arguably, the expansion of migration control carried out by private actors at offshore locations may be seen as an exercise of governmental authority sanctioned by and parallel to that carried out by states themselves at the border and elsewhere. Yet whether or not the control performed by an actor such as a private carrier substitutes for an otherwise necessary exercise of government authority is at least more debatable.

The correctness of the latter reading is indirectly supported by the commentary. While acknowledging that the specific thresholds or criteria for defining government authority are to some degree dependent on the particular society, it is suggested that the test does not rely only on the content of powers conferred, but equally on the way in which powers are conferred, the purpose for which they are exercised and the extent to which entities are accountable to governments in their exercise of

---

[87] Ibid., p. 102.   [88] Ibid., p. 100.

such powers.[89] Second, to clear any doubts that the application of Article 5 is relevant in some cases relating to the privatisation of migration control, the commentary explicitly mentions the delegation of 'certain powers in relation to immigration control or quarantine' to '[p]rivate or state-owned airlines' as an example of private actors exercising governmental authority.[90] As a sovereign prerogative of the state, the exercise of migration control may thus undoubtedly be characterised as an exercise of 'governmental authority'.

The general requirements set out above will, however, have to be fulfilled in regard to each type of delegation and the specific circumstances of the arrangement. Only in a few instances is delegation of migration control functions specifically and explicitly provided for in national law.[91] The situation is most likely to arise where private agents are formally incorporated to work alongside official border agents. An example is the use of private contractors by the United Kingdom both at its territorial borders and under the juxtaposed controls scheme. In both cases, the role of contractors is explicitly provided for in the Immigration, Asylum and Nationality Act 2006.[92] The authority of contractors is further narrowly circumscribed (searching vehicles, detaining irregular entrants and escorting them to national authorities), and private agents undergo both an authorisation process and ongoing monitoring. Together, this makes a strong case that any exercise of authority by private search officers is directly attributable to the United Kingdom. The implementation of

---

[89] Ibid., p. 101. [90] Ibid., p. 100.

[91] The concept of 'national law' remains debatable, however. Within the human rights context the 'law' requirement appears in a number of instruments to ensure the principle of legality and rule of law. It is, however, well established that administrative decrees, incorporated international law and well-established customary law may equally amount to national law within the meaning of e.g. the European Convention on Human Rights. Nevertheless, it remains decisive that rules of authority are accessible and reasonably clear (P. Lorenzen, L. A. Rehof, T. Trier, N. Holst-Christensen and J. Vedsted-Hansen, *Den Europæiske Menneskerettighedskonvention: med kommentarer (art 1–10)* (Copenhagen: Jurist- og Økonomforbundets Forlag, 2003), pp. 49–50). It is clear that too restrictive an interpretation of what constitutes 'empowered by national law' may lead some states to circumvent responsibility by delegating authority to private actors by other means. On the other hand, situations of de facto authorisation and instruction are covered by Art. 8 of the ILC Articles as dealt with in the subsequent section. While it may thus in some instances be hard to draw a firm line between situations where non-state actors are empowered to exercise governmental authority and situations where private agents are merely authorised to exercise certain powers by a state, it is nonetheless reasonable to assume that the respective applications of the two Articles are intended to close any gap.

[92] Ss. 40 and 41.

monitoring mechanisms to oversee the operations and address any complaints or failings could be taken as an indirect acknowledgement of this conclusion, and, importantly, private search officers may not themselves reject irregular entrants, but only escort them to governmental border officers.

A more contentious issue is whether, and under what circumstances, the widespread delegation of control functions to carriers may amount to an exercise of governmental authority in the meaning of Article 5. On the one hand, the legislative link is likely to be established in most cases. While national rules and requirements vary, the imposition of fines and sanctions is normally provided for by national law. On the other hand, whether such legislation amounts to an obligation actually to enforce controls remains debatable.[93] Sanctions constitute a third-party liability mechanism that may compel carriers to take on migration control functions,[94] yet to establish attribution it must be shown that legislation itself confers governmental authority in this respect.

As carrier liability has developed, however, legislation not only provides for a fines system but also imposes a number of direct duties on carriers to perform document and identity checks as well as an obligation to remove from the host country passengers without proper documentation.[95] In the EU context, Article 26(1)(b) of the Schengen Convention requires member states to incorporate into national legislation that

> The carrier shall be obliged to take all the necessary measures to ensure that an alien carried by air or sea is in possession of the travel documents required for entry into the territories of the Contracting State.

Further evidence of enforcement obligations can also be found in international aviation and maritime law. Under the 1944 Chicago Convention on Civil Aviation, standards have been developed essentially replicating key requirements of many states' national legislation.[96] Carriers are thus required to co-operate in establishing the validity of documents and visas

---

[93] Feller, 'Carrier sanctions'.

[94] Scholten and Minderhoud, 'Regulating immigration control', 134.

[95] Nicholson, 'Immigration Act 1987', 601; Cruz, *Shifting Responsibility*; Feller, 'Carrier sanctions', 51.

[96] Abeyratne, 'Air carrier liability', 679; Nicholson, 'Immigration Act 1987', 618. The ICAO Standards and Recommended Practices on Facilitation were first adopted in 1949 pursuant to Art. 37 of the 1944 Chicago Convention, designated as Annex 9 and subsequently developed and revised. While it is clear that recommendations are not binding, the legal status of standards has sometimes been questioned. According to Art. 38 of the Convention, 'standards' are 'recognized as necessary to facilitate and improve some aspects of international air navigation' and any non-compliance must be notified

and 'take necessary precautions at the point of embarkation to ensure that passengers are in possession of the documents prescribed by states of transit and destination for control purposes'.[97] Carriers are further responsible for the cost of custody and care of persons found to be inadmissible by national immigration authorities and for ensuring their return flight.[98] Similar requirements have been introduced in regard to maritime carriers under the 1965 Convention on Facilitation of International Maritime Traffic.[99]

More than the mere conditionality of sanctions, carrier legislation thus introduces a set of mandatory obligations under which carriers must act and report.[100] The detailed provisions in this regard reinforce the notion that carriers are expected and empowered to perform migration control on the express requirement of national authorities.[101] Rather than the sanctions themselves, the adjoined obligation placed on carriers to exercise certain functions of migration control may thus be argued to constitute a legislative conferral of governmental authority.

It has been objected that the extent of authority conferred does not amount to an express obligation by the carrier to reject passengers and in particular protection-seekers. Yet under Article 5 of the ILC Articles it is not necessary to show that a private agent actually acts on the instructions of the state, as long as they act in the capacity or pursuit of the governmental functions conferred.[102] If it is accepted that carrier legislation in at least some respects empowers carriers to exercise elements of governmental authority to check and inspect documents, the state therefore remains responsible even if a carrier or other private agent acts in excess of their authority or exercises independent discretion.[103] The mere inclusion of provisions in, for example, European legislation to honour the obligations under the Refugee Convention and other human rights instruments is not sufficient to relieve states of their obligations. Any actual instance of *refoulement* by carriers may give rise to state responsibility, and more

---

to the Council. As such, standards are generally considered binding and an integral part of the Convention.

[97] Annex 9, Standard 3(33).   [98] Annex 9, Standards 5(9) and 5(11).

[99] Standards concerning carrier responsibility regarding inadmissible persons and immigration pre-arrival clearance were introduced in the 1996 amendments. In 2005 recommended practices expanded this responsibility to include digital transfer of pre-departure and pre-arrival information to the destination state (12th edition, Annex 9, Chapter 3(K)).

[100] Scholten and Minderhoud, 'Regulating immigration control', 135.

[101] Abeyratne, 'Air carrier liability'.

[102] Crawford, *Articles on State Responsibility*, p. 101.   [103] Ibid., p. 102.

concrete steps are thus required to ensure that private migration control does not amount to violations of international refugee and human rights obligations.

In principle states thus remain responsible for some types of private migration control where, through a combination of national legislation and actual conferral of powers on private agents, the latter can be shown to exercise governmental authority. The criteria are most clearly fulfilled in cases where private contractors are granted direct powers or are incorporated into otherwise national border functions. However, an argument could also be made that carrier legislation as it has developed may equally amount to a delegation of governmental authority.

The extent to which Article 5 on State Responsibility can be made applicable in other cases concerning private migration control is more uncertain. From a legal perspective, it is doubtful that the activities of self-proclaimed border patrol groups, for example, or private visa handling agents can be argued to constitute governmental authority. Furthermore, in many instances the involvement of private actors for the purpose of migration control is not facilitated through law but, rather, administrative or otherwise de facto arrangements between authorities and the individuals or corporations involved.[104]

Second, it should be remembered that the notion of private actors exercising 'governmental authority' has deliberately been constructed as a narrow category under the ILC Articles, according to some scholars even 'exceptional',[105] and that case law substantiating the principles set out in the ILC Articles on this issue is still limited, especially in the human rights field. In particular, the lack of a definition of what constitutes 'governmental authority' opens up another point of contestation. For example, the United States, claiming to follow an overall principle not to outsource 'inherently governmental functions', is unlikely to accept that any actual privatisation of migration control functions amounts to this.[106]

5.6 Private conduct authorised, directed or controlled by a state

Beyond situations where private actors can be established to exercise governmental activity, state responsibility may also arise where individuals

---

[104] These instances may, however, be covered by Art. 8, dealt with below.
[105] H. Duffy, *The "War on Terror" and the Framework of International Law* (Cambridge University Press, 2005), p. 66.
[106] Verkuil, *Outsourcing Sovereignty*, pp. 58–60.

or corporations are controlled or directed by a state. According to Article 8 of the ILC Articles on State Responsibility,

The conduct of a person or group of persons shall be considered an act of State under international law if the person or group of persons is in fact acting on the instructions of, or under the direction or control of, that State in carrying out the conduct.

Unlike Article 5, the applicability of this article depends on establishing not a de jure relation through national law, but rather a 'real link' or the de facto power exercised by a state over the private actor in question.[107] Following the commentary, this relationship may arise in two types of instance: first, where conduct of private actors is in fact *authorised* by a state and thus acts on its instructions and, second, where private agents act under the *direction* or *control* of a state.[108]

State responsibility in situations where private actors have been authorised has been established in a number of cases where individuals or groups have been engaged or recruited to supplement or act as auxiliaries to state organs while still remaining outside the official state structures.[109] Attention has been brought to this situation particularly in the context of private military and security companies (PMSCs) employed to carry out offshore tasks in, for example, Iraq.[110]

That a state incurs responsibility when it instructs or authorises private actors has also been affirmed in the context of the European Convention on Human Rights. In *Stocke* v. *Germany*, the German police enlisted the help of a private individual, Mr Köster, to help retrieve Mr Stocke from France, where he had fled following German allegations of tax offences. Köster managed to divert to Germany a private aircraft carrying both of them, and Stocke was arrested there. While the case was rejected on its merits, the European Commission of Human Rights as a general principle established that

In the case of collusion between State authorities, i.e. any State official irrespective of his hierarchical position, and a private individual for the purpose of returning against his will a person living abroad, without the consent of his State of

---

[107] Crawford, *Articles on State Responsibility*, p. 110.   [108] Ibid.   [109] Ibid.

[110] McCorquodale and Simons, 'Responsibility beyond borders', 610; M. Bina, 'Private Military Contractor Liability and Accountability after Abu Ghraib', (2005) 39 *John Marshall Law Review* 1237–50; J. R. Coleman, 'Constraining modern mercenarism', (2004) 55 *Hastings Law Journal* 1493–537.

residence, to its territory where he is prosecuted, the High Contracting Party concerned is responsible for the acts of the private individual who *de facto* acts on its behalf.[111]

While it does not matter whether the delegation is carried out through national law, some degree of formalised agreement or pre-existing authorisation or instruction must, however, be shown in regard to the specific conduct carried out in these instances.[112]

In the context of migration control, states would thus only be responsible in situations where contracts or other explicit arrangements are made authorising or instructing private agents to carry out tasks that may violate refugee or human rights. The first criterion is likely to be fulfilled where private individuals or corporations are formally employed or awarded contracts or grants related to migration control or migration management. This would include the incorporation of private search officers, such as in the United Kingdom, the wholesale privatisation of certain checkpoints, as in the Israeli contract with private security firms along the West Bank wall, and the involvement of private contractors in setting up and running border control systems as in the case of the United States' contracts with Boeing. Following the *Stocke* case, it could further be argued that more practical arrangements may suffice as well – for example, cases where states ask or demand that private carriers ensure the forced return of passengers refused embarkation.

The second criterion, however, narrows application; it must be established that the contract or instructions clearly relate to any human rights violation in question.[113] In many instances, authority and instructions of private contractors are explicitly limited to avoid the exercising of power by non-officials that may breach national or international law. Thus tasks delegated to Boeing, for example, in setting up the SBInet are unlikely to amount to human rights violations in themselves, nor are the limited powers given to private search officers in the United Kingdom likely

---

[111] *Stocke v. Germany*, para. 168. Neither the Commission nor the Court found any violations of the Convention based on the facts, and the Court has yet to reaffirm the principle set out above. See further Lawson, 'Out of control', p. 104.

[112] In this sense, the cases where private actors act under the instructions of or have been authorised by the state do seem to share a number of features with the cases where states exercise governmental authority under Art. 5, and may perhaps usefully be thought of in close connection hereto. While Art. 5 concerns situations where states de jure delegate public functions, the first part of Art. 8 concerns situations where private actors are de facto authorised.

[113] Crawford, *Articles on State Responsibility*, p. 113.

to result in *refoulement*. Yet this is not to say that instructions explicitly have to authorise or demand conduct violating refugees' rights. Where a privately contracted border guard has the authority to reject an asylum-seeker directly, or where a carrier under orders returns a possible refugee to persecution, these actions and their consequences remain attributable to the state.[114]

State responsibility under Article 8 may, however, also arise in situations where private agents are not directly authorised, but nonetheless act 'under the direction or control' of a state. In principle this may cover a wider set of instances, as it does not depend on any contract or formal attachment between the state and the private actors in question. Yet, conversely, it must be established that the state directed or controlled the specific actions or operations in question.[115]

Determining when private conduct is in fact controlled or directed by a state moreover raises difficulties at both the abstract and practical levels. So far, the threshold has been set rather high. Thus in the *Nicaragua* case the International Court of Justice took the view that even though the United States had financed, supported and trained the *contras* fighting against the Nicaraguan government, this did not amount to 'such a degree of control in all fields as to justify treating the *contras* as acting on its behalf',[116] and that for legal responsibility to arise it would have to be proved that the United States had 'effective control of the military or paramilitary operations in the course of which the alleged violations were committed'.[117] Although the United States was held responsible for its own actions and support to the *contras*, the acts of the *contras* themselves could not be attributed to the United States.

The reasoning of the International Court of Justice in *Nicaragua* underscores that the control must be specifically related to the actions or tasks leading to a possible rights violation or unlawful act.[118] Unlike under

---

[114] That the latter case falls under the scope of Art. 8 can be verified by recourse to the suggested format for documents relating to the return of inadmissible persons set out in the ICAO standards. Following personal information regarding the returnee, the suggested format thus reads, 'The incoming carrier was instructed to remove the passenger from the territory of this State on flight (flight number) departing on (date) at (time) from (name of) airport.' Appendix 9 of Annex 9.

[115] Crawford, *Articles on State Responsibility*, p. 110.   [116] *Nicaragua* case, para. 17.   [117] Ibid.

[118] In this context, the notion of 'effective control' should not be confused with its use for the purpose of establishing extraterritorial jurisdiction as dealt with in chapter 4. In his Separate Opinion to the *Nicaragua* case, Judge Ago subscribed to the judgment as a whole but pointed to the need to define 'effective control', which in his opinion must involve some kind of specific instructions to commit a particular act or carry out a

Article 5, arguments that control and direction only concern limited and inherently lawful functions related to migration control cannot therefore prima facie be disregarded. On the other hand, preventing access to seeking asylum has been an explicit justification by a number of states for introducing carrier sanctions.[119] Even where reasons for privatisation are not so bluntly expressed, this requirement is likely to be fulfilled where it can be shown that violations of refugee rights are an unavoidable or foreseeable consequence of the state-controlled private conduct.[120]

Control or direction over the specific actions or operations leading to a violation would still, however, have to be established. Where the involvement of private actors is based on contracts or grants with clear descriptions of tasks and corresponding monitoring and reporting of activities, this may be less of an issue. Yet where arrangements are less tightly state-governed, it becomes difficult in practice to show that states direct or control specific conduct leading to human rights violations.

A case in point concerns migration control functions performed by carriers. On the one hand, carrier legislation and general requirements to check documents and so on are in themselves unlikely to be sufficient to meet the specificity requirement set by the International Court of Justice in the *Nicaragua* case. On the other hand, the increasing involvement of state officials in the way in which controls are carried out may amount to 'direction' or 'control', even within a restrictive interpretation of Article 8. As Scholten and Minderhoud evidence, not only does the Dutch government ensure general training of employees of KLM, the Dutch national airline, but also deployed immigration liaison officers to support and advise carriers in individual cases.[121] While the carrier remains responsible for effecting any rejections, a passenger allowed to board against the advice of immigration liaison officers will be subjected to an additional check directly after disembarkation to ensure that a potential fine can be linked to the carrier in question.[122] In practice, it may thus be hard to distinguish between 'advising' and direct 'instructions'. In the

---

particular task (paras. 188–9). C. Lehnart, 'Private military companies and state responsibility', IILJ Working Paper 2007/2, Institute for International Law and Justice, New York University School of Law, 2007, p. 13.

[119] Nicholson, 'Immigration Act 1987', 588–90; Vedsted-Hansen, 'Privatiseret Retshåndhævelse', pp. 171–2; Cruz, *Shifting Responsibility*, p. 85.

[120] Crawford, *Articles on State Responsibility*, p. 113.

[121] Scholten and Minderhoud, 'Regulating immigration control', 137–40.   [122] Ibid., 140.

Netherlands airlines have thus been shown to follow immigration liaison officer advice in more than 99 per cent of all cases.[123]

Recently developed systems to pre-authorise passengers in, for example, the United Kingdom and the United States may provide an even clearer example. Under the Secure Flight and APIS schemes operated by the United States, carriers are obliged to forward advance passenger information (API) data no later than thirty minutes prior to departure. The Transportation Security Administration will then vet passengers, and any passenger on a federal watch list or with insufficient information forwarded will result in a 'not-cleared' message prohibiting boarding being relayed back to the carrier.[124]

It should be noted that the test for 'control' or 'direction' established in the *Nicaragua* case has been challenged as being too inflexible in a world where privatisation is becoming prevalent in an increasing number of fields.[125] In the *Tadić* case,[126] the International Criminal Tribunal for the former Yugoslavia (ICTY) thus explicitly rejected the *Nicaragua* test, arguing that

The requirement of international law for the attribution to States of acts performed by private individuals is that the State exercises control over the individuals. The degree of control may, however, vary according to the factual circumstances of each case. The Appeals Chamber fails to see why in each and every circumstance international law should require a high threshold for the test of control.[127]

Similarly, in *Ilaşcu* the European Court of Human Rights was of the view that Russia's 'decisive influence over' and 'military, economic, financial and political support to' the separatist regime in Moldova was sufficient to attribute the actions of the Moldavian Republic of Transnistria to Russia and thus establish Russian jurisdiction and responsibility.[128] How much can be gained from these cases is, however, still uncertain. The

---

[123] Ibid., 138.
[124] Department of Homeland Security, Bureau of Customs and Border Protection, Advance Electronic Transmission of Passenger and Crew Member Manifests for Commercial Aircraft and Vessels, Final rule, 19 CFR Parts 4 and 122, 7 December 2005; Department of Homeland Security. Transportation Security Administration, Secure Flight Program, Final rule, 49 CFR Parts 1540, 1544, and 1560, 28 October 2008.
[125] Lehnart, 'Private military companies', p. 14; McCorquodale and Simons, 'Responsibility beyond borders', 609.
[126] *Prosecutor v. Tadić*, International Criminal Tribunal for the former Yugoslavia (Appeals Chamber), IT-94-1-A, 15 July 1999.
[127] *Prosecutor v. Tadić*, para. 117.   [128] *Ilaşcu and Others v. Moldova and Russia*, para. 392.

ICTY was arguably set up to consider issues of individual criminal responsibility, not state responsibility.[129] The International Court of Justice thus expressly rejected the 'overall control' test applied in *Tadić*, and instead reaffirmed the notion of 'effective control' and principles for attribution set out in *Nicaragua*.[130] Even if the test applied in *Ilaşcu* is adopted, many cases where states engage private actors for the purpose of migration control will still fall below this threshold.

The criteria for attribution and state responsibility in respect of actions by private agents thus evidently remain higher than in the case of outsourcing or relations between states, where merely 'aiding or assisting' another state in committing an internationally wrongful act is sufficient to establish collaborative or derivative state responsibility.[131]

Moreover, establishing the 'real link' between an outsourcing state, the private actor and the human rights violation in question becomes further complicated when public/private relationships grow more complex and multi-layered. The widespread use of sub-contractors by airline companies and large-scale border contractors such as Boeing adds another layer to the attribution analysis, both as a matter of law and in the often complex matter of ascertaining the facts of the case. The determination of state responsibility in these instances will have to rely either on directly

---

[129] Crawford, *Articles on State Responsibility*, p. 112.

[130] *Bosnia and Herzegovina v. Serbia and Montenegro*, para. 403. See also *Case concerning Armed Activities on the Territory of the Congo (DR Congo v. Uganda)*, International Court of Justice, 19 December 2005.

[131] ILC Articles on State Responsibility, Art. 16. See further Crawford, *Articles on State Responsibility*, pp. 148–51. Nonetheless, some scholars have argued that while Art. 16 covers only inter-state relations, the increased direct liability of corporations and private actors under international law may extend it to apply in relations between outsourcing states and private corporations as well. McCorquodale and Simons, 'Responsibility beyond borders', 613–4. If this view is correct, it would substantially lower the threshold for attributing private conduct to states and corresponding legal responsibility. The argument, however, seems to build on at least two assumptions. First, as discussed above, it is still questionable to what extent private corporations do incur direct responsibility under international law, and although one may point to specific examples, the position hardly finds general support or any precedent within refugee law. Second, it seems uncertain at best whether the requirements laid down in Art. 16 even lend themselves to extending their application to private actors. In particular, application of Art. 16 requires that the act is considered 'internationally wrongful' both by the acting and by the aiding or assisting state. This would seem to require a firm legal basis for the international liability of the private actor that matches that of the state in the specific case. Consequently, one would have to conclude that if the International Law Commission intended to set a similar threshold for establishing state responsibility in the case of private actors as in the cases of outsourcing or of assisting third states, the Commission would have used similar language.

showing that the sub-contractor is acting under state instructions or control, or on a two-step analysis, first attributing the conduct of the main contractor to the state and, second, establishing the relationship of the sub-contractor vis-à-vis the main contractor.[132]

Additional complications arise where private actors act as intermediaries between two or more states. As noted above, this is the case in countries like Ukraine, where a number of private companies funded by EU member states assist Ukrainian authorities in reinforcing border control between Ukraine and Russia.[133] Such situations are likely to become more typical as co-operation with third countries on migration is increasingly facilitated through financial framework programmes predominantly implemented by non-state actors.[134] Establishing any legal responsibility of the outsourcing or funding state in these situations is complicated by the fact that private involvement often only amounts to assistance to third-country national authorities, which remain the agents carrying out actual controls. If such co-operation is facilitated directly between the national authorities of two states, the first state may be held responsible if it is found to assist or aid the second state in committing an internationally wrongful act.[135] Yet, where non-state entities act as intermediaries, it would have to be proved, first, that the private company is acting under the direction and control of the funding state and, second, that the attributable conduct of that company aids or assists foreign authorities in violating refugee law or other international norms.[136]

5.7 The concomitant requirement of jurisdiction

So far, state responsibility for the conduct of private actors has been considered in general terms, with little consideration as to geography and territorial sovereignty principles. But what happens to the assessment of

---

[132] For a parallel issue, McCorquodale and Simons discuss the problems of 'penetrating the corporate veil' and establish state responsibility for transnational corporations with legally separate sub-entities. McCorquodale and Simons, 'Responsibility beyond borders', 616–17.

[133] Gatev, 'Border security in the eastern neighbourhood'.

[134] In the EU context, see in particular the AENEAS programme and the succeeding Thematic Programme of Cooperation with Third Countries in the Areas of Migration and Asylum.

[135] ILC Articles on State Responsibility, Art. 16. See further Crawford, *Articles on State Responsibility*, pp. 148–51.

[136] McCorquodale and Simons, 'Responsibility beyond borders', 611; Clapham, *Human Rights Obligations*, p. 263.

state responsibility when private migration control is carried out extraterritorially as opposed to at the border or inside the territory? As was noted above, the privatisation of migration control has a strong extraterritorial component. This concerns not only carrier sanctions but also the use of contractors at offshore migration control zones, privately operated holding zones and the increased use of private visa-handling agents.

For the initial step of attributing the conduct of private actors to a state it does not matter whether this conduct takes place within or outside the state's territory.[137] Yet in the second step of establishing state responsibility under international refugee and human rights law, jurisdiction – territorial or extraterritorial – in most cases remains a requirement. When attributing otherwise private conduct to a state, this conduct becomes an 'act of state', and thus for all purposes under international law such conduct is considered as if it were carried out by the state itself. It logically follows that the scope of state responsibility *ratione loci* for attributed conduct of private actors cannot extend beyond that of state responsibility for the actions of its own agents and authorities.

Since the applicability of the *non-refoulement* principle and other key human rights norms remains limited to a state's jurisdiction, any instance where private migration control attributable to a state is carried out extraterritorially thus refers analysis back to the jurisdictional assessment dealt with in the previous chapter. As in the case of extraterritorial acts by a state's own agents, the threshold for establishing state responsibility will depend on the legal geography and jurisdictional test applied. Where private migration control is enacted on the high seas or in international airspace, or a functional approach to jurisdiction for other reasons is applied, there is a strong argument that, for example, denial of boarding by carrier personnel would amount to an exercise of jurisdiction and the state attributable may thus be held responsible for any violations of extraterritorially applicable refugee and human rights obligations.

Yet where private agents act within the sovereign territory of a third state, the relevant tests for establishing personal or geographical control must be borne in mind. Overall control of a place or location could be argued to apply, for example, in the case of the US enforcement of pre-embarkation controls at designated zones within foreign airports or of the United Kingdom's juxtaposed controls scheme. Equally, in situations where the rejection of passengers either at the country of destination or in transit countries is followed by detention or forced return, this would

---

[137] Lawson, 'Out of control', pp. 95–6.

in all likelihood bring about extraterritorial jurisdiction in the personal sense. Reports regarding the restraint of unwilling deportees through drugs, physical restraint aids and other measures of physical force not only cause concern in themselves, but also clearly underline the fact that forced return flights may well amount to full and physical control over individuals.[138] Whether or not detention and return flights are managed by private actors or the outsourcing state in principle does not matter. If rejection of embarkation by a private airline can be attributed to the state, jurisdiction and a possible violation of the *non-refoulement* principle may be established in combination with subsequent measures, for example where refugees are detained in waiting zones or during forced removal.

Not all conduct by private actors in regard to migration control, even though attributable to the outsourcing state, may, however, amount to jurisdiction. As in the case of pre-clearance schemes operated directly by national immigration officers, it is at least debatable whether similar rejections by airline officials are sufficient to establish extraterritorial jurisdiction in the personal sense.[139] Furthermore, in some instances the use of private agents clearly works to distance asylum-seekers further from otherwise established jurisdictional bases. A case in point is the increased use of commercial visa-handling agents and concomitant plans to out-source entirely to private contractors the running of common EU visa application centres. The private intermediary means that asylum-seekers not only are prevented access to embassy or consulate premises, but are even denied any direct contact with consulate or other government officials – both something that may otherwise be at least partly relied on to establish jurisdictional commitments and thus in some instances human rights obligations of the sending state.[140]

Where privatised migration control operates extraterritorially, over-coming the public/private distinction to rebut the basic presumption against attributing responsibility for private conduct to the state is thus only the first step. In addition, extraterritorial jurisdiction of the state in question will have to be established. Even though the analysis above points to the conclusion that both carrier sanctions and other forms of private migration control may under certain circumstances be attributed to

---

[138] International Transport Workers Federation, 'Controlling travel document fraud and illegal migration', working paper presented at the ICAO FAL Division meeting in Cairo, 22 March–2 April 2004.

[139] *R. (European Roma Rights Centre and Others) v. Immigration Officer at Prague Airport and Another*, House of Lords. See further above, section 4.3.3.

[140] Noll, 'Seeking asylum at embassies'. See further above, section 4.3.3.

the outsourcing state, it may not always amount to extraterritorial jurisdiction. In effect, what is created is another barrier. At least under more
doctrinal analyses of both attribution and extraterritorial jurisdiction,
access to refugee and human rights protection thereby becomes doubly
'exceptional'.

That being so, it should be borne in mind that a jurisdictional assessment would have to be carried out looking at the combined degree of
control exercised by both private and public actors. Thus where private conduct can be attributed to a state, this adds to any assessment
of extraterritorial control exercised by a government's own agents. This is
particularly relevant in cases where private and public forms of migration
control are exercised in close connection or take the shape of hybrid pub-
lic/private partnerships. One could thus imagine situations where neither
the degree of authority exercised by immigration liaison officers nor the
controls performed by carriers on their own might suffice to establish
extraterritorial jurisdiction, but where the close inter-operation between
the two means that they cumulatively reach the threshold for extraterritorial jurisdiction.

5.8 Due diligence and indirect responsibility for conduct of private actors

While the principles of state responsibility may be a useful starting point
for analysing when the conduct of private actors is directly attributable
to a state, the law on state responsibility should not be considered a
straitjacket.[141] Under human rights law states also maintain certain positive or due diligence obligations to ensure the fulfilment of human rights
protection, not just in regard to its own actions, but also where human
rights violations are carried out by private individuals or other non-state
actors.[142] These obligations do not stem from the conduct of private actors
being attributed to the state, but from the requirement of states to exercise due diligence in preventing human rights violations or investigating

---

[141] Lawson, 'Out of control', p. 109.
[142] A. Reinisch, 'The changing international framework for dealing with non-state actors',
in P. Alston (ed.), *Non-State Actors and Human Rights* (Oxford University Press, 2005), pp.
37–89, at pp. 79–80. The concept of due diligence is retained here as opposed to positive
obligations. The duty to exercise due diligence actually entails both positive and
negative obligations. As discussed below, the latter may be particularly important
where the locus of rights violations is to be found outside a state's territory and
jurisdiction.

and providing remedies for them when they occur, regardless of who commits them.[143]

As a matter of general international law, the due diligence principle has been affirmed by the International Court of Justice in several cases concerning inter-state relations. In the *Corfu Channel* case, the Court thus held Albania responsible because of its 'grave omissions' in not removing mines in its territorial waters or at least warning foreign states of their existence and location.[144] In the human rights context, the Inter-American Court of Human Rights in *Velásquez Rodríguez* v. *Honduras* similarly found that the widespread occurrence of disappearances in Honduras, even though it could not be proved that these were directly imputable to the Honduran government, nonetheless engaged the responsibility of Honduras, not 'because of the act itself, but because of the lack of due diligence to prevent the violation or to respond to it as required by the convention'.[145] Similarly, the European Court of Human Rights in *Osman* v. *United Kingdom* recognised that core obligations such as the right to life protected under Article 2 of the European Convention on Human Rights may imply a 'positive obligation for states to take preventive operational measures to protect an individual whose life is at risk from criminal acts of another individual'.[146] As emphasised in *Velásquez Rodríguez*, it is this omitting to exercise due diligence on behalf of the state that is decisive, and not the establishment of any causal relationship between the state and privately committed human rights violations.

The exact content of due diligence obligations is hard to determine in the abstract. The extent of a state's responsibility will depend both on the

---

[143] McCorquodale and Simons, 'Responsibility beyond borders', 617–8; Barnidge, *Non-state Actors and Terrorism*, pp. 55–112; Clapham, *Human Rights Obligations*, p. 239; Evans, 'State responsibility and the European Convention on Human Rights', pp. 151, 157.

[144] *Corfu Channel Case*, International Court of Justice, 9 April 1949. See further *United States Diplomatic and Consular Staff in Tehran*, International Court of Justice, 24 May 1980. Similarly, the notion that an occupying power has certain positive obligations towards civilians within the occupied territory was reaffirmed by the International Court of Justice in the *Congo* case.

[145] *Velásquez Rodríguez v. Honduras*, Inter-American Court of Human Rights, Series C, No. 4 (1988), 29 July 1988, para. 88.

[146] *Osman v. United Kingdom*, European Court of Human Rights, Application No. 23452/94, 28 October 1998, para. 1. See further D. M. Chirwa, 'The doctrine of state responsibility as a potential means of holding private actors accountable for human rights', (2004) 5 *Melbourne Journal of International Law* 1–36, at 9–11; M. Scheinin, 'State responsibility, good governance and indivisible human rights', in H.-O. Sano and G. Alfredsson (eds.), *Human Rights and Good Governance: Building Bridges* (The Hague: Martinus Nijhoff, 2002), pp. 29–45, at p. 35.

actual power of the state to intervene and the possibility of so doing, and on the foreseeability and knowledge of any human rights violations. Thus the Inter-American Court of Human Rights in *Velásquez Rodríguez* points out that a state must

take reasonable steps to prevent human rights violations and to use the means at its disposal to carry out a serious investigation of violations committed within its jurisdiction, to identify those responsible, to impose the appropriate punishment and to ensure the victim adequate compensation.[147]

While such a reasonability test is inherently malleable, it does emphasise that due diligence obligations must be assessed in the light of the issue at hand and the state's practical ability to prevent and to investigate human rights violations.[148] In *A. v. United Kingdom*, the European Court thus found that the existing UK criminal law was insufficient to ensure protection against child abuse.[149] In *Z. v. United Kingdom*, the Court argued that the United Kingdom had a positive obligation to remove children from abusive situations.[150] And in *Siliadin v. France*, the Court established a due diligence obligation under Article 4 that states must apply effective criminal sanctions to prevent the occurrence of situations where persons are held in slavery, servitude or forced labour by private individuals or groups.[151]

Further, in *Osman v. United Kingdom* the European Court of Human Rights underlined that while positive obligations do flow from, in this case, Article 2 of the Convention,

it must be established to its satisfaction that the authorities knew or ought to have known at the time of the existence of a real and immediate risk to the life of an identified individual or individuals.[152]

The obligation incumbent on states to exercise due diligence in securing and protecting human rights is equally established to extend not only

---

[147] *Velásquez Rodríguez v. Honduras*, para. 174.

[148] Chirwa, 'Doctrine of state responsibility', 10.

[149] *A. v. United Kingdom*, European Court of Human Rights, Application No. 25599/94, 23 September 1998.

[150] *Z. v. United Kingdom*, European Court of Human Rights, Application No. 29392/95, 10 May 2001.

[151] *Siliadin v. France*, European Court of Human Rights, Application No. 73316/01, 26 July 2005.

[152] *Osman v. United Kingdom*, para. 116. Both reasonableness and knowledge of the violation were similarly emphasised by the International Court of Justice in establishing the positive obligations of Iran in regard to the US embassy staff held hostage in Tehran. *United States Diplomatic and Consular Staff in Tehran*, paras. 32–33.

to situations within a state's territory but also to where states exercise extraterritorial jurisdiction through effective control over a geographical area. As was noted by the European Court of Human Rights in the *Cyprus* case, the mere

acquiescence or connivance of the authorities of a Contracting State in the acts of private individuals which violate the Convention rights of other individuals within its jurisdiction may engage that State's responsibility under the Convention.[153]

To what extent does such indirect responsibility arise in the context of privatised migration control? Notably, the *non-refoulement* principle itself is essentially a due diligence obligation. It requires states to prevent individuals from being subjected to persecution, torture or other inhuman treatment, even when these human rights violations are carried out in another country outside the jurisdiction of the state in question. Barring intervention in the sovereign sphere of another state, what may reasonably be expected from states in this regard is primarily couched in a negative preventive obligation: not to expel or turn back asylum-seekers where there is a substantial risk that they may be subjected to such treatment on return.

Yet there is nothing to support a reading that this obligation applies only to situations where persons are rejected or sent back by a state's own authorities. On the contrary, the inclusive language employed in Article 33 of the 1951 Refugee Convention prohibiting *refoulement* 'in any manner whatsoever' could be interpreted as providing an obligation even when rejection or returns are carried out by non-state actors. This does not turn on interpreting 'in any manner whatsoever' to imply a geographical extension of the *refoulement* prohibition itself, but rather that a state has an obligation to prevent *refoulement* no matter how and by whom it is carried out.[154]

Equally, the *Soering* line of cases establish a due diligence obligation as part of the prohibition against torture and inhuman and degrading treatment enshrined in Article 3 of the European Convention on Human Rights.[155] The *Soering* case involved the pending extradition of a murder

---

[153] *Cyprus v. Turkey*, para. 81.   [154] See above, section 3.2.1.

[155] Crawford, *Articles on State Responsibility*, pp. 145–6; Lawson, 'Out of control', p. 110; R. B. Lillich, 'The *Soering* case', (1991) 85 *American Journal of International Law* 128–49, at 142. As early as the 1960s, Art. 3 of the European Convention was interpreted as encompassing a *non-refoulement* principle (Goodwin-Gill and McAdam, *Refugee in International Law*, p. 210). See e.g. *X v. Belgium*, European Commission on Human Rights, Application No. 984/61, 29 May 1961. The principle has been affirmed since; see e.g. *Chahal v. United Kingdom*. On the general nature of the *Soering* doctrine see further

suspect from the United Kingdom to face trial and a possible death sentence in the United States. The United Kingdom flatly rejected having any responsibility for ill-treatment taking place in the United States clearly outside its jurisdiction. Nor could the United Kingdom be held to have facilitated a violation of Convention rights by the United States, since the United States is not a party to the Convention. Nonetheless, the European Court of Human Rights in effect established a due diligence obligation and held that through the act of extradition itself, the United Kingdom would have breached its obligations under Article 3 of the Convention not to act in a way that carried a 'real risk' of exposing individuals to ill-treatment by another state.[156]

That states may incur responsibility if they by acts or omissions fail to exercise due diligence in preventing rights violations carried out by non-state actors was more directly affirmed in *Elmi* v. *Australia*. Here, the Committee against Torture argued that the return of a Somali national to a situation where he had a well-founded risk of being subjected to torture by Somali clans would constitute *refoulement* in violation of Art. 3 of the Convention, despite the submission by the Australian government that these clans did not constitute public authorities or act in any official capacity.[157]

As regards private involvement in migration control, the notion of due diligence may be argued to impose indirect obligations on states in a number of scenarios where the private conduct cannot be directly attributed to the state in question. This concerns, first of all, cases where migration control or border patrols are carried out on private initiative with no official links to the authorities, such as the self-proclaimed Minutemen in the United States. Following from the above, the United States is not only under an obligation to examine and prosecute any alleged abuse of

---

above, section 4.2.2, and UNHCR, Interception of Asylum-Seekers and Refugees: The International Framework and Recommendations for a Comprehensive Approach, UN Doc. EC/50/SC/CRP.17, 9 June 2000, para. 62.

[156] *Soering*, paras. 88–91.

[157] *Sadiq Shek Elmi v. Australia*, Committee against Torture, Comm. No. 120/1998, 25 May 1999. A similar question was brought before the European Court of Human Rights in *H.L.R. v. France*, concerning the return of a Colombian drug trafficker who feared repercussions for co-operating with the French police. While the Court did not find any violation of Art. 3 in the present instance, it did note that

> Owing to the absolute character of the right guaranteed, the Court does not rule out the possibility that Article 3 of the Convention may also apply where the danger emanates from persons or groups or persons who are not public officials. However, it must be shown that the risk is real and that the authorities of the receiving State are not able to obviate the risk by providing appropriate protection. (*H.L.R. v. France*, European Court of Human Rights, Application No. 24573/94, 29 April 1997, para. 40)

immigrants or asylum-seekers by these groups, but also has a responsibility to intervene preventively in respect of groups or individuals where there is knowledge that their activities are likely to result in violations of the rights of immigrants and asylum-seekers.

Moreover, within a state's jurisdiction the due diligence principle may impose an obligation on states in respect of private border or immigration contractors, even where these clearly act outside or in excess of instructions and their conduct thus cannot be directly attributed to the state. In practical terms, this may require states to, for example, ensure strict regulatory frameworks for all such contractors, as well as relevant training and regular monitoring.[158]

Lastly, the due diligence principle could be argued to impose a responsibility on the territorial states hosting private contractors or other agents carrying out elements of migration control on behalf of or instructed by other states. This may close an important legal gap in putting an obligation on transit countries in respect of carriers or other private migration control companies operating at their borders, ports or airports. States hosting private migration control agents may thus in principle be held indirectly liable for not regulating the conduct of such agents and looking into any claims of unlawful detention or refusal to travel.[159]

While the existence of due diligence obligations in regard to private migration control is unquestionable for actions occurring within a state's jurisdiction, a more vexing question is whether due diligence obligations may similarly be extended in respect of private conduct and human rights violations taking place outside the state's jurisdiction. In principle, the application of positive human rights obligations does not depend on whether the violation occurs within the jurisdiction of the state. As noted above, the obligation to exercise due diligence may be violated wherever there is a failure to act or, as in the case of *Soering*, where a state's own actions will evidently lead to a human rights violation by other actors. The obligation to exercise due diligence is in this sense tied to the state's own actions or omissive delicts, not the state's control over the private actor (attribution) or the human rights victim (jurisdiction).[160]

---

[158] C. Hoppe, 'Passing the buck: state responsibility for private military companies', (2008) 19 *European Journal of International Law* 989–1014, at 993.

[159] Of course, like all due diligence obligations, a host state's responsibilities in this regard would be tempered by its actual powers to intervene, something that might not always be fulfilled. Furthermore, such interventions may naturally create tensions in regard to the countries demanding that carriers perform immigration checks.

[160] Cerone, 'Out of bounds?', p. 27.

Although such a view has still to find a foothold in human rights case law, the argument that states may retain certain obligations regarding rights violations or harm inflicted by non-state actors outside their jurisdiction has been affirmed more generally by the International Court of Justice. In *Nicaragua*, the Court thus held the United States to be 'under an obligation not to encourage persons or groups engaged in the conflict in Nicaragua' to act in violation of the Geneva Conventions and general principles of international humanitarian law, even though the acts of the *contras* could not in themselves be attributed to the United States.[161] Parallels may also be drawn with the principle of good neighbourliness and environmental law. As early as 1938, the *Trail Smelter* case established that

> no State has the right to use or permit the use of its territory in such a manner as to cause injury by fumes in or to the territory of another or the properties or persons therein, when the case is of serious consequence and the injury is established by clear and convincing fact.[162]

Both these cases support the general notion that states may carry due diligence obligations in regard to the conduct of non-state actors and where rights violations or harm occur outside its jurisdiction.

In the human rights context this has so far only been confirmed in cases concerning extraterritorial effect. As the European Court concluded in *Soering*, state parties are responsible 'for all and any foreseeable consequences of extradition suffered *outside their jurisdiction*'.[163] Arguably, however, the *Soering* line of cases differs from most cases of extraterritorial migration control in that the applicant was already within the territorial jurisdiction of the state at the time of application. While Mr Soering's presence in the United Kingdom is naturally a precondition for extradition, the court, however, emphasised that it was the act of extradition itself that triggered the responsibility of the United Kingdom and that this act was within its jurisdiction.[164] Seen in this light, it has thus been

---

[161] *Nicaragua*, para. 220.
[162] *Trail Smelter Arbitral Decision (United States v. Canada)*, Trail Smelter Arbitral Tribunal, Reports of International Arbitral Awards 3 1938, 1941, p. 1965. For a more contemporary affirmation of this principle see further *Legality of the Threat or Use of Nuclear Weapons*, Advisory Opinion, International Court of Justice, 8 July 1996, para. 29.
[163] *Soering*, para. 86 (emphasis added).
[164] Lillich, 'The *Soering* case', 133. This was expressed most clearly by the Commission:
> If, for example, a Convention State deports or extradites a person to a country where it is certain or where there is a serious risk that the person will be subjected to torture or inhuman treatment the deportation or extradition would, in itself, under such circumstances constitute inhuman treatment for

argued that the *Soering* doctrine may, *mutatis mutandis*, equally serve as a basis for evaluating the scope of the due diligence principle in situations where a state's conduct in regard to private actors carrying out migration control abroad has a foreseeable risk of entailing *refoulement* or other human rights violations.[165]

The content of due diligence obligations in such situations would, however, be somewhat more limited. Where a state does not exercise overall control of the territory in question, what may 'reasonably be expected' in this regard would be much more narrowly circumscribed by the degree of influence and power exercised over private actors and the knowledge and foreseeability of rights violations.[166]

Where more direct forms of control are exercised over the conduct of carriers or other private agents, for example by the positioning of immigration liaison officers to advise and check airline controls, the due diligence principle could be argued to impose on states a positive requirement to ensure that in the implementation of privatised controls, reasonable measures are taken to avoid the summary rejection of protection seekers, including vetting procedures, regular monitoring of performance and ensuring that relevant personnel have received

> which the deporting or extraditing State would be directly responsible under Article 3 of the Convention. The basis of State responsibility in such cases lies in the exposure of a person by way of deportation or extradition to inhuman or degrading treatment in another country. (*Soering*, para. 96. See further the similar reasoning of the Court on this matter, 7 July 1989, paras. 88–91)

[165] Lawson, 'Out of control', p. 111. This reading is indirectly supported by the ruling in *Al-Adsani v. United Kingdom*. The case involved concerned a claim that by granting the state of Kuwait immunity in a case concerning the alleged torture by Kuwait authorities of the applicant during his stay in Kuwait, the United Kingdom had failed to secure his right not to be tortured and denied him access to a court contrary to Arts. 3 and 6 of the Convention. While the Court rejected that there was a violation of Art. 3, in doing so it specifically reflected on the precedent set by *Soering*. According to the Court, Art. 3 imposes an obligation to 'secure' the rights under the Convention and thus both 'to take certain measures to ensure that individuals within their jurisdiction are not subjected to torture' (para. 38), and also where the 'Contracting State by reason of its having taken action which had as a direct consequence the exposure of an individual to proscribed ill-treatment' (para. 39). According to the Court, 'the applicant does not contend that the alleged torture took place within the jurisdiction of the United Kingdom or that the UK authorities had any causal connection with its occurrence' (para. 40). *A contrario*, it may then be argued that an obligation to prevent persons being returned to torture and inhuman or degrading treatment may persist even where the violation occurs outside the state's jurisdiction, but where a 'causal connection with its occurrence' can nonetheless be established.

[166] See, *inter alia*, *United States Diplomatic and Consular Staff in Tehran*, para. 68.

adequate training to carry out their task in respect of international legal obligations.[167]

But even where such control or influence cannot be established, certain negative and preventive obligations may remain with states which, through incentives or otherwise, encourage private actors to engage in migration control. Rick Lawson takes the broad view that a state may be held responsible under the European Convention on Human Rights 'if it has encouraged individuals to engage in acts contrary to human rights'.[168] The International Court of Justice in its *Wall* opinion has similarly suggested that a negative obligation 'not to raise any obstacle to the exercise' of fundamental human rights may remain even where the state does not exercise effective control.[169]

This is exactly what emerges from the *Soering* case – an obligation to abstain from acts that indirectly may lead to human rights violations by other actors. Such a principle is likely to be particularly relevant where conduct of private actors exercising extraterritorial migration control cannot be directly attributed to sanctioning states or where jurisdiction cannot be established. In the instance of carrier sanctions, states arguably retain a negative obligation not to pass legislation or in practice to refrain from implementing sanction schemes that carry a 'real risk' that asylum-seekers or refugees will be summarily rejected or turned back by private airline officers.

The notion of due diligence obligations may thus go some way to closing the responsibility gap, especially in situations where states have only limited control over private agents operating migration control within its jurisdiction, but also possibly in situations where privatised

---

[167] The extraterritorial dimension of due diligence obligations has also found expression in regard to the parallel issue of private military contractors. Art. 4 of the Montreux Document, currently signed by seventeen states and aimed at restating relevant obligations under international law, establishes that

> Contracting States are responsible to implement their obligations under international human rights law, including by adopting such legislative and other measures as may be necessary to give effect to these obligations. To this end they have the obligation, in specific circumstances, to take appropriate measures to prevent, investigate and provide effective remedies for relevant misconduct of PMSCs and their personnel. (Montreux Document on Pertinent International Legal Obligations and Good Practices for States related to Operations of Private Military and Security Companies during Armed Conflict, UN Doc. A/63/467, 17 September 2008)

[168] Lawson, 'Out of control', p. 104.

[169] *Legal Consequences of the Construction of a Wall in the Occupied Palestinian Territory*, para. 112. See further Cerone, 'Out of bounds?', pp. 23–6.

migration control is clearly linked to a state's own actions yet does not suffice to establish extraterritorial jurisdiction. It should be borne in mind, however, that the content of such obligations is not unaffected by considerations similar to those faced when directly attributing private conduct under the ILC Articles on State Responsibility: what may reasonably be expected from a state is likely to be considerably more limited in respect of private conduct taking place where the state exercises only more temporary or limited authority abroad than in respect of private conduct taking place within a state's territory.

Furthermore, determining the exact content of due diligence obligations is essentially a matter of interpretation and concrete assessment. Although the existence of a due diligence principle is not disputed in itself, it is hard, if not impossible, to give the concept and its content a clear-cut definition. Any application of the due diligence principle is highly dependent on the factual circumstances of the case, its legal geography and the content of the relevant norms. As a result, assessing what may reasonably be expected from a state is inherently open to contestation at both the normative and the evidentiary level.

This is especially true in situations where states do not exercise direct control over the act in question or effective control over the space in which it is carried out. In such situations states are more likely to argue that they lack the practical capabilities or means at their disposal required to honour due diligence obligations under refugee and human rights law, either for lack of actual control over the private actors in question or for lack of knowledge of their activities. The lack of specific case law so far testing the due diligence content of relevant norms under refugee and human rights law further exacerbates this problem and leaves the principled arguments with few anchor points for establishing the exact content of state obligations in regard to private migration control.

5.9 Conclusion

The involvement of private actors in migration control is a growing phenomenon. Over the last twenty years the widespread implementation of carrier liability legislation has turned all the world's major airlines into de facto pre-frontier border guards rejecting thousands of travellers each year. Today, however, the privatisation of migration control is far from limited to airlines or other transport companies. From the use of private contractors to run immigration detention facilities and enforce returns to the use of private search officers both at the border and at offshore control zones, private involvement in migration management is both expanding and taking new forms.

Asylum-seekers are thus increasingly likely to encounter the entry management mechanisms of the host state in the form of non-state actors. In the case of carriers, it is already well documented that the control carried out by employees of these companies constitutes a major impediment for any asylum-seeker wishing to reach his or her country of refuge by air or sea. About other types of private migration control knowledge is still scarce, yet it is safe to assume that similar problems may occur where asylum-seekers are refused entry by contracted migration officers or private groups carrying out border control on their own initiative.

This chapter has set out when and under what circumstances states may be held responsible under international refugee and human rights law when migration control functions are handed over to or taken up by private actors. While the traditional starting point remains that states cannot be held responsible for the conduct of private actors, a number of principled exceptions nonetheless apply. Under the ILC Articles on State Responsibility, private conduct may thus be attributed to states in two sets of circumstances: when private actors in reality constitute para-statal entities and thus exercise governmental authority, and when states can be shown to have authorised, controlled or directed the actions of private individuals or groups.

Both instances may be relevant to the case of migration control. In at least some cases the control functions performed by carriers may thus be argued to constitute an exercise of governmental authority within the meaning of Article 5 of the ILC Articles. So may the incorporation of private border guards or outsourcing of immigration detention centres to private contractors as long as these powers are provided for by national law. Even where this is not the case, states may still be held responsible under Article 8 for the conduct of private contractors where they can be shown to have authorised such conduct, for example through contracts, grants or other specific administrative arrangements. Lastly, the close monitoring of carrier control duties and case-by-case 'advice' by immigration liaison officers or national authorities may well amount to de facto 'control' or 'direction'.

In each case, however, the requirements for attributing private conduct to the outsourcing state remain substantial. Far from all private involvement in migration control is likely to be regulated through national law, and the notion of 'governmental authority' remains undefined and open to contestation. Similarly, states must be shown to exert a high degree of control or direction over the specific actions leading to, for example, *refoulement*, something that may be hard to prove in practice as few public accountability and monitoring mechanisms tend to exist in these situations.[170]

The high threshold for attribution shows that while the public/private distinction is not set in stone, it nonetheless retains importance even though it appears more and more artificial in relation to the reality surrounding us. By starting out presuming the separateness between public and private, an extra legal operation is demanded in order to rebut this presumption. In this sense, the public/private distinction continues to constitute a *Grundnorm*, an underlying or basic normative ordering that has to be overcome before the somewhat more exceptional situation of state responsibility for private actions can occur. While case law and interpretation are likely to continue to develop, analysis of the ILC Articles and current international case law points to the conclusion that many, but probably not all, instances where states engage private actors for the purpose of migration control may be attributed to the outsourcing state under international law.

Furthermore, where private migration control is carried out extraterritorially attribution is only the first step in holding states accountable under refugee and human rights law. For the purpose of international law, private conduct attributed to a state may be equated with an act of that state's own authorities. As such, even though human rights responsibility may be attributed to a state, refugee or human rights obligations do not extend further than they would in respect of a state's own actions. This basically refers analysis back to the preceding chapter and the question of what constitutes extraterritorial jurisdiction. While the relevant tests for effective control over individuals or geographical areas may be fulfilled in some cases, in others they may not. Even though the control functions carried out by airlines may be attributed to the sanctioning state, the rejection of an asylum-seeker at the departure gate does not necessarily amount to an exercise of jurisdiction and thus an obligation to respect the *non-refoulement* principle.

Beyond questions of direct attribution, the notion of due diligence obligations may, however, go some length to fill the responsibility gap left above. State responsibility in this regard is not dependent on attributing the private conduct to the state, nor on whether migration control is carried out within the state's territory or jurisdiction. Rather, it stems from

---

[170] See below, chapter 6.

the state's own actions or omissions in not taking reasonable steps to prevent or react to a given human rights violation. While the exact nature of due diligence obligations is difficult to determine in the abstract, it has been shown that certain positive or due diligence obligations flow from both the *non-refoulement* principle enshrined in the 1951 Refugee Convention and similar obligations under other human rights instruments.

Again, however, the assessment of such obligations is not independent of legal geography. More may naturally be expected in terms of a state's ability to prevent or react to any violation of refugees' rights by private actors within a state's territory or where extraterritorial jurisdiction is exercised through overall control over a geographical area. Yet even where states do not exercise such control or jurisdiction, certain negative obligations not to encourage or actively assist human rights violations by private actors could be argued to remain.

More generally, the growing privatisation and delegation of regulatory functions away from the state has been argued to lead to a loss of control from the perspective of the state.[171] Yet nothing in the above analysis indicates that the privatisation of migration control entails a loss of state influence. On the contrary, through a mixture of law, economic incentives and direct authority, the state in most instances retains close managerial powers or behavioural influence in terms of how privatised migration control is enacted and carried out.

From a governance perspective, the appeal of privatisation may have several aspects. Privatisation and deregulation are often carried out to obtain flexibility, efficiency or cost-efficiency in service delivery. As such, the privatisation of migration control is of course not an isolated phenomenon, but embedded in a much larger tendency to outsource and privatise even core sovereign functions that not long ago could not be imagined as separate from the state. Yet, as Alston correctly points out, in the pursuit of these objectives, the element of accountability, central to the human rights regime, may be significantly reduced.[172]

The privatisation of migration control is no exception. Crossing the public/private divide makes it both legally and institutionally more difficult to establish responsibility of the outsourcing state under international

---

[171] Verkuil, *Outsourcing Sovereignty*; Flinders, 'Politics of public–private partnerships', 245.

[172] P. Alston, 'Downsizing the state in human rights discourse', in N. Dorden and P. Grifford (eds.), *Democracy and the Rule of Law* (Washington, DC: Congressional Quarterly Press, 2001), pp. 357–68, at p. 361. Furthermore, accountability and government control may even be considered as an enemy to privatisation, as it may reduce rather than add to these objectives. Clapham, *Human Rights Obligations*, p. 12.

refugee law. Moreover, unlike situations where a state's own migration control is carried out in the territory or territorial waters of another state, the inability to establish such responsibility does not simply mean that refugee protection obligations are shifted to the territorial state, with all that may follow in terms of the quality of protection from such a shift. Rather, as long as private actors do not incur direct responsibility under international refugee law, the privatisation of migration control easily risks deconstructing refugee protection altogether.

From the perspective of the lawyer hoping to mend the responsibility gap brought about by the increasingly blurred distinction between the state and private actors in the management of migration, the outlook is mixed. On the one hand, because privatisation of otherwise sovereign functions is a more general phenomenon, heightened attention to human rights issues in other contexts – for example, the use of private military companies – may bring about a push for codification of principles and both national and international judicial review that positively spills over into other areas. The ILC Articles themselves could be considered an example of this. On the other hand, the specificity demanded in attributing private conduct to states and establishing the content of due diligence obligations is closely tied to the relevant norms as well as the factual circumstances of the issue at hand. As such, attempts to ensure state responsibility for private conduct have so far been marred by ad hoc solutions.

6 'Hic abundant leones': the institutional reach of refugee protection

In the British Library hangs one of the earliest maps of Europe. The Cotton Tiberius Map[1] bears few resemblances to modern maps, but it represents the world as it was known at around the first millennium AD. The cartographer may have been aware that some areas were a little sketchy and largely unexplored. In the top left corner, near the east coast of Asia, one thus finds a drawing of a lion and the inscription, 'Hic abundant leones'. Since then, the expression 'here lions abound' has been copied by several cartographers to describe partly or wholly uncharted territories. More generally, the expressions 'here be lions' or 'here be dragons' have occasionally been used to imply that on this or that issue little is known and less can thus be said with any degree of certainty.[2]

Today, few such places remain on geographical maps. Satellite images and the Global Positioning System (GPS) ensure that we have constant access to an updated picture of the world around us. Not only is this knowledge used to ensure our own navigation, it has also become a key tool in the attempt by governments to control or manage migration flows and international travel. Examples of the surveillance technologies employed for this purpose have already been mentioned in the previous chapters: carriers and visa consulates forward biometric data, immigrant and asylum-seeker databases are growing, and radar stations, satellites, warships and airborne warning and control systems (AWACS) are being used to monitor irregular migrants at many of the world's migratory hot spots. In the current migration management strategies, global

---

[1] Cotton MS Tiberius B.V., fol. 56v. British Library, approximately AD 1025.
[2] The variation 'Hic sunt dracones' has appeared on a number of later maps and globes.

surveillance and data collection are a necessary prerequisite for all following interventions.[3]

Where a parallel to the Tiberius Map may nonetheless be drawn is in regard to the invisibility of the encounter between the asylum-seeker and states exercising offshore or outsourced migration control. Accessing and comprehensively documenting concrete cases and practices of offshore and outsourced migration control is notoriously difficult. Despite the communications revolution and all the surveillance technology available to render the irregular traveller visible and thereby subject to control, the control performance itself remains strangely opaque. As has been seen throughout the previous chapters, very little case law exists regarding offshore and outsourced migration control specifically, which is surprising given the dimension and proportions these practices have taken on.

Albeit a challenge for legal analysis, the lack of knowledge and visibility of state practice in this regard could also be said, however, to constitute an important observation in itself. While the preceding chapters have sought to trace the boundaries of legal responsibility, this penultimate chapter inquires into the possibility of and barriers to the practical realisation of protection obligations. In other words, how is access to asylum institutionally secured or denied when the encounter between the refugee and the state moves off the territory or when migration control is carried out by private actors?

The following is a brief sketch which draws out a few examples and highlights the general issues at stake. A comprehensive investigation of this area would easily take up a separate volume; nonetheless, a legal analysis of offshore and outsourced migration control would be incomplete without some considerations as to how refugee and human rights are accessed in practice by those entitled to them.

In the following it is first suggested that there is an 'out of sight, out of mind' effect attached to offshore and outsourced migration control, which makes it particularly difficult for refugees effectively to claim their rights and which also, to a large extent, leaves states unchecked as to how this control is being exercised. Second, it is argued that there is a close interrelation between the continued contestation of legal responsibility and the lack of mechanisms ensuring accountability, monitoring and de facto access to rights. The institutional structures facilitating the implementation of refugee rights and human rights, to perhaps an even greater extent than legal norms, reflect state-centric and territorial principles of organisation. This has important consequences, not only for

---

[3] Gammeltoft-Hansen, 'Filtering out the risky migrant'.

those asylum-seekers who find themselves unable to access rights that are in principle owed to them. It also affects the legal understanding, as rather than the legal uncertainties pertaining to this area being closed by the emergence of relevant cases to set before national and international judiciaries, the exact scope of refugee and human rights obligations may remain contested.

6.1 The 'out of sight, out of mind' effect

On 26 September 2006, thirty-one migrants, including a number of asylum-seekers from Iraq and the Palestinian territories, were picked up from the open sea by Turkish coastguards and brought ashore. Six others were later found drowned and another three are still missing. The survivors claimed that they had paid a human-smuggler to take them to Europe and that their original destination had been Greece. Off the Greek island of Chios they had been stopped by Greek coastguards, who had sailed them back to Turkish territorial waters and thrown them overboard to swim ashore.

Legally speaking this situation is simple. There is no doubt that Greece exercised jurisdiction, territorially and subsequently extraterritorially, in this scenario. The problem is that no one but the migrants themselves has been able to confirm it. There were no independent witnesses and no one had seen the Greek vessel. Greece subsequently rejected the migrants' story in the strongest possible terms, while Turkey conversely used the incident to accuse Greece of systematically 'dumping' irregular migrants in their territorial waters.[4]

In other cases such pushbacks are fortuitously documented. In January 2009, tourists managed to take photographs of Thai army officers rounding up arriving Rohingya asylum-seekers from Myanmar and

---

[4] 'Greece denies dumping illegal immigrants into the sea', *Spiegel Online*, 28 September 2006, available at www.spiegel.de. NGO reports have, however, detailed a number of similar stories. According to testimony, Greek authorities even appear to have gone to some lengths to conceal any objective evidence that migrants have entered Greek jurisdiction or had contact with Greek authorities. Returned migrants thus describe how Greek authorities have removed any aid or materials supplied and punctured inflatable boats that may link migrants to Greece before forcibly returning migrants and asylum-seekers to Turkish waters or islands. See, e.g., Pro-Asyl, 'The truth may be bitter, but it must be told: the situation of refugees in the Aegean and the practices of the Greek coast guard', October 2007, available at www.proasyl.de; and Human Rights Watch, 'Stuck in a revolving door: Iraqis and other asylum seekers and migrants at the Greece/Turkey entrance to the European Union', November 2008, available at www.hrw.org, pp. 42–4.

subsequently dragging them and their boats back to international waters.[5] Knowledge may also come from the agents of control themselves. Speaking against the unfair imposition of control responsibilities on carriers, a representative of British Airways thus regretted that the company had no idea how many among those denied boarding by the airline might have had a claim to refugee status, but that in the period 1987–2001 no fewer than 400 improperly documented passengers nonetheless carried into the United Kingdom had subsequently received full refugee status.[6]

While the above may be examples of particularly harsh conduct, there is little to suggest that similar practices do not occur elsewhere. What may be most surprising is that we even hear about them. In many other situations either private actors are unlikely to have an interest in revealing details about rejected passengers, control is carried out further away from the coast, far from the cameras of curious tourists, or those turned back may simply not be able subsequently to tell their story to anyone.

Problems in assuring the realisation of rights are nothing new to refugees. Examples of states not respecting national and international obligations are, regrettably, plentiful.[7] The asylum-seeker is almost inevitably a stranger to his or her host country, unfamiliar with legal and bureaucratic structures, with limited personal networks or none, and may not speak the language. In recent years, a trend may further be observed in a number of countries to isolate asylum-seekers in remote or inaccessible locations, and the mandatory detention of asylum-seekers has been introduced by a number of countries.[8] Thus Australia has been known to confine asylum-seekers not only at offshore processing facilities, but also in detention centres in the Australian desert.[9] Likewise, asylum-seekers intercepted by the Italian authorities in the Mediterranean have

---

[5] Dan Rivers, 'Probe questions fate of refugees in Thailand', CNN, 26 January 2009, available at www.cnn.com.

[6] Remarks by James Forster, British Airways, Round Table on Carriers' Liability Related to Illegal Immigration, Brussels, 30 November 2001, available at www.iru.org.

[7] Hathaway, *Rights of Refugees*, pp. 279–93.

[8] A. Edwards, 'The Optional Protocol to the Convention against Torture and the Detention of Refugees', (2008) 57 *International and Comparative Law Quarterly* 789–825, at 790.

[9] The most notorious example concerns the Woomera Immigration Reception and Processing Centre located in the South Australian desert, approximately 300 km from Adelaide, established in 1999. Following accusations of human rights abuses and a number of riots and protests outside the centre, the culmination of which involved a mass breakout in 2002 aided by protesting social activists, it was finally closed down in 2003.

been detained on the small island of Lampedusa, 200 km south of Sicily.[10] While such places are not offshore in the legal sense, they nonetheless have a similar effect of distancing migrants and refugees further from the ordinary institutions guaranteeing the rule of law. As well as this, journalists, NGOs and even the UN High Commissioner for Human Rights have on several occasions been barred access to such facilities and locations.[11]

The question remains as to what extent extraterritorialisation and privatisation may exacerbate these problems. Shifting jurisdiction eclipses many of the ordinary institutional mechanisms for securing the realisation of refugee and human rights, just as privatisation may shortcut ordinary procedures of public transparency and scrutiny. Offshore and privatised migration control may thus create an 'out of sight, out of mind' effect, where actual control practices and any violations of refugee and human rights that may ensue remain largely invisible.

6.2 Looking beyond the fence: offshore and institutional protection capacity

International refugee law, like other areas of human rights law, operationally functions through a complex network of institutions and actors to ensure both clarification of legal norms and the monitoring of state performance. Internationally these include organisations such as UNHCR, other UN agencies and the UN human rights treaty bodies. Regionally, adjudicatory bodies include the Inter-American Court of Human Rights and the European Court of Human Rights, as well as international institutions such as the Council of Europe Human Rights Commissioner, the European Parliament, the EU Fundamental Rights Agency, the Inter-American Commission on Human Rights and the African Commission on Human

[10] While the Lampedusa facility was originally merely a reception centre, since December 2008 the Italian government appears to have ceased transferring asylum-seekers to other processing centres on the Italian mainland. The conditions at the centre, lack of access to legal advice and counselling contrary to Italian law and summary expulsions to Libya have received substantial criticism from both NGOs and the European Parliament. See e.g. European Parliament, Resolution on Lampedusa, P6_TA(2005)0138, 14 April 2005.

[11] The UN High Commissioner for Human Rights, Mary Robinson, was denied access to Woomera in 2002, though she was later admitted. Similarly, UNHCR was in 2004 'for security reasons' denied access to the Lampedusa centre during certain periods of large-scale arrivals and expulsions. Amnesty International, 'Italy: Lampedusa, the island of Europe's forgotten promises', EUR 30/008/2005, 5 July 2005. UNHCR has gained access since then and the centre has received inspection visits from, among others, delegations from the European Parliament.

and Peoples' Rights. At the national level one may equally point to public institutions such as domestic courts and ombudsman institutions, to quasi-public actors such as national human rights institutions and publicly employed academics, and last, but not least, civil society, including national and international NGOs, grass-roots organisations, associations, lawyers and journalists.

At the core of all these activities is the gathering of precise and updated information about human rights conditions, both generally and in regard to individual cases.[12] Each of the institutions and actors mentioned above are in that sense part of a 'food chain', sharing and passing on such information. It is well recognised that even the most resourceful and well-established organisations ensuring refugee protection, such as UNHCR or the international human rights bodies, are closely dependent on the information gathered and attention given to individual cases by national NGOs and human rights activists.[13] It is only through the interplay between these very different institutions that the international refugee and human rights regime can be said to achieve any kind of efficiency at all.

Concern arises since the central links in this chain may often be nationally anchored and territorially limited in their outlook and accessibility. From the perspective of the individual refugee, offshore migration control means that it is harder to access human rights institutions. While an asylum-seeker arriving at the border or already within the territory of the potential host state will normally have access to the whole range of existing human rights institutions, an asylum-seeker rejected on the high seas or by an immigration officer posted abroad will have obvious difficulties in both identifying and accessing the UNHCR, refugee-assisting NGOs,

---

[12] D. P. Forsythe, *Human Rights in International Relations* (Cambridge University Press, 2000), p. 166.

[13] Tomuschat, *Human Rights*, pp. 184, 285–90; B. Fernando, 'The role of NGOs in policy-making: campaigns against torture as an illustration', in L. Dhundale and E. A. Andersen (eds.), *Revisiting the Role of Civil Society in Promoting Human Rights* (Copenhagen: Danish Institute for Human Rights, 2004), pp. 143–63, at p. 154; L. S. Wiseberg, 'The role of non-governmental organizations (NGOs) in the protection and enforcement of human rights', in J. Symonides (ed.), *Human Rights: International Protection, Monitoring, Enforcement* (Aldershot: Ashgate, 2003), pp. 347–72, at p. 349; H. Steiner and P. Alston (eds.), *International Human Rights in Context: Law, Politics, Morals*, 2nd edn (Oxford University Press, 2000), pp. 938 ff.; B. Lindsnæs and L. Lindholdt, 'National human rights institutions: standard setting and achievements', in H. Stokke and A. Tostensen (eds.), *Human Rights Development Yearbook 1998* (The Hague: Kluwer Law International, 1998).

national human rights institutions or lawyers of the state carrying out control.[14]

The same is true of public institutions. Offshore migration control typically entails a physical distancing of different specialised authorities. A border guard is first and foremost trained to exercise control and check documents, and any knowledge of asylum will be secondary to this task.[15] Under ordinary circumstances cases that raise any doubt will be referred to the competent national asylum authorities. Where migration control moves to the high seas and asylum authorities remain ashore, this exchange of knowledge and mutual appraisal is made more difficult, and the asylum-seeker is unlikely to be able to access specialised asylum authorities, including translators.

Authority specialisation may be compounded by limited and incoherent mandates and jurisdictions. During the preparations for the Frontex operations outside the Canary Islands in 2006, Denmark offered to assist Spain by sending a number of Danish asylum experts to the Canary Islands.[16] This was refused by Frontex as lying outside the organisation's mandate, which is limited to border management.

The disconnect between asylum and border authorities increases the risk of overlooking or wrongly rejecting asylum-seekers. The Spanish immigration authorities at the Canary Islands have repeatedly stressed that the vast majority of those intercepted were 'illegal immigrants'. Despite an increase in irregular immigration, the number of asylum-seekers has hardly risen and the rate of recognition has even gone down, leading NGOs to suggest that asylum claims are being allowed to fall on deaf ears or prevented from being made.[17]

Even where referral mechanisms are formally in place for asylum-seekers as part of offshore migration control, the lack of competent

---

[14]   M.-M. Mohamedou, 'The effectiveness of national human rights institutions', in B. Lindsnæs, L. Lindholdt and K. Yigen (eds.), *National Human Rights Institutions: Articles and Working Papers* (Copenhagen: Danish Institute for Human Rights, 2001), pp. 49–58, at pp. 52–3.

[15]   UNHCR Executive Committee, Determination of Refugee Status, Conclusion No. 8 (XXVII), 1977.

[16]   C. Krag, 'EU-lande i aktion mod folkevandring fra Afrika', *Berlingske Tidende*, 3 June 2006.

[17]   Amnesty International, 'Spain: the southern border', EUR 41/008/2005, 2005. The low percentage of asylum-seekers may also, however, be a result of strategic choice. Applying for asylum in the Canary Islands normally entails detention for the duration of the procedure, yet irregular migrants who cannot be identified or for whom there is no return agreement with Spain are typically transferred to the mainland after forty days and allowed freedom of movement.

asylum authorities on the spot may render them practically ineffective. From 1981 to 1990, the period before the *non-refoulement* principle was declared strictly intra-territorially applicable, the United States maintained a referral mechanism for asylum-seekers interdicted on the high seas provided that their case was not considered manifestly unfounded. Yet, despite the grave human rights situation in Haiti during this period, the US coastguard found only six out of more than 21,000 persons intercepted to have a case that merited referral to a full asylum procedure.[18]

From the perspective of national institutions, gathering knowledge about offshore activities is often equally challenging. By definition *refoulement* can only be established *post facto*, after rejection or expulsion to another country, and for this reason many cases never come to public attention.[19] Few institutions, public or private, are able or have the means to follow up the fate of rejected asylum-seekers. Even well-established national human rights organisations are often in their organisation and mandate focused on monitoring human rights conditions within the country in question.[20]

For organisations that do try to follow up asylum-seekers post-return, it is typically a precondition that the person is identified before rejection. For an asylum-seeker arriving at the territory a case file will usually be opened by the public authorities and/or refugee-assisting organisations such as UNHCR or national NGOs. In cases where it is suspected that rejection or return may result in *refoulement*, the more resourceful human rights organisations may try to trace individuals using this information, either following the person back or contacting the relevant country office or partner organisations in the country of return.

Where asylum-seekers are rejected before they reach the territory, however, the likelihood that any national human rights institutions will even

---

[18] Legomsky, 'USA and the Caribbean interdiction programme', 679.

[19] M. Lynch, 'Forced Back: International Refugee Protection in Theory and Practice', Refugees International, Washington, 2004.

[20] Wilde, 'Legal "black hole"?', 754. An exception being international NGOs like Amnesty International which, exactly to avoid complaints from national authorities, always assign investigation and lobbying for political prisoners to groups outside the country of imprisonment. Nothing very similar is known among refugee NGOs, although in Europe the introduction of 'safe third country' policies prompted a number of NGOs to establish 'early warning' systems in order to follow chain deportations, a practice that more recently has been replicated and sought to be expanded to EU neighbouring countries under the co-ordination of the European Council for Refugees and Exiles in order to monitor the results of offshore migration control and returns.

know about the incident is greatly reduced. And even where such knowledge is available, the lacking registration makes tracing the fate of those rejected a most difficult task. Even though Frontex reported that in 2006, 3,665 persons were directly returned after being intercepted in Senegalese or Mauritanian waters, European refugee organisations have little knowledge of who these persons are and which among them might have had a well-founded asylum claim. Those intercepted did not have access to UNHCR or other refugee-assisting organisations, or access to any public authorities allowing them to launch an asylum claim or appeal against their return.[21]

Lastly, even where cases are brought before national courts, offshore may entail certain problems. Domestic courts do not always have adjudicative jurisdiction over extraterritorial acts of government authorities. The controversy over whether Guantánamo detainees have access to habeas corpus is perhaps the strongest example in this regard, but the lack of remedy before domestic courts has long been an issue in regard to carrier enforced controls.[22] Moreover, national courts have on occasion rejected requests for investigations of extraterritorial actions. In *Al-Skeini* the applicants demanded a full, open and independent investigation of the shooting incidents and the related facts of the case in line with other Strasbourg case law relating to Articles 2 and 3 of the European Convention on Human Rights. The UK House of Lords, however, turned down this demand as unfeasible, given the 'real practical difficulties' in carrying out a technical investigation of this sort in Basra, Iraq.[23]

6.3 Penetrating the corporate veil: privatisation of migration control and institutional protection capacity

Similar barriers to access may arise where migration control is delegated to private actors. As the privatisation of governmental functions

---

[21] In addition, requests for public access to the Memoranda of Understanding between Spain and Senegal/Mauritania have so far been refused. On the domestic and EU law implications of this see Rijpma, 'Building borders', pp. 341–3.

[22] Under the Military Commissions Act 2006, prisoners held at Guantánamo Bay were stripped of their right to habeas corpus under US district courts based, among other things, on the argument that the constitutional right to habeas corpus does not extend to non-citizens outside the sovereign territory of the United States. This provision of the Act was declared unconstitutional by the Supreme Court by 5–4 in *Boumediene*. See further the dissent by Judge Scalia upholding the territorialist interpretation. See also Nicholson, 'Immigration Act 1987', 623–7.

[23] *Al-Skeini and others v. Secretary of State for Defence*, para. 26.

has become more prevalent, the impact of privatisation on public transparency and accountability has received increasing attention. On the one hand, proponents of privatisation argue that accountability may be increased by governing through market mechanisms. Noting that control and accountability of governmental actors and institutions is often far from perfect, it has been argued that clear economic incentives and contracts may actually prove more efficient in regulating agent behaviour. Second, the distance between governments and private contractors makes it easier to carry out a critical appraisal, and private entities may be more open to reform and change. Third, the competitive environment surrounding private contractors may lead major corporations in a given market themselves to develop codes of conduct and accept accountability mechanisms in order to create a market brand vis-à-vis potential customers.[24]

On the other hand, those more sceptical of privatising governmental functions argue that by its very nature the market is inherently difficult to govern. Thus the corporate veil works not only to separate legal responsibilities but also to cloak the practices of private actors.[25] Even where clear contracts or other regulatory frameworks are in place, the legal barrier between states and private actors breaks the ordinary administrative chain of command.[26] Even the best of contracts may not foresee the full need for appraisal and monitoring and may thus equally become a straitjacket preventing further action and scrutiny.[27] Second, public employees are both more visible and in many countries have explicit guarantees against repercussions for expressing their opinions in public or acting as whistle-blowers. Third, practice in regard to private military companies seems to indicate that even where legal provisions for public scrutiny are in place, the resources for governmental monitoring often lag behind the pace and scale of privatisation itself.[28] Lastly, private companies seldom have a direct interest in public oversight, as any criticism may entail negative economic consequences and be detrimental to the company's competitive position. Where such an interest convergence, for example for

---

[24] L. Dickinson, 'Contract as a tool for regulating PMCs', in Chesterman and Lehnart, *From Mercenaries to Markets*, pp. 217–38, at p. 230; D. McDonald (ed.), *Private Prisons and the Public Interest* (Piscataway, NJ: Rutgers University Press, 1991), p. 189; C. H. Logan, *Private Prisons: Cons and Pros* (Oxford University Press, 1990).

[25] Verkuil, *Outsourcing Sovereignty*; Leander, *Eroding State Authority?*, pp. 98–103.

[26] McDonald, *Private Prisons*, p. 188.   [27] Leander, *Eroding State Authority?*

[28] D. Isenberg, 'A government in search of cover', in Chesterman and Lehnart, *From Mercenaries to Markets*, pp. 82–93, at 87–8.

image reasons, nonetheless exists, voluntary codes of conduct or soft law accountability mechanisms have so far not proven particularly efficient.[29] Rather, the danger of such arrangements is that accountability is further removed from state authority and 'ceremonialised' by offering lip service to official principles without any efficient enforcement mechanisms.[30]

As far as carriers are concerned, little has generally been done to ensure accountability or monitoring of those refused embarkation by airline staff. As several scholars have noted, governments have been reluctant to make publicly available the figures regarding the amount of fines imposed and seldom systematically gather data in regard to numbers and the identity of those rejected.[31] Sanctions legislation is by design weak in terms of democratic control, accountability and judicial remedies for those rejected.[32] Save for reasons of protesting against the imposition of fines mentioned above, carriers themselves have little further incentive for giving out information on these issues which may convey a negative picture of companies to customers. Even where airlines are asked by governments or NGOs to provide 'denied boarding' figures, they do not always do so.[33]

Rejection by a private company such as an airline is, further, not subject to national administrative regulations. It is not a public decision, and those rejected can thus be sent back with no notification needed of the decision made and in principle without leaving any trace.[34] As has been covered in the previous section, the extraterritorial venue of most rejections makes it even more difficult for both national institutions and civil society to access those rejected.[35] As a result, only a handful of cases concerning carrier controls have ever been brought before national courts,

---

[29] J. Cockayne, 'Make or buy? Principal–agent theory and the regulation of private military companies', in Chesterman and Lehnart, *From Mercenaries to Markets*, pp. 196–216, at p. 207; A. Leander, 'The impunity of private authority: understanding PSC accountability', paper presented at Standing Group of International Relations, ECPR, University of Turin, 12–15 September 2007. The privately contracted interrogators involved in the Abu Ghraib prisoner abuse thus clearly acted contrary to the self-imposed Standards of Ethics and Business Conduct of the employing company, CACI.

[30] Cockayne, 'Make or buy?', pp. 207–8.

[31] Guiraudon, 'Enlisting third parties'; Nicholson, 'Immigration Act 1987', 598.

[32] Scholten and Minderhoud, 'Regulating immigration control', 131.

[33] Nicholson, 'Immigration Act 1987', 598.   [34] Guiraudon, 'Enlisting third parties', p. 8.

[35] Nicholson, 'Immigration Act 1987', 598, and Vedsted-Hansen, 'Privatiseret Retshåndhævelse', p. 176. In principle, this problem could be somewhat remedied by the development of close monitoring procedures and the positioning of national immigration liaison officers as detailed in the previous chapter. Yet this does not seem to be within the intended mandate of such officers.

despite modern carrier legislation having been in place for more than twenty years.[36]

Where privatisation of migration control is governed by contracts, the possibilities for monitoring and visibility are improved somewhat. The higher likelihood of state responsibility for any human rights violations in these situations as compared with the mere use of economic sanctions may first of all give a greater incentive for governments to ensure accountability. Second, contracts give added possibilities for states to require vetting, adequate training of privately employed personnel, regular monitoring and performance reports. As was seen in the previous chapter, the United Kingdom has thus introduced clear contractual limits for responsibility and a national supervisory function for the use of privately contracted immigration search officers.[37]

Nonetheless, even where a clear contractual relationship is established, accountability and public scrutiny may still remain insufficient. This is particularly evident in the growing number of cases concerning privately operated detention facilities. In Australia, the conditions in some privately managed asylum and immigration detention centres have been described as gravely lacking in external accountability and monitoring.[38] Access to information about conditions in the centres has been further hampered by attempts by those managing them to prevent outsiders from gaining access. Australasian Correctional Management, which runs four detention centres in Australia, has thus been known to require all external professionals, such as medical staff or teachers, who enter ACM facilities to sign confidentiality agreements preventing them from disclosing any information regarding detainees or the administration of the centres.[39]

Parallels may be found in other countries using private contractors to run asylum and immigration detention facilities. Following a BBC documentary documenting racism and physical abuse of immigrant detainees at Oakington detention centre, the UK Prisons and Probation Ombudsman issued a report pointing to several cases of misconduct by Group 4 Securicor in running the centre and carrying out forced escorts and removals. The report further pointed to a number of problems relating

---

[36] See above, section 5.3.   [37] See above, section 5.5.
[38] Professor Richard Harding, speaking of Curtin detention centre. Speech delivered at International Corrections and Prisons Association on 30 October 2001, excerpt available at www.refugeeaction.org.
[39] Australian Lawyers for Human Rights, Submission to the National Inquiry into Children in Immigration Detention, Submission No. 168, Australian Human Rights Commission, 10 October 2002.

to monitoring and oversight.[40] Similarly, in a 2007 lawsuit in the United States, the American Civil Liberties Union pointed to the lack of oversight of privately operated detention facilities and accused Corrections Corporation of America of overcrowding cells and cutting supplies and medical care to save costs.[41]

To some extent, pushes for better monitoring of private actors may be facilitated through developments in general human rights law. The Optional Protocol to the Convention against Torture[42] both establishes an international subcommittee with authority to visit places of detention (Art. 2) and requires states to set up or designate national bodies with similar powers to conduct visits and comment on general conditions of detention (Art. 3). In both cases, the Protocol states explicitly that visits may be conducted to

any form of detention or imprisonment or the place of a person in a *public or private* custodial setting which that person is not permitted to leave at will by order of any judicial, administrative or other authority. (Art. 4(2), emphasis added)

The formulation is clearly relevant not only to asylum and immigration detention facilities in general but also to situations where asylum-seekers are detained by non-state actors, whether in privately operated detention centres or through confinement in airport transit zones.[43]

In sum, even where privatised migration control is clearly contractually regulated and carried out within the territorial jurisdiction, there is still a risk of effective monitoring being hampered. This situation is only exacerbated when private actors are engaged in migration control extraterritorially, as in the case of carrier sanctions. An important lesson in this regard may be learned from the related field of private military companies. Despite an apparent desire on the part of governments to regulate PMSC activities and a number of national and international efforts to implement regulatory frameworks, accountability mechanisms and various standards and codes of conduct, it has been difficult to implement them effectively, very few cases have been brought against PMSCs, and

---

[40] Report by the Prisons and Probation Ombudsman for England and Wales, Inquiry into Allegations of Racism and Mistreatment of Detainees at Oakington Immigration Reception Centre and While under Escort, July 2005.

[41] L. Berestein, 'Immigration agency, contractors are accused of mistreating detainees', *San Diego Union Tribune*, 4 May 2008. *Kiniti et al. v. Myers et al Second Amended Complaint*, US District Court of the Southern District of California, filed 24 January 2007. The case was settled with the Department of Homeland Security and CCA 4 June 2008.

[42] UN Doc. A/RES/57/199 (2002), entered into force 22 June 2006.

[43] Edwards, 'Optional Protocol', 799.

even companies with an established record of mismanagement continue to receive new contracts.[44]

The engagement of private actors in migration control shares a number of similarities in these respects. One may even fear that governments have less of an interest in ensuring effective oversight and monitoring in this area, and that the consequences of private migration control are easier to keep invisible than the actions of private military operators. So far this area has certainly received much less public attention. The privatisation of migration control in this sense thus serves not only as a legal barrier to establishing state responsibility, but also as an institutional distancing of control practices from the state.

6.4 Capacity and limits of international human rights bodies

Lastly, it may be worth considering how offshore and outsourcing practices and the constraints identified at the national level affect the litigation and monitoring practices of international human rights institutions. Establishing proper and impartial evidence or facts in international human rights cases is a general concern and arguably particularly pertinent for the international refugee regime. The Refugee Convention is one of the few major human rights treaties without a dedicated independent mechanism to facilitate inter-state accountability. Nonetheless, refugee rights violations are routinely brought to the attention of general human rights bodies and regional human rights courts, both as general issues and in the context of the specific instruments.[45]

Until recently, the very idea of international human rights bodies seeking to obtain facts other than, and possibly contradicting, those submitted by governments was close to unthinkable.[46] Nonetheless, most international bodies today in principle retain fairly wide scope for drawing on a range of independent sources for ascertaining the facts of a given case or country report and may undertake independent fact-finding missions. The limited resources of such bodies and their position in the human rights machinery, however, means that review of evidence and facts is highly dependent on national institutions, NGOs and domestic courts.[47]

---

[44] Leander, 'Impunity of private authority'; Leander, *Eroding State Authority?*; P. W. Singer, *Corporate Warriors: The Rise of the Privatized Military Industry* (Ithaca: Cornell University Press, 2003).

[45] Hathaway, *Rights of Refugees*, pp. 994–7.

[46] Steiner and Alston, *International Human Rights in Context*, p. 602.

[47] Tomuschat, *Human Rights*, pp. 184, 285–90.

The procedure of the European Court of Human Rights may serve as an example. Following the admissibility stage, the relevant facts of a case will have to be established 'beyond reasonable doubt', and the Court may for this purpose in principle draw on all available sources. In practice, however, the Court applies a subsidiarity principle maintaining that domestic authorities have the primary role in the assessment of evidence.[48] The requirement to exhaust domestic remedies (Art. 35) means that a case will normally already have been through national courts, and the Court has emphasised that it does not see it as its purpose to replace national courts' assessments of the facts with that of its own.[49] Where evidence is clearly lacking or the assessment of the facts is contested the Court will normally exercise more caution in how assessments of the parties are used and make more efforts to carry out oral interviews of witnesses and investigations in the relevant location.[50]

Similar issues arise under other human rights bodies, and some may even face further constraints. As a rule the individual communications procedures under the human rights monitoring bodies are carefully limited to written evidence of the parties when considering the facts of the case.[51] The inability to conduct oral interviews and inspect locations for alleged human rights abuses considerably limits the gathering of evidence, which becomes particularly problematic in situations where

---

[48] J. Christoffersen, 'Fair balance: a study of proportionality, subsidiarity and primarity in the European Convention on Human Rights', University of Copenhagen, 2008, p. 272; *Vidal v. Belgium*, European Court of Human Rights, Application No. 12351/86, 22 April 1992, para. 33; and *Edwards v. United Kingdom*, European Court of Human Rights, Application No. 13071/87, 16 December 1992, para. 34. See Christoffersen, 'Fair balance', pp. 273–4 for further examples and discussion.

[49] J. F. Kjølbro, *Den Europæiske Menneskerettighedskonvention – for praktikere*, 2nd edn (Copenhagen: Jurist- og Økonomforbundets Forlag, 2007), p. 73; *Klaas v. Germany*, European Court of Human Rights, Application No. 15473/89, 22 September 1993, para. 29.

[50] Kjølbro, *Den Europæiske Menneskerettighedskonvention*, p. 74. On-site investigations remain infrequent. For an example, see *N v. Finland*, in which the court undertook a fact-finding mission to Finland to take oral evidence to assess whether the expulsion of an asylum-seeker to the Democratic Republic of the Congo would constitute a violation under Art. 3 of the Convention. *N v. Finland*, European Court of Human Rights, Application No. 38885/02. 26 July 2005.

[51] Tomuschat, *Human Rights*, pp. 215–16. See e.g. Art. 5(1) of the Optional Protocol 1 to the International Covenant on Civil and Political Rights. The specific limitation to 'written information' is, however, absent in Art. 22(4) of the Convention against Torture and Art. 7(1) of the Optional Protocol to the Convention on the Elimination of All Discrimination against Women.

the state and individuals submit conflicting depictions of the facts.[52] The Optional Protocol to the Convention against Torture may perhaps be taken as an example to the contrary. As mentioned above, the protocol established both a subcommittee of international experts and a national monitoring mechanism to visit places of detention, private and public.

In cases involving private actors and/or an extraterritorial locus, these issues gain additional dimensions. Carrying out fact-finding is substantially harder when alleged human rights abuses take place in a foreign jurisdiction of a state possibly not even party to the convention in question.

The question also arises in connection with the subcommittee established under the Optional Protocol to the Convention against Torture. In principle the protocol provides that visits may be conducted to 'any place under [a state's] jurisdiction or control where persons are or may be deprived of their liberty' (Art. 4(1)). Since deprivation of liberty or physical custody, as discussed in chapter 4, will normally always bring about jurisdiction, this must be interpreted equally to cover situations of extraterritorial detention, confinement and control, whether managed by private or public authorities. Yet the application of these mechanisms to offshore asylum detention facilities or processing centres remains a question of practical access. Even though the state responsible for detention may be obliged to allow visits, if the state on whose territory or in whose territorial waters detention is taking place is not a party to the Optional Protocol, it will have no obligation to co-operate with the subcommittee or allow inspection visits.[53]

Cases concerning interception on the high seas entail similar issues. To the extent that rejected asylum-seekers or immigrants even get the chance to bring a case before an adjudicatory body, it is likely to remain a question of the state party's word against that of the asylum-seeker. In doubtful cases it may, further, be difficult to establish whether

---

[52] Nowak, *UN Covenant*, p. 692.

[53] Edwards, 'Optional Protocol', 819. A different scenario, however, is the situation where the territorial state is a party to the Optional Protocol but the state responsible for offshore detention is not. Arguably, the territorial jurisdiction of the former imposes an obligation under the protocol to allow visits by the subcommittee as well as national institutions, despite the fact that it may not be responsible for these detentions. This point may be important not just in regard to situations of immigrant detentions, but also to extraordinary rendition flights for example, or extraterritorial military detention facilities.

interception occurred in the territorial sea of the acting state, international waters, or in foreign territorial waters, just as it may be difficult to determine objectively whether an encounter on the high seas is an act of interception or of search and rescue, the definition of which is left to the master of the 'rescuing' vessel.[54]

The problems are no less onerous in situations where private actors are involved in migration control. International human rights bodies are likely to have limited possibilities for independently probing into the actual relations between governmental authorities and private actors, especially where these are not explicitly regulated by national legislation or contracts. Assessing the facts of cases concerning airline staff denying boarding to asylum-seekers thus faces a double evidentiary challenge. First, the facts surrounding the actual rejection and the relation between the applicant and the private actor have to be established. Second, the relationship between the private airline and the destination state would have to be assessed and thus whether the specific rejection may be attributed to the state and thereby give rise to state responsibility.

Both treaty law and human rights institutions nonetheless emphasise the obligation to conduct proper investigations in connection with suspicions of *refoulement*, torture or other inhumane treatment. Article 12 of the 1984 Convention against Torture sets out that contracting states must ensure that competent authorities undertake 'a prompt and impartial investigation, wherever there is reasonable ground to believe that an act of torture has been committed in any territory under its jurisdiction'.[55] Likewise, General Comment 20 to the 1966 International Covenant on Civil and Political Rights establishes that any complaint of *refoulement* to torture as set out in Article 7 'must be investigated promptly and impartially by competent authorities'. Similar requirements have been set out by the European Court of Human Rights, which has, further, emphasised that the responsibility for carrying out an efficient investigation

---

[54] See further above, section 4.3.4. In 2009 a case against Italy, *Hirsi and Others* v. *Italy*, was nonetheless launched by twenty-three persons intercepted by Italian vessels and returned to Libya.

[55] Thus presumably also cases of alleged *refoulement* prohibited under Art. 3. The formulation is, of course, curious, as it would seem to rule out exactly those situations where states exercise non-territorial jurisdiction, such as when carrying out interdiction on the high seas or carrying out individual migration control in the territory of third states.

into human rights violations cannot be removed by the circumstances for doing so being particularly difficult or dangerous.[56]

Nonetheless, lack of evidence has been decisive in the rejection of some cases concerning extraterritorial jurisdiction. In *Issa*, the European Court of Human Rights held that the Turkish military operations could in principle bring about extraterritorial jurisdiction of Turkey over certain geographic areas of Iraq. However, the facts of the case were insufficient to establish that the shepherds who were killed were within an area over which Turkey exercised effective control.[57] One may further speculate whether practical concerns may also have influenced the much-debated passage in the *Banković* case professing that the Convention is intended to apply

in an essentially regional context and notably in the legal space (*espace juridique*) of the Contracting States ... The Convention was not designed to be applied throughout the world, even in respect of the conduct of Contracting States.[58]

As a matter of law, the notion that the Convention only applies within a certain regional *espace juridique* has been convincingly refuted by scholars as well as by prior and subsequent judgments of the Court.[59] However, this reference to the 'design' of the Convention may perhaps be better interpreted as a concern that the already overburdened Court would have to take on an additional range of complicated complaints over the actions of contracting states in countries outside the Council of Europe.[60]

6.5 Conclusion: the chicken and the egg, law and institutions

As noted at the outset of this chapter, specific case law related to offshore and outsourced migration control is sparse at both the domestic and the

---

[56] See e.g. *Ergi v. Turkey*, European Court of Human Rights, Application Nos. 66/1997/850/1057, 28 July 1998. These cases concerned deaths (Art. 2) in south-east Turkey, but it would not be unreasonable to assume that a similar principle would apply to cases of *refoulement* under Art. 3, and to situations involving extraterritorial jurisdiction.

[57] *Issa and Others v. Turkey*, para. 76.   [58] *Banković*, para. 80.

[59] *W.M. v. Denmark; Issa and Others v. Turkey*. See further Gibney, *International Human Rights Law*, pp. 73–5; Kessing, 'Terrorbekæmpelse og menneskeret', p. 225; Roxstrom et al., 'NATO bombing case', 79; Wilde, 'Opinion', 115–24; Lawson, 'Life after *Banković*', p. 114.

[60] Roxstrom et al., 'NATO bombing case', 135. At time of writing, the European Court of Human Rights had a backlog of more than 100,000 cases, corresponding to somewhere between two and three years at its annual working capacity. Tomuschat, *Human Rights*, p. 245.

international levels. Beyond constituting a methodological challenge for the legal analysis, this chapter has proceeded to ask why that may be. One answer may of course be that offshore and privatisation do achieve a legal shifting of responsibility away from the acting state so successfully that claims against it become fruitless. While the preceding chapters point to the sometimes insufficient reach of international refugee rights and human rights in this regard, it should nonetheless be clear that this is far from always true. To the extent that the exact scope of legal obligations remains contested, if anything this ought to bring about an increased interest in achieving legal clarification from national and international courts.

When this has not been the result, it is perhaps because offshore and privatisation also in a more institutional sense appear to eclipse a number of the mechanisms that normally ensure the individual asylum-seeker's access to rights, monitor state behaviour and ensure accountability for the exercise of power. As soon as migration control is carried out extraterritorially it becomes inherently harder for asylum-seekers to access civil-society actors, national asylum authorities and international organisations. The complex human rights enforcement machinery is still largely organised around territorial delineations and ensuring oversight of extraterritorial actions encounters a number of difficulties.

Similarly, the privatisation of migration control raises a number of issues regarding accountability and transparency. While privatisation in general has been argued by some to lead to increased accountability, this does not seem to be the case for migration control. The control performed by carriers is largely invisible to public scrutiny, and little is done to register or keep track of those denied onward travel. The situation may be somewhat better where private actors are governed through a clear contractual relationship. Yet the case of privately operated immigration detention centres still points to several shortcomings that reinforce the notion of a 'corporate veil' complicating both governmental and civil-society monitoring.

The issues are essentially replicated at the international level. With limited resources, UNHCR and human rights bodies are closely dependent on information provided by governments and national civil-society organisations. Regional human rights courts are often worse positioned than national institutions when it comes to independently establishing the facts of a given case, and have thus exercised some caution in embarking on independent fact-finding missions. As a result, cases may end up being a matter of the applicant's word against that of the accused state party, and situations of impunity persist due to lack of evidence.

In short, offshore and outsourced migration control creates an 'out of sight, out of mind' effect. Because the ordinary institutional human rights mechanisms seldom pick up on what goes on when states leave their territory or delegate authority to private entities, it is less often picked up on. When Grahl-Madsen wrote in his commentary to the *non-refoulement* principle that refugees who have not yet crossed into the territory are 'only seen as shadows or moving figures at the other side of the fence ... not [yet] materialized as human beings', this may be much more true as a matter of practice than as matter of law.[61] The refugee encountering the state outside its territory and/or in the form of a private agent does have certain rights in most instances and as such has already materialised as a subject under refugee and human rights law. Yet offshore and privatisation of migration control will often mean that he or she is likely to have a much harder time physically accessing asylum and de facto claiming any legal entitlement owed.

At this stage it is almost impossible not to draw parallels to the Foucauldian notion of 'biopolitics' or Agamben's concept of 'bare life'. Following Carl Schmitt, Agamben argues that the sovereign is defined precisely by deciding who are included in the legal order and who are refused access to the rule of law.[62] The sovereign is in this sense constituted in a position beyond the law, and the rejected are reduced to *homo sacer* – life without the protection of the law – or bodies to be controlled and disciplined at will.[63] Where states cannot wholly rid themselves of legal obligations through offshore or outsourced migration control, the limited

---

[61] Grahl-Madsen, *Commentary on the Refugee Convention.*

[62] C. Schmitt, *The Nomos of the Earth in the International Law of the Jus Publicum Europaeum* (New York: Telos Press, 2003); Schmitt, *Political Theology: Four Chapters on the Concept of Sovereignty* (Boston: MIT Press, 1985); G. Agamben, *Homo Sacer: Sovereign Power and Bare Life* (Stanford University Press, 1998).

[63] Agamben, *Homo Sacer*; M. Foucault, *The History of Sexuality* (London: Penguin Press, 1976), vol. 1. Several authors have previously employed the Foucauldian notion of biopolitics to the issue of migration control. See in particular the contributions in D. Bigo and E. Guild (eds.), *Controlling Frontiers: Free Movement Into and Within Europe* (London: Ashgate, 2005). Similarly, Gregor Noll has convincingly employed Agamben's concept of bare life to the analysis of offshore asylum processing centres and regional protection zones. Noll, 'Visions of the exceptional'. Yet, where Noll's analysis is based on a primarily legal analysis as the premise of bare life and on Agamben's use of Hannah Arendt's notion of the 'camp' as a closed site for exceptional measures beyond the law, it may be more correct to identify the premise of the exceptional not only at the level of law but equally, and often more importantly, at the level of institutions. Moreover, in the

reach of the institutional mechanisms ensuring their accessibility may be an even more important factor in realising migration control unfettered by the ordinary constraints imposed by international refugee law. In the unchecked encounter between the individual and offshore or privatised migration control, state authorities (or their delegates) are free to label those encountered as 'illegal migrants', 'rescuees' or 'asylum-seekers' – all of which produce and institutionalise very different legal entitlements.

The present chapter has attempted to sketch only a few issues pertaining to the issue of institutional enforcement of refugee rights. Yet it is important to realise that the question of institutional capacity is not separate from, but endemic to, the question and determination of legal norms. The two are intrinsically connected. On the one hand, the lack of institutional capacity means that few cases ever reach domestic or international human rights courts and, even if they do, difficulties in establishing objective facts entail a strong risk that cases fail. Little judicial clarity is thus provided to help resolve the existing contestation of the exact scope and application of relevant norms, which in turn leaves states with a wider scope for national interpretation and domestic implementation of international obligations.[64]

On the other hand, the lack of institutional capacity to create accountability in situations of offshore and outsourcing is also partly a reflection of the somewhat unclear or only recently developed norms in this area. Extraterritorialisation and privatisation still remain somewhat the exception. The vast majority of human rights abuses still pertain to a state's *own* actions *within* its territory. Extending institutional capacity beyond this may not only be very costly but also hard to argue, as long as the legal need is not clearly established.

In effect, the clarification of legal norms and institutional monitoring capacity thus becomes a 'chicken and egg' problem. Lack of institutional oversight and monitoring may reflect legal ambiguity, yet legal clarity can only be obtained with the availability of knowledge of practices and of concrete cases that may be brought before national courts and international human rights bodies.

context of extraterritorial migration control, the offshore venue is seldom a closed site. Rather, the national realm becomes the bounded sphere of justice.

[64] As Jonas Christoffersen points out, countries such as Denmark normally require a fairly high degree of clarity for implementing human rights obligations in national adjudication. National courts tend to await developments from the European Court of Human Rights. Christoffersen, 'Fair balance', pp. 523–4.

Breaking this cycle is, however, not impossible. Lessons from other fields indicate that the effect of simply casting light on situations of offshore and outsourcing may create a political impetus for accountability beyond legal and institutional barriers.[65] There is a link between visibility and political and societal acceptance. When offshore arrangements become too exposed in terms of the way in which they elude ordinary norms and standards of regulation, it creates a tension that may eventually lead to their demise. Individual offshore and outsourcing schemes are in that sense fickle things that seldom hold up well in the face of exposure. As the practice becomes more visible, political tension builds to achieve a re-normalisation of regulation that may end up making offshore and outsourcing arrangements purposeless.[66]

The actual practices of offshore and privatised migration control thus continue to be largely uncharted and opaque. International organisations, journalists and, in particular, NGOs have made several efforts to change this and bring visibility to the consequences of offshore and outsourced migration control. Ultimately, however, casting light on these practices and ensuring accountability mechanisms depend on the political will of those governments engaged in offshore and privatised migration control, which has so far been limited.

Until that happens, lions continue to abound.

---

[65] Fernando, 'Role of NGOs in policy-making'; W. Brittain-Catlin, *Offshore: The Dark Side of the Global Economy* (New York: Picador, Farrar, Straus and Giroux, 2005), pp. 170–5.

[66] The US prison programme at Guantánamo and the related Supreme Court rulings form a case in point. Similarly, following a change in government, Australia in 2008 decided to end the 'Pacific solution' scheme developed following the *Tampa* incident. The practice of intercepting asylum-seekers and transferring them to camps in Nauru or other island states for offshore asylum procedures had been substantially criticised by both national and international organisations.

7   Conclusion

7.1 Recapitulation

This book started by asking the simple question: when does a refugee encounter the state? As a matter of practice something is clearly changing in the encounter between the asylum-seeker and the potential asylum state. Rather than the traditional image of the refugee arriving at the border and claiming asylum with national authorities, more and more often asylum-seekers find themselves confronted with measures of migration control before arriving at their prospective destination state and with controls carried out by agents other than the state's own authorities.

Throughout the preceding chapters an attempt has been made to give examples of these practices. It has been argued that 'offshore' and 'outsourcing' migration control is not just a growing trend among both old and new asylum and immigration countries; it may well be a systemic feature of the world we currently inhabit and as such finds parallels in a number of other fields.

The driving force behind this volume has been to ask whether this de facto shift in location and actors for the encounter between the refugee and the state is accompanied by an equal de jure shift in the reach of international refugee law. To what extent are states bound by international refugee and human rights obligations when carrying out extraterritorial migration control or delegating control functions to private actors? The preceding chapters have attempted to probe critically the boundaries of international refugee law in this respect, in particular the geographical application of the *non-refoulement* principle, the bases of extraterritorial jurisdiction in cases of offshore migration control and the principles for establishing state responsibility when outsourcing migration control to private parties.

The outcome of this inquiry may be read in several ways, however. The next part of this chapter (7.2) relates to the above questions at the most immediate level. It affirms that in many situations of extraterritorial or privatised migration control states do retain core obligations under refugee and human rights law. Seen thus, the legality of the current practice of many states is highly questionable and the general lack of protection safeguards as an integral part of offshore and outsourced migration control begs to be remedied.

The next part of the chapter (7.3) reflects on the responsibility gaps nonetheless identified in the legal analysis. While a critical analysis goes some way towards bringing international obligations to bear on situations of extraterritorial and privatised migration control, some situations remain legally unclear, and certain legal and evidentiary thresholds must be overcome in order for international refugee rights and human rights obligations to apply. To understand why this is so, three dynamics can be identified that permeate this field: the contestability of norm application, the instrumentalisation of sovereignty norms and the invisibility of control practices. All contribute to the ongoing difficulty in establishing human rights responsibility in situations of offshore and outsourcing.

The final part of the chapter (7.4) is devoted to a few considerations regarding the wider perspectives of the analysis above.

7.2 The reach of international refugee law

The most important conclusion of the present investigation is that states do not rid themselves of international obligations simply by offshoring and outsourcing migration control. Contrary to the vivid claims that extraterritorial actions or privatisation are carried out in a 'human rights vacuum' or 'legal black hole', the preceding chapters have affirmed that core norms under international refugee law and human rights law, even under the most restrictive reading, undeniably remain applicable in many of these situations.

The geographical scope of the 1951 Refugee Convention, and in particular the *non-refoulement* principle, have been the subject of debate since the very inception of the Refugee Convention. Even though a number of rights under this instrument are clearly reserved for refugees already present or staying within the territory, the prohibition against *refoulement* set out in Article 33 does not carry such a limitation. Looking at the wording, object and purpose as well as the drafting documents, an interpretative scope does exist regarding the applicability *ratione loci* of this article. A comprehensive interpretation, taking account of subsequent developments in other human rights instruments, soft law and state practice points to a development in favour of a more expansive interpretation. Even if it was not the case fifty years ago, it is today clear that the *non-refoulement* principle must be interpreted to apply everywhere a state exercises jurisdiction.

This brings Article 33 of the Refugee Convention into line with the majority of international and regional human rights instruments, yet necessarily begs a more general analysis of the concept of jurisdiction as used and conceived in human rights law. As shown in chapter 4, even though jurisdiction is understood in primarily territorial terms, a growing body of case law provides a firm basis for extending jurisdiction to a number of situations where states act outside their territory. Thus states will normally bring about jurisdiction when carrying out migration control and rejecting asylum-seekers in international waters or in designated 'international zones'. Where migration control is carried out within the territory or territorial waters of another state, establishing extraterritorial jurisdiction depends on the level of control exercised over the area, place or individual concerned. In cases where offshore migration control involves exclusive control over areas of another state's territory, such as through the establishment of closed camps or control facilities, or physical apprehension of asylum-seekers and migrants on board ships, aircraft or elsewhere, there is little doubt that this will equally entail jurisdiction and thus responsibility under both refugee and human rights law.

The same conclusion applies regarding the outsourcing of migration control to private actors. Even though the public/private distinction has been a key feature of international law, it is far from impenetrable. While there is little specific human rights case law in this area, general principles of international and human rights law may be relied on to provide a basis for establishing state responsibility in cases of private involvement in migration control. As can be seen in chapter 5, the use of private contractors for the purpose of migration control or immigration detention will thus entail responsibility of the outsourcing state in most instances. A strong case may equally be made that carrier liability legislation, combined with the degree of supervision and case-by-case 'advice' provided by immigration liaison officers, gives rise to state responsibility either as an exercise of governmental authority or as situations where states may be said to direct or control the conduct of otherwise private actors. In both instances the conduct of private actors may be considered an 'act of state' for the purpose of international law and thus entails human rights obligations on a par with a state's own actions in similar circumstances.

Lastly, the preceding chapters have pointed to a dynamic potential both within the law on state responsibility and regarding the establishment of extraterritorial jurisdiction. While gaps may thus still exist regarding human rights accountability for offshore and outsourcing policies, there is little to suggest that these areas of law are at a standstill. Several judgments regarding extraterritorial jurisdiction already seem to suggest something of a revision of the strict 'effective control' test applied in cases like *Banković*. As is suggested in chapter 4, we may yet see the emergence of a more functional approach to jurisdiction, not just to cases on the high seas but also to situations where migration control is carried out within the territorial jurisdiction of another state. Similarly, the concept of due diligence, although difficult to operationalise in the abstract, has already been relied on in a number of human rights cases to establish state responsibility for the conduct of private actors. As argued in chapter 5, such obligations not only are likely to be important in cases where private migration control within the territory cannot be directly attributed to the state, but may also extend at least a negative obligation not to aid or assist rights violations by other actors in cases where private migration control takes place extraterri-torially.

Even under a more restrictive reading of current international law, the analysis carried out above seriously questions the legality of many current practices of offshoring and outsourcing migration control. Accepting the conclusion that international refugee and human rights law applies to at least some situations of extraterritorialisation and privatisation, it is hard to see how, for example, current interception schemes on the high seas or the systematic rejection of asylum-seekers in so-called 'international zones' can be carried out without violating the *non-refoulement* obligation and other core human rights norms.

Offshore and outsourced migration control generally operates with few, if any, protection safeguards. The legal analysis of the present work suggests that if conformity with international law is to be ensured, a number of current practices must either be abandoned or, perhaps more realistically, adequate protection mechanisms implemented that ensure access to asylum for refugees among general migration flows. A num-ber of recommendations and best practices to achieve the latter have already been put forward by UNHCR, NGOs and scholars.[1] Proposals for 'protection-sensitive' migration control include legislative and regulative changes to allow such measures as the issuing of 'protection visas' by immigration liaison officers or embassies, imposing clearer monitoring and reporting obligations on both government officials and private actors involved in migration control, and establishing referral mechanisms for asylum-seekers stopped by carriers. Second, there is a clear need for training of both border authorities and private actors involved in migration control, the better to identify protection-seekers and ensure proper procedures to avoid *refoulement*.[2] Third, UNHCR in particular has pushed for better dialogue and co-operation between the authorities of territorial and offshoring/outsourcing states as well as co-operation with and the involvement of NGOs and UNHCR in border management programmes. And lastly, several suggestions for creating alternative pathways ensuring access to asylum, for example by way of 'protected entry procedures' allowing asylum applications to be lodged at embassies in third states, have been tabled.[3]

The implementation of such protection safeguards would no doubt go a long way to facilitating access to asylum as part of offshore and outsourced migration control. Whether it would be sufficient to ensure that situations of *refoulement* or other rights violations are avoided completely remains a more open question. Save a few positive examples, the political will to implement protection safeguards as part of offshore and outsourced migration control has largely been missing. Indeed, such safeguards may go against the very reason for introducing such offshoring and outsourcing policies in the first place. Even where such political will is present, offshore and outsourced migration control will inevitably continue to eclipse many of the ordinary institutions ensuring access to asylum, accountability and human rights monitoring. To some extent, refugees encountering the state outside its territory or by proxy are thus

---

[1] See e.g. European Council for Refugees and Exiles, 'Defending refugees' access to protection in Europe', Brussels, December 2007); Refugee Council, 'Remote controls'; and UNHCR, Refugee Protection and Mixed Migration: A 10-point Plan of Action, 1 January 2007.

[2] See further UNHCR Executive Committee, Protection Safeguards in Interception Measures, Conclusion No. 97 (LIV), 2003.

[3] The Commission released a study on protected entry procedures in 2003 based on the existing practice of a number of EU member states. See Noll et al., 'Processing asylum claims outside the EU'.

likely to keep on experiencing additional barriers in claiming their legal entitlements.

Finally, attention should be paid to the possible wider effects of carrying out offshore and outsourced migration control without adequate protection safeguards for refugees and asylum-seekers. By preventing access to asylum, refugee protection is at worst entirely deconstructed and at best shifted to the countries in which controls are conducted. This strategic shifting of protection obligations places an extra burden on countries in the region of origin and countries of transit, states that often already host large numbers of refugees.

Where protection obligations are deflected to less developed countries, states with poor human rights records or undeveloped asylum systems, the quality of protection provided to individual refugees may be severely eroded. As is shown in chapter 2, the structure of the Refugee Convention is such that the more substantial protection obligations owed are specifically granted relative to the human rights and socio-economic situation in the specific host country. To the extent that extraterritorial and privatised migration control works to strategically shift protection obligations to states where the cost of protection is perceived to be lower, the result may be the emergence of 'protection lite', a market for realising refugee protection at the lowest level still possible within a restrictive reading of the obligations owed under the Refugee Convention.

Ultimately, the effect of offshore and outsourced migration control seems destined to create a mimicry effect in the states where such controls are carried out. Faced with increased protection burdens, these countries are likely to adopt similar policies and mechanisms to restrict access to asylum and push protection obligations further away. Interception policies, carrier sanctions, safe country rules and readmission agreements are already flourishing in east European, north African, central American and some Asian countries. Often such policies are implemented with the active help and assistance of the countries originally implementing offshore and outsourcing mechanisms in exchange for co-operation, readmission agreements and/or access to operate control within foreign territory. In the long run, the extraterritorialisation and privatisation of migration control is thus unlikely to prove sustainable. Rather, these policies seem constantly to push refugees back to sites closer and closer to the state of persecution, a development that ultimately threatens to undermine the very concept of refuge.

7.3 The limits of international refugee law

While a positive appraisal shows that international refugee and human rights do extend to encompass a wide range of offshore and outsourcing practices, the analysis carried out in the preceding chapters also merits a more critical assessment of the legal framework. As has been seen, establishing extraterritorial jurisdiction or attributing conduct of private actors to a state is often a complicated legal manoeuvre and subject to a number of limitations. States may not be bound in all situations of offshore or outsourced migration control, and in particular under the Refugee Convention the content and extent of obligations change as migration control is moved outside the territory. This is particularly worrying as a number of recent offshore and outsourcing practices seem to be carefully designed expressly to avoid establishing extraterritorial jurisdiction or attribution of private conduct.

If we accept that the legal framework as it stands at present does allow certain responsibility gaps where migration control can be carried out with no, or substantially reduced, obligations under refugee and human rights law, it is natural to ask why this is so. If a basic tenet of human rights law is that wherever there is power there should be constraint of that power, why, then, is it so difficult for refugee and human rights law to encompass the obvious developments in state practices? The answer suggested in this volume is that the otherwise universal aspirations of human rights law must, in its application, be reconciled with core norms of general international law, in particular the principle of territoriality and the public/private distinction. In this clash a new playing field is opened up, where legal interpretation may be challenged from both sides and thus constantly has to balance universalist and particularist claims. Specifically, three interrelated dynamics can be traced throughout the analysis that may help us to understand the difficulties in fully bridging remaining responsibility gaps and bringing more legal clarity to this field.

7.3.1 Contesting the applicability of refugee and human rights law

What is perhaps most remarkable about the legal discourse pertaining to refugee and human rights in cases of offshore and outsourcing is the difficulty in reaching general consensus on even basic issues of legal interpretation. The meaning of and exact principles for establishing 'jurisdiction' are subject to intense debate among both lawyers and governments. Equally, while general principles for attributing private conduct to states may be agreed on, their concrete application is marred by a range of different interpretations as regards both the meaning of the international norms and their applicability to concrete cases. Furthermore, the exact scope of application of different human rights instruments and specific articles within them continues to spur disagreement.

In the academic world the result has been a recent wave of writing on the extraterritorial application of human rights norms and state responsibility for the conduct of private actors. From proclamations of 'legal black holes' to arguments that human rights apply everywhere and to everyone – states, corporations and individuals alike – there seems to be an inherent scope for contesting the applicability of refugee and human rights law when states act beyond their territory or delegate power to private actors.

In the context of refugee law this is probably best seen in connection with the continuing disagreement over the scope of application *ratione loci* of the *non-refoulement* principle as enshrined in Article 33 of the Refugee Convention. As is evidenced in chapter 3, this issue has been a bone of contention even during its drafting, with no clear resolution. Differing interpretations, ranging from the strictly territorial to border, jurisdictional and universal application, have since been proposed by governments, UNHCR, national courts and scholars. The lack of specific foresight about current practices of offshore migration control may well be to blame, and no clear and convincing answer thus appears from the wording of the article itself or the drafting history.

While the present work proposes a jurisdictional interpretation based on a more thorough analysis of subsidiary sources and subsequent developments, the tension between territorialist and universalist arguments remains evident throughout every stage of interpretation. And while a growing consensus seems to be mounting in favour of a jurisdictional interpretation, this has not prevented individual states from maintaining strong positions in favour of a more restrictive reading. Most notably, the United States has expressed criticism of UNHCR's Advisory Opinion on this matter and instead maintained that not only is the *non-refoulement* obligation under the Refugee Convention strictly territorially limited, so are obligations under the International Covenant on Civil and Political Rights in general.[4]

---

[4] US Mission, Observations of the United States on the advisory opinion of the UN High Commissioner for Refugees.

The inherent contestability of refugee and human rights norms in situations of offshore and privatisation may ultimately point back to a deeper conflict within human rights law itself. In their idea and inception, human rights are conceived of as universal. Yet in their codification and institutionalisation as treaty law, this aspiration has to be reconciled with general principles of international law, which inevitably ties the human rights project to a legal conceptualisation of the state still largely built on the principle of territoriality and the public/private distinction.

7.3.2 Instrumentalising sovereignty norms against responsibility

To a certain extent related to the contestation of refugee and human rights obligations is what could be termed the instrumentalisation of sovereignty norms to avoid protection obligations. Rather than contesting or refusing the applicability of human rights norms as such, the attempt to reduce protection obligations is, in this dynamic, made by reference to the territorial and state-centric structure of refugee and human rights law in order to shift or deconstruct protection burdens. What becomes essential here is the instrumentalisation of another state or private entity as part of the offshoring and outsourcing process in order to limit or disclaim the sovereign responsibility and obligations over the polity or acts concerned.

Under the EU Frontex operations to prevent irregular migrants from arriving at the Canary Islands, Spanish vessels not only carry out interdiction in Senegalese waters but also take on board Senegalese coastguards. In each case Senegal's sovereignty is instrumentalised to boost the claim that not only does interception take place within the jurisdiction of Senegal, but also that any migrants intercepted are also rejected by Senegalese authorities, and any protection obligations thus fall to Senegal. Similarly, governments have been keen to emphasise that immigration liaison officers posted to foreign airports do not exercise direct authority and maintain only an advisory role. In this way, the posting state maintains the claim that the territorial state still holds exclusive jurisdiction and that the control carried out by airlines remains legally distinct from the state imposing fines and advising on which passengers to carry.

The introduction of another sovereign in this way may severely affect the application of legal norms. As is seen in chapter 4, moving interdiction from the high seas to foreign territorial waters substantially changes the thresholds for establishing extraterritorial jurisdiction. As long as states are operating in the *res communis*, a more functional approach has so far been applied, in which the mere cause-and-effect relationship appears to be enough to invoke the human rights responsibility of the acting state. But where another sovereign is added to the equation, the tests for establishing extraterritorial jurisdiction become more demanding. In these cases the extraterritorially acting state must be shown to exercise 'effective control' in a way that de facto excludes the authority of the territorial state over the geographical area or the individual involved.

This is where the two basic norms of international law – the territoriality principle and the public/private distinction – come most clearly to the fore. They do not limit state responsibility in cases of offshore and privatisation per se, yet they create a strong presumption for the exclusivity of the territorial sovereign and distinctiveness of private actors. Only when these presumptions are successfully rebutted does responsibility arise on behalf of the offshoring or outsourcing state.

These legal structures are what give rise to the political commercialisation of sovereignty and, more specifically, to the increasing market for migration control. Horizontally, the market for migration control takes the form of jurisdiction shopping, as states purchase access to exercise migration control in foreign jurisdictions where corresponding refugee and human rights obligations are perceived to be lower or less precise. Vertically, a market is similarly created for private actors, in which the very label of being 'private' may be exploited to shed responsibility by outsourcing governmental functions through tenders or threats of economic sanctions.

7.3.3 Rendering migration control invisible

The third dynamic concerns the lack of knowledge of offshore and outsourced migration control. The distinct invisibility of actual practices in this field fundamentally affects both legal interpretation and the effectiveness of legal entitlements owed. The previous chapter identifies an 'out of sight, out of mind' effect surrounding much of what takes place when states extraterritorialise or privatise migration control. Information about these practices may be obtained through press coverage of certain incidents, testimonies of migrants, NGO reports and field research. Yet what goes on in the actual control situation generally remains opaque, and it is only incidental information about states carrying out control that tends to reach the media and the public.

The lack of knowledge is in part a reflection of the institutional structures facilitating the realisation and monitoring of human rights. These are, to an even greater extent than legal norms, organised along state-centric and territorial principles. Shifting jurisdiction thus eclipses many of both the public and private mechanisms normally facilitating access to asylum, and privatisation may shortcut the traditional accountability procedures ensuring public oversight. These limitations not only pose important problems for the individual asylum-seeker, who in these situations does not have access to any of the ordinary institutions: the specialised authorities, translators, UNHCR or refugee-assisting NGOs who normally guide and aid the launching of an asylum application. From the perspective of refugee and human rights institutions working to monitor state performance in this field, offshoring and outsourcing also tend to render the effects of migration control largely invisible.

Save the occasional stories from asylum-seekers and migrants themselves, very little is known of what goes on when migrant vessels are intercepted on the high seas or in foreign territorial waters. Independent monitors, the press or NGOs are rarely allowed on board vessels carrying out offshore interdiction programmes, and authorities themselves seldom if ever document the interception situation itself. Situations where migrant and authority accounts of events differ are thus inherently difficult to resolve objectively or to verify. Similarly, following the fates of asylum-seekers rejected as part of offshore migration control is nearly impossible if their identities have not been established and recorded prior to rejection.

Even where controls are operated within the territory, privatisation may create a distance for both governmental accountability mechanisms and independent monitoring. The numerous reports of the alleged mistreatment of asylum-seekers and immigrants in privately operated detention centres are a case in point and fully illustrate the difficulties of penetrating the 'corporate veil', even where private actors are governed by strict contracts, are subject to public inspection and are located within the territory. In the case of extraterritorially operated controls such as those enacted by carriers, the problems are only exacerbated. A refusal of embarkation by an airline official is not considered to be a public decision, and no record or justification is thus given. As a result, very little is known about rejected persons and how many may have had a valid protection claim.

The invisibility of offshore and outsourced migration control has important consequences, not only for the effective enforcement of refugee and human rights law, but also for the possibilities of establishing legal clarity. Resolving existing legal gaps or interpretative uncertainties is crucially dependent on concrete cases being taken forward and placed before national and international judiciaries. Even where this is possible, evidentiary problems are likely to persist for both national courts and international human rights bodies in assessing the facts of extraterritorial actions or specific power relations between governments and private actors. In sum, even beyond the de jure constraints, offshore and outsourced migration control seems to create a number of de facto barriers for accessing asylum.

7.4 Wider perspective and implications

The above has sought to draw together the more immediate conclusions of the legal analysis as well as to address the wider explanatory research questions posed at the outset of this volume. Before it comes to an end, however, a few remarks are in order as regards the possible wider significance of the questions raised by the present analysis. What follows should not thus be read by way of a conclusion, but rather as an attempt to point onwards and to spark further debate.

7.4.1 The role and importance of refugee and human rights law

The above analysis may have painted a somewhat bleak picture of state practices hardly in conformity with international refugee and human rights obligations, and of offshore and outsourcing as deliberate strategies to avoid legal constraints otherwise imposed by national and international law. At face value this could be taken to support the growing realist critique of refugee and human rights law as increasingly irrelevant and powerless to constrain state behaviour. As political concerns over immigration and refugees have increased, refugee and human rights, at least in these areas, no longer constitute a 'self-enforcing equilibrium' where the states participating have clear interests and where there are obvious pay-offs for abiding by the rules.[5]

Such a reading would, however, overlook one of the most important premises for the globalisation of migration control. As has been seen, offshore and outsourcing policies are often costly affairs and may demand substantial concessions, for example to territorial states to achieve access and co-operation. While some effectiveness benefits may accrue from intercepting persons pre-arrival and enlisting private actors, the logic of offshore and outsourcing cannot be understood in purely managerial

---

[5] S. D. Krasner, 'The hole in the whole: sovereignty, shared sovereignty, and international law', (2004) 25 *Michigan Journal of International Law* 1075–1101, at 1075; Watson, *Theory and Reality*; Goldsmith and Posner, *Limits of International Law*, pp. 177–80.

or economic terms. At least in the field of migration control a key purpose rather seems to be to reduce, shift or deconstruct legal obligations otherwise owed, de jure and/or de facto.

Yet such ambitions necessarily assume that refugee responsibilities imposed by national and international law do actually, under ordinary circumstances, constrain state behaviour. If governments felt that they could simply flout international refugee and human rights law, there would be little need to engage in cumbersome and costly offshore and outsourcing exercises. The contestability of legal norms, burden-shifting possibilities and invisibility achieved by offshore and outsourcing is exactly what makes it possible for some states to avoid protection obligations but nonetheless still situate themselves as countries abiding by their international refugee and human rights commitments. As such, the very existence of offshore and outsourcing migration control may be taken as an argument that norms do still matter and as a reaffirmation of refugee and human rights law in a more general sense.

Such policies, however, hardly conform to the liberal or cosmopolitan vision of international law as bringing about a legalisation of world politics and global human rights applications normally contrasted with the more political realist accounts. Rather, offshoring and outsourcing states appear to be much more instrumental in their relationship with refugee and human rights norms. While international refugee and human rights obligations may be accepted as such, their applicability to certain situations is contested and legal gaps are deliberately exploited to realise sovereign power and prerogatives unconstrained by refugee and human rights law.

Second, the normative framework may not only constrain but also enable certain policies. When states shift migration control to third-state territory or territorial waters, it is exactly by claiming the sovereign jurisdiction and concomitant refugee protection obligations of the territorial state that the offshoring state seeks to avoid taking responsibility. Similarly, traditional asylum countries have been keen to exploit the territorial structure of the refugee regime in order to realise protection in third countries at perceived lower costs.

To the extent that these observations hold true for other fields, a new position between the dominant black and white readings of human rights law may need to be staked out, one that on the one hand acknowledges the basic assumption that refugee and human rights law does influence state behaviour despite the lack of any effective enforcement mechanisms, but on the other hand appreciates that states simply submit to human rights obligations as they might have been intended. The emergence of offshore and outsourcing policies are indicative that states are much more creative and instrumental in their relationship to international refugee and human rights law than is normally assumed.

7.4.2 The sollen and the sein of refugee and human rights law

The impression that states are constantly seeking to influence legal interpretation to their own advantage and to position practices to avoid legal constraints points back to a deeper conflict in refugee and human rights law. Inherent in the very idea of human rights is the assumption of their universality, or at least a normative ideal that they ought to be respected everywhere and regardless of who is exercising power. At the same time, however, human rights are put forward as positive law, clad and locked in the form of international treaties. In becoming positive international law, normative ideals may first of all be cut down to what states in the end are willing to sign up to. The difficulty in codifying an actual 'right to asylum' as a matter of binding international law is an example in point. But, equally, in becoming positive law the universal principles are somewhat awkwardly sought to be reconciled with a normative framework structured around idealised but ever strong principles of national sovereignty.

It is around this tension between the '*sollen*' and the '*sein*' of refugee and human rights that interpretation in cases concerning offshoring and outsourcing revolves. The particularity of human rights law is that it necessarily remains both a normative ideal and a body of positive law, simultaneously both the *sollen* and the *sein*. The present analysis has initially advanced from the latter, taking heed of both the territorial structure of instruments like the Refugee Convention and the limitations posed by national sovereignty principles in establishing extraterritorial jurisdiction or state responsibility for private conduct. Yet, as should also be clear from the preceding analysis, the ideal of universality is equally present at every stage of interpretation, and has in several respects served to extend the scope of refugee and human rights responsibility in the light of new practices, beyond what drafters might originally have intended or foreseen.

The *sein* and the *sollen* of human rights law could be argued to constitute a double structure that may help in understanding not just the enduring conflicts over interpretation, but also the particular dynamic quality of refugee and human rights law. How an issue is framed within this double structure is crucial, as the perspective from which arguments are advanced will often be determinative of the interpretative outcome. Those who hope to expand the reach of human rights law will tend to start from a conceptualisation of human rights as a universal ideal and from there emphasise their relevance and application to the reality of current-day practices. Conversely, from the perspective of states engaged in offshore and outsourcing, an argument advancing from national sovereignty may be employed to superimpose territorial and public/private divisions of authority, regardless of de facto practices to the contrary, in order to shed or limit corresponding human rights responsibilities.

Just as international refugee and human rights law may be seen to constrain or condition the politics of migration control, deciphering the legal structures surrounding the extraterritorial application of human rights and state responsibility for private conduct conversely lays bare a playing field for the political in the interpretation of the exact scope of human rights obligations. In this process international human rights law no longer merely serves to harness the exercise of political power; it may also be sought instrumentalised as a juridical cover in order to exercise power unconstrained by ordinary obligations.

7.4.3 Reconciling national sovereignty and the effectiveness of human rights law

In the light of these considerations, the final question, of course, remains how this field will develop in the future. This concerns not only the offshoring and outsourcing of migration control, but more generally the application of human rights law to situations of extraterritorial action and where private actors are involved in the exercise of otherwise public powers.

Arguably, the stakes are high. On the one hand there is a real risk to the effectiveness of international refugee and human rights law from those building an interpretation entirely based on principles of national sovereignty. As Theodor Meron concluded in response to the US Supreme Court judgment in the *Sale* case, '[n]arrow territorial interpretation of human rights treaties is anathema to the basic idea of human rights'.[6] A blind refusal of state responsibility in cases of privatisation and extraterritorial application of refugee and human rights instruments would only create a further incentive for states to move the less palatable issues of governance to foreign territories and private actors, with all that follows from this in terms of a shrinking of the rule of law and breaking of the

---

[6] Meron, 'Extraterritoriality of human rights treaties', 82.

link between legitimacy and power. Even the current status quo may be argued to constitute a severe legitimacy crisis allowing obvious gaps in which states seem to position interception measures strategically.

On the other hand, however, only relying on the *sollen* of human rights and completely giving up geographical and public/private boundaries for state responsibility may entail equal complications. This does not relate solely to the tricky issue of dividing up and tailoring responsibility between states – if all states are responsible everywhere, is anyone in particular in practice liable anywhere, and how are positive and more material human rights obligations effectively guaranteed beyond borders? It also relates to the more practical and resource-based arguments sometimes put forward by national administrations, that opening up human rights instruments for extraterritorial application would unleash a wealth of hard-to-assess complaints on already overburdened international and national judiciaries. More fundamentally, simply doing away with the principle of territoriality and the public/private distinction in order to realise human rights responsibility in situations of offshoring and outsourcing is unlikely to be compatible with general international law. Claiming that human rights is a legal regime *sui generis* will almost inevitably undermine the claim of human rights to be positive law. Even more than offshore and outsourcing policies themselves, such a move may risk overstretching the politico-legal conception of 'the state' and thereby shake the very foundations on which not just international refugee and human rights law but our entire political imaginary is founded.

A balanced approach may ultimately be both most desirable and most realistic. The contours of one such may already be appearing. The developing case law and writings on both extraterritorial jurisdiction and attribution of private conduct suggest that clearer legal principles for both of these are being developed and reinforced through each concrete case application. Yet, rather than these becoming 'mainstream' or 'business as usual', certain thresholds are still being upheld and instances are repeatedly presented as *extra*-ordinary or as exceptions to the ordinary modus operandi. While human rights jurisprudence in cases of offshore and outsourcing may be hoped to develop a more functional conception of extraterritorial jurisdiction and make wider references to due diligence obligations, these developments do not seem to simply overturn more traditionalist approaches. It is as if there is a fundamental barrier that is hard to move past, a conceptual history that makes it cognitively difficult to conceive of jurisdiction not tied to territorial claims or human rights obligations not exclusively concerned with the actions of states' own authorities.

In that sense, one might expect extraterritorial human rights obligations and state responsibility for private actions to develop more as a 'border theorem' – that is, a conceptual framework employed to describe a certain confined field or issue that does not replace the ordinary paradigm but merely limits its field of application.[7] The concept has been used to describe the relation between Newtonian physics and quantum mechanics. Quantum mechanics was developed because classical physics theory proved insufficient to explain phenomena at the atomic level. Quantum mechanics dissolves the distinction between waves and particles, light and matter, much as a notion of functional jurisdiction dissolves the distinction between each polity's exclusive sphere of authority and state attribution of private conduct overcomes the private/public distinction. Yet, as Niels Bohr was acutely aware, even though the phenomena he wanted to explain fell outside existing theory, the very description of his theory, and of the experimental set-up, would have to conform to the language and rules of traditional physics for others to accept it.[8] Thus the distinction between particles and waves has survived both in everyday usage and as epistemically distinct categories.

Similarly, the language of national sovereignty and its associated norms of territorial exclusivity and distinction between public and private do not appear to falter, despite the advent of offshore and outsourcing. Territorial jurisdiction and state-centrism have remained the epistemic starting points and form a normative framework which is still appropriate and sufficient to guide the majority of situations where the exercise of public power is carried out by states' own authorities and effected within their respective national boundaries. When confronted with the, albeit growing, exception of extraterritoriality and privatisation, this framework is the backdrop for any judiciary.

This is not to say that the law on jurisdiction and state responsibility will remain the status quo, far from it. Within their spheres of application we may well see gradual and potentially far-reaching developments in both. Yet there is little to suggest that such developments will substantially alter the ordinary modus operandi of international law, which springs from a conception of the state as defined through geographical boundaries and a sovereign–subject dichotomy. To the extent that refugee and human

---

[7] S. Rozental, 'Om komplementaritet i atomfysikken', (1955) *Fysisk Tidsskrift* 325–42, at 327.
[8] N. Bohr, *Atomfysik og Menneskelig Erkendelse* (Copenhagen: Schultz, 1957), p. 88.

rights law wants to remain a genuine part of general international law, these norms are likely to continue to exercise importance. It will thus remain the challenge for both national and international judiciaries to develop a concept of jurisdiction and attribution that fits our global age while still couching it within the language of national sovereignty.

Bibliography

Aalberts, Tanja E., and Werner, Wouter, 'Sovereignty beyond borders: sovereignty, self-defense, and the disciplining of the state', in R. Adler-Nissen and T. Gammeltoft-Hansen (eds.), *Sovereignty Games: Instrumentalizing State Sovereignty in Europe and Beyond* (New York: Palgrave Macmillan, 2008), pp. 129–50.

Abeyratne, R. I. R., 'Air carrier liability and state responsibility for the carriage of inadmissible persons and refugees', (1998) 10 *International Journal of Refugee Law* 675–87.

Adler-Nissen, Rebecca, and Gammeltoft-Hansen, Thomas (eds.), *Sovereignty Games: Instrumentalizing State Sovereignty in Europe and Beyond* (New York: Palgrave Macmillan, 2008).

Agamben, Giorgio, *Homo Sacer: Sovereign Power and Bare Life* (Stanford University Press, 1998).

Allains, Jean, 'The *jus cogens* nature of *non-refoulement*', (2001) 13 *International Journal of Refugee Law* 533–58.

Alston, Philip (ed.), *Human Rights Law* (Aldershot: Dartmouth, 1996).

'The myopia of handmaidens: international lawyers and globalization', (1997) 8 *European Journal of International Law* 435–48.

'Downsizing the state in human rights discourse', in N. Dorden and P. Grifford (eds.), *Democracy and the Rule of Law* (Washington, DC: Congressional Quarterly Press, 2001), pp. 357–68.

'The "not-a-cat" syndrome: can the international human rights regime accommodate non-state actors?', in P. Alston (ed.), *Non-state Actors and Human Rights* (Oxford University Press, 2005), pp. 3–36.

Amerasinghe, Chittharanjan F., *Local Remedies in International Law* (Cambridge University Press, 1990).

Andrisani, P. J., Hakim, S., and Savas, E. S., *The New Public Management: Lessons from Innovating Governors and Mayors* (Norwell, MA: Kluwer, 2002).

Anker, Deborah E., 'Refugee law, gender and the human rights paradigm', (2002) 15 *Harvard Human Rights Journal* 133–54.

Armstrong, D., Farrell, T., and Lambert, H., *International Law and International Relations* (Cambridge University Press, 2007).

Ayling, J., and Grabosky, P., 'Policing By command: enhancing law enforcement capacity through coercion', (2006) 28 *Law and Policy* 420–43.

Bacon, Christine, 'The evolution of immigration detention in the UK: the involvement of private prison companies', RSC Working Paper No. 27, Refugee Studies Centre, Oxford (2005).

Barnes, Richard, 'Refugee law at sea', (2004) 53 *International and Comparative Law Quarterly* 47–77.

Barnett, Laura, 'Global governance and the evolution of the international refugee regime', New Issues in Refugee Research No. 54, United Nations High Commissioner for Refugees, Geneva, 2002.

Barnidge, Robert P. Jr, *Non-state Actors and Terrorism: Applying the Law of State Responsibility and the Due Diligence Principle* (The Hague: Asser Press, 2008).

Barutciski, Michael, and Suhrke, Astrid, 'Lessons from the Kosovo refugee crisis: innovations in protection and burden-sharing', (2001) 14 (2) *Journal of Refugee Studies* 95–134.

Beck, Robert J., 'Britain and the 1933 Refugee Convention: national or state sovereignty?', (1999) 11 *International Journal of Refugee Law* 597–623.

Bello, Judith Hippler, and Kokott, Juliane, '*Amuur* v. *France*', (1997) 91 (1) *American Journal of International Law* 147–52.

Bem, Kazimierz, 'The coming of a "blank cheque" – Europe, the 1951 Convention and the 1967 Protocol', (2004) 16 *International Journal of Refugee Law* 609–27.

Bem, K., Field, N., and Meyer, S., 'A price too high: the cost of Australia's approach to asylum-seekers', A just Australia and Oxfam Australia, August 2007.

Berman, Franklin, 'Jurisdiction: the state', in P. Capps, M. D. Evans and S. Konstadinidis (eds.), *Asserting Jurisdiction* (Portland: Hart Publishing, 2003), pp. 2–15.

Betts, Alexander, 'International cooperation between North and South to enhance refugee protection in regions of origin', RSC Working Paper No. 25, Refugee Studies Centre, Oxford, 2005.

  'Towards a Mediterranean solution? Implications for the region of origin', (2006) 18 *International Journal of Refugee Law* 652–77.

Bigo, Didier, 'When two become one: internal and external securitisations in Europe', in M. Kelstrup and M. C. Williams (eds.), *International Relations and the Politics of European Integration: Power, Security and Community* (London: Routledge, 2000), pp. 171–205.

  'Security and Immigration: towards a critique of the governmentality of unease', (2002) 27 *Alternatives* 63–92.

Bigo, Didier, and Guild, Elspeth (eds.), *Controlling Frontiers: Free Movement Into and Within Europe* (London: Ashgate, 2005).

Bina, Mark, 'Private military contractor liability and accountability after Abu Ghraib', (2005) 39 *John Marshall Law Review* 1237–50.

Bohr, Niels, *Atomfysik og Menneskelig Erkendelse* (Copenhagen: Schultz, 1957).

Bostock, Chantal Marie-Jeanne, 'The international legal obligations owed to the asylum seekers on the MV *Tampa*', (2002) 14 *International Journal of Refugee Law* 279–301.

Boswell, Christina, 'The "external dimension" of EU immigration and asylum policy', (2003) 79 *International Affairs* 619–38.

Brittain-Catlin, William, *Offshore: The Dark Side of the Global Economy* (New York: Picador, Farrar, Straus and Giroux, 2005).

Brouwer, Andrew, and Kumin, Judith, 'Interception and asylum: when migration control and human rights collide', (2003) 21 (4) *Refuge* 6–24.

Brownlie, Ian, *Principles of Public International Law* (Oxford University Press, 1998).

Buergenthal, Thomas, 'The UN Human Rights Committee', (2001) 5 *Max Planck Yearbook of United Nations Law* 341–98.

Bullard, Alice, *Human Rights in Crisis* (Aldershot: Ashgate, 2008).

Burchill, Richard, 'International human rights law: struggling between apology and Utopia', in A. Bullard (ed.), *Human Rights in Crisis* (Aldershot: Ashgate, 2008), pp. 49–68.

Byrne, R., Noll, G., and Vedsted-Hansen, J., *New Asylum Countries? Migration Control and Refugee Protection in an Enlarged European Union*, vol. 4 of E. Guild and J. Niessen (eds.), *Immigration and Asylum Law and Policy in Europe* (The Hague: Kluwer Law International, 2002).

Cacciaguidi-Fahy, S., 'The Law of the Sea and Human Rights', (2007) 19 *Sri Lanka Journal of International Law* 85–107.

Camilleri, Joseph A., and Falk, Jim, *The End of Sovereignty? The Politics of a Shrinking and Fragmenting World* (Aldershot: Edward Elgar, 1992).

Capps, P., Evans, M. D., and Konstadinidis, S. (eds.), *Asserting Jurisdiction* (Portland: Hart Publishing, 2003).

Carling, Jørgen, 'The merits and limitations of Spain's high-tech border control', *Migration Information Source*, June 2007.

Cassarino, Jean-Pierre, 'Informalising readmission agreements in the EU neighbourhood', (2007) 42 (2) *International Spectator* 179–96.

Cassel, Douglass, 'Extraterritorial application of inter-American human rights instruments', in F. Coomans and M. T. Kamminga (eds.), *Extraterritorial Application of Human Rights Treaties* (Antwerp: Intersentia, 2004), pp. 175–82.

Cassese, Antonio, *Terrorism, Politics and the Law* (Cambridge: Polity Press, 1989).

Castles, Stephen, and Miller, Mark J., *The Age of Migration: International Population Movements in the Modern World*, 3rd edn (New York: Palgrave Macmillan, 2003).

Cerna, Christina, 'Extraterritorial application of the human rights instruments of the inter-American system', in F. Coomans and M. T. Kamminga (eds.), *Extraterritorial Application of Human Rights Treaties* (Antwerp: Intersentia, 2004), pp. 141–74.

Cerone, John, 'Out of bounds? Considering the reach of international human rights law', Working Paper No. 5, Center for Human Rights and Global Justice, New York, 2006.

Chimni, B. S., 'The geopolitics of refugee studies and the practice of international institutions: a view from the South', (1999) 11 (4) *Journal of Refugee Studies* 350–74.

Chimni, B. S. (ed.), *International Refugee Law – A Reader* (New Delhi: Sage Publications, 2000).

Chinkin, Christine, 'A critique of the public/private dimension', (1999) 10 (2) *European Journal of International Law* 387–95.

Chirwa, Danwood Mzikenge, 'The doctrine of state responsibility as a potential means of holding private actors accountable for human rights', (2004) 5 (1) *Melbourne Journal of International Law* 1–36.

Christoffersen, Jonas, 'Fair balance: a study of proportionality, subsidiarity and primarity in the European Convention on Human Rights', University of Copenhagen, 2008.

Clapham, Andrew, *Human Rights in the Private Sphere* (Oxford: Clarendon Press, 1993).

Human Rights Obligations of Non-state Actors (Oxford University Press, 2006).

Clapham, Christopher, 'Sovereignty and the third world state', (1999) 47 (3) *Political Studies* 522–37.

Clark, Tom, 'Rights-based refuge, the potential of the 1951 Convention and the need for authoritative interpretation', (2004) 16 *International Journal of Refugee Law* 584–608.

Cockayne, James, 'Make or buy? Principal–agent theory and the regulation of private military companies', in S. Chesterman and C. Lehnart (eds.), *From Mercenaries to Markets* (Oxford University Press, 2007), pp. 196–216.

Coleman, James R., 'Constraining modern mercenarism', (2004) 55 *Hastings Law Journal* 1493–537.

Coleman, Nils, *European Readmission Policy* (The Hague: Martinus Nijhoff Publishers, 2009).

Collinson, Sarah, 'Visa requirements, carrier sanctions, "safe third countries" and "readmission": the development of an asylum "buffer zone" in Europe', (1996) 21 (1) *Transactions* 76–90.

Coomans, Fons, and Kamminga, Menno T. (eds.), *Extraterritorial Application of Human Rights Treaties* (Antwerp: Intersentia, 2004).

la Cour Bødtcher, Anne, and Hughes, Jane, 'The effects of legislation imposing fines on airlines for transporting undocumented passengers', in Kjærum, M. (ed.), *The Effects of Carrier Sanctions on the Asylum System* (Copenhagen: Danish Refugee Council and the Danish Center of Human Rights, 1991), pp. 6–13.

Craven, Matthew, 'Human rights in the realm of order: sanctions and extraterritoriality', in F. Coomans and M. T. Kamminga (eds.), *Extraterritorial Application of Human Rights Treaties* (Antwerp: Intersentia, 2004), pp. 233–58.

Crawford, James, *The International Law Commission's Articles on State Responsibility: Introduction, Text and Commentaries* (Cambridge University Press, 2002).

Crawford, James, and Hyndman, Patricia, 'Three heresies in the application of the Refugee Convention', (1989) 1 *International Journal of Refugee Law* 155–79.

Crawford, James, and Olleson, Simon, 'The continuing debate on a UN convention on state responsibility', (2005) 54 (4) *International and Comparative Law Quarterly* 959–68.

Cruz, Antonio, 'Carriers' liability in the member states of the European Union', CCME Briefing Paper No. 17, Churches' Commission for Migrants in Europe, Brussels (1994).

Shifting Responsibility: Carriers' Liability in the Member States of the European Union and North America (Stoke-on-Trent: Trentham Books, 1995).

Davy, Ulrike, *Asyl und Internationales Flüchtlingsrecht*, vol. I, *Völkerrechtlicher Rahmen* (Vienna: Österreichische Staatsdruckerei, 1996).

Dickinson, Laura, 'Contract as a tool for regulating PMCs', in S. Chesterman and C. Lehnart (eds.), *From Mercenaries to Markets* (Oxford University Press, 2007), pp. 217–38.

Duffy, Helen, *The "War on Terror" and the Framework of International Law* (Cambridge University Press, 2005).

Dupuy, Pierre-Marie, 'International law: torn between coexistence, cooperation and globalization. General conclusions', (1998) 9 (2) *European Journal of International Law* 278–86.

Durieux, François, and McAdam, Jane, '*Non-Refoulement* through time: the case for a derogation clause to the Refugee Convention in mass influx emergencies', (2004) 16 *International Journal of Refugee Law* 4–24.

Edwards, Alice, 'The Optional Protocol to the Convention against Torture and the Detention of Refugees', (2008) 57 *International and Comparative Law Quarterly* 789–825.

Elias, T., *New Horizons in International Law* (Dordrecht: Martinus Nijhoff, 1992).

Evans, Malcolm D., 'State responsibility and the European Convention on Human Rights: role and realm', in M. Fitzmaurice and D. Sarooshi (eds.), *Issues of State Responsibility before International Judicial Institutions* (Oxford: Hart Publishing, 2004), pp. 139–60.

Falk, Richard, 'Human rights: a descending spiral', in R. A. Wilson (ed.), *War on Terror* (Cambridge University Press, 2005), pp. 225–41.

Fastenrath, Ulrich, 'Relative normativity in international law', (1993) 4 *European Journal of International Law* 305–40.

Feller, Erika, 'Transport carriers and refugee protection', in M. Kjærum (ed.), *The Role of Airline Companies in the Asylum Procedure* (Copenhagen: Danish Refugee Council, 1988), pp. 6–13.

'Carrier sanctions and international law', (1989) 1 *International Journal of Refugee Law* 48–66.

'Asylum, migration and refugee protection: realities, myths and the promise of things to come', (2006) 18 *International Journal of Refugee Law* 509–36.

Fernando, Basil, 'The role of NGOs in policy-making: campaigns against torture as an illustration', in L. Dhundale and E. A. Andersen (eds.), *Revisiting the Role of Civil Society in Promoting Human Rights* (Copenhagen: Danish Institute for Human Rights, 2004), pp. 143–63.

Fischer-Lescano, Andreas, and Löhr, Tillmann, *Border Control at Sea: Requirements under International Human Rights and Refugee Law* (Berlin: European Center for Constitutional and Human Rights, 2007).

Fitzpatrick, J., 'Revitalizing the 1951 Refugee Convention', (1996) 9 *Harvard Human Rights Journal* 229–53.

'Temporary protection of refugees: elements of a formalized regime', (2000) 94 (2) *American Journal of International Law* 279–306.

Flinders, Matthew, 'The politics of public–private partnerships', (2006) 7 (2) *British Journal of Politics and International Relations* 215–39.

Ford, Richard T., 'Law's territory (a history of jurisdiction)', (1999) 97 *Michigan Law Review* 843–930.

Forsythe, David P., *Human Rights in International Relations* (Cambridge University Press, 2000).

Foucault, Michel, *The History of Sexuality* (London: Penguin Press, 1976).

Fourlanos, Gerassimos, *Sovereignty and the Ingress of Aliens* (Stockholm: Almquist and Wiksell International, 1986).

Friedmann, Wolfgang, *The Changing Structure of International Law* (London: Stevens & Sons, 1964).

Furuseth, Rita, 'Creating security through immigration control: an analysis of European immigration discourse and the development towards a common EU asylum and immigration policy', NUPI Report 274, Norsk Utenrikspolitisk Institutt, Oslo, 2003.

Gammeltoft-Hansen, Hans, *Flygtningeret* (Copenhagen: Jurist- og Økonomforbundets Forlag, 1984).

Gammeltoft-Hansen, Thomas, 'The risk of migration control: a reflexive analysis of the common EU asylum and immigration policy', master's thesis, University of Copenhagen, 2005.

'Outsourcing migration management: EU, power, and the external dimension of asylum and immigration policy', DIIS Working Paper 2006/1, Danish Institute for International Studies, Copenhagen, 2006.

'Filtering out the risky migrant: migration control, risk theory and the EU', AMID Working Paper 52/2006, Academy for Migration Studies in Denmark, Aalborg, 2006.

'EU's Umulige Grænsekontrol', (2006) 2 *Udenrigs* 69–79.

'The extraterritorialisation of asylum and the advent of "protection lite"', Working Paper 2007/2, Danish Institute for International Studies, Copenhagen, 2007.

'The refugee, the sovereign and the sea: EU interdiction policies in the Mediterranean', in R. Adler-Nissen and T. Gammeltoft-Hansen (eds.), *Sovereignty Games: Instrumentalizing State Sovereignty in Europe and Beyond* (New York: Palgrave, 2008), pp. 171–96.

Gammeltoft-Hansen, Thomas, and Aalberts, Tanja, 'Sovereignty at sea: the law and politics of saving lives in the Mare Liberum', DIIS Working Paper 2010/18, Danish Institute for International Studies, Copenhagen, 2010.

Gammeltoft-Hansen, Thomas, and Adler-Nissen, Rebecca, 'An introduction to
sovereignty games', in R. Adler-Nissen, and T. Gammeltoft-Hansen (eds.),
Sovereignty Games: Instrumentalizing State Sovereignty in Europe and Beyond (New
York: Palgrave, 2008).

Gammeltoft-Hansen, Thomas, and Gammeltoft-Hansen, Hans, 'The right to seek
revisited: on the UN Human Rights Declaration Article 14 and access to
asylum procedures in the EU', (2008) 10 (4) *European Journal of Migration and
Law* 439–59.

Garlick, Madeline, 'The EU discussions on extraterritorial processing', (2006)
18 *International Journal of Refugee Law* 601–30.

Gatev, Ivaylo, 'Very remote control: policing the outer perimeter of the EU
neighbourhood', paper presented at the External Dimension of European
Immigration Policies, European University Institute, Florence, 23–24
November 2006.

    'Border security in the eastern neighbourhood: where biopolitics and
geopolitics meet', (2008) 13 *European Affairs Review* 97–116.

Gavouneli, Maria, *Functional Jurisdiction in the Law of the Sea* (The Hague: Martinus
Nijhoff Publishers, 2007).

Geddes, Andrew, 'Migration as foreign policy? The external dimension of EU
action on migration and asylum', SIEPS Report 2009:2, Swedish Institute for
European Policy Studies, Stockholm, 2009.

Gibney, Mark, 'In search of US refugee policy', in D. P. Forsythe (ed.), *The United
States and Human Rights: Looking Inward and Outward* (Lincoln: University of
Nebraska Press, 2000), pp. 52–72.

    International Human Rights Law: Returning to Universal Principles (Lanham,
Maryland: Rowman & Littlefield, 2008).

Gibney, Mark, and Skogly, Sigrun (eds.), *Universal Human Rights and Extraterritorial
Obligations* (University of Pennsylvania Press: 2010).

Gibney, Mark, Tomaševski, Katarina, and Vedsted-Hansen, Jens, 'Transnational
state responsibility for violations of human rights', (1999) 12 *Harvard Human
Rights Journal* 267–96.

Gibney, Matthew J., and Hansen, Randall, 'Asylum policy in the West: past trends,
future possibilities', WIDER Discussion Paper, UNU/WIDER, Helsinki, 2003.

Gil-Bazo, Maria-Teresa, 'The practice of Mediterranean states in the context of
the European Union's Justice and Home Affairs External Dimension: the safe
third country concept revisited', (2006) 18 *International Journal of Refugee Law*
571–600.

Goldsmith, Jack L., and Posner, Eric A., *The Limits of International Law* (Oxford
University Press, 2005).

Gondek, Michal, 'Extraterritorial application of the European Convention on
Human Rights: territorial focus in the age of globalization', (2005)
Netherlands International Law Review 348–87.

    *The Reach of Human Rights in a Globalising World: Extraterritorial Application of
Human Rights Treaties* (Antwerp: Intersentia, 2009).

Goodwin-Gill, Guy, *The Refugee in International Law* (Oxford: Clarendon Press, 1983).

'Non-refoulement and the new asylum seekers', in D. Martin (ed.), *The New Asylum Seekers: Refugee Law in the 1980s* (Dordrecht: Martinus Nijhoff Publishers, 1986).

'The Haitian *refoulement* case: a comment', (1994) 6 *International Journal of Refugee Law* 103–9.

The Refugee in International Law, 2nd edn (Oxford University Press, 1996).

'The right to leave, return and remain', in V. Gowlland-Debbas (ed.), *The Problem of Refugees in the Light of Contemporary International Law Issues* (The Hague: Martinus Nijhoff Publishers, 1996), pp. 93–108.

'Article 31 of the 1951 Convention Relating to the Status of Refugees: non-penalisation, detention, and protection', in E. Feller, F. Nicholson and V. Türk (eds.), *Refugee Protection in International Law: UNHCR's Global Consultations on International Protection* (Cambridge University Press, 2003), pp. 185–252.

Goodwin-Gill, Guy, and McAdam, Jane, *The Refugee in International Law*, 3rd edn (Oxford University Press, 2007).

Gorlick, Brian, 'The Convention and the Committee against Torture: a complementary protection regime for refugees', (1999) 11 *International Journal of Refugee Law* 479–95.

Gornig, Gilbert-Hanno, *Das Refoulement-Verbot im Völkerrecht* (Vienna: Wilhelm Braumüller, 1987), vol. XVIII.

Grahl-Madsen, Atle, *Commentary on the Refugee Convention 1951 Articles 2–11, 13–37* (Geneva: Division of International Protection of the United High Commissioner for Refugees, 1963 (republished 1997)).

Territorial Asylum (Stockholm: Almqvist & Wiksell International, 1980).

Greenwood, Christopher, 'Jurisdiction, NATO and the Kosovo conflict', in P. Capps, M. D. Evans and S. Konstadinidis (eds.), *Asserting Jurisdiction* (Portland: Hart Publishing, 2003).

Guild, Elspeth, 'Moving the borders of Europe', inaugural professorial lecture delivered at CPO Wisselleerstoel at the University of Nijmegen, 30 May 2001.

'The border abroad – visas and border controls', in K. Groenendijk, E. Guild and P. Minderhoud (eds.), *In Search of Europe's Borders* (The Hague: Kluwer Law International, 2002), pp. 87–104.

'Jurisprudence of the ECHR: lessons for the EU asylum policy', in M. C. D. U. de Sousa and P. de Bruycker (eds.), *The Emergence of a European Asylum Policy* (Brussels: Bruylant, 2004), pp. 329–42.

'Seeking asylum: storm clouds between international commitments and EU legislative measures', (2004) 29 *European Law Review* 198–218.

'The Borders of the European Union: Visas and carrier sanctions', (2004) 7 (3) *Tidsskriftet Politik* 34–43.

'What is a neighbour? Examining the EU neighbourhood policy from the perspective of movement of persons', paper presented at Western NIS Forum for Refugee-Assisting NGOs, Yalta, 1–3 June 2005.

'The Europeanisation of Europe's asylum policy', (2006) 18 *International Journal of Refugee Law* 630–52.

Guilfoyle, Daniel, *Shipping Interdiction and the Law of the Sea* (Cambridge University Press, 2009).

Guiraudon, Virginie, 'Before the EU border: remote control of the "huddled masses"', in K. Groenendijk, E. Guild and P. Minderhoud (eds.), *In Search of Europe's Borders* (The Hague: Kluwer Law International, 2002), pp. 191–214.

'The constitution of a European immigration policy domain: a political sociology approach', (2003) 10 *Journal of European Public Policy* 263–82.

'Enlisting third parties in border control: a comparative study of its causes and consequences', paper presented at Managing International and Inter-Agency Cooperation at the Border, Geneva, 13–15 March 2003.

Guiraudon, Virginie, and Lahav, Gallya, 'The state sovereignty debate revisited: the case of migration control', (2000) 33 *Comparative Political Studies* 751–78.

Haddad, Emma, 'The refugee: the individual between sovereigns', (2003) 17 *Global Society* 297–322.

Hailbronner, Kay, 'Asylrecht in Völkerrecht', in W. Beitz and M. Wollenschläger (eds.), *Handbuch des Asylrechts* (Baden-Baden: Nomos, 1980).

'*Non-refoulement* and "humanitarian" refugees: customary international law or wishful legal thinking?', in D. Martin (ed.), *The New Asylum Seekers: Refugee Law in the 1980s* (Dordrecht: Martinus Nijhoff Publishers, 1988), pp. 128–36.

'Comments on the rights to leave, return and remain', in V. Gowlland-Debbas (ed.), *The Problem of Refugees in the Light of Contemporary International Law Issues* (The Hague: Martinus Nijhoff Publishers, 1996), pp. 109–18.

Hänggi, H., and Tanner, F., 'Promoting security sector governance in the EU's neighbourhood', Chaillot Paper No. 80, European Union Institute for Security Studies, Paris, 2005.

Harvey, Colin, 'Regionalism, asylum and solidarity in Europe', in C. Harding and C. M. Lim (eds.), *Renegotiating Westphalia* (The Hague: Martinus Nijhoff, 1999), pp. 219–56.

Harvey, C., and Barnidge, R. P. J., 'Human rights, free movement, and the right to leave in international law', (2007) 19 *International Journal of Refugee Law* 1–21.

Hathaway, James, 'The emerging politics of non-entrée', (1992) 91 *Refugees* 40–1.

'New directions to avoid hard problems: the distortion of the palliative role of refugee protection', (1995) 8 *Journal of Refugee Studies* 288–94.

The Rights of Refugees under International Law (Cambridge University Press, 2005).

'Forced migration studies: could we agree just to "date"?', (2007) 20 *Journal of Refugee Studies* 349–69.

'Leveraging asylum', (2010) 45 *Texas International Law Journal* 503–36.

Hathaway, James (ed.), *Reconceiving International Refugee Law* (The Hague: Kluwer Law International, 1997).

Hathaway, James, and Dent, John A., *Refugee Rights: Report on a Comparative Survey* (Toronto: York Lanes Press, 1995).

Held, D., McGrew, A., Goldblatt, D., and Perraton, J., *Global Transformations: Politics, Economics, and Culture* (Stanford University Press, 1999).

Henkin, Louis, 'International law: politics, values and functions', (1989-IV) 216 *Recueil des cours, Collected Courses*.

'Notes from the President', *ASIL Newsletter*, Sept.–Oct. 1993.

International Law: Politics and Values (The Hague: Kluwer Law International, 1995).

'That "S" word: sovereignty, and globalization, and human rights, etc.', (1999) 68 (1) *Fordham Law Review* 1–14.

Higgins, Rosalyn, 'The legal bases of jurisdiction', in C. J. Olmstead (ed.), *Extra-territorial Application of Laws and Responses Thereto* (Oxford: International Law Association/ESC Publishing, 1984), pp. 3–14.

Problems and Process: International Law and How We Use It (Oxford: Clarendon Press, 1994).

Hoppe, Carsten, 'Passing the buck: state responsibility for private military companies', (2008) 19 *European Journal of International Law* 989–1014.

Hughes, Jane, and Liebaut, Fabrice (eds.), *Detention of Asylum-Seekers in Europe: Analysis and Perspectives* (The Hague: Martinus Nijhoff, 1998).

Hurwitz, Agnès, *The Collective Responsibility of States to Protect Refugees* (Oxford University Press, 2009).

Huysmans, Jef, 'The European Union and the Securitization of migration', (2000) 38 *Journal of Common Market Studies* 751–77.

ICMPD, *Irregular Transit Migration in the Mediterranean – Some Facts, Futures and Insights* (Vienna: ICMPD, 2004).

Isenberg, Davis, 'A government in search of cover', in S. Chesterman and C. Lehnart (eds.), *From Mercenaries to Markets* (Oxford University Press, 2007), pp. 82–93.

Kamminga, Menno T., and Scheinin, Martin, *The Impact of Human Rights Law on General International Law* (Oxford University Press, 2009).

Keohane, R. O., 'Hobbes's dilemma and institutional change in world politics: sovereignty in international society', in H. H. Holm and G. Sørensen (eds.), *Whose World Order? Uneven Globalization and the End of the Cold War* (Boulder: Westview, 1995).

Kessing, Peter Vedel, 'Skal danske styrker i udlandet overholde Danmarks menneskeretlige forpligtelser?', (2007) 1 *Juristen*.

'Terrorbekæmpelse og menneskeret', Ph.D. dissertation, Faculty of Law, Copenhagen University, 2008.

Kjær, Kim U., *Den retlige regulering af modtagelsen af asylansøgere i en europæisk kontekst* (Copenhagen: Jurist- og Økonomforbundets Forlag, 2001).

Kjærum, Morten, 'The role of airline companies in the asylum procedure', Group of Experts under the Auspices of European Consultation on Refugees and Exiles (ECRE), Danish Refugee Council, Copenhagen, 1988.

Kjølbro, Jon Fridrik, *Den Europæiske Menneskerettighedskonvention – for praktikere*, 2nd edn (Copenhagen: Jurist- og Økonomforbundets Forlag, 2007).

Klaauw, Johanne Van Der, 'European asylum policy and the global protection regime: challenges for UNHCR', in S. Lavenex and E. M. Ucarer (eds.), *Migration and the Externalities of European Integration* (Lanham: Lexington Books, 2002), pp. 33–54.

Klepp, Silja, 'A double bind: Malta and rescue of unwanted migrants at sea', paper presented at Exploratory Workshop: The Human Costs of Border Control in the Context of EU Maritime Migration Systems, Vreije University, Amsterdam, 25–27 October 2009.

Kneebone, Susan, 'The Pacific plan: the provision of "effective protection"?', (2006) 18 *International Journal of Refugee Law* 696–722.

Koh, Harold Hongju, 'The "Haiti paradigm" in United States human rights policy', (1994) 103 *Yale Law Journal* 2391–435.

Koskenniemi, Martti, *From Apology to Utopia: The Structure of International Legal Argument* (Helsinki: Finnish Lawyers' Publishing Company, 1989).

  'Hierarchy in international law: a sketch', (1997) 8 *European Journal of International Law* 566–82.

Krasner, Stephen D., *Sovereignty – Organized Hypocrisy* (Princeton University Press, 1999).

  'The hole in the whole: sovereignty, shared sovereignty, and international law', (2004) 25 *Michigan Journal of International Law* 1075–101.

Kratochwil, Friedrich V., *Rules, Norms, and Decisions: On the Conditions of Practical and Legal Reasoning in International Relations and Domestic Affairs* (Cambridge University Press, 1989).

Kruse, Inke, 'Creating Europe outside Europe: externalities of the EU migration regime', paper presented at ECPR Conference, Theories of Europeanisation. Marburg, 18–21 September 2003.

Lahav, Gallya, 'Migration and security: the role of non-state actors and civil liberties in liberal democracies', Second Coordination Meeting on International Migration, United Nations, Department of Economic and Social Affairs, Population Division, New York, 2003.

Lambert, Hélène, 'Protection against *refoulement* from Europe: human rights law comes to the rescue', (1999) 48 *International and Comparative Law Quarterly* 515–44.

Landgren, Karin, 'Deflecting international protection by treaty: bilateral and multilateral accords on extradition, readmission and the inadmissibility of asylum requests', New Issues in Refugee Research No. 10, UNHCR, Geneva, 1999.

Larsen, Kjetil M., 'Territorial non-application of the European Convention on Human Rights', (2009) 78 *Nordic Journal of International Law* 73–93.

Lassen, Nina, and Hughes, Jane, *'Safe Third Countries': Policies in European Countries* (Copenhagen: Danish Refugee Council, 1997).

Lassen, N., Selm, J. v., and Doomernik, J., 'The transfer of protection status in the EU, against the background of the common European asylum system and the goal of a uniform status, valid throughout the Union, for those granted asylum', European Commission, Brussels, 25 June 2004.

Lauterpacht, Elihu, and Bethlehem, Daniel, 'The scope and content of the principle of *non-refoulement*: opinion', in E. Feller, V. Türk and F. Nicholson (eds.), *Refugee Protection in International Law: UNHCR's Global Consultations on International Protection* (Cambridge University Press, 2003), pp. 87–177.

Lauterpacht, Hersch, *The Development of International Law by the Permanent Court of Justice* (New York: Longman, Green & Co., 1934).

The Development of International Law by the Permanent Court of International Justice, 2nd edn (London: Stevens & Sons, 1958).

'Restrictive interpretation and the principle of effectiveness in the interpretation of treaties', (1949) 26 *British Yearbook of International Law* 48–85.

Lavenex, Sandra, *Safe Third Countries: Extending the EU Asylum and Immigration Policies to Central and Eastern Europe* (New York: Central European University Press, 1999).

'Shifting up and out: the foreign policy of European immigration control', (2006) 29 *West European Politics* 329–50.

Lavenex, Sandra, and Ucarer, Emek U., 'The External Dimension of Europeanization: The Case of Immigration Policies', (2004) 39 (4) *Cooperation and Conflict* 417–45.

Lavenex, Sandra, and Ucarer, Emek U. (eds.), *Migration and the Externalities of European Integration* (Lanham: Lexington Books, 2002).

Lawson, Rick, 'Out of control – state responsibility and human rights: will the ILC's definition of the "act of state" meet the challenges of the nation state in the 21st century?', in M. C. Castermans-Holleman, G. Hoof and J. Smith (eds.), *The Role of the Nation State in the 21st Century: Essays in Honour of Peter Baehr* (The Hague: Martinus Nijhoff, 1998), pp. 91–116.

'Life after *Banković*: on the extraterritorial application of the European Convention on Human Rights', in F. Coomans and M. T. Kamminga (eds.), *Extraterritorial Application of Human Rights Treaties* (Antwerp: Intersentia, 2004), pp. 83–123.

'The concept of jurisdiction in the European Convention on Human Rights', in P. J. Slot and M. Bulterman (eds.), *Globalisation and Jurisdiction* (Leiden: Kluwer Law International, 2004), pp. 202–18.

'Moving beyond *Banković*: the gradually expanding reach of the European Convention on Human Rights', paper presented at International Society for Military Law and the Law of War, XVIIth Congress, Scheveningen, 16–21 May 2006.

Leander, Anna, *Eroding State Authority? Private Military Companies and the Legitimate Use of Force* (Rome: Centro Militare di Studi Strategici, 2006).

'The impunity of private authority: understanding PSC accountability', paper presented at Standing Group of International Relations, ECPR, University of Turin, 12–15 September 2007.

Leben, Charles, 'Symposium: the changing structure of international law revisited: by way of introduction', (1997) 8 *European Journal of International Law* 399–408.

Legomsky, Stephen H., 'Secondary refugee movements and the return of asylum seekers to third countries: the meaning of effective protection', (2003) 15 *International Journal of Refugee Law* 567–667.

'The USA and the Caribbean interdiction programme', (2006) 18 *International Journal of Refugee Law* 677–96.

Lehnart, Chia, 'Private military companies and state responsibility', IILJ Working Paper 2007/2, Institute for International Law and Justice, New York University School of Law, New York, 2007.

Lillich, Richard B., 'The *Soering* case', (1991) 85 *American Journal of International Law* 128–49.

Linderfalk, Ulf, *Om tolkningen av traktater* (Lund: Lund University, 2001).

Lindsnæs, Birgit, and Lindholdt, Lone, 'National human rights institutions: standard setting and achievements', in H. Stokke and A. Tostensen (eds.), *Human Rights Development Yearbook 1998* (The Hague: Kluwer Law International, 1998).

Logan, Charles H., *Private Prisons: Cons and Pros* (Oxford University Press, 1990).

Longo, Michael, *Constitutionalising Europe: Processes and Practices* (Aldershot: Ashgate, 2006).

Lorenzen, Peer, Rehof, Lars A., Trier, Troels, Holst-Christensen, Nina, and Vedsted-Hansen, Jens, *Den Europæiske Menneskerettighedskonvention: med kommentarer (art 1–10)* (Copenhagen: Jurist- og Økonomforbundets Forlag, 2003).

Loucaides, Loukis G., 'Determining the extra-territorial effect of the European Convention: facts, jurisprudence and the *Banković* case', (2006) 4 *European Human Rights Law Review* 391–407.

Lowe, Vaughan, 'Jurisdiction', in M. D. Evans (ed.), *International Law*, 2nd edn (Oxford University Press, 2006), pp. 335–60.

International Law (Oxford University Press, 2007).

Lucht, Hans, 'Ud af den globale verdens skygger', (2007) (2) *Den Ny Verden* 73–82.

Lutterbeck, Derek, 'Policing Migration in the Mediterranean', (2006) 11 (1) *Mediterranean Politics* 59–82.

Lynch, M., *Forced Back: International Refugee Protection in Theory and Practice* (Washington, DC: Refugees International, 2004).

McAdam, Jane, 'Seeking asylum under the Convention on the Rights of the Child: a case for complementary protection', (2006) 14 *International Journal of Children's Rights* 251–74.

Complementary Protection in International Refugee Law (Oxford University Press, 2007).

MacCormick, Neil, *Institutions of Law: An Essay in Legal Theory* (Oxford University Press, 2007).

McCorquodale, Robert, and La Forgia, Rebecca, 'Taking off the blindfolds: torture by non-state actors', (2001) 1 *Human Rights Law Review* 189–218.

McCorquodale, Robert, and Simons, Penelope, 'Responsibility beyond borders', (2007) 70 *Modern Law Review* 598–625.

McDonald, Douglas, (ed.), *Private Prisons and the Public Interest* (Piscataway, NJ: Rutgers University Press, 1991).

McGoldrick, Dominic, 'Extraterritorial effect of the International Covenant on Civil and Political Rights', in F. Coomans and M. T. Kamminga (eds.), *Extraterritorial Application of Human Rights Treaties* (Antwerp: Intersentia, 2004).

McKenzie, Evan, *Privatopia* (New Haven: Yale University Press, 1994).

Magner, Tara, 'The less than "Pacific" solution for asylum seekers in Australia', (2004) 16 *International Journal of Refugee Law* 53–90.

Malanczuk, Peter, *Akehurst's Modern Introduction to International Law* (Oxford: Routledge, 1997).

Mandal, Ruma, 'Protection mechanisms outside the 1951 Convention ("complementary protection")', Legal and Protection Policy Research Series, UNHCR, Geneva, 2005.

Mantouvalou, Virginia, 'Extending judicial control in international law: human rights treaties and extraterritoriality', (2005) 9 *International Journal of Human Rights* 147–63.

Matas, David, 'Carrier sanctions: alternatives or amendments to existing legislation', in M. Kjærum (ed.), *The Effects of Carrier Sanctions on the Asylum System* (Copenhagen: Danish Refugee Council and the Danish Center of Human Rights, 1991), pp. 27–34.

Mathew, Penelope, 'Australian refugee protection in the wake of the *Tampa*', (2002) 96 *American Journal of International Law* 661–76.

Meijers, H., 'Possibilities for guaranteeing transport to refugees', in M. Kjærum (ed.), *The Role of Airline Companies in the Asylum Procedure* (Copenhagen: Danish Refugee Council, 1988), pp. 16–23.

Meron, Theodor, 'Extraterritoriality of human rights treaties', (1995) 89 *American Journal of International Law* 78–82.

Milano, Enrico, *Unlawful Territorial Situations in International Law* (The Hague: Martinus Nijhoff, 2006).

Milanovic, Marco, 'From compromise to principle: clarifying the concept of state jurisdiction in human rights treaties', (2008) 8 *Human Rights Law Review* 411–48.

Miltner, Barbara, 'Rescue-at-sea and maritime interceptions: issues of refugee protection', paper presented at Talking across Borders: New Dialogues in Forced Migration Studies, 10th Conference of the International Association for the Study of Forced Migration, Centre for Refugee Studies, York University, Toronto, 18–22 June 2005.

'Case comment: broadening the scope of extraterritorial application of the European Convention on Human Rights', (2007) 2 *European Human Rights Law Review* 172–82.

Mohamedou, Mohammad-Mahmoud, 'The effectiveness of national human rights institutions', in B. Lindsnæs, L. Lindholdt and K. Yigen (eds.), *National Human Rights Institutions: Articles and Working Papers* (Copenhagen: Danish Institute for Human Rights, 2001), pp. 49–58.

Mole, Nuala, 'Case analysis: *Issa v. Turkey*: delineating the extra-territorial effect of the European Convention on Human Rights', (2005) *European Human Rights Law Review* 86–91.

Morgenthau, Hans J., 'The problem of sovereignty reconsidered', (1948) 48 *Columbia Law Review* 341–65.

Morris, Jessica, 'The spaces in between: American and Australian interdiction policies and their implications for the refugee protection regime', (2003) 21 (4) *Refuge* 51–62.

Nicholson, Frances, 'Implementation of the Immigration (Carriers' Liability) Act 1987: privatising immigration functions at the expense of international obligations', (1997) 46 *International and Comparative Law Quarterly* 586–634.

Nicholson, Frances, and Türk, Volker, 'Refugee protection in international law: an overview', in E. Feller, V. Türk and F. Nicholson (eds.), *Refugee Protection in International Law* (Cambridge University Press, 2003).

Nicolaidis, Kalypso, and Tong, Joyce L., 'Diversity or cacophony? The continuing debate of new sources of international law', (2004) 25 *Michigan Journal of International Law* 1349–75.

Niessen, Jan, and Schibel, Yongmi, 'International migration and relations with third countries: European and US approaches', MPG Occasional Paper, Migration Policy Group, Berlin, May 2004.

Noll, Gregor, *Negotiating Asylum: The EU Acquis, Extraterritorial Protection and the Common Market of Deflection* (The Hague: Martinus Nijhoff, 2000).

'Visions of the exceptional: legal and theoretical issues raised by transit processing centres and protection zones', (2003) 5 *European Journal of Migration and Law* 303.

'Seeking asylum at embassies: a right to entry under international law?', (2005) 17 *International Journal of Refugee Law* 542–73.

'Asylum claims and the translation of culture into politics', (2006) 41 *Texas International Law Journal* 491–501.

'The politics of saving lives: interception, search and rescue and the question of human rights at sea', paper presented at The Future of Asylum Policy in the European Union, Turku, 10 October 2006.

Noll, G., Fagerlund, J., and Liebaut, F., 'Study on the feasibility of processing asylum claims outside the EU against the background of the common European asylum system and goal of a common asylum procedure', European Commission, 2003.

Noll, G., and Vedsted-Hansen, J., 'Non-communitarians: refugee and asylum policies', in P. Alston (ed.), *The European Union and Human Rights* (Oxford University Press, 1999).

Nowak, Manfred, *UN Covenant on Civil and Political Rights: CCPR Commentary* (Kehl am Rhein: Engel, 1993).

O'Boyle, Richard, 'The European Convention on Human Rights and Extraterritorial Jurisdiction: a comment on life after *Banković*', in F. Coomans and M. T. Kamminga (eds.), *Extraterritorial Application of Human Rights Treaties* (Antwerp: Intersentia, 2004).

Okoth-Obbo, Georges, 'Coping with a complex refugee crisis in Africa: issues, problems and constraints for refugee and international law', in V. Gowlland-Debbas (ed.), *The Problem of Refugees in the Light of Contemporary International Law: Papers Presented at the Colloquium Organized by the Graduate*

Institute of International Studies in Collaboration with the United Nations High
    Commissioner for Refugees, Geneva 26 and 27 May 1994 (Dordrecht: Martinus
    Nijhoff Publishers, 1996).
Olmstead, Cecil J. (ed.), Extra-territorial Application of Laws and Responses Thereto
    (Oxford: International Law Association/ESC Publishing, 1984).
Oppenheim, Lassa, Oppenheim's International Law, 9th edn (Harlow: Longman,
    1992).
Orakhelashvili, Alexander, 'Restrictive interpretation of human rights treaties in
    the recent jurisprudence of the European Court of Human Rights', (2003) 14
    European Journal of International Law 529–68.
Osbourne, Davis, and Gaebler, Ted, Reinventing Government (New York:
    Addison-Wesley, 1992).
Palan, Ronen, 'Tax havens and the commercialization of state sovereignty',
    (2002) 56 International Organization 151–76.
    The Offshore World: Sovereign Markets, Virtual Places and Nomad Millionaires (Ithaca:
    Cornell University Press, 2003).
Pastore, Ferruccio, 'Aeneas' route: Euro-Mediterranean relations and
    international migration', in S. Lavenex and E. M. Ucarer (eds.), Migration
    and the Externalities of European Integration (Lanham: Lexington Books, 2002),
    pp. 105–23.
Pedersen, Michael Purchardt, 'Territorial Jurisdiction in Article 1 of the
    European Convention on Human Rights', (2004) 73 Nordic Journal of
    International Law 279–305.
Pellet, Alain, '"Human rightism" and international law', (2000) Italian Yearbook of
    International Law 3–16.
Peral, Luis, 'EU protection scheme for refugees in the region of origin: problems
    of conditionality and coherence', paper presented at ESIL Research Forum
    on International Law: Contemporary Issues, Geneva, 26–28 May 2005.
Plender, Richard, and Mole, Nuala, 'Beyond the Geneva Convention: constructing
    a de facto right of asylum from international human rights instruments', in
    F. Nicholson and P. Twomey (eds.), Refugee Rights and Realities (Cambridge
    University Press, 1999), pp. 81–105.
Pugh, Michael, 'Drowning not waving: boat people and humanitarianism at sea',
    (2004) 17 Journal of Refugee Studies 50–68.
Reinisch, August, 'The changing international framework for dealing with
    non-state actors', in P. Alston (ed.), Non-state Actors and Human Rights (Oxford
    University Press, 2005), pp. 37–89.
Reydams, Luc, Universal Jurisdiction: International and Municipal Legal Perspectives
    (Oxford University Press, 2003).
Riedel, Eibe, 'Standards and sources: farewell to the exclusivity of the sources
    triad in international law', (1991) 2 European Journal of International Law
    58–84.
Rijpma, Jorrit J., 'Building borders: the regulatory framework for the
    management of the external border of the European Union', doctoral
    dissertation, European University Institute, Florence, 2009.

Robinson, Nehemiah, *Convention Relating to the Status of Refugees: Its History, Contents and Interpretation – A Commentary* (New York: Institute for Jewish Affairs, 1953).

Rodger, Jessica, 'Defining the parameters of the *non-refoulement* principle', LLM research paper international law, Faculty of Law, Victoria University, Wellington, 2001.

Rodier, Claire, 'Analysis of the external dimension of the EU's asylum and immigration policies', European Parliament, Directorate-General for External Policies of the Union Directorate B – Policy Department, 2006.

Ross, Alf, *Lærebog i Folkeret*, 4th edn (Copenhagen: Munksgaards Forlag, 1961).

Roxstrom, Erik, Gibney, M., and Einarsen, T., 'The NATO bombing case (*Banković et al. v. Belgium et al.*) and the limits of Western human rights protection', (2005) 23 *Boston University International Law Journal* 56–136.

Rozental, S., 'Om komplementaritet i atomfysikken', (1955) *Fysisk Tidsskrift* 325–42.

Rudolph, Christopher, 'Globalization and security: migration and the evolving conceptions of security in statecraft and scholarship', (2003) 13 (1) *Security Studies* 1–32.

Ruff, Anne, 'The Immigration (Carriers' Liability) Act 1987: its implications for refugees and airlines', (1989) 1 *International Journal of Refugee Law* 481–500.

Ruggie, John Gerard, 'Territoriality and beyond: problematizing modernity in international relations', (1993) 47 (1) *International Organization* 139–74.

Rutinwa, Bonaventure, 'The end of asylum? The changing nature of refugee policies in Africa', New Issues in Refugee Research Working Paper No. 5, UNHCR, Geneva, 1999.

Sakellaropoulos, Spyros, 'Towards a declining state? The rise of the headquarters state', (2007) 71 (1) *Science and Society* 7–34.

Salcedo, Juan A. C., 'Reflections on the existence of a hierarchy of norms in international law', (1997) 8 *European Journal of International Law* 583–95.

Salter, Mark B., 'Governmentalities of an airport: heterotopia and confession', (2007) 1 (1) *International Political Sociology* 49–66.

Samers, Michael, 'An emerging geopolitics of illegal immigration in the European Union', (2004) 6 (1) *European Journal of Migration and Law* 27–45.

Sassen, Saskia, *Losing Control? Sovereignty in an Age of Globalization* (New York: Columbia University Press, 1995).

Territory, Authority, Rights: From Medieval to Global Assemblages (Princeton University Press, 2006).

Scheinin, Martin, 'State responsibility, good governance and indivisible human rights', in H.-O. Sano and G. Alfredsson (eds.), *Human Rights and Good Governance: Building Bridges* (The Hague: Martinus Nijhoff, 2002), pp. 29–45.

'Extraterritorial effect of the International Covenant on Civil and Political Rights', in F. Coomans and M. T. Kamminga (eds.), *Extraterritorial Application of Human Rights Treaties* (Antwerp: Intersentia, 2004), pp. 73–82.

Schmitt, Carl, *Political Theology: Four Chapters on the Concept of Sovereignty* (Boston: Massachusetts Institute of Technology Press, 1985).

The Nomos of the Earth in the International Law of the Jus Publicum Europaeum (New York: Telos Press, 2003 [1950]).

Scholten, Sophie, and Minderhoud, Paul, 'Regulating immigration control: carrier sanctions in the Netherlands', (2008) 10 *European Journal of Migration and Law* 123–47.

Schutter, Olivier De, 'Extraterritorial jurisdiction as a tool for improving the human rights accountability of transnational corporations', Background paper to the SRSG on human rights and transnational corporations, UN High Commissioner for Human Rights, New York, 2006.

Schwarz, Rolf, and Jütersonke, Oliver, 'Divisible sovereignty and the reconstruction of Iraq', (2005) 26 *Third World Quarterly* 649–65.

Scobbie, Ian, 'The theorist as a judge: Hersch Lauterpacht's concept of the international judicial function', (1997) 8 *European Journal of International Law* 264–98.

Selm, Joanne van, 'Access to procedures, "safe third countries", "safe countries of origin" and "time limits"', Global Consultations on International Protection, Third Track, Background Paper, UNHCR, Geneva, 2001.

Shahabuddeen, Mohammed, 'Developing countries and the idea of international law', in R. Macdonald (ed.), *Essays in Honour of Wang Tieya* (Dordrecht: Martinus Nijhoff, 1994), pp. 721–36.

Sianni, Areti, 'Interception practices in Europe and their implications', (2003) 21 (4) *Refuge* 25–34.

Simma, Bruno, 'International human rights and general international law: a comparative analysis', in *Collected Courses of the Academy of European Law*, Vol. 4, Book 2 (The Hague: Kluwer Law International, 1995), pp. 153–236.

Singer, Peter W., *Corporate Warriors: The Rise of the Privatized Military Industry* (Ithaca: Cornell University Press, 2003).

'War, profits, and the vacuum of law: privatized military firms and international law', (2004) 42 *Columbia Journal of Transnational Law* 521–49.

Sinha, S. Prakash, *Asylum and International Law* (The Hague: Martinus Nijhoff, 1971).

Skogly, Sigrun, *Beyond National Borders: States' Human Rights Obligations in International Cooperation* (Antwerp: Intersentia, 2006).

Skogly, Sigrun, and Gibney, Mark, 'Transnational human rights obligations', (2002) 24 *Human Rights Quarterly* 781–98.

Smith, Brian D., *State Responsibility and the Marine Environment: The Rules of Decision* (Oxford: Clarendon Press, 1988).

Sørensen, G., 'Sovereignty: change and continuity in a fundamental institution', (1999) 47 *Political Studies* 590–604.

Spiermann, Ole, *Enten & Eller: Studier i suverænitetsbegreber* (Copenhagen: Jurist- og Økonomforbundets Forlag, 1995).

International Legal Argument in the Permanent Court of International Justice: The Rise of the International Judiciary (Cambridge University Press, 2005).

Moderne Folkeret, 3rd edn (Copenhagen: Jurist- og Økonomforbundets Forlag, 2006).

Spijkerboer, Thomas, 'The human cost of border control', (2007) 9 *European Journal of Migration and Law* 127–39.

Steiner, Henry, 'International protection of human rights', in M. D. Evans (ed.), *International Law*, 2nd edn (Oxford University Press, 2006), pp. 753–82.

Steiner, Henry and Alston, Philip (eds.), *International Human Rights in Context: Law, Politics, Morals*, 2nd edn (Oxford University Press, 2000).

Sterkx, Steven, 'Curtailing the comprehensive approach: governance export in EU asylum and migration policy', paper presented at ECPR Joint Sessions of Workshops, Uppsala, 13–18 April 2004.

Steyn, Johan, 'Guantánamo Bay: the legal black hole', (2004) 53 *International and Comparative Law Quarterly* 1–15.

Strange, Susan, *The Retreat of the State* (Cambridge University Press, 1996).

Stuart, Allison, 'The inter-American system of human rights and refugee protection: post 11 September 2001', (2005) 24 (2) *Refugee Survey Quarterly* 67–82.

Sur, Serge, 'The state between fragmentation and globalization', (1997) 8 *European Journal of International Law* 421–35.

Takkenberg, A., and Tahbaz, C., *The Collected Travaux Préparatoires of the 1951 Geneva Convention Relating to the Status of Refugees* (Amsterdam: Dutch Refugee Council, 1990).

Taylor, Savitri, 'Australia's implementations of its *non-refoulement* obligations under the Convention against Torture and Other Cruel, Inhuman or Degrading Treatment or Punishment and the International Covenant on Civil and Political Rights', (1994) 17 *University of New South Wales Law Journal* 432–74

'Protection elsewhere/nowhere', (2006) 181 *International Journal of Refugee Law* 283–312.

Teubner, Günther (ed.), *Global Law without a State* (Aldershot: Dartmouth, 1997).

Tomuschat, Christian, 'State responsibility and the country of origin', in V. Gowlland-Debbas (ed.), *The Problem of Refugees in the Light of Contemporary International Law Issues* (The Hague: Kluwer, 1996), pp. 59–80.

Human Rights: Between Idealism and Realism, 2nd edn (Oxford University Press, 2008).

Turner, Simon, Munive, Jairo, and Sørensen, Ninna N., 'European attitudes and policies towards the migration/development nexus', in N. N. Sørensen (ed.), *Mediterranean Transit Migration* (Copenhagen: Danish Institute for International Studies, 2006), pp. 67–100.

Turpin, James, 'The jurisdictional art of separation: the role of jurisdiction in the management of territorial and self-determination disputes – mixed jurisdiction in the Anglo-French condominium of the New Hebrides 1906–1980', doctoral dissertation, European University Institute, Florence, 2002.

UNHCR, *The State of the World's Refugees: In Search of Solutions* (Oxford University Press, 1995).

The State of the World's Refugees: Human Displacement in the New Millennium (Oxford University Press, 2006).

Vandvik, Bjarte, 'Extraterritorial border controls and responsibility: a view from ECRE', (2008) *Amsterdam Law Forum* 27–36.

Vattel, E. de, *The Law of Nations* (Philadelphia: T. & J.W. Johnson & Co., 1883).

Vedsted-Hansen, Jens, 'Transporters' responsibilities under the Chicago Convention on International Civil Aviation', in M. Kjærum (ed.), *The Role of Airline Companies in the Asylum Procedure* (Copenhagen: Danish Refugee Council, 1988), pp. 14–16.

'Sanktioner mod transportselskaber med "inadmissible passengers"', (1989) 71 *Juristen* 219–33.

'Privatiseret Retshåndhævelse og Kontrol', in L. Adrian (ed.), *Ret og Privatisering* (Copenhagen: Gad Jura, 1995).

'Europe's response to the arrival of asylum seekers: refugee protection and immigration control', New Issues in Refugee Research No. 6, United Nations High Commissioner for Refugees, Geneva, 1999.

'Non-admission policies and the right to protection: refugees' choice vs. states' exclusion?', in F. Nicholson and P. Twomey (eds.), *Refugee Rights and Realities: Evolving International Concepts and Regimes* (Cambridge University Press, 1999), pp. 269–88.

Verdross, Alfred, and Simma, Bruno, *Universelles Völkerrecht: Theorie und Praxis* (Berlin: Duncker & Humblot GmbH, 1984).

Verkuil, Paul R., *Outsourcing Sovereignty: Why Privatization of Government Functions Threatens Democracy and What We Can Do about It* (Cambridge University Press, 2007).

Walker, Neil, 'Late sovereignty in the European Union', in N. Walker (ed.), *Sovereignty in Transition* (Oxford: Hart Publishing, 2003), pp. 3–32.

Wasem, Ruth Ellen, 'Cuban migration policy and issues', CRS Report for Congress RS20468, Congressional Research Service, Washington, DC, 2007.

Watson, James Shand, *Theory and Reality in the International Protection of Human Rights* (New York: Transnational Publishers, 1999).

Weil, Prosper, 'Towards relative normativity in international law?', (1983) 77 *American Journal of International Law* 413–42.

Weiner, Myron, 'Ethics, national sovereignty and the control of immigration', (1996) 30 *International Migration Review* 171–97.

Weinzierl, Ruth, *Border Management and Human Rights: A Study of EU Law and the Law of the Sea* (Berlin: Deutches Institut für Menchenrechte, 2007).

Weis, Paul, *The Refugee Convention, 1951: The Travaux Préparatoires Analysed with a Commentary by the Late Dr Paul Weis* (Cambridge University Press, 1995).

Werlau, Maria C., 'International law and other considerations on the repatriation of the Cuban balseros by the United States', (2004) 14 *Cuba in Transition* 202–12.

Werner, Wouter, 'State sovereignty and international legal discourse', in W. Werner and I. F. Dekker (eds.), *Governance and International Legal Theory* (Leiden: Brill Academic Publishers, 2004).

Werner, Wouter, and Wilde, Jaap De, 'The endurance of sovereignty', (2001) 7 *European Journal of International Relations* 283–313.

Wilde, Ralph, 'Legal "black hole"? Extraterritorial state action and international treaty law on civil and political rights', (2005) 26 *Michigan Journal of International Law* 739–806.

'Opinion: The "legal space" or "*espace juridique*" of the European Convention on Human Rights: is it relevant to extraterritorial state action?', (2005) 2 *European Human Rights Law Review* 115–24.

Willheim, Ernst, 'MV *Tampa*: The Australian Response', (2003) 15 *International Journal of Refugee Law* 159–91.

Wiseberg, Laurie S., 'The role of non-governmental organizations (NGOs) in the protection and enforcement of human rights', in J. Symonides (ed.), *Human Rights: International Protection, Monitoring, Enforcement* (Aldershot: Ashgate, 2003), pp. 347–72.

Zolberg, Aristide, 'The formation of new states as a refugee-generating process', (1983) 467 (1) *The Annals of the American Academy of Political and Social Science* 24–38.

'Matters of State', in C. Hirschman, P. Kasinitz and J. DeWind (eds.), *The Handbook on International Immigration* (New York: Russell Sage Foundation, 1999), pp. 71–93.

'Beyond the crisis', in P. M. Benda and A. Zolberg (eds.), *Global Migrants, Global Refugees* (New York: Berghahn Books, 2001), pp. 1–19.

Index

CAMBRIDGE STUDIES IN INTERNATIONAL AND COMPARATIVE LAW

Books in the series

Access to Asylum: International Refugee Law and the Globalisation of Migration Control Thomas Gammeltoft-Hansen

Trading Fish, Saving Fish: The Interaction between Regimes in International Law Margaret Young

The Individual in the International Legal System: State-Centrism, History and Change in International Law Kate Parlett

The Participation of States in International Organisations: The Role of Human Rights and Democracy Alison Duxbury

'Armed Attack' and Article 51 of the UN Charter: Evolutions in Customary Law and Practice Tom Ruys

Science and Risk Regulation in International Law: The Role of Science, Uncertainty and Values Jacqueline Peel

Theatre of the Rule of Law: The Theory, History and Practice of Transnational Legal Intervention Stephen Humphreys

The Public International Law Theory of Hans Kelsen: Believing in Universal Law Jochen von Bernstorff

Vicarious Liability in Tort: A Comparative Perspective Paula Giliker

Legal Personality in International Law Roland Portmann

Legitimacy and Legality in International Law: An Interactional Account Jutta Brunnée and Stephen J. Toope

The Concept of Non-International Armed Conflict in International Humanitarian Law Anthony Cullen

The Challenge of Child Labour in International Law Franziska Humbert

Shipping Interdiction and the Law of the Sea Douglas Guilfoyle

International Courts and Environmental Protection Tim Stephens

Legal Principles in WTO Disputes Andrew D. Mitchell

War Crimes in Internal Armed Conflicts Eve La Haye

Lightning Source UK Ltd.
Milton Keynes UK
UKOW02f1909290716

279509UK00001B/72/P